NEW BEGINNINGS

D0705881

John Deely presents a compelling argument in the history of philosophy – that there is a way of looking at modern philosophy that is very different from the received opinions, one which profoundly affects our understanding of the contemporary situation in philosophy and the shape of its immediate future.

Deely contends that the direction modern philosophy took did not make full or even good use of the Latin resources available to the classical modern authors. Part I of his book examines the mainstream Latin context of philosophy at the time of Descartes in order to show that there were important speculative developments of the Latin tradition under way, especially in Iberia, of which Descartes himself had no knowledge. Notable among these strains of influence was the semiotic thought of John Poinsot (1589–1644) in his *Tractatus de Signis*. These Latin developments were subsequently screened out of the mainstream of modern philosophy, but have central relevance for the contempoary postmodern context of discourse analysis and culture studies in general. In particular, Deely shows that more than a century of late Latin development anticipated John Locke's proposal for a 'doctrine of signs' or 'semiotic' which would give us a logic and critique of knowledge different from that which the mainstream of modern thought presaged.

Part II of the book develops the speculative connections between late Latin philosophical developments and postmodern thought. Deely provides a synthesis of late Latin scholasticism and Peircean philosophy, which bears upon the role of signs as experiential reference to human knowledge. It is noteworthy that Deely traces the historical developments surrounding the concept of 'cause' in science and philosophy; this provides what may well be the most complete outline for the concept of causality to be found in current literature.

John Deely is a professor in the Department of Philosophy, Loras College, Dubuque, Iowa.

JOHN DEELY

with a Preface by Lúcia Santaella-Braga

New Beginnings
Early Modern Philosophy
and Postmodern Thought

UNIVERSITY OF TORONTO PRESS
Toronto Buffalo London

© 1994 by John Deely
Printed in Canada

ISBN 0-8020-0624-8 (cloth)
ISBN 0-8020-7583-5 (paper)

Printed on acid-free paper

Toronto Studies in Semiotics
Editors: Marcel Danesi, Umberto Eco, Paul Perron, and
Thomas A. Sebeok

Canadian Cataloguing in Publication Data

Deely, John N.
  New beginnings : early modern philosophy and
  postmodern thought

  (Toronto studies in semiotics)
  Includes bibliographical references and index.
  ISBN 0-8020-0624-8 (bound) ISBN 0-8020-7583-5 (pbk.)

  1. Philosophy, Modern.   2. Postmodernism.   I. Title.
  II. Series.

  B832.1.D44 1994   190   C94-932008-0

University of Toronto Press acknowledges the
financial assistance to its publishing program
of the Canada Council and the Ontario Arts Council.

This book is dedicated

to the recovery of the Iberian intellectual culture

of the Late Latin Age,

which provides the deepest continuity

between the High Middle Ages and Postmodern times

Principal Early Modern Figures:
Schematic List

(from Columbus' discovery to the American revolution)

Francisco de Vitoria, 1492/3–1546

Domingo de Soto, 1495–1569

Pedro da Fonseca, 1548–1599

Francisco Suárez, 1548–1617

Francisco de Araujo, 1580–1664

João Poinsot, 1589–1644

René Descartes, 1596–1650

John Locke, 1632–1704

Gottfried Wilhelm Leibniz, 1646–1716

George Berkeley, 1685–1753

David Hume, 1711–1776

Contents

List of Illustrations

Preface

The Way to Postmodernity

We have here a work which is required reading for anyone interested in ideas and their history, a work which will unavoidably provide a focal point for years of controversy. Deely's main claim is an argument in the history of philosophy as such: that there is a way of looking at modern philosophy very different from the received opinions, one which profoundly affects our understanding of the contemporary situation in philosophy and the shape of its immediate future. So powerfully is the argument made that even a reader who resists the claim will forever think differently about his or her own counter-claim and how to stake it.

Suffice to point out by way of preface to this work that, despite the difficulty or even the impossibility of definitively assigning the meaning and the frontiers of what is being called postmodernity, there is nevertheless a nearly indisputable consensus that the word "post" can only exist in opposition, continuity, or complementarity with the universe which it presupposes, that is, the universe of modernity. To delimit this latter, scholars of the new Frankfurt school have tried to establish a consensus which considers Kant's famous essay of 1784, *Was Ist Aufklärung* ("What is Enlightenment"), as the inaugural event of modernity. Without denying the importance, historical and otherwise, of this essay by Kant, to consider that modernity begins with Kant, in the Enlightenment, creates a dead end by making impossible or, at the very least, restricting gratuitously, alternative understandings of the tangle of relationships linking modernity and postmodernity.

Although it is certain that to cultivate misunderstandings and irrelevant ambiguities is a typical tendency of the minds of many so-called postmoderns, for those who continue to recognize the necessity of clarification and do not confuse fertile complexity with the opacity of sheer confusion, this challenging book by John Deely brings a great and very original contribution to our understanding of the oppositions, continuities, and complementarities that constitute the postmodern milieu.

The first great merit of this book lies in its freedom respecting all the intellectual fashions (deconstruction, anti-foundationalism, relativism, anarchism) to which American academic minds generally show themselves keen nominalistically to adhere under the label ''postmodernism''. Despite the fact that the fashions in question are, no doubt, part of the postmodern environment, Deely, in this veritable *tour de force*, is wise and transnationalist enough not to mistake the partial and characteristically North American aspects of postmodernity for postmodernity *tout court*.

The second, equally great, merit of John Deely's book is in locating the starting point of philosophical modernity exactly where it has to be situated if we are to find any source of understanding in all that has been insistently put under the label of postmodernity. For Deely, modernity began with the Cartesian Rationalism and Lockean Empiricism, finding together their most accomplished synthesis in Kant. At the same time, as a good reader of Heidegger, Deely makes of this point only the beginning of a search for what Descartes put into oblivion, showing that what was lost surely included much of the richest speculative materials developed in the late Latin Age. His investigation of the achievements of the closing Latin centuries uncovers the beginnings of a path all but untraveled, which yet reveals enough of itself to show that it leads into the crucial issues of discourse analysis posed by postmodernity, and does so by questioning some basic presuppositions and prejudices of the modern age more profoundly than contemporary postmoderns have so far achieved.

The third and greatest merit of this work is to show in a new way how the past is not a heavy and brute unmovable stone but a source of insights which can be put into movement according to the pressures and necessities of the present. The ordering in present understanding of past deeds, events, and ideas is not unchangeable. New and better orders can be created if we are not deaf to the claims of the present and not blind to the arrows that point toward the future. Deely forces on the reader nothing less than a rethinking of the accepted story of modern philosophy.

For if the classical history of modern philosophy began with Descartes, then, in our postmodern age, that *history* has to be rewritten in the light of what Descartes left aside. And what was that? I will not anticipate the answers given by Deely nor spoil the excitement of a text which pulls the reader along much in the fashion of a mystery tale. It is enough to say by way of preface that the unexpected historical path opened by Deely is a sapient, lucid one, able to lead us beyond the vicious circles of the realism versus idealism debates, the foundationalism versus anti-foundationalism quarrelings, and the dilemmas of objectivism versus relativism. This is no small feat, but to profit from it, you, *lecteur mon semblable,* will have to free yourself from the pre-possession of the sacred canonical authors and texts of modernity and postmodernity, and penetrate into this new terrain while watching its landscape unfold with rinsed eyes.

The path of thinking Deely has provided us, it may be said, appears unmistakable once it has been traversed; but before Deely, neither the moderns nor the postmoderns were able to see it at all. As in every successful voyage of discovery, the traveler's hardships are recompensed with delights of unexpected vistas and pleasures of newfound goods. The sign-vessel which is this book vindicates its title throughout its passage, both from Latinity to modernity and from modernity to postmodernity. Remarkably, Deely's conjunction of late Latin Iberian scholasticism with contemporary developments in epistemology and the theory of signs produces an original, exciting, and compelling program for postmodernism, a new paradigm under which to think the term.

Professora Lúcia Santaella-Braga, Livre-Docente
Universidade de São Paulo

Technical Prenote

and Acknowledgements

This book is written for anyone, including an undergraduate, who is seriously interested in the historicity of human understanding as expressed in philosophy. Although the language of the book itself is end-of-the-twentieth-century American English, there is no getting around the fact that, in the part of the book that concerns early modern philosopy, much, indeed most, of the problematic is bound up with the Latin language. For any author who would deal with ideas not expressed in the author's own language, there is no way to gainsay Augustine's maxim (c.397: lib. 2, cap. 13) that "quoniam et quae sit ipsa sententia, quam plures interpretes pro sua quisque facultate atque judicio conantur eloqui, non apparet, nisi in ea lingua inspiciatur quam interpretantur"—that is to say, "we do not clearly see what the actual thought is which the several translators endeavor to express, each according to his or her own ability and judgment, unless we examine it in the language which they translate."

For this reason, for the reader's musement, I have included in the original language also whatever is said herein in translation, usually in notes appended to the text. And, for the reader's convenience, I have placed all notes at page bottom. In a few cases, the citations were too lengthy to include as bilingual notes. Where necessary, therefore, for typesetting purposes, I have removed the lengthiest Latin quotations to an Appendix of Longer Citations at the end of the book. This appendix is preceded by another appendix "Contrasting Transcendental and Ontological Relatives", which is my latest attempt to explain the tangled opposition of the Latin terms *relatio secundum dici* and *relatio secundum esse*. I have kept this distinction as much in the background as possible in the main text, but serious students pursuing the sources will soon find it crowding the foreground, so some direct discussion seemed in order.

A particular boon that may come to scholarly life with the aid of computers is that we shall put an end to the scholarly disgrace of publishing translations without at the same time providing the hapless reader with the original as well. In any event, the present work, like the edition of Poinsot 1632a without which the present work would hardly have been feasible, points in the right direction for future work.

The last step in the releasing of a book into print has an importance which is outweighed only by its difficulty and its tedium: proofreading. This is the stage at which most authors, and certainly this one, desperately need assistance. I am most grateful to Kevin Berg, Roman Ciapalo, Richard Schaefer, and Brooke Williams for providing that much needed help. Even though in vain, we now hope together to have caught every error!

And how many authors have the privilege of their typesetter's friendship? Warmest thanks to Bud MacFarlane, master compositor of the pages of Poinsot's *Tractatus de Signis* published by the University of California Press, who came out of retirement to typeset the present book.

I have intellectual acknowledgements to make, but these I defer to the notes as the book unfolds.

John Deely
completed with the
1993 Omas *Club Internazionale della Stilografica "Armando Simoni"* penna
con numero 266
4 August 1994

NEW BEGINNINGS

Introduction

On Reading This Book

This book concerns the theme of new beginnings within philosophy, the changes of age which define philosophical epochs. The theme is taken up not in its full scope as a speculative issue, but concretely in terms of the two most recent such turning points: the origins of modern philosophy out of Latin times and the origins of postmodern philosophy out of modern times. Each of these eras arises out of and defines itself against the backdrop of the paradigm of philosophy accepted in the background period. But what is unusual in the case I am considering is that the modern paradigm was so formed as to conceal from the outset fundamental themes of premodern Latin thought which are, in effect, resumed and foregrounded (with new accents and emphases, to be sure) by the postmodern development. Between the late Latin matrix of early modern philosophy and postmodernism there is a measure of speculative continuity which the classical modern development conceals. That underarching continuity or subtension is what I want to bring to the surface.

Even so restricted and concretized, the transitions at issue are large. To make their handling manageable, in Part I of the book I have focused on them as they are embodied in key figures: especially René Descartes, 1596–1650, and John Locke, 1632–1704 (and, to a lesser extent, George Berkeley, 1685–1753, and David Hume, 1711–1776), for the understanding of the origins of distinctively modern philosophy; Charles Peirce, 1839–1914, and Martin Heidegger, 1889–1976, for the understanding of the central thrust of postmodernism in philosophy; and John Poinsot, 1589–1644, for demonstrating speculative links which bind the matrix of the two at either end—the dawn and the dusk—of essentially modern philosophy.[1]

Thus there are five key figures in the book, but Poinsot is the central one. He is central, however, not as an isolated thinker but as a representative—a unique and uniquely qualified representative, as the reader will learn—of the Latin Age both in its last phase as providing the matrix of early modern philosophy and in its full extent so far as it was a development of the logical, physical, and metaphysical writings of Aristotle assimilated to the milieu of medieval and renaissance Latin culture. In the same way, Descartes and Locke, Peirce and Heidegger, appear in these pages not as individual thinkers but as paired thinkers representative, respectively, of modernism and postmodernism in philosophy. All five figures, then, are personifications of the theme, and are presented as instantiating it.

By this device of personification, I hope to have achieved three goals: to help a broad readership appreciate the importance of philosophical ideas in defining any age of humanity; to expose to reflection a number of presuppositions and prejudices which have not served us well in the teaching of philosophy since Descartes; to bring to light neglected materials relevant to the problematic of knowledge and experience.

The personification device simplifies the argument, to be sure, because it allows each figure, as representing an age, to speak for more than himself alone. In particular, Poinsot as the central figure eventually comes to personify the continuity between early modern philosophy and postmodernism itself.

A simplified argument always runs the risk of misleading, and the reader who came to see this book as about figures as such, even about this central figure, would be misled. The book is about the state of the problem of knowledge and experience at the time that modern

---

1 Since in this list of principals the name "John Poinsot" is the only one that the reader is likely to be encountering for the first time, it may be noted that a fuller discussion of the identity of Poinsot and of the reasons why Poinsot should be made a central figure for any postmodern evalutation of early modern philosophy in relation to the Latin Age begins below on pp. 21–26, and will be elaborated throughout the book. For a complete discussion of the name, national origin, historical period, and life of Poinsot the reader is referred to the Editorial AfterWord (Deely 1985) of the bilingual critical edition of Poinsot 1632a, esp. pp. 421–444.

philosophy was formed and its direction set. This book is about the fact that the direction modern philosophy took did not make good use of the full Latin resources available in the period of its early course-setting, because the classical modern authors ignored Iberian developments germane to their project of establishing the foundations of philosophy in human experience. And the book is about the fact that the postmodern development in philosophy seems to call for just the sort of material that those neglected sources provide.

Part II of the book is no longer concerned with historical material and personages as such, but purely with the development for their own sake of speculative points and themes that pertain centrally to the postmodern problematic in philosophy and culture.

Part I and Part II alike underscore the point that both the history of philosophy and the speculative contours of modern philosophy itself have been distorted, even deformed, as a consequence of Descartes' having succeeded in screening out the semiotic developments in the Latin milieu of his day. As this book makes clear, Poinsot is not the only one involved in the Iberian semiotic development; but he happens to be the last in the line, and he provided a comprehensive speculative synthesis. He was alive, morever, precisely when Descartes himself was alive.

This book sets out to redress the imbalances and correct some distortions, in order to motivate philosophers and historians of philosophy to see and review their materials in a new light—and above all to start reading some new texts which will not only make it possible to tell, but will shortly compel us to tell, a quite different ''story of modern philosophy'' than the stale one-sided tale we have been repeating to generations upon generations of students since the 1800s.

Thus the plan for the two-part unfolding of the book as a whole may be stated as follows. Part I establishes the historical contacts necessary to see something like the full scope of the speculative possibilities of early modern times in contrast with the much narrower range of speculative development actually undertaken by the modern authors. Part II is written from the postmodern standpoint already adumbrated by the early modern Iberian late Latins, to wit, a standpoint transcending the impasse which modern thought has reached in idealisms at loggerheads with realisms. The aim of Part II is to expand upon and make unmistakable the speculative links proper to such a transcendence which give relevance today to the forgotten semiotic development of late Latin (or early postmodern) Iberian intellectual culture. Through these two parts, the book unfolds in eight Chapters.

Chapter 1 proposes that we are at a turning point in the history of philosophy, a turning point forced upon us by the exhaustion of the classical modern paradigm. At the same time, the exhaustion of the modern paradigm was, as it were, self-ordained by the attitudes and orientation determined by the work of Descartes, to a degree that need not have been. In Descartes' own time, the materials and themes which are today forcing the supplanting of the classical modern paradigm were already nascent, but were ignored by and perhaps unknown to Descartes. But to see this, it is necessary to begin to look at the Latin writings, here personified in Poinsot, which modernity consigned to oblivion. That is the statement of the problem in Chapter 1.

Chapter 2 argues that the Latin Age needs to be seen in terms of an organic and wholistic outline, which has not been done in modern times because the true visage of Latin times has been obscured by a number of prejudices and distorting historical influences, as stated in the chapter.

Chapter 3 states simply what a true outline of the Latin Age should look like, through the proposal that once we begin to look at the totality of the Latin writings, we find that they represent an organic development which did *not* culminate in the high middle ages, as is commonly assumed. On the contrary, the so-called high middle ages were themselves a period of a new beginning within the Latin matrix, separating the early development (Augustine to Abelard) from the late development (roughly, Albertus Magnus to Poinsot). Poinsot stands at this juncture as a pivotal figure for three very fundamental reasons: *first*, by his juxtaposition to Suárez as presenting a culminating synthesis of Latin thought, narrower (in that Suárez's synthesis includes law, political philosophy, ethics, and metaphysics independently treated), but speculatively more reliable in what it does treat; *second*, by virtue of his consequent value as an index of where best to look among the Latin authors for valuable but lost insights; *third*, and mainly, by the focus in his treatise on signs on exactly the epistemological problematic which would become the preoccupation of modern philosophy after Descartes. This chapter is short, but it has as its purpose only to present a proper outline of the Latin Age, not to argue it in full detail.

Chapter 4 sets the development of late Latin ideas (between Ockham, c.1285–1347, and Descartes) as synthesized by Poinsot in counterpoint to the classical early modern authors, beginning with Descartes, but including also Locke, Berkeley, and Hume. The point of the chapter is to show that, among the historical figures of the time when modern philosophy took shape, Poinsot is both the one whose arguments on the philosophical requirements of the problematic of epistemology are the most penetrating and far-reaching, and the one whose work is the least known. Enough here is said to demonstrate that the problematic common to the classical early moderns is also a problematic directly addressed among the Latins as represented by Poinsot, who, therefore, though not by current standards considered among the early moderns, is nonetheless an actual historical figure of the formative early modern years that needs to be brought into the picture of early modern philosophy. What is said in this chapter enables the reader to see the familiar "broad picture" of early modern philosophy more broadly still, and in a striking new light which reveals unsuspected deficiencies in the "standard picture" and unsuspected speculative possibilities for a rethinking of the period. This chapter constitutes nothing less than a "retrieve" of the early modern period in the precise technical sense defined by Heidegger:

By the re-trieving of a fundamental problem we understand the disclosure of those original possibilities of the problem which up to the present have lain hidden. By the elaboration of these possibilities, the problem is transformed and thus for the first time is conserved in its proper content. To preserve a problem, however, means to retain free and awake all those interior forces that render this problem in its fundamental essence possible.[2]

The chapter not only requires readers to look to new sources, but also to see the old ones in a light that comes only from those new sources.

---

2 "Unter der Wiederholung eines Grundproblems verstehen wir die Erschliessung seiner ursprünglichen, bislang verborgener Möglichkeiten, durch deren Ausarbeitung es verwandelt und so erst in seinem Problemgehalt bewahrt wird. Ein Problem bewahren heisst aber, es in denjenigen inneren Kräften frei und wach halten, die es als Problem im Grunde seines Wesens ermöglichen."—Martin Heidegger, *Kant und das Problem der Metaphysik* (Frankfurt: Klostermann, 1951), p. 185; cf. p. 211 of the trans. by James S. Churchill, *Kant and the Problem of Metaphysics* (Bloomington, IN: Indiana University Press, 1962).

Chapter 5 does something no classical modern philosopher, including Locke, ever did: it takes seriously the 1690 text of Locke's proposal for the division of the sciences concluding his *Essay Concerning Humane Understanding*, in which text the name "semiotic" first appears.[3] This discussion follows naturally from the demonstration in Chapter 4 that Poinsot's semiotic approach to the problem of experience and knowledge is exactly what sets his work philosophically apart from Descartes and the other classical moderns, and affords an opportunity to bring into the light one of the least understood and yet philosophically richest aspects of Latin philosophy, namely, the doctrine of *"species"* or forms as specificative within cognition. What Locke merely proposed and the rest of the moderns ignored is one of the main things the late Latins, at least in Iberia, were about; and what Locke proposed, taken up anew by philosophers in our day, is what is proving to be the undoing of modern philosophy.

The "Epilogue" (or "concluding note") which follows Chapter 5 directly addresses the point that what is fundamental about Heidegger's thought in *Being and Time* ¶1 is exactly what is central to Poinsot's semiotic. Without attempting to rewrite my earlier book on Heidegger, I point that out here, leaving the arguments pro and con to other places (and probably other authors: I find the Heideggerean sect at the moment one of the least open to dialogue). This is my "wave good-bye" after laying out in the preceding chapters what I see as no more than a seminal proposal calculated to spark a revolution in the handling of early modern philosophy and to shape the understanding of the term "postmodernism" over the coming years on historical grounds.

---

3 Professor Barry Allen, in his curiously mistitled essay "Is Locke's Semiotic Inconsistent?" (*The American Journal of Semiotics*, 10.3/4, forthcoming), quite misses the point that Locke *has* no semiotic doctrine as such, only the *proposal for* and *naming of* such a doctrine which, when developed, proves to be flatly inconsistent with Locke's and Descartes' assumption that ideas as psychological realities ("modes of our consciousness") are the direct objects of our experience. That Locke "does not formally define the sign in the *Essay*" is not, as Barry would have it, something "odd"; it is a natural consequence of the fact that a doctrine of signs is not what Locke essays. Whether, of course, the philosophy that Locke does essay is one consistent with semiotic—consistent, that is to say, with the proposal he makes for a doctrine of signs—is quite another question that does not seem to occur to Barry. See my reply to his article, "Locke's Philosophy *versus* Locke's Proposal for Semiotic" (*ibid.*).

There follows upon this in Chapter 6, the beginning of Part II, a lengthy discusssion of "how signs work" (a revision for the present work of Deely 1991, which treats in a much schematized form the richer discussion developed in Deely 1994). The opening six paragraphs of this chapter state the occasion and reasons for the discussion here. This chapter shows how much the modern philosophers arbitrarily and unnecessarily narrowed the notion of cause, and shows that only in the overlap of late Latin and early modern times was the original causal scheme of Aristotle refined to the point of being applicable to the problematic of experience and knowledge. The content of the chapter, thus, is singularly relevant to the main argument of the earlier chapters, since it reinforces the claim of the preceding chapters that the late Latin development of epistemology not only was given short shrift by Descartes (and the classical moderns after him) but also contains ideas that need to be reintroduced into philosophy today, not just for purposes of historical justice, but also for the sake of speculative progress. The chapters of Part I set fundamental ideas of Descartes, Locke, and Poinsot in counterpoint. This chapter opening Part II, by contrast, despite its historical interest, opens in effect a collateral line of inquiry, for there is practically nothing in Locke or Descartes to set in counterpoint with the ideas here introduced.

Chapter 7 (a revision of Deely 1989) continues the collateral discussion by showing how the unusual sense of causality required to explain the action of signs also serves to justify in particular Peirce's intuition that semiosis is an action coextensive with the whole of nature, reaching "even to the stars", as Lúcia Santaella-Braga once finely put the matter.

Chapter 8, adapted to the present volume from my Thomas A. Sebeok Fellowship Inaugural Lecture (Deely 1993b), rounds out the parallel discussion as my attempt to speak most directly in my own voice rather than through historical figures in laying out, through an appropriation of the Jakobsonian notion of "renvoi", what seem to me at present some of the most important terms and distinctions for the postmodern development of semiotics.

The work as a whole should make clear that I see in postmodernism above all an opportunity that has only begun to be grasped, based on the possibility of a philosophical response to the shortcomings of the modern paradigm which at once remedies those shortcomings and

retrieves for philosophy its lost history in the context of—and as supremely relevant to—the postmodern period which all agree we are entering
without much agreement on how it is to be defined. This lost history
is the period from Ockham to Descartes, when the first florescence of
semiotic consciousness occurred in the Iberian peninsula, involving not
only Poinsot but also Soto (1495–1560), Araújo (1580–1664), and Fonseca (1548–1599), to name only the principal predecessors to Poinsot's synthesis. In the approach of these thinkers is found the way to deal with
Heidegger's original and abiding central concern with the unity of being prior to its division into categories, as with Peirce's central concern
with the nature of semeiosis.

No doubt this approach amounts to a retrieve also of the very term
''postmodernism''. As a fashionable term, at least in the United States,
''postmodern'' has come to be frequently used as a label for the results
of a so-called ''deconstruction'' consisting in a kind of literary/sophistic
attempt to eviscerate rational discourse in philosophy through a forced
control of signifiers, made rather to dismantle than to constitute some
text taken precisely as severed from any vestige of authorial intention.
An abstraction as such need not be a lie, but neither is the lie precluded
from abstraction; and this is what the in-itself semiotically neutral method
of deconstruction results in when it is used ideologically to express
primarily the cleverness and will of the interpreter rather than the
possibilities inherent in the text as a coherent whole aimed at expressing some historically conditioned understanding of its object and linked
always to a larger than linguistic semiosis (see Deely 1994: Gloss 8 on
¶96).

In the present work, ''postmodernism'', without precluding deconstruction, is far from synonymous therewith; still less is the term
''postmodern'' employed with an ideological intent. The argument here
is to employ the term through juxtaposition with the internal dimensions of the classical modern paradigm so as to establish thereby a
philosophical sense of ''postmodernism'' defined historically but able
to link contemporary requirements of speculative understanding with
late Latin themes omitted from the repertoire of analytic tools developed
by modernity. In order to make so complex a historical situation intellectually manageable without oversimplification, the book refers mainly
to the five figures I consider to be at the interface, first of modern philo-

sophy in its break with the Latin Age (Descartes, Poinsot, and Locke), and then of postmodern philosophy in its break with the classical modern development (Peirce and Heidegger), initially according to the device of personification as explained above, but finally on the strength of the argument and the clarity arrived at concerning key distinctions and terms constitutive of semiotic as a doctrine. This doctrine—alas!, and in spite of Poinsot's best efforts—proves to be revolutionary for philosophy.

Standard modern treatments generally concern the past in its relatively unchangeable aspect: how it actually went down in a certain region among certain writers. *New Beginnings* is concerned rather with the past in its eminently changeable aspect, namely, our perception of it, and how that perception affects present and future thought. This third "new beginning", a reshaping of our perception of the modern past and its relations to Latinity as bearing on the future course of contemporary thought, is the ultimate portent of the present work's title.

PART I

The Historical Contacts

"If the classical history of modern philosophy

began with Descartes,

then, in our postmodern age, that history has to be rewritten

in the light of what Descartes left aside."

— Lúcia Santaella-Braga, from the *Preface* —

1

Stating the Question

Classical modern philosophy began in the writings of Descartes. At least, it was from Descartes' work that the modern mainstream known as "rationalism" took rise, and it was from John Locke's rejection of rationalism that the alternative modern mainstream called "empiricism" took rise. These two powerful movements developed in counterpoint up to the mighty synthesis effected by Immanuel Kant (1724–1804), the high point, by almost any reckoning, of the modern period. For even though the synthesis of modernity's philosophical paradigm by Kant was almost immediately exposed by Hegel (1770–1831) as depending on an inherent contradiction in the notion of noumenon (as Kant technically garbed the mainstream early modern assumption that objects are equivalent to ideas), Hegel's demonstration of the point, perhaps because it was too entangled in the coils of his own elaborate system, did not become effective in a sociological sense until it was taken up by Peirce as a central corollary to his understanding of semiosis, the action of signs, in the acquisition and development of knowledge. It is not too much to say that the intellectual capital of the rationalist-empiricist debate has continued to bankroll the main movements of late modern philosophy in its guise as phenomenology on the one hand and analytic philosophy on the other.

Postmodern philosophy, by contrast, has yet to achieve a positive characterization, as its very name—provisional, therefore, to be sure—indicates. Indeed, the competition for the name among conflicting trends usually characterized by a keen penchant for the arbitrary and irrational comes near to comedy; but the one thing postmodern thought is not, is modern: it is what comes *after* or (better) *consequent upon* the modern period. It is neither Cartesian, nor empiricist, nor Kantian.

What we now call the "modern period", too, began as a reaction against an earlier age, not, of course, as earlier, but as the currently established paradigm fully developed on the basis of philosophical suppositions adopted many centuries before and still regnant in their developed fruits. These suppositions of the age against which modernity reacted can be variously articulated, but they all centered on the idea of *being* as the focus and center of gravity of philosophical thought. Being, moreover, especially in the Latin Age as the matrix and background for the rise of modern philosophy, was understood in a very precise sense: what had reality and existence independently of the activities of human thought and feeling.

Modernity took no less interest in this reality than did the Latins, but sought to bring into the account precisely another aspect of reality which the Latin focus left in the background, namely, the very activity itself of the human mind in reaching its understanding of "being" supposed as independent of that reaching. In this way a kind of shift in focus was introduced, which at the same time shifted the philosophical center of gravity *away from* being as such *to* discourse, the rational activity of the human mind whereby it is able to know whatever it comes to know. From the beginning of distinctively modern thought, in the writings of Descartes and Locke alike, as later in the grand synthesis effected by Kant, the basic assumption at work is that the mind directly knows only its own products, and from this assumption arose the whole "problem of the external world" methodologically outlined by Descartes, but substantively articulated especially by David Hume.

The emphasis on method in modern thought was a natural outgrowth of the focus on the mind's own workings. Postmodern thought has made its own claims to methods, but these are distinctively not "modern" methods concerned with rationality and sensibilia so much as they are methods of exploring what stands in opposition to rationality and the idea of a given at the foundations of experience in sense. *Postmodernism seeks to make a place for yet further aspects of reality* that modernity left in the background, much as modern thought began by seeking to make a place for the aspect of the mind's rational working left in the background by the Latin period. These are the realities of feeling, deception, and illusion, which are every bit as much a piece with our experience as are the "realities" of rational communication and order and sensible intrusions from the environment upon our experience, such as the rising and setting of the sun, the phases of the moon, and the patterns of the stars.

We can see in this way a progression of sorts in philosophical concern, from the bare "realism" of ancient Greek and later Latin thought, to the stark "idealism" of modern thought, to the comprehensive confrontation with the whole of experience, including the irrational, in postmodern developments. Just as the Greeks and Latins reduced philosophy's concern to what they supposed to be what it is, independent of human thought, so the moderns reduced philosophy's concern to what was supposed to be distinctively rational or natural in the content of the mind's workings. Postmodernism rejects all such reduction, and for the first time insists on bringing to the foreground the whole of experience, not just a distortion of it made in view of a selected part.

In this progression we see a growth in the very notion of experience itself. In the Greek period the notion did not exist much beyond the bare term ἐμπειρία, which occurs, for example, in the *Metaphysics* and *Ethics* of Aristotle as a kind of semantic seed for his commentators to develop. Perhaps following this lead, the notion of experience in the Latin period was confined to the action of the sensible thing making itself an object by its own action upon the organ of sense. Even the developed notion of *experimentum* through which the results of sensation are preserved and incorporated in the activities of perception[1] was, among the Latins, more an analysis of the manner in which the cognitive powers enhanced the subjectivity of the cognitive organism than it was an appreciation of objectivity in its full-scale contrast with the subjective.[2] Mainly in the modern period was the notion of experience expanded to cover the cognitive workings of mind in their entirety. Postmodernism takes the further step of thematizing within experience its entire contents in

---

[1] See my analysis of "Animal Intelligence and Concept-Formation", *The Thomist* XXXV.1 (January, 1971), esp. pp. 55–83.

[2] Cf. the discussion in Tachau 1988: 135ff., 180ff., 319ff., of the Latin reactions to Peter Aureol's attempt to establish a notion of *esse apparens*, an attempt, however, which looks more like an anticipation of modern idealism than an anticipation of objective being in a postmodern semiotic context.

contrast to any supposed prejacent given "real", the affective no less than the cognitive, the conative no less than the intellective, the cultural and artifactual no less than the natural.

In a word, postmodernism is the opening of a passageway from the age of classical modern philosophy to an epoch as distinct from the modern age as the modern age was from Latin times, or Latin times from the ancient Greek period. The opposition of modernity to Latin (and Greek) times eventually took the form of the opposition of *idealism* to *realism* in philosophy. Postmodern thought begins, properly speaking, not so much by rejecting this opposition as by transcending it, for in experience integrally taken, mind-dependent and mind-independent being assert themselves equally—not "equally" in the quantitative sense, but "equally" in the sense of components both asserting themselves in different ways at different times and in different proportions throughout the course of human life, both together making up the one fabric of our lives we call "experience".

Now experience is the proper locus for any understanding of reality, be "reality" understood in whatever way. This realization, hard and slowly won in the history of these questions, constitutes a decisive gain within philosophy. For even granting that there be a world of nature prior to and independent of human concerns, the only way to such a world is through experience, and hence experience itself, relative to any reality so conceived, stands as a prior reality on which reality (the mind-independent reality) depends insofar as it comes to be actually known. In other words, reality in the Latin sense is something derivative from and within experience, a part of its content, but by no means the whole of it. The content of experience is that which has to be first sorted out in order for the notion of something real in the sense of mind-independent to emerge and be singled out within the objectivity of experience. From the standpoint of experience, not only what is mind-independent is real, and hence the medieval equation of reality with mind-independent being (*ens reale*) is clearly a reductive notion.

The moderns, in rejecting the dominant paradigm for the study of nature among the Latins, namely, Aristotelianism with its central notion of substance as "that which being primarily and essentially is", did not reject the medieval ideal of reality as mind-independent being. What they did reject was the naive notion that this reality is the very stuff of experience or a self-evident given within that stuff. Instead, they insisted on an analysis of how reality as the mind-independent might be attained from within the mind's own workings. Only much later, and in spite of their preferences, did late modern philosophers realize with amazement that, if the results and orientation of the early modern founding figures of the new period in philosophy were sound, they pointed finally not toward the long-sought reality but to the emptiness of the original ideal.

Thus the master of the modern era, the great Kant, rejected the label of "idealism" for himself. In the Preface to the second edition of his central *Critique of Pure Reason*, he even proposed to have removed the "scandal to philosophy and to human reason in general", whereby "the existence of things outside us ... must be accepted merely on *faith*" (1787: 34 note α; cf. Deely 1992: esp. Note 1, 316–318).

In this regard, subsequent thinkers have not agreed that Kant in any meaningful sense escaped the coils of the modern idealism. Idealism and realism, in their struggle through legions of proponents, have come to have as many divisions and subdivisions as the snakes on the head of Medusa. But the bottom-line thread uniting the varieties of "realists" remains the conviction, not that *there is* a reality in the sense of mind-independent being, but *that this very reality can be known* in *what* it is. And precisely this Kant denied, and thought he proved must be denied in the mighty work of his *Critiques*.

Postmodernism properly begins with a dawning realization that the shift from being narrowly understood to discourse equally narrowly understood, which took place at the beginning of modern times, was something of a misbegotten choice. What was needed for philosophy to mature was not so much a shift as an expansion, an expansion of the notion of reality—and with it, being—to include the whole of experience as the prior ground out of which human understanding arises and on which it throughout depends. From the start, being should have been an inclusive, not an exclusive and oppositional notion. Being is not only "that which can only be said in many ways" (Aristotle), but that out of which the division between what is and what is not independent of the mind arises (Aquinas), and not in any finally fixed way, but differently according to the time and circumstances of the one experiencing such a contrast among objects.

Hence the central importance for the nascent postmodernism of ideas of illusion, irrationality, and deconstruction, even though these fashionable preoccupations are far from the whole story and, in the nature of the case, incapable of adequately defining the contours of what postmodern philosophy must inevitably move toward realizing, namely, an adequate appreciation of the richness of human experience as the ground of all art and science, and the only means we have for testing what is true.

For the purposes of this study, I take Heidegger and the Heideggerian philosophy of being to be the purest expression of the initial requirement of postmodernism, namely, the requirement that human experience be understood as the ground out of which idealism and realism alike arise as reductions or, often enough, distortions, and that this ground be understood as having a unity peculiar to itself which is prior to, not just the Aristotelian categories of substance and accident, but any categorial scheme whatever. I take Charles Sanders Peirce with his pragmaticism[3] to be, in this regard, the key transitional figure. As I envision our situation, Peirce stands at the interface of modernity with postmodernity, the last of the moderns and first of the postmoderns, as Augustine stood at the interface of the ancient and the medieval worlds, "last of the fathers and first of the medievals".

None of these choices are made arbitrarily, but the reasons for making them are the purpose of the study itself to reveal. They are dictated by what I have found to be the situation of early modern philosophy when viewed not in terms of its classical mainstream development, as is usually done in speaking of the early modern period, but in terms of the actual relations obtaining in the age of Descartes between the choices which led to the classical modern development and the wider possibilities for choice which the speculative Latin context of that period provided. These wider possibilities were destined to fall through the cracks of history until Charles Peirce, inspired by Locke's anomalous conclusion to his *Essay* of 1690 (which otherwise launched modern empiricism), gave them life again in our time as the inevitable trajectory along which postmodern thought must rise and eventually achieve definition of itself in positive terms.

The history of early modern philosophy is much more interesting—

---

[3] Pragmaticism as emphatically distinguished from the pragmatisms of James and Dewey, which remain quintessentially tied to the consequences of the presuppositions defining the classical modern paradigm.

and relevant to postmodernism—than the standard studies narrowly focused on Descartes and Leibniz, or Locke and Hume, could have us believe. The history of early modern philosophy can be something much richer than a mere study over again, in ever greater detail, of the classical modern sources as giving rise to the classical modern development with its culmination in the Kantian synthesis. But to see this, it is necessary to look in the other direction, so to speak; that is to say, it is necessary to consider Descartes and Locke in relation to the then-current Latin speculations, which is a context wider than either the father of rationalism or the father of empiricism actually drew upon in fixing the direction for the future of philosophy.

Not only does the early modern Latin milieu provide a wider context of speculative possibility than either Descartes, Locke, or their mainstream modern successors realized, but, as we can now see regarding it from the advantage of a nascent postmodernism, that Latin milieu provides a richer context as well, one which arguably adumbrates the full requirements of a philosophy which has experience integrally understood for its center of gravity.

The reader has to be warned that the period of early modern philosophy approached from its Latin side, rather than from the side of its emergence out of Latin into the national language traditions of classical modern thought, is a dismaying maze of the greatest difficulty to navigate. We need a compass and a guide to gain an initial orientation, or the whole landscape dissolves into a morass of material repetitions of terms (i.e., the constant use of same terms to convey actually different points) and multiplication of abstruse distinctions, leaving the visitor practically without a clue beyond the engrained modern prejudices toward the Latins which every contemporary has imbibed with the air one breathes. Needless to say, the orientation more or less unconsciously provided by such prejudices is not particularly helpful if it is to be a question of attaining a new understanding of the possibilities inherent in the Latin matrix of early modern philosophy, and eventually seeing those possibilities with rinsed eyes in their bearing on the future of thought.

Hence it is that a familiar guide, one who orients us in terms of the classical modern development as it actually came about, is perforce the least useful one. We need instead an unfamiliar guide, unfamiliar in terms of the actual modern development after Descartes, but intimately familiar with the Latin developments leading up to the period of Descartes and providing us with the full intellectual context of Descartes' time. The reader needs to be open to the possibility that there could be such a "neglected figure" capable of orienting us in terms of the intrinsic possibilities of the Latin development and proving that those possibilities are not what Descartes and the moderns have heretofore led us to believe they were. For as far as the history of early modern philosophy goes, it is impossible to study it while leaving out the standard figures, and indeed Descartes and Locke will figure throughout our remarks in these pages, but it is equally impossible to enlarge the early modern context through the Latin sources if we regard them solely from the standpoint to which the standard figures have accustomed us. We need a non-standard figure—a non-standard primary source—as a guide, one who knew the whole early modern Latin context, and therefore who knew the Latin development far better than Descartes himself. In particular, with a view to the postmodern development, we need a guide who is able to show within the late Latin context an orientation toward a notion of being understood within experience as prior to the categories and to any division of being into what is mind-independent and mind-dependent.

Allow me to introduce John Poinsot, 1589–1644, as our orienting figure and guide. A contemporary of Descartes neglected in the standard histories of the modern period, Poinsot was a central figure of the Latin matrix within which early modern philosophy gestated. To students of the modern mainstream, this name is, practically speaking, wholly unfamiliar. It sounds French, but is in fact Burgundian, dating back to a time when the Duchy of Burgundy was an independent region. Moreover, the name contains no hint of the fact that the man bearing it was born and raised in the Portuguese city of Lisbon, of Maria, a Portuguese woman of the Garcez family married to Peter Poinsot. Peter had journeyed from Vienna to Madrid as Secretary to the Archduke Albert the VI, and thence with the Archduke to Lisbon, where he settled for some years and took Maria Garcez as his wife. The difficulty that Poinsot is a name and figure unfamiliar to the mavens of early modern philosophy in its classical development is compounded by the further difficulty that no less than eighteen different versions and variations of this name (Deely 1985: 423n33) are required to locate in scholarly sources what has been written about him, here and there, over the centuries since his passing.

In all the variants, counterparts to the English "John" are verified.
That his family name, his surname, was "Poinsot" is certain. His own
later substitution of "a Sancto Thoma" for "Poinsot" in religious life
has created a number of more or less needless problems both within and
outside the Hispanic milieu where he produced his Latin writings. Within
the world of Hispanic and Latin philosophy, his work sometimes came
to be confused with that of two other authors using the same religious
name. To remove this confusion, it was necessary to recur to the proper surnames of all three authors, to wit, Buccretius, Sarasetenus, and
Poinsot. Outside the Hispanic milieu, the practice of the substitution
of names reflects religious customs and ideological orientations which
are at best poorly understood, and which at worst are the objects of hostili-
ty and bigotry.

It is thus for good reason that the best contemporary and, I would
expect, future work on this author turns to the one name that provides
an invariant reference across all the national language lines of contemporary discussion—Poinsot.

Poinsot was completely unknown to Peirce, which is a pity, because
Poinsot was the first to systematically demonstrate the foundations of
logic and knowledge in the sign in just the sense that Peirce thought of
logic as semiotic. He was likewise unknown, it would appear, to Heidegger, which is again a pity, in that Poinsot's *Tractatus de Signis* was in effect the answer to Heidegger's foundational question concerning the
notion of truth as a correspondence of thought with thing: what is the
basis of the prior possibility of such a correspondence? By demonstrating
how signs are indifferent to the mind-dependent and mind-independent
dimensions of objects within experience, Poinsot was the first to establish
a unified subject matter for semiotic inquiry, and to show how the fabric
of experience at all levels is woven of sign relations. But this is to get
ahead of the story.

At this point, we need do no more than establish Poinsot's credentials
as a credible guide to the full extent of Latin thought in the age of Descartes, and as a reasonably reliable commentator on the bearing of that
thought toward emergent distinctively modern concerns with discourse
in its contrast with being considered as a mind-independent reality.

Between the years 1631 and 1635, as professor of philosophy at the
University of Alcalá, then-rival to Salamanca as Spain's greatest center

of higher learning, writing under his name in religion, "Joannes a Sancto Thoma", John Poinsot brought to publication a two-volume treatment of logic and a three-volume treatment of natural philosophy. All of the volumes, except the first in natural philosophy, which was published in Madrid, were published at Alcalá.

In 1637–1638 the first general edition of the contents of the original five volumes was published in Rome as nine volumes in a two-part set, wherein the volumes on logic bore their original title of *Ars Logica, Prima et Secunda Pars*, and the volumes on natural philosophy were assigned the common title—whether by Poinsot or by his publisher we do not know—of *Cursus Philosophicus*.

In 1638, in Cologne, this time in three volumes, the second general edition of the contents of the original five volumes was published under the care of Thomas of Sarria. For this second general edition the modifier *Thomisticus* was added, presumably by Sarria, to the Rome title assigned to the treatment of natural philosophy, and the general title so modified was extended to the whole of the work, including the treatment of logic. Thus was born the *Cursus Philosophicus Thomisticus* of John Poinsot.

In the best modern edition of this work, that of B. Reiser issued in three volumes between 1930 and 1937, the modified general title from Sarria's 1638 second complete edition, *Cursus Philosophicus Thomisticus*, again appears. Reiser's decision on this point is subject to debate, inasmuch as the title in question is not one known to have been assigned by Poinsot himself (Deely 1985: 399n4).

In favor of Reiser's decision is the negative fact that the title in question appeared well within Poinsot's lifetime without raising any known objection on his part; and the positive fact that the title is certainly consistent with the attitude of an author reported by an intimate friend and biographer (Ramirez 1645: xl) to have said, on his deathbed the 17th of June, 1644, that he had "never, in thirty years, written or taught anything he did not judge to be consonant with truth and conformed with the teaching of the Angelic Doctor". On the other hand, there is the fact that the author chose *Cursus Theologicus* without the partisan particle *Thomisticus* for the general title of his systematic eight volumes of theological writing, even though such a qualification would be more appropriate to a theological than to a philosophical context (see Poinsot's

"Tractatus de Approbatione et Auctoritate Doctrinae D. Thomae", 1637: S I, 221–301).[4]

We can only guess, but my guess (spelled out in the 1985 edition of the *Tractatus de Signis*, p. 399n5) would be that the simple title *Cursus Philosophicus*, or even *Cursus Artium*, is what Poinsot himself saw as the best general title for the set of volumes, notwithstanding his indubitable concern for their Thomistic lineage. The last title, *Cursus Artium*, in fact, was actually used by Poinsot in his 1640 Preface to the second edition of the *Artis Logicae Secunda Pars* (reproduced in the 1985 edition of the *Tractatus de Signis*, p. 35), and also by his first biographer, Didacus Ramirez (1645: xxxvij). In any event, under whatever general title, Poinsot's *Cursus Philosophicus* stands as one of the most complete speculative syntheses (presupposing the Aristotelian contrast of speculative with practical thought) that we have of Latin philosophy in its final stage of development as an indigenous, linguistically homogeneous tradition. It stands also as a work written explicitly from the point of view of that development as it took inspiration from the *opera omnia* of Thomas Aquinas.

Upon completion of his philosophical *Cursus*, Poinsot set to work at once on the publication of his *Cursus Theologicus*, an even more massive synthesis of theology in the Latin Age. This work originally appeared in eight volumes between 1637 and 1667. The first three volumes were brought to press by Poinsot himself, and the remaining five posthumously.[5] These works have considerable philosophical interest in their own right, to be sure, but the explicitly theological horizon of their project places detailed discussion of their contents and overall structure outside our present purview.

---

4 Thomas Merton (1951: 334), well familiar with the traditions and writings in question, gives the opinion that Poinsot's "most admirable characteristic is the completeness with which he proposed to submerge his own talents and personality in the thought of the Angelic Doctor ... John of St. Thomas sought only the pure doctrine of St. Thomas Aquinas, which he opposed to the 'eclectic' Thomism of those who, though they may have acquired great names for themselves, never rivalled the Angelic Doctor himself."

5 Details of the publication history and contents of Poinsot's *Cursus Theologicus* can be found in the Latin "Editorum Solesmensium Praefatio" of 1931; they have also been gathered in English in the "Editorial AfterWord" to the 1985 Deely edition of the *Tractatus de Signis*, beginning at 398n3.

These two syntheses of Latin philosophy and Latin theology—
Poinsot's *Cursus Philosophicus* of 1631–1635 and his partially posthumous
Cursus Theologicus of 1637–1667—are perhaps the two latest and most
authoritative presentations of Latin thought at its most advanced stage
that are available to us, and as such they are veritable mines of gold for
any postmodern effort to retrieve and understand from our own perspective and for our own interests what were the achievements of the Latin
Age. I have no doubt that that is exactly how they will eventually be
perceived by future scholars. But in the meantime, some formidable
obstacles have to be overcome, and I see the work of this book as an initial contribution to that prior task of clearing away an accumulation
of historical stereotypes and prejudices of various kinds, including racial
ones, which stand in the way of a full and just assessment of the
achievements of the Latin Age, especially in its final Hispanic phase,
for what concerns early modern philosophy and postmodern
developments.

Given the synoptic achievement and historically privileged position
of Poinsot's work in time, why is he today a virtually unknown and
thoroughly neglected figure in the history of philosophy, and in the
history of early modern philosophy in particular? The next two chapters
are my guess at this riddle, while Chapter 4 begins the work of making
such guessing unnecessary for future generations of students.

2

The Historical Prejudices

A. The Cartesian Heritage

If we except the powerful filter of Anglo-American bias against things
Hispanic in general, so well documented today in the work of Philip
Powell[1] and best defined historically for philosophy by Jorge Gracia (a
bias which I am not equipped to discuss in the full scholarly manner required for its diminution and eventual dissolution), no doubt the most
effective obstacle in contemporary consciousness to the appreciation of
the work in philosophy of John Poinsot is the heritage of René Descartes
(1596–1650). By this I mean the general prejudice Descartes engendered
against the importance of history for the philosopher, fancied by Descartes to be a man rightly concerned only with the book of the world
in its present state of existence as open directly to personal experience,
and especially with what can be found within himself. Descartes himself, of course, did not see himself as engendering against history a general
prejudice of the sort most harmful to the human mind in its search for
truth in matters philosophical. On the contrary, he saw himself as opening the way to philosophical wisdom and truth. "Resolving to seek no
knowledge other than that which could be found in myself or else in the
great book of the world", he tells us (1637: 115), "I have had much more
success, I think, than I would have had if I had never left my country
or my books."

---

[1] Notably his 1971 study of propaganda and prejudices affecting the United States'
relations with the Hispanic world: see References at the end of this book.

Philosophy itself in its historical dimension Descartes saw as the paradigm case for dismissal in the search for philosophical truth. Whereas Aristotle's meditations on first philosophy (c.348–330BC) led Aristotle first to consider the views of his predecessors, the meditations of Descartes (1641) led Descartes first to dismiss his predecessors, as he had so frankly told us they would (1637: 114–115):

Regarding philosophy, I shall say only this: seeing that it has been cultivated for many centuries by the most excellent minds and yet there is still no point in it which is not disputed and hence doubtful ... And, considering how many diverse opinions learned men may maintain on a single question—even though it is impossible for more than one to be true—I held as well-nigh false everything that was merely probable.

Of course, historicity as an irreducible condition of human knowledge was no less a part of the human situation in Descartes' day than in our own. If Descartes had merely been anticipating the contemporary insight that all history is present history, or that present experience inevitably colors our understanding of the past and evaluation of its sources, his heritage in this area would be anything but pernicious. Yet Descartes promotes lack of insight regarding tradition (1637: 112): "when I cast a philosophical eye upon the various activities and undertakings of mankind," he tells us, "there are almost none which I do not consider vain and useless."

Descartes' illusion that he was beginning philosophy anew with his own experience and consciousness free from any dependence on history was no less an illusion for his commitment to it as true. All the work accomplished in this area beginning with Gilson has not yet been enough to free our colleagues, particularly in the so-called analytic tradition or school of philosophy, of the crippling assumption that the history of philosophy is essentially peripheral to philosophy's main task (whatever that task may be).

Poinsot, although of Descartes' same generation, could not have stood in fuller contrast in his attitude toward history. He was irrevocably committed to the importance of tradition in philosophy at the very historical moment when the exuberance of modern discoveries in areas we now call science, in contrast to philosophy, was encouraging men to dismiss tradition as an obstacle to the adoption of new methods and to concentration on problems framed in a way alien to traditional concerns. At just the moment that Poinsot was determined, as Simonin rightly said (1930: 145), "to remain a man of the past and to arrange his work in its totality according to the pattern and methods of long-standing tradition", Descartes—and with him, modernity—was determined to jettison the pattern and methods of Latin tradition in favor of a new pattern and new methods better suited to the interests of understanding the world in its empirical guise as accessible to present experience and to control through experimental designs.

There is great irony in this situation. For while it is true that these two emphases are clearly opposed as attitudes of mind, it is equally true that the opposition, philosophically considered, is a superficial one, reducible to the difference between philosophical doctrine and scientific theory as complementary theoretical enterprises, as the latter cannot develop without being based on assumptions whose validity can be adjudicated only with recourse to the former. The principles for resolving the conflict of attitudes were equally available to Descartes and to Poinsot in the traditional writings Descartes chose to turn away from, even if the differing attitudes themselves were too little understood to allow for such application in detail. *Prise de conscience* always requires some reflective distance, and this was not available to the men caught up in the present of that time.

Today we see clearly that the object of science, while transcending perception, always concerns and essentially depends upon what can be directly sensed within perception, whereas the object of philosophy concerns rather the framework as such of understanding according to which whatever is sensed and perceived is interpreted. This object is not reducible to language, but is nonetheless accessible only through language. Debating whether the atom can be split, the scientist can ultimately resort to an experiment *demonstrando ad sensus* as happened at Hiroshima. Debating whether God exists, or what the nature of signs is that they can be used to debate about objects such as atoms (which depend upon material conditions) or spirits (which by nature would not depend upon matter, especially in the case of God), the philosopher never has the privilege of falling back upon such a "crucial experiment". From first to last, philosophy has only a *demonstratio ad intellectum* whereupon to rest its case. Science is the domain of experiments. Intellectual doctrine as irreducible to what can be manifested as decisive in an empirical frame is the domain of philosophy. There are many areas in the development of hypotheses and the elaboration of frameworks for the testing of hypotheses where, to be sure, philosophy and science overlap. But ultimately there is always the difference between *scientia* as what can in some measure be reduced to a crucial experiment *demonstrando ad sensus*, and *doctrina* as a body of thought sensitive to its own implications and striving for consistency throughout, while achieving explanations (however provisional) at a level beyond what can be empirically circumscribed in unambiguous ways.[2]

Today, we would be more inclined to admire Poinsot's attempt "to let no new achievements be lost, and to profit from the final developments of a scholasticism which had exhausted itself in the plenitude of its refinements" (Simonin 1930: 145) and less inclined to be taken in by Descartes' denigration of "the various activities and undertakings of mankind" as "vain and useless" (1637: 112). But habits which have taken hold for three centuries die hard. In our classrooms today and for the foreseeable—but perhaps not indefinite—future, it is still the meditations of Descartes that are likely to be read and discussed rather than the tractates of Poinsot, for two principal reasons. First, the comparative poverty of Descartes' texts makes them much easier to grasp: on the surface at least, no more is required of the reader than conversance with the language in which the text itself is presented. By contrast, in the case of Poinsot's work, even on the surface, "the reader is not granted dispensation from knowledge of the dialogue, implicit in the work, with the centuries-old strata of commentaries and discussions of the Aristotelian corpus" (Santaella-Braga 1991: 156). Second, the style of the Cartesian texts better suits the modern frame of mind, though this may be changing: "The supremely professional character of Poinsot's extensive text, along with the dazzling scope revealed by the huge synoptic table of the work", remarks D. P. Henry (1987: 1201), "are, one feels, immensely superior to the rather chatty tone of his contemporary

---

2   On the contrast of *doctrina* with *scientia* in the modern sense, see the terminological entry "Doctrine" in the *Encyclopedic Dictionary of Semiotics* (Deely 1986b), and Appendix I, "On the Notion 'Doctrine of Signs'", in *Introducing Semiotic* (Deely 1982: 127–130).

Descartes—a tone symptomatic of philosophy's decline towards the drawing-rooms of 'well-bred company and polite conversation' favored by Locke.'' We are already in a postmodern period, to be sure, but we have not been there long enough to achieve the reflective distance presupposed for a general *prise de conscience* appropriate to this change of age.

From this point of view, Descartes and Poinsot, contemporaries in the glorious seventeenth century, are alike doorways to the past. The past onto which Poinsot's work gives entry spans the full twelve-hundred years of the Latin Age, but brings into particular focus its last three centuries as seen from Iberia. The past onto which Descartes' work gives entry spans, by contrast, no more than an anticipation and launching of the three centuries of modernity's determined effort to present itself as the once and future truth owing nothing to history.

B. Extensions of the Cartesian Heritage: Scholarly, Religious, and Ideological Prejudices

A substantive point about ideology needs to be made regarding the last three centuries of the Latin development, which are (ab)normally neglected in the standard presentations to date of so-called ''medieval philosophy''. In the standard discussions of the period, serious presentation ends with William of Ockham (c.1285–1349), and takes up again with Descartes, whence follows the discussion of the classical modern development as culminating in Kant's work. Though seldom so nakedly stated, the common attitude of scholars for decades has been that of Matson (1987: II, 253): ''William of Ockham was the last of the great creative scholastics. The three centuries following his death are a philosophical desert.'' Desmond FitzGerald (1986: 430) has rightly characterized this remark as ''an absurd comment''.[3] Yet its absurdity does not gainsay its accuracy as a summation of the standardized attitude toward and treatment of Latin thought of the late fifteenth to early seventeenth century.

---

[3] Matson's comment strikes me as an illustration of what Pérez-Ramos (1993: 141) floridly labels ''the sort of cultural consensus which transcends the limits of what can be reasonably termed 'philosophy' and adopts the sweeping pathos of an all embracing ideology.''

When a prejudice is this naked, how does it manage to take root in the first place, let alone survive and thrive even in the most learned circles of academe? The answer to this question lies in the details of the history of the period, no doubt, and in the political, social, and economic dimensions even more than in the intellectual dimensions, as Powell (1971) has made clear. Intellectual history pertains to culture as such; yet culture as such depends upon and develops through—in a word, *lives* by—the sociological realities of social interaction. Hence it is that only long after the passions and occupations of sociological life have faded and altered in their basic constellations that intellectual history is normally able successfully to double back on itself and to recover what had always been available to it just beyond the gulf created by passions of the historical moment.

Such is decidedly the case with the missing period in philosophy's history between Ockham and Descartes. Appropriate categories for understanding this gap in the standard general histories are only beginning to be developed by scholars.[4] The most important work in this problem area, so far as concerns the present study, is Jorge Gracia's recent establishment (1993: 480) of the category of "Hispanic philosophy" as "a general category [essential] to bring out the philosophical reality encompassed by the Iberian peninsula and Latin America", and to "do justice not only to the historical relations between Iberian and Latin American philosophers, but also to the philosophy of Spain, Catalonia, Portugal, and Latin America". The diverse elements which make up the philosophy of Spain, Catalonia, Portugal, and Latin America, and which uniquely bind the Iberian peninsula and Latin America, have either been ignored completely in standard histories of philosophy, or have been inappropriately parcelled out along political, territorial, racial, or national linguistic lines which do not convey the cluster of historical

---

4 For example, the work of Tachau (1988), as cited in note 1 of Chapter 3 below, reveals that Questions 1 and 2 in Book III of Poinsot's *Tractatus de Signis* (1632a), which deal extensively with so-called "intuitive" and "abstractive" awareness, provide one of the best ways—and an as yet unexplored one at that—of situating Poinsot's thought on the theory of knowledge in terms of the mainstream Continental and English developments between the time of Scotus (d. 1308) and the return of Soto to Iberia from his studies in Paris of the early 1500s. Here is material for a valuable doctoral dissertation. Cf. Raposa 1994.

ties which constitute the universe of Hispanic philosophy. Yet just these are the elements which, *properly arranged and understood*, make up, as Gracia puts it (1993: 486), "the thought of the world created by the European discovery of America".

It is from this forgotten late Latin Hispanic universe, in fact, that the work of Poinsot comes, and to which it belongs as a boundary point relative to the classical early modern period, as becomes clear from the following list of the principal figures definitive of "the first period of philosophical development that properly merits being called Hispanic" (Gracia 1993: 486–487):

Its first notable figure is Juan de Zumárraga (1468?–1548) and its last is Juan de Santo Tomás (John Poinsot) (1589–1644). In between are Bartolomé de las Casas (1484–1566), Vasco de Quiroga (1487?–1568), Juan Luis Vives (1492–1540), Francisco de Vitoria (1492/3–1546), Domingo de Soto (1494–1560), Alonso de Castro (1459–1558), Alonso de la Vera Cruz (1504?–1584), Francisco de Salazar (1505–1575), Melchior Cano (1509–1560), Pedro da Fonseca (1528–1599), Domingo Bañez (1528–1604), Tomás de Mercado (1530–1575), Francisco Toletus (1532–1596), Luis de Molina (1535–1600), Benito Pereira (1535?–1610), Juan de Mariana (1536–1624), Antonio Rubio (1548–1615), Francisco Suárez (1548–1617), Gabriel Vazquez (1549–1604), Antonio Arias (1564–1603), and Alfonso Briceño (1587–1699), among many others. Territorially, it covers the Iberian peninsula and the Iberian colonies in the New World. In the Iberian peninsula certain universities stand out, such as Salamanca and Coimbra, but others, like Valladolid, Segovia, Alcalá, and Evora, follow closely. In the New World, the most important centers of activity are found in Mexico and Peru, particularly in the capital cities of Mexico City and Lima, although there are also developments in other areas.

Thus, while the neglect of these figures and their period, as Gracia says (1993: 478–479), "makes no historical sense" intellectually speaking, it makes all too much sense when we consider ideology and religious prejudice that stem precisely from that period. In particular, ideological religious prejudices on both sides of the "Reformation" have independently conspired in modern times to consign the period in question to intellectual oblivion, both in the English speaking world and in cultural zones dominated by central European civilization.

On one side, Protestant scholars have tended to neglect this period because it was dominated by thinkers associated with the Roman Catholic Church. On the other side, Catholic scholars have neglected this period because it does not fit at all with a general preoccupation to find ways of disentangling the concerns of Church and State in secular political life.

On top of this general preoccupation, the nineteenth century revival of the study of St. Thomas Aquinas by Leo XIII translated into a concern—more or less narrow-minded as it actually developed in the contemporary period—to achieve a kind of material demonstration of what was the thought of Thomas Aquinas by using his *actual vocabulary* as a criterion of purity. A procedure flawless in itself as a historical device respecting the determination of what a given thinker actually said or wrote, however, becomes an instrument of reductivism when it is used to cut off discussion of the ideas expressed insofar as implications can be developed or applications made which require the introduction of new vocabulary, an evolution and development of the material sign-vehicles conveying the original thought being discussed.[5] Such practice excluded from serious consideration work of later Latins who departed from that vocabulary, perforce, in applying philosophical principles to new questions (and new emphases on old questions) generated within their own social and cultural contexts.

My description of this practice might seem exaggerated, but it is attested to by the greatest historian of the revival, Etienne Gilson. "I myself, who have lived in the familiarity of St. Thomas Aquinas," Gilson wrote me (letter of 10 July 1974), "have not continued reading [John of St. Thomas] when I realized that he was not using the same language as that of our common master."[6]

---

[5] See discussion of "Aquinas' Texts as Boundary" vs. "Aquinas' Texts as Centre" in Deely 1995.

[6] In this context, as we will see in Chapter 4, it is ironic to find, in "A History of Philosophy" series sponsored by Gilson himself, criticism of Ockham by one of Gilson's principal disciples (Maurer 1962: 285) on the ground that he has "no signs or likenesses whose whole function is to lead to a knowledge of something else, and which are not themselves direct objects of knowledge". The irony is heightened by Gilson's own identification, perhaps tongue in cheek, of Ockham's notion of concepts as "natural signs" as "the only difficulty there is in understanding Ockham" (Gilson 1955: 491). The almost exceptionless use of the notion of concepts as natural signs under the designation "formal sign" by the contemporary "realists" determined

I suspect that we find in this attitude of linguistic limitation an evidence of the Cartesian influence even across the divide of Catholic from Protestant religious scholars both agreeing for different reasons to neglect the closing centuries of Latinity. Surely it is a notable example of self-referential inconsistency that the Thomists of Gilson's school have applied to the matter of interpreting Aquinas a method in effect Cartes-

to vanquish idealism from the philosophical arena (e.g., Simon, Wild, Veatch, Adler) surely compounds this "only difficulty".

For it is not enough simply to posit such a sign as the formal sign is alleged to be— one which signifies without itself being objectified. It is necessary to show how such a distinction is more than merely *ad hoc*, by establishing *how it is possible* for a sign to function in the way the formal sign is postulated to function, as Poinsot uniquely does (Rasmussen 1994: 432). Dalcourt (1994) and Cahalan (1994) have recently shown once again how seductive the mainly dialectical use of the formal sign can be. But too often, such use amounts to an avoidance of getting to the bottom of what is really at stake in the notion, as the late modern history of this question amply illustrates (cf. Deely 1978: 22–23 n. 10; and see note 13 in Chapter 8, p. 229 below, for some conceptual problems in the designation of sign as "formal"). Nor is it only in recent times, but in the Latin time as well, that many have paid lip service to the notion of "formal signifying" (e.g., see Deely 1982a: 55–57; Doyle 1984a) without in the end being able to give a satisfactory account of what they were postulating.

Nor are signs in the requisite sense—"signs or likenesses whose whole function is to lead to a knowledge of something else, and which are not themselves direct objects of knowledge", as Maurer puts it—found unequivocally in the work of Aquinas himself (see the listing of principal Aquinian texts in Chapter 4, note 9, p. 58 below).

John Poinsot is the only thinker in the long history of these questions who actually undertook to systematize the multifaceted writings of Aquinas on this specific point and reduce them to a thematic unity. He did so not *in vacuo*, but precisely as a respectful student not only of Aquinas' own texts but also of those authors before him who had integrally studied those texts, and further as a rational animal confronted with the data of experience (in the light of which above all any text needs to be evaluated if it is to be a question of philosophy). A man of Portuguese education and birth principally introduced to the thought of Aquinas as a graduate student at Louvain, Poinsot thereafter devoted himself to the exposition and rationalization of Thomistic thought for the remainder of his life. To Poinsot Jacques Maritain turned for his principal illumination in reading the texts of Aquinas on epistemological questions (see, for example, Maritain 1922, 1959), although always from the perspective of what he himself (1962: 32) would later call "Cyclopean Thomists", i.e., Thomists who "have their eyes fixed solely on the perspective of being", or, more specifically in late modern times, I would say rather Thomists obsessed with the modern opposition of realism to idealism in philosophy (see the discussion in Deely 1986c and 1995).

ian: there is but a single optic, discovered only in our day, which allows for a correct reading of the Aquinian corpus. Viewed through this optic, each of the commentators of the period of Classical Thomism[7]—Capréolus (c.1380–1444), Thomas de Vio Cajetan (1468–1534), Ferrariensis (c.1474–1528), Francisco Vitoria (1492/3–1546), Dominic Soto (1494–1560), Melchior Cano (1509–1560), Domingo Bañez (1528–1604), and John Poinsot (1589–1644)—appears to be an unreliable interpreter, either for failure to stress enough the centrality of *esse*, as became the fashion of the Thomistic revival (limited exception on this point is made for Bañez), or because, as has been said, the commentator, in dealing with problems beyond the purview of Aquinas' focal concerns in any given text, perforce introduces terminology not to be found in the master, and therefore suspect. In a letter of 28 August 1968, Gilson wrote to me in this regard that " 'A thomist' of whatever brand should find it superfluous to develop a question which Thomas was content to pass over with a few words", because

it is very difficult to develop such a question with any certitude of doing so along the very line he himself would have followed, had he developed it. If we develop it in the wrong way, we engage his doctrine in some no thoroughfare, instead of keeping it on the threshold his own thought has refused to cross, and which, to him, was still an assured truth.

Years later, when I was charged with the organization of the 1994 Special Issue of *The New Scholasticism*[8] in honor of John Poinsot (Deely Ed. 1994), I again encountered this attitude. A distinguished alumnus of the Toronto school Gilson founded, a fellow Dominican with Poinsot, declined to participate in the Special Issue on the ground that his own approach to all questions "is not through John Poinsot but through Thomas Aquinas", and therefore, he felt, it would take him too far afield

---

7 I have explained the designation "Classical Thomism" in an article titled "Metaphysics, Modern Thought, and 'Thomism'" written for *Notes et Documents* (Deely 1977a), which, unfortunately was published from uncorrected proofs, but provides nonetheless a sound outline of what is at issue.

8 The name of this journal was subsequently changed to the *American Catholic Philosophical Quarterly*, a change difficult to understand after sixty-three years of publication.

from his concern with the thought of Aquinas to delve deeply into the texts of Poinsot. To count for nothing is the fact that Poinsot himself is among the historical handful who had developed an intimate acquaintance with the complete range of Aquinas's writings and made this acquaintance, along with reason itself,[9] his own reference point in the evaluation of theoretical issues in philosophy. Only the author's own reading of Aquinas, solipsistically undertaken and maintained, is to count. Of course, the solipsism is an illusion, insofar as the reader thinks himself to be a pristine interpreter of whatever truth Aquinas has to convey, just as the presumption of Descartes that he had shriven his mind of all influence from society and history was an illusion (a transcendental one at that in Poinsot's sense of *relativum transcendentale*, inasmuch as it contained within itself the clues of previous—by definition historical—influences, as Gilson was to demonstrate in his doctoral work published in 1913).

Bergson used to speak of the ''natural geometry of the human intellect'' in order to explain its resistance to time and to seeing the development of things in time. Perhaps the Cartesian prejudice is nothing more than the formalization and explicitation of a resistance to history that is engrained in human understanding as part of its natural proclivity for seeing parts as wholes and present phenomena as eternal species. However that may be, the resistance of philosophers themselves to recognizing the historicity of human thought in all particulars—powerfully reinforced by the belief Descartes fostered as the father of modern philosophy that Latin philosophy is a nest of errors that can be safely ignored in beginning philosophy anew on the basis of individual experience and modern scientific methods—has tended to promote secular historians of philosophy who look back to the Latin Age only insofar as it can be made to reflect the narrow linguistic and logical concerns of recent Anglo-American philosophy. Among other things, this bias has led to a natural focus on William of Ockham as the reputed father of Nominalism in modern thought.

Thus, by a curious confluence of independent reasons, those scholars interested in philosophy's history, both secular and religious, have unwittingly conspired to neglect the key figures important to the develop-

---

9 I.e., in the sense of ''doctrina'' (p. 30 above, note 2).

ment of thought in the last centuries of the Latin Age. This neglect has been a pity for two reasons. First, because speculative thought in the closing Latin centuries saw powerful developments in epistemological theory which resonate with the central developments of postmodern contemporary thought. Second, because of the truth of Gilson's analogy (1937), according to which history provides for the philosopher what the laboratory provides for the scientist, namely, the arena in which the consequences of ideas are played out.

Miller (1993: 41) describes this idea that the work of philosophy must proceed through a study of history in order to achieve its best results as among "the most lasting lessons Foucault learned from his teacher", Jean Hyppolite. In any event, it is one of the defining ideas of postmodernism.

3

Outlining Latinity with Rinsed Eyes

It needs to be said that the absence of a proper outline for the Latin Age in philosophy as a whole is a major obstacle to appreciating the work of John Poinsot, which exists precisely as a final detail on the capstone of such an outline. The standard treatment of the Latin Age, to begin with, is misleadingly labelled "medieval philosophy", and extends, in the standard coverage (in a hodge-podge selection of writings), from Augustine to William of Ockham. Despite Tachau's work establishing Scotus' distinction between so-called intuitive and abstractive awareness (*notitia intuitiva/notitia abstractiva*) as the initial frame for the shift of emphasis from being to discourse in the closing Latin centuries,[1] Latin

---

[1] "... the notion of intuitive cognition was still inchoate when Scotus adopted it, and subsequent medieval readers credited him with its invention. If their attribution is not precisely accurate, it is indicative of the fact that virutally everyone who employed the terminology to the mid-point of the fourteenth century took Scotus's definition as his starting point." "Despite the difficulties presented by his innovation in grafting intuition onto the process induced by species, the dichotomy of intuitive and abstractive cognition was rapidly and widely adopted by Parisian trained theologians. Within a decade of the Subtle Doctor's death, its acceptance on the other side of the English Channel was also ensured. That is not to say that his understanding was uniformly employed; nor, indeed, that all who employed the terminology of intuitive and abstractive cognition considered Scotus's an adequate delineation of the modes of cognition; nevertheless, the history of medieval theories of knowledge from ca. 1310 can be traced as the development of this dichotomy." Katherine H. Tachau, *Vision and Certitude in the Age of Ockham. Optics, epistemology, and the foundations of semantics 1250–1345* (Leiden: E. J. Brill, 1988), pp. 70, and 80–81. See note 4 in Chapter 2, p. 32 above.

authors after Ockham are given only the most superficial treatment or are ignored entirely in the standard coverage, till philosophy is supposed to "begin again" with Descartes or shortly before (Parkinson 1993: 5–6; Deely and Russell 1986), with Francis Bacon (1561–1626), who shared Descartes' passion for a new beginning and a jettisoning of Latin tradition. Time may be a good partner in advancing the development of a subject-matter that has once been well-outlined, as Aristotle claimed (c.335–334BC: *Ethics* 1098a20–25), but the situation of teaching medieval philosophy in modern times bears witness rather to Aristotle's inverse point (ibid.) that in the absence of such an outline, progress in the area tends toward a standstill.

Yet for all its conspicuous absence in today's academy, a proper outline of the Latin Age is not difficult to draw. In fact, the development of philosophy in Latin after the fall of the Roman empire is an indigenous, multi-faceted, and highly organic development which falls naturally into two main periods or phases.

The first period extends from Augustine in the fifth century to Peter Abelard (1079–1142) and John of Salisbury (1115–1180) in the twelfth. In this interval, the logical treatises of Aristotle and such related Greek writings as Porphyry's *Quinque Verba* (the *Isagoge*) were the only works of Greek philosophy surviving in translation from the Greek, whence philosophy in its own right (that is, as relatively unmixed with theology) developed around mainly logical and methodological questions. The second period extends from Albertus Magnus (1193–1280) to Francis Suárez (1548–1617) and John Poinsot (1589–1644), when the full range of Aristotle's writings, along with such influential Arabic commentaries as those of Avicenna and Averroes, provided the newly emerging universities with the substance of their curriculum across the full range of philosophical subject matter—including those areas we now see as specifically scientific.

This accounts for the great emphasis in the second phase on philosophy of nature, an emphasis which developed into a special focus on the place in nature of the human species.[2] In the Italian peninsula, this focus led to advances in medicine and to a preparation of the ground for

2 The "philosophy of human nature" courses in curricula today are the principal vestige of this last development.

the framing of nature's details in mathematically calculable terms which climaxed in the work of Galileo and the establishment of sciences in the modern sense, as the work of William Wallace (1977–1992) has shown in particular. In the Iberian peninsula, the focus led rather to a concentration on social, political, and religious questions more in direct continuity with the theological emphases of the central European "high middle ages", though in logic and psychology (see Gannon 1991) breakthrough developments took place especially in the areas we now recognize generically as epistemological and specifically as semiotic.

Thus, just as in the first period of the Latin Age there was a concentration especially on methodological tools (the "liberal arts") and concepts of logic, so in the second period there was a concentration initially on the substantive matters of natural philosophy broadly treated so as to provide also the foundations for ethics and metaphysics—matters treated thematically according to the customs and *Weltanschauung* of the period more within theology than within philosophy itself—and on the expansion of logical questions to include the whole of what is called today philosophy of science, epistemology and criteriology, as well as much of ontology.[3]

---

3 Writing of the volumes of Poinsot's *Cursus Philosophicus*, Reiser (1930: XII) remarks: "On the showing of his volumes' titles, Poinsot treats of Logic and Natural Philosophy. As a matter of public avowal he treats neither of Metaphysics nor of Ethics, whence to one inspecting the work superficially will it readily appear that Poinsot has said nothing or next to nothing on these matters. But to anyone who not only looks at the index of questions and articles, but who also reads the text attentively in its entirety, will find that practically everything expounded by modern authors under the title of Ontology can be found in Poinsot under his treatment of material Logic and under his treatment of causes and the ground of motion in the Natural Philosophy. Likewise for the fundamentals of Criteriology, which can be found treated in the Second Part of the Logic in the questions on foreknowledge and premises, demonstration and scientific knowledge. The fact that our author does not provide a specific dissertation on Metaphysics and especially on Ethics within the compass of his Cursus Philosophicus, while unfortunate from our point of view, should not lead anyone to think that Poinsot has written little or nothing on these matters in other places. Matters pertaining to natural theology and to ethics were left for thematic treatment in the Cursus Theologicus, according to the custom of that age, and, specifically, the matters of natural theology to the *Commentary on the First Part* [Poinsot, 1637, 1643], those of Ethics to the *Commentary on the Second Part* [Poinsot 1645, 1649] of the *Summa Theologiae* of St. Thomas, where all these matters

Worthy of special mention is the fact that, in the last two Latin centuries (the period of coalescence of Gracia's "Hispanic philosophy"), intellectual foundations were laid in the university world of the Iberian peninsula for the development of international law and for dealing with the general problems of cultural conflict and assimilation. The work of Francisco de Vitoria (1492–1536), which helped frame the imperial legislation for Spain's New World territories comes to mind, as does the figure of Francisco Suárez (1548–1617) with his rethinking of natural law. In the areas of social and political philosophy, as well as in the areas of ontology and theory of knowledge, the scholastic faculties of the principal universities of Portugal and Spain in the fifteenth, sixteenth, and seventeenth centuries left behind a vein of pure philosophical gold which has only begun to be mined as the prejudices of contemporary scholarship in Anglo-American and Continental philosophy have begun to crumble in the face of historical facts at first grudgingly, now with increasing exuberance, brought to light in the academy. It is to this later, substantive period, that the work of Poinsot belongs.

From our point of view today, Poinsot as the author of the *Cursus Philosophicus* of 1631–1635 appears alongside Francisco Suárez as author of the *Disputationes Metaphysicae* of 1597, in providing what Jack Miles describes (1985) as "one of the two great seventeenth-century summations of medieval philosophy". From the point of view of the classical

are found treated at great length" ("Titulis demonstrantibus agit de Logica et de Philosophia naturali. Ex professo neque Metaphysicam neque Ethicam tractat, quare obiter inspicienti de his rebus nihil vel prope nihil dixisse facile videtur. Qui quidem non tantum indicem quaestionum et articulorum, sed ipsum textum eumque totum attente perlegerit, inveniet paene omnia, quae a recentioribus in Ontologia exponuntur, apud ipsum in Logica totum tractatum de causis et de prima motore in Philosophia haberi. Imo et fundamenta Criteriologiae in secunda parte Logicae, in quaestionibus de praecognitis et praemissis, de demonstratione et scientia tangit. Quod auctor de Metaphysica et praesertim de Ethica intra ambitum Cursus philosophici propriis dissertationibus non egit, quamvis dolendum sit, nemini tamen persuadere licet ipsum nihil vel pauca solummodo de his materiis aliis locis scripsisse. Quae ad Theologiam naturalem et ad Ethicam spectant, ad morem illius aetatis ad Cursum theologicum ex professo tractanda remittit, et quidem quae sunt Theologiae naturalis ad primam [Poinsot 1637, 1643a&b], quae sunt Ethicae ad secundam partem Summae theologicae [Poinsot 1645a&b, 1649], ubi haec omnia plene evoluta inveniuntur").

modern development, however, as Miles goes on to note, while Suárez "remained the textbook philosopher of Europe long after Descartes had given philosophy a new *point de départ*, Poinsot, by contrast, was nearly without intellectual issue until he was rediscovered in this century by Jacques Maritain."[4]

Again we are faced with an ironic situation. Not only was Suárez the textbook philosopher through whose *Disputationes Metaphysicae* almost alone was the philosophic thought of the Latin Age filtered into modern European learning, but he was also generally taken to be, in this regard, a faithful expositor of Thomas Aquinas.[5] In the early decades of the late nineteenth century Thomistic revival, many and heated debates arose over the question of Suárez' reliability as a guide to the views of Thomas Aquinas. These debates were generally and decisively decided in the negative. But fidelity to St. Thomas was not Suárez' principal concern, and his contribution to philosophy on other grounds is equally beyond question. Still, as far as concerns the question of what is and is not consistent with the views of Aquinas in philosophy, as Nuchelmans well put it (1987: 149), the *Cursus Philosophicus* of John Poinsot presents itself as an exemplar "of the powerful tradition to which he belonged and wholeheartedly wanted to belong".[6] Fidelity to St. Thomas was a principal concern of Poinsot. In contrast with the procedure of Suárez, Poinsot made this concern co-ordinate with the exercise of philosophical reason, a co-ordination exhibited in the literary forms of his *Cursus Philosophicus* (see Deely 1985: 417–420).

We see, thus, on several grounds, that the work of Poinsot occupies a heuristically unique position respecting contemporary efforts to rediscover and understand the Latin Age in its integrity, particularly as regards its condition at the time of the formation of early modern philosophy.

---

4 For details, see "Semiotic in the Thought of Jacques Maritain" (Deely 1986c) and "Quid Sit Postmodernismus" (Deely 1995). This latter essay, despite its improbable title, is basically about the work of Gilson and Maritain in relation to Poinsot.

5 "Thomism as formulated by the Jesuit Suárez was universally taught and finally supplanted the doctrine of Melanchthon, even in the universities of Protestant countries" (Bréhier 1938: 1).

6 See Thomas Merton's remarks in Chapter 1, note 4, p. 25 above.

This problem of properly outlining the Latin Age is related to a fact which, in my estimation, has not been taken note of to the extent that it needs to be. I have in mind the fact that the major changes in philosophical epochs happen to correspond in general with the major linguistic changes in Western civilization. The natural macro-units for the study of philosophy are the major changes in the situation of the natural languages. Thus, the period of Greek philosophy extends from the pre-Socratics to the end of the dominance of Greek as the language of learning at the end of the Roman empire in the fifth century. At that moment the Latin speaking peoples were thrown back on their own resources, and the indigenous development of philosophy from a Latin linguistic base began. This development would dominate until the seventeenth century, when again a linguistic sea-change occurs with the emergence of the European national languages as the principal medium of mainstream philosophical discourse. Modern philosophy, not coincidentally, rises against Latin scholasticism on the tide of the emerging natural languages.

The postmodern period, again, coincides with a breakdown of the modern national linguistic compartmentalizations, as a new global perspective begins to emerge beyond national differences of language. This emerging perspective is based not on a unity of natural language, as in the previous three epochs, but on the achievement of an epistemological paradigm capable of taking into account the very mechanisms of linguistic difference and change as part of the framework of philosophy itself. This movement, the postmodern development, is coming to be based especially in the work of the American philosopher Charles Sanders Peirce, with its leading premiss that "the highest grade of reality is only reached by signs" (Peirce 1904: 23). This foundational thrust of Peirce's work takes up again themes in logic and epistemology that developed strongly in the last two centuries or so of Latin thought.

In this particular connection Poinsot makes a very specific contribution, as noted by Jack Miles (1985):

Within Poinsot's great *Cursus Philosophicus*, there stands a clearly distinct smaller work, a kind of excursus, entitled *Tractatus de Signis*, a "Treatise on Signs." ... in this forgotten document, Poinsot anticipated in a most extraordinary way the modern linguistic/philosophical movement called semiotics.

In this *Treatise*[7] in three books—"On the Sign in Its Proper Being", "The Division of Sign", and "Modes of Awareness and Concepts")— we confront in a particularly exaggerated form the paradox of Poinsot's work as constituting, in Simonin's description (1930: 145–146), "a synthesis of irreconcilables":

On the one hand, Poinsot is determined to let no new achievements be lost, and to profit from the final developments of a Scholasticism which has exhausted itself in the plenitude of its refinements; but on the other hand, he is determined further still to remain a man of the past and to arrange his work in its totality according to the pattern and methods of long-standing tradition ... Whatever sympathy one may have for the attempt, it seems equally clear that it was not destined to develop and fulfill itself normally.[8]

---

[7] Thomas Merton points out (1951: 335) a tract that stands out within Poinsot's *Cursus Theologicus*, and I am inclined to add that it does so in much the way that the *Treatise on Signs* stands out within the *Cursus Philosophicus*: "One tract of John of Saint Thomas stands out above all the rest. His study of the Gifts of the Holy Ghost is of capital importance. It contains the solution to some of the problems that have most exercised mystical theologians in our day. The claims of modern writers like Father Garrigou-Lagrange, Father Gardeil, and others who hold that the mystical life is the normal fulfillment of the Christian life of grace, rest almost entirely on the teaching of Saint Thomas about the Gifts of the Holy Ghost as it has been developed by John of Saint Thomas. There can be no question that the seventeenth-century Dominican has given us, with absolute clarity and fidelity, the true doctrine of Saint Thomas Aquinas."

This treatise within Poinsot's theology did not escape the notice of his contemporaries as did the *Tractatus de Signis* within the philosophy, as the early testimony of the Salmanticenses witnesses: "de hac materia tam docte, tam profunde et luculenter agit ut palmam aliis immo et sibi alia scribenti praeripere videatur"—"Poinsot has treated of this matter with such wisdom, depth and clarity, that he surpasses all others, and indeed even himself, making it seem impossible for anyone to write after him." See the Editorial AfterWord (Deely 1985) to the *Tractatus de Signis*, pp. 443–444, text and notes 68 and 69, for historical context.

[8] Simonin, 1930: 145–146: "L'ouvrage de Jean de St.-Thomas se presente donc comme un ouvrage de transition; c'est là la marque de son originalité ... Aussi n'est-ce pas sans émotion que l'on voit Jean de St.-Thomas s'essayer à faire la synthèse de l'inconciliable. D'un côté il n'entend laisser perdre aucune des acquisitions nouvelles, et profiter des derniers développements d'une scolastique qui s'épuise elle même à force de raffinements, mais d'autre part il entend, davantage encore, rester un homme du passé et disposer l'ensemble de son oeuvre selon le plan ancien et les anciennes méthodes. Il y fallait évidemment le coup d'oeil et la main d'un artiste ex-

In no part of the *Cursus Philosophicus* is Simonin's observation better verified than in the particular detail of Poinsot's *Tractatus de Signis* considered in relation to the whole of which it was originally crafted as a part. First of all, as a part, it is strikingly anomalous. Despite occupying only about 7.1% of the whole work quantitatively speaking, qualitatively the *Treatise on Signs* unites the opening questions of the *Ars Logica* and the concluding questions of the *Philosophia Naturalis*—that is to say, the opening and the closing passages of the *Cursus Philosophicus* as a whole—in a new perspective, the perspective of relations as required to ground our experience of signs in constituting experience itself in its proper and irreducible being, which transcends the division of the two parts of the whole (Logic and Natural Philosophy) as concerned, respectively, with mind-dependent and mind-independent being. As such, it is not too much to say that the *Tractatus de Signis* subsumes the structure of the whole of which it is part and renders that whole, to borrow a not inapt term from Hegel's lexicon, *aufgehoben*—synthesized in a higher way.

Thus, the miniscule part the *Tractatus de Signis* occupies on the second of the seven folds comprising the giant fold-out "synoptic table" of the *Cursus Philosophicus* (pp. 371–375 in the Deely edition of Poinsot 1632a) can be quite misleading. For the *Summulae* or introductory logic books, which open the *Ars Logica* and the *Cursus Philosophicus*, begin with a chapter defining what a term is, followed by a chapter on the definition and division of signs, and a third chapter dividing terms in various ways. These initial three Summulae chapters, each less than two pages in length, turn out, however, to be pregnant with all the metaphysical and psychological difficulties that Poinsot considers susceptible of a systematically unified treatment such as they have heretofore not received, and which he thinks he has "removed to their proper place" by dealing with them (as befits "uncommon difficulties") in Part II rather than in Part I of the *Ars Logica*, and in particular by relating them to the discussion of interpretation (*perihermenias*).

ceptionnel, et, quelque sympathie que l'on puisse avoir pour la tentative, il semble bien qu'elle n'était pas appelée à se développer et à s'épanouir normalement ... Ainsi comprise et située à sa place dans l'ensemble d'une evolution, l'oeuvre de Jean de St.-Thomas prend une signification spéciale, et peut-être un intérêt notable en un moment où l'on retrouve le goût du style ancien."

Similarly, if one compares the contents of Books II and III of the *Treatise* (*Ars Logica*, Qq. XXII–XXIII, "On the Division of Sign", and "On Modes of Awareness and Concepts") with the contents of Questions IV–IX ("On External and Internal Sense Powers and Objects") and Question XI ("On Understanding and Conception") of the concluding Fourth Part of the *Philosophia Naturalis*, one discovers that the very same material covered from a semiotic point of view under the rubric of "signum formale" (formal sign) and "notitia" (awareness) is also covered from an ontological point of view (the point of view of the then-traditional natural philosophy and metaphysics) under the rubric of sensation and intellection in the questions which conclude the discussions of cognition in the natural philosophy (and *Cursus Philosophicus* as a whole).

These remarks serve to illustrate concretely how the theoretical requirement that a doctrine of signs develop from a standpoint superior to the classical division of being into mind-independent and mind-dependent (*ens reale* and *ens rationis*) is realized in the development of Poinsot's *Tractatus*. The *Treatise on Signs* returns to the beginnings of traditional logic to reconceptualize the foundations proper to discourse in its entirety, but, at the same time, it incorporates into that new beginning results that were only reached in traditional philosophy through the ontological analysis of substance and of living beings as substances capable of perception and concept formation. It is not just the beginnings but also the conclusions of the traditional *Cursus Philosophicus* that are transcended in the point of view proper to the consideration of signs. The whole of philosophy traditionally conceived proves to be embryonic to the point of view of the *Treatise on Signs*.

A vignette from the history of Poinsot's logical writings may serve to illustrate Simonin's contention that Poinsot's attempt to contain all new achievements within the pattern and methods of long-standing tradition amounted to 'a synthesis of irreconcilables not destined to develop and fulfill itself normally'. I am thinking of the case of the *Quaestiones minoris dialecticae* of Michael Comas (1661), where Poinsot's ideas on signs are taken over and applied to the organization of a traditional logic textbook in ways quite unanticipated by Poinsot. To appreciate the case, a little background on the organization of Poinsot's *Treatise on Signs* in relation to the *Logic* and *Natural Philosophy* of the *Cursus Philosophicus* is in order.

The story begins in 1529, when Dominic Soto, who had completed his graduate studies in Paris, published his influential *Summulae*, as the introductory logic text in those days was commonly called, therewith introducing into the Iberian university world the custom of treating of signs in the early part of formal logic. His treatment of signs, however, was set out through a series of more or less *ad hoc* distinctions which had the effect of disrupting the treatment of logic and diverting it into metaphysical and psychological issues which had by no means been digested in semiotic terms. Soto's example and influence resulted in a kind of curricular chaos to which Poinsot, in his capacity as teacher of introductory logic, made objection. The first task, as he saw it, was the proper assimilation of traditional metaphysics and natural philosophy to the perspective required for a doctrine of signs, not the consideration of these matters within the context of an introductory logic curriculum.

In his own *Summulae* text, i.e., the First Part of his *Logic* (1631), Poinsot devoted the opening three chapters, the second of the three in particular, to a discussion of the sign. This opening treatment indeed indicates the foundational status the sign has in relation to logical enquiry integrally conceived. However, this opening treatment in Poinsot is highly schematic and abstract. Detailed and substantive treatment of the matter he postponed to the Second (or ''material'') Part of his *Logic* (1632), where he introduces his full-scale treatment of the doctrine of signs with the following observation (1632a: 38/11–21):

The materials covered in the introductory logic of the *Summulae* books pertain without exception to the analysis of discourse in terms of its logical elements and their interrelation.

Yet because in the introductory logic courses the subject matter is treated throughout by way of interpretation and signification, since indeed the universal instrument of Logic is the sign, from which are constituted all of logic's instruments, therefore, lest the foundations of logical form go unexamined, the project of the present work is to treat of these things which were brought into the introductory course for the purpose of explaining the nature and division of signs, but which have been set aside for special treatment here. For the grasp of beginners is not proportioned to these questions about signs.[9]

---

9 Poinsot 1632a: 8–21: ''De his egimus in libris Summularum; haec enim omnia ordinantur et pertinent ad prioristicam resolutionem. Sed tamen, quia haec omnia

This last remark about the ''grasp of beginners'' bears some scrutiny, for it provides us with a remarkably rich historical illustration of what we would call today ''curricular development''. Writing barely twenty-nine years after the publication of Poinsot's *Treatise*, Michael Comas was able to point out that one main result of Poinsot's advanced doctrinal synthesis was to demonstrate how the full discussion of signs in their proper being could be integrated, without disruption, into the introductory treatment of logic. In Comas' view, Poinsot's strictures against treating logic from the start in terms of the sign were justified by the pedagogical situation at the time, rather than by the nature of the subject matter itself.

In other words, when the realization of the foundational role of the sign in logical studies was new and undeveloped, it was inappropriate to impose it on beginners in the subject matter, who could hardly be expected to assimilate and master material that even the professors were only just beginning to understand. Once further research—in this case, Poinsot's own *Treatise*—had succeeded in systematizing the requirements and clarifying the nature of the new perspective, the manner of its proper introduction into, and integration with, the beginner's logic course also becomes apparent. Comas expressed himself on this point as follows (1661: 17):

Following the order of doctrine, we begin with the sign; for it is more universal than terms and logically structured discourse, and is something necessarily prerequisite thereto. For every logical instrument used for knowing and speaking is a sign: the understanding knows through the significations of ideas and speaks through the significations voiced. Thus, if the student of logic is to master his instruments, namely, terms and arguments, he must perforce understand the nature of the sign; and as the *Summulists* [the Professors of Formal Logic] commonly say that right doctrinal order requires that Logic begin with terms, because the term is the smallest unit of logical discourse and pertains to the simple awareness presupposed in every cognitive operation, so it

tractantur in his libris per modum interpretationis et significationis, commune siquidem Logicae instrumentum est signum, quo omnia eius instrumenta constant, idcirco visum est in praesenti pro doctrina horum librorum ea tradere, quae ad explicandam naturam et divisiones signorum in Summulis insinuata, huc vero reservata sunt. Nec enim tironum captui quaestiones istae de signis proportionatae sunt.''

strikes me that that very same order of doctrine and the identical line of reasoning dictates that Logic begin with the sign: for just as terms formally connote discourse, so must they have the rationale of signs.[10]

Poinsot himself clearly recognized the semiotic foundations of logic, and how these foundations called for a broader understanding of logic in the traditional sense. Yet, until the exact nature of those foundations had been worked out, a task he himself undertook to execute, he rightly deemed the matter too difficult to bring to the attention of beginners in logic ("Nec enim tironum captui quaestiones istae de signis proportionatae sunt"). In proceeding thus he provided the theoretical remedy for a pedagogical problem, a remedy which needed to be understood and assimilated before its practical applications could be made.

Michael Comas, expressly basing his treatment of logic on the requirements proper to the order of doctrine precisely as these had been systematized and clarified by Poinsot's work, felt that Poinsot had prepared the way sufficiently for just such a practical, curricular application. In making this application, indeed, Comas provided a kind of anticipation of the Peircean project of deriving even the traditional concerns of formal logic and syllogistic directly from the prior consideration of the sign in its proper being (further specified as this and that kind of sign—in the case of logic as then conceived, "second intentions").

In other words, Comas uses Poinsot's arguments on the nature of signs in relation to traditional logic to begin the treatment of that very logic, *especially* for beginners, with the discussion of signs. Furthermore, Comas justifies this change in the starting point for beginners' logic in

10 Miguel Comas del Brugar ("Michael Comas") 1661: 17: "Ordine doctrinae servato incipimus a signo; quia est universali termino, & oratione logicali, & quid necessario praerequisitum; omnia enim instrumenta logicalia, utimur ad cognoscendum, & loquendum sunt signa; intellectus namque per conceptus significativos cognoscit, & per voces significativas loquitur; ideoque, ut logicus bene intelligat sua instrumenta scilicet terminos, & orationes, necesse est naturam signi intelligat, & sicut dicunt communiter Summulistae, quod recto ordine Doctrinae incipit logica a termino, quia terminus est pars orationis logicalis, & pertinet ad primam operationem intellectus, quae praesupponitur ad alias operationes; eodem ordine incipiendum putavi a signo propter eandem rationem: quia ut formaliter orationes terminus connotat, debet habere rationem signi, licet hoc sit fundamenta secundae intentionis termini, in quo resolutio logicalis proprie sistit."

a way that is systematically derived from Poinsot's advanced theoretical work. Comas's derived way offered an alternative both to the way that Poinsot had chosen, following his teachers, and to the way chosen by Soto that Poinsot had criticized as a premature introducion of the perspective of the sign into the traditionally established subject matter.

At the time he undertook to write his own *Tractatus* on the subject Poinsot expressly and with justice held the opinion that the treatment of signs in the courses introductory to the philosophy curriculum (that is, the courses of "minor", "formal", or "summulist" logic) was eclectic and confused, disrupting the order of traditional introduction without commensurate gain. The problem, then, i.e., at that historical moment of the doctrine's development, was to systematize the treatment of signs and to discover the unity proper to the problematic of *signum* providing the foundations for interpretation in general and logical interpretation in particular. As a research matter, this is a subject for advanced study, not for the introductory course.

If this problematic could be systematized and the unity and treatment proper to it assimilated, the problems constituting it could then be presented clearly and in their proper relation to logical studies—and to other studies insofar as they are "sign-dependent". At that point, it would be possible to restore even to the traditional introduction a fuller consideration of signs, without creating confusion and resorting to eclecticism. This way of handling signs would also require a change in the order of traditional introduction, but now the change would be integrative rather than disruptive—it could effect the commensurate gains that clarity and a higher order of synthesis in the subject matter offer to beginning students.

The alternatives pursued by Poinsot and Comas, in sum, alike repugned a confused eclecticism. But, in relation to one another, the opposition of their ways is not repugnantial but sequential. What we have here is a detail illustrative of the evolution of intellectual culture. Today's graduate seminars have a way of shaping even the most traditional of tomorrow's introductory textbooks for undergraduates.

Yet in Poinsot's own organization of his work, it was not the novel or revolutionary aspect of questions that he wished to emphasize, but rather a skilful balance and integration of novel with traditional concerns that would enable him, by preserving "the accustomed framework of philosophical teaching'', as Simonin said (1930: 144–145), ''to situate his work in the totality of analogous undertakings''.

Yet, in the case of his *Treatise on Signs*, the truly ''analogous undertaking'' for what Poinsot essays is less to be found in earlier works of Aristotelian commentary than it is in the work of his contemporary Descartes, who of deliberate purpose sets his hand to the laying of a new foundation for the whole of philosophy. For if, as I have indicated above, both the beginnings and the conclusions of the traditional *Cursus Philosophicus* are transcended in the point of view proper to the *doctrina signorum*, then it is the whole of philosophy that is embryonic to the semiotic point of view, ''it is'', exactly as Winance summarized (1983: 515) in his review of Poinsot's *Tractatus de Signis*, ''in the tradition of Peirce, Locke, and Poinsot that Logic becomes semiotic, able to assimilate the whole of epistemology and natural philosophy as well.''

The case needs to be examined in considerably more detail if we are to show how all this is at stake in the detail of Poinsot's analyses of the sign. Let us try to see in the next chapter what this specific contribution on Poinsot's part within his would-be traditional *Cursus* implies for the understanding on our part of philosophy itself, both in the context of the seventeenth century and in the contemporary context of nascent postmodernism.

4

The Problem of Novelty
in the Writings of Late Latin Scholasticism

By comparison with Descartes, Poinsot's contribution to the seventeenth century search for a new beginning in philosophy is difficult to access. Descartes proposed, as the necessary solution to the muddle of the Latin past, adoption of a new method without which "the pursuit of learning would, I think, be more harmful than profitable" (1628: 17). "By 'a method'", he explained (ibid.: 16),

I mean reliable rules which are easy to apply, and such that if one follows them exactly, one will never take what is false to be true or fruitlessly expend one's mental efforts,[1] but will gradually and constantly increase one's knowledge till one arrives at a true understanding of everything within one's capacity.[2]

As to the writings of the ancients, insofar as they contain, by virtue of the natural light, scattered glimmers of the Cartesian method, they

---

[1] Hence Descartes' assurance to Mersenne in his letter of February 1637 (cited from Stoothoff 1985: 109; cf. Kenny 1970: 30) that his method "consists much more in practice than in theory" and "extends to every kind of subject-matter."

[2] The requisite rules, of course, Descartes set himself to supply, and with the hindsight of three centuries I can confidently report that, while Descartes' various discourses in this area are still widely read by philosophy students, they have nowhere served for the complete rebuilding of the edifice of human knowledge that Descartes envisioned for them. The issuance of "promissory notes" in philosophy, still popular in analytic circles today, may be said to have been begun by Descartes; hence, if the witness of history counts for anything in such a matter, the last three hundred years tend to discredit the practice.

perhaps deserve to be read, "but at the same time there is a considerable danger that if we study these works too closely traces of their errors will infect us and cling to us against our will and despite our precautions" (Descartes 1628: 13).

In other words, what is proposed as novel in the Cartesian system is the system itself, in particular the method of analysis of objects into their simplest components, buttressed by methodical doubt maintained at each step of the way. Adoption of the Cartesian approach, moreover, is recommended as necessary from the outset if "the pursuit of learning" is not to be, as by implication it has perforce always heretofore been, "more harmful than profitable" (Descartes 1628: 17).

The desire for a new approach to philosophy that characterized the birth of modern philosophy in the seventeenth century, moreover, was not something vague and general, but quite specific. Those desiring to be moderns knew not only what they were looking for, but where they expected to find it. Descartes (1628: 31) spoke for the entire period when he asserted that "the most useful inquiry we can make at this stage is to ask: What is human knowledge and what is its scope?", and that the task for such inquiry is "to seek to encompass in thought everything in the universe, with a view to learning in what way particular things may be susceptible of investigation by the human mind."

Poinsot's approach to the problems of philosophy, including this one, was in almost every respect contrary to that of Descartes. To begin with, he did not think that there was any sure and easy method, old or new, that would lead to the infallible discovery of philosophical truth. For him, there was no substitute for studying the works of those who had gone before, and the method for doing this was to reduce the arguments to be found in previous authors to their logical core and express this core in strict logical form as the means whereby hidden assumptions and unsound premisses could best be brought to light.[3]

Hence Poinsot rejected Descartes' view (1628: 37) that "ordinary dialectic is of no use whatever to those who wish to investigate the truth of things", though he agreed completely with Descartes (1628: 36) in

---

3 See Poinsot's "Prologus Totius Dialecticae, Praeludium Primum: quo proponitur dialecticae disputationis exercitium et praxis", in the *Artis Logicae Prima Pars* (1631), 3a1–5a3 (= *Tractatus de Signis*, "First Prologue: Wherein is set forth the exercise and practice of dialectical disputation", 10/1–13/12).

repudiating those who prescribed the forms of dialectic as a means for taking, "as it were, a rest from considering a particular inference clearly and attentively". The forms of dialectic, for Poinsot—the necessary aspect of even probable syllogisms—are merely the preliminary instrument for positioning ourselves to adjudicate what is philosophically sound or unsound in the views of another, ancient or modern.

The disagreement between Poinsot and Descartes over method extended also to the object of our knowledge. Poinsot was not a reductionist. He did not believe that higher orders of difficulty in knowledge could be reduced to complex arrangements of ultimately simple objects, so that the complex could be deduced from the simple merely by a careful observation of the proper ways in which simple objects combine to form complex wholes. Poinsot accepted rather a doctrine of substance according to which ontological unities in nature do not ordinarily correspond and can seldom be made to correspond in one-to-one fashion with objective unities represented in knowledge, a point which Cajetan had clarified better than anyone. In his *Commentariam in Summam Theologicam. Prima Pars* (1507), Quaestio 1, Articulus 3, Cajetan enunciates the principle that differences among things are quite another matter than differences among objects. Poinsot takes up this principle as one of the fundamental principles of the doctrine of signs.[4] Knowledge, Poinsot considered, consisted essentially in the establishment, for any given case, of a correspondence in relationships between objective representation and ontological reality, allowing in particular for objective states of affairs which have no ontological counterpart existing apart from their representation.[5] To know the truth in any given case is critically to determine

---

4 See the *Tractatus de Signis*, Book I, Question 2, 149/41–151/21, Question 4, 187/28–190/23 and note 33 thereto, p. 187; especially Book II, Question 1, 235/36–236/46, Question 5, 270/37–271/21. See also Cajetan's comments on q. 28, art. 1, of this same part of the *Summa*, partially cited in note 18, p. 95 of the 1985 Deely edition of the *Tractatus de Signis*.

5 Poinsot 1635: 77b26–78a46 (cited in Deely edition of Poinsot 1632a: 190n35): "In the object of a power the focus of attention is not formally mind-independent or entitative reality, according as the object has being in itself, but the proportion and adaptation to the power. This proportion indeed as it subjectively exists in a thing must be mind-independent; but in terms of the relation to the power, that it exists subjectively in the thing itself is not what is regarded, but rather that it exists *objectively*

which pattern of objectivity we are dealing with in this or that aspect of experience.[6]

relative to the power in question—although on other grounds, if the power itself respects only mind-independent being [as the external senses], it will also require a mind-independent being in the object, not as existing, but as related to the power. For existence is always in an order to itself and subjectively, whereas to a power it always pertains objectively. Whence a mind-dependent being, although in itself it has subjectively no reality, can still be the object of an act of understanding and specify that act by reason of an objective proportion which it takes on in an order to the understanding when it has a real fundament and is conceived on the pattern of mind-independent being. For then it can perfect and specify the understanding by a mind-independent perfection, not one innate to itself or existing in itself, but one borrowed and appropriated from mind-independent entity, on whose pattern it is objectively conceived, as we have said in the Logic 2. p. q. 1. art. 3 [Reiser ed., 265b44–266b12]. Thus, even though reality and the character of being belongs to mind-independent and mind-dependent being analogically, and not simply in the same way, nevertheless, objectively it can be found in a mind-dependent being simply in the same way as in a mind-independent being, because, presupposing a borrowing from mind-independent being and from its fundament, the very proportion and adaptation to a cognitive power which alone pertains essentially to an objective rationale is there, for the mind-dependent being is truly and properly coapted, so that it terminates a true and proper act of understanding exactly as do other objects.

"Nor does it matter that the mind-dependent being has existence from the act itself of understanding; therefore it does not perfect and specify that act, but is perfected by it. The answer to this is that the mind-dependent being has existence from the understanding after the manner of an existence not mind-independently, but denominatively, that is to say, as regards the denomination of 'known thing', which follows upon an act of understanding. And for this reason such a consequent denomination is not a rationale perfecting the understanding, but as one effected and consequent, yet the mind-dependent being does perfect the understanding insofar as, antecedently to this denomination, by reason of its fundament, it takes on an objective adaptation and proportion whereby it truly and properly terminates as an object of understanding, by the fact that, even though it is a constructed or fictive being, it is nevertheless not fictively objectified and understood, but terminates a true act by a true termination, although by a fictive entity." (Latin cited in Appendix of Longer Citations, pp. 255–256 below.)

The same basic notions hold for the higher powers of purely sensory life, as Poinsot shows in Article 3 of the First Preamble to the *Treatise on Signs*.

6   The Latin context in which Poinsot is concerned to synthesize his views, the landscape he surveys in the area we call epistemology, is rich beyond imagining. "Like some great philosophical Indies, it now lies in wait for its Columbus'', wrote

In other words, Poinsot was a quintessential scholastic, at the historical moment when the very complexity of the results arrived at by the scholastic method and the very multiplicity of authorities established in the scholastic line were experienced by most as a crushing burden more trouble to learn than it was worth. Scholastic logic, the point of entry into the system of philosophy in the mainstream university curricula against which Descartes and the moderns rebelled, demanded seven years' study in Poinsot's university, three in formal logic and four in so-called "material" logic, which was the study of logic as an instrument not merely for restating arguments in form but for adjudicating therewith the truth of their contents.

Imbued with the deepest respect for tradition, Poinsot felt charged with a double mission: not only to advance the truth, but to do so in a way that carried with it the whole of past truth. Simonin has described the dilemma well (1930: 145):

Poinsot is determined to let no new achievements be lost, and to profit from the final developments of a scholasticism which had exhausted itself in the plenitude of its refinements.

A. Finding a Focus

If, therefore, we are to find from Poinsot a contribution to the modern demand for a new beginning in philosophy, it will be hidden among the plenitude of refinements made in the final developments of scholastic philosophy, the mainstream philosophy of the Latin Age. There may of course be more than one such contribution in the vast synthesis of Poinsot's *Cursus Philosophicus*. But the most promising area in which to look would naturally concern the nature and extent of human knowledge. For Poinsot was inevitably a man of his own time as well as a figure of tradition. He worked from one of the most vital centers of seventeenth century university life, cognizant of all the currents of modernity,[7] and

a current Marco Polo of studies in Latin philosophy (Doyle 1984a: 121). See Doyle 1987–1988, 1990.

[7] That Poinsot clung to the discredited empirical beliefs of the ancients (Lavaud 1928: 416–417) and knew nothing of the works of Galileo and Descartes (Simon 1955: xix)

breathing the atmosphere of the period. It is no accident that Latin scholasticism, no less than the peripheral currents which would replace it as mainstream on the Continent and in England, had undergone in its later development a shift in emphasis from ontological questions to questions of epistemology, as we would call them today.

In this regard, the decisive influence on Poinsot's thought came from the University of Paris, where his predecessor at Alcalá, Dominic Soto, had done his graduate study.[8] At Paris, Soto had been steeped in the controversy begun by followers of Ockham over the adequacy of Augustine's classical definition of sign, enshrined in the fourth book of Lombard's *Sentences* as the focus for sacramental theology, according to which a sign is something which, on being perceived, brings into awareness another besides itself. The Parisian logicians developed at length a point that Aquinas had passingly touched on in a number of contexts but never thematized, the point that this definition from Augustine is too narrow, because intellectual notions and phantasms alike—in a word, concepts and percepts, ideas and images—function precisely to bring into our awareness something that they themselves are not.[9] And not only, for example, is it the case that an idea of a dog

are myths that need to be exploded, as I have pointed out in my Editorial After-Word to the *Tractatus de Signis* (Deely 1985: 399–404, esp. 403n8). Suffice it here to point out that the structure Poinsot finally gave to his *Cursus* as published, both in what it omits in natural philosophy and what it incorporates in logic (Deely 1985: 404), is inexplicable except on the assumption of Poinsot's intimate awareness of the philosophical trends developing in Italy and central Europe.

8 An excellent brief summary of the general historical context, based on the many works of Muñoz Delgado and Ashworth 1974, 1978, is provided in Angelelli 1992, esp. Section 3, "From Montaigu to Alcalá and Salamanca".

9 Aquinas had qualified in passing in a number of contexts but never thematized this point that the classical definition of sign from Augustine is too narrow to cover the function of concepts as *aliquid stans pro alio*, a point that would be fiercely taken up by later Parisian doctors who would influence Soto as a student there (and thence, through Soto, the whole of Iberia: see preceding note). Poinsot identifies a variety of contexts in which Aquinas touches on these points. It is interesting to notice that these contexts cover the full span of Aquinas' professorial career: c.1254–1256: the *Commentary on the Sentences of Peter Lombard*, Book IV, dist. 1, q. 1, quaestiunc. 2; c.1256–1259: the *Disputed Questions on Truth*, q. 4. art. 1 ad 7, q. 9. art. 4 ad 4 and ad 5; c.1269–1272: the *Questions at Rando*, q. 4 art. 17; c.1266–1273/4: the *Summa*

is not a dog, but also is it the case that a dog thought of may or may not be a dog existing. Nascent here is not merely the dyadic distinction emphasized by the Paris logicians between signs as vehicles of awareness themselves sometimes perceptible and sometimes not, but, more fundamentally, a triadic distinction among concepts as psychological states, objects as apprehended terms of cognitive relations, and things existing physically whether or not objectively. But the immediate focus of the controversy in Paris was on the question of whether the sign is rightly defined when being perceptible to sense is made part of its definition; and to this question the decisive answer was made in the negative.

From this answer arose a new definition of *signum* as *anything* which brings into awareness what it itself is not, and a corresponding new division into signs which perform the act of signifying only on condition that they are themselves objective terms of apprehension, hereafter among the Latins called *instrumental signs*, and signs which perform the act of signifying without themselves being objects first apprehended as such, hereafter among the Latins called *formal signs*. The actual coinage of this terminology historians have yet to attribute to a specific individual. What seems certain is that the terminology was in use in Paris by the time Soto studied there, and it is certain that Soto introduced the terminology and the controversy into the Iberian university world early in the sixteenth century, where it became, over the next century, a matter of daily dispute in the schools (cf. Poinsot 1632: 194/39-40).

theologiae III, q. 60, art. 4 ad 1. (It will be interesting to check this list via an electronic search of a CD-ROM version of Aquinas' *Opera Omnia*, which I hope to do in the near future.) Synthesizing the import of these passages, Poinsot concludes soberly that "in sententia S. Thomae probabilius est signum formale esse vere et proprie signum, atque adeo univoce cum instrumentali"—"In the opinion of St. Thomas, the more probable reading is that a formal sign is truly and properly a sign, and therefore univocally with an instrumental sign, even though formal signs and instrumental signs greatly differ in mode of specifying" (*Artis Logicae Secunda Pars*, Q. XXII, Art. 1, "Utrum sit univoca et bona divisio signi in formale et instrumentale", 694b1-4; = *Tractatus de Signis*, Book II, Question 1, "Whether the Division of Signs into Formal and Instrumental is Univocal and Sound", 225/11-14). The carefully nuanced wording here nicely illustrates Maritain's observation (1953: vi) that "Men like Cajetan and John of St. Thomas set such an example of exacting respect for the genuine thought of Aquinas that their guidance is a most effective protection against the risk of ignoring the historical evolution of problems".

The problem was, from Poinsot's point of view, that Soto had introduced this discussion into the Iberian curriculum in a disruptive fashion. For he had made the discussion of signs a part of the opening chapters in his introductory logic text or *Summulae* (Soto 1529, 1544), and this example had been followed by other Iberian professors, giving rise to "a vast forest of intractable questions and a thorny thicket of sophisms" which have served mainly "to burden and abrade the minds of students, causing no little harm".[10] For "the grasp of beginners is not proportioned to these questions about signs"[11]—"swarming with so many and extraordinary difficulties"[12]— which, "for the slower wits", have "raised a fog".[13] Poinsot's solution to this problem was to remove "the metaphysical and other difficulties from the books *On the Soul* which the ardor of disputants has caused to intrude into the very beginning of the *Summulae* books"[14] and "to publish separately, in place of a Commentary on the books *On Interpretation*" a "treatise on signs and modes of awareness".[15] This treatise cannot be appropriately

---

10 Poinsot's 1631 Preface (*Lectori*) to the *Artis Logicae Prima Pars*, p. 1 (= *Tractatus de Signis*, "To the Reader of 1631", p. 5): "immensam inextricabilium quaestionum silvam et spinosa sophismatum dumeta excidere curavimus, quae audientium mentibus onerosae et pungentes utilitatis nihil, dispendii non parum afferebant".

11 *Artis Logicae Secunda Pars* (1632), remarks "super libros Perihermenias", 642a22–24 (= *Tractatus de Signis*, 38/20–21): "Nec enim tironum captui quaestiones istae de signis proportionatae sunt."

12 Poinsot's 1640 Preface (*Lectori*) to the second separate edition of his *Artis Logicae Secunda Pars*, p. 249 (= *Tractatus de Signis*, "To the Reader of 1640", p. 35): "... tractatum de signis, pluribus nec vulgaribus difficultatibus scaturientem, ne hic iniectus aut sparsus gravaret tractatus alio satis per se graves ...": for full text, see note 15 below on this page.

13 Ibid.: "... fateor sic me ista tractasse, ut accuratioribus oculis haud quaquam praeluxisse praesumam, at nec tardioribus offudisse caliginem ..."

14 Poinsot's 1631 Preface (*Lectori*) to the *Artis Logicae Prima Pars*, p. 1 (= *Tractatus de Signis*, "To the Reader of 1631", p. 5): "Ad haec metaphysicas difficultates pluresque alias ex libris de Anima, quae disputantium ardore in ipsa Summularum cunabula irruperant, suo loco amandavimus et tractatum de signis et notitiis in Logica super librum Perihermenias expedimus."

15 Poinsot's 1640 Preface to the second separate edition of his *Artis Logicae Secunda Pars*, 249 (= *Tractatus de Signis*, "To the Reader of 1640", 35): "We have now covered

introduced—introduced, that is, without causing undue confusion and perplexity—until mind-dependent being and relation have first been thoroughly treated, for the reason that it is on these two notions, and especially the notion of relation, that successful "inquiry concerning the nature and definable essence of signs principally depends".[16]

Here we see one of the best illustrations of the manner in which the work of Poinsot attempts what Simonin (1930: 145) has called "a synthesis of irreconcilables": "On the one hand, Poinsot is determined to let no new achievements be lost", while, "on the other hand, he is determined further still ... to arrange his work in its totality according to the pattern and methods of long-standing tradition."

Poinsot does not disagree with Soto's emphasis on the importance of a doctrine of signs. "Since the universal instrument of logic is indeed the *sign*," he tells us, "the very foundation of the exposition of logic goes unexamined" until and unless the project of a doctrine of signs has been

---

as we promised the several questions traditionally dealt with in the first part of Logic, except that, for good reasons, the treatise on signs, swarming with so many and extraordinary difficulties, and in order to free the introductory texts of the pervasive presence of its uncommon difficulties, we have decided to publish separately in place of a commentary on the books On Interpretation and together with questions on the books of Posterior Analytics; and for the more convenient use of the work, we have separated the treatise on signs from the discussion of the Categories."—"Quod in prima Logicae parte promisimus de quaestionibus pluribus, quae ibi tractari solent, hic expediendis, plane solvimus, excepto quod iustis de causis tractatum de signis, pluribus nec vulgaribus difficultatibus scaturientem, ne hic iniectus aut sparsus gravaret tractatus alio satis per se graves, seorsum edendum duximus loco commentarii in libros Perihermenias simul cum quaestionibus in libros Posteriorum, et pro commodiori libri usu a tractatu Praedicamentorum seiunximus."

16 Poinsot, *Artis Logicae Secunda Pars* (1632), remarks "Super libros Perihermenias", 642a22–24 (= "Remarks on Aristotle's *Books on Interpretation*, Explaining the Relation of the *Treatise on Signs* to the Aristotelian Tradition, Its Philosophical Justification, and Its Presuppositions within the *Ars Logica*", *Tractatus de Signis*, 38/21–39/4): "[these questions concerning signs] now, however, in this work, may be authentically introduced, following a consideration of mind-dependent being and of the category of relation, on which considerations this inquiry concerning the nature and definable essence of signs principally depends"—"[quaestiones istae de signis] nunc autem in hoc loco genuine introducuntur, post notitiam habitam de ente rationis et praedicamento relationis, a quibus principaliter dependet inquisitio ista de natura et quidditate signorum".

completed.[17] Moreover, as the unfolding of his treatment of the questions on relation and mind-dependent being as they pertain to the doctrine of signs makes clear, in Poinsot's view, interpretation is an activity coextensive with the life of the mind.[18] Hence a *Treatise on Interpretation*, strictly and properly so-called, cannot be restricted to the logical interpretation of terms and propositions, but must extend itself to the instrument of interpretation as such, whether logical or otherwise, and this instrument is the sign. Hence, in view of the full requirements of philosophical tradition, the proper place for a consideration of signs in their entire amplitude is not merely in connection with or as part of a traditional commentary on the Aristotle's *De Interpretatione*, as Poinsot's Coimbra teachers and others in the milieu had essayed, but *instead of* and *supplanting* the traditional commentary entirely.[19]

---

17 "... commune siquidem Logicae instrumentum est signum, quo omnia eius instrumenta constant, idcirco visum est in praesenti pro doctrina horum librorum ea tradere, quae ad explicandam naturam et divisiones signorum ..." ("Super libros Perihermenias", in *Artis Logicae Secunda Pars*, 642a615–21; = *Tractatus de Signis*, 38/13–19).

18 See note 30, p. 75 below.

19 Poinsot 1640 Preface (*Lectori*): "Our promise to resolve in the first part of Logic the several questions customarily treated there has now been fulfilled, except that, for just reasons, we have decided to publish separately the treatise on signs—swarming with many and uncommon difficulties—in place of a commentary on the Perihermenias books, and together with some questions on the books of the Posterior Analytics; and for the more convenient use of the work we have separated the treatise on signs from the treatment of the Categories."—"Quod in prima Logicae parte promisimus de quaestionibus pluribus, quae ibi tractari solent, hic expediendis, plane solvimus, excepto quod iustis de causis tractatum de signis, pluribus nec vulgaribus difficultatibus scaturientem, ne hic iniectus aut sparsus gravaret tractatus alio satis per se graves, seorsum edendum duximus loco commentarii in libros Perihermenias simul cum quaestionibus in libros Posteriorum, et pro commodiori libri usu a tractatu Praedicamentorum seiunximus." (Cited in Deely edition of Poinsot 1632a: 35, with discussion in the "Fourth Semiotic Marker" [see note 28 on p. 74 below for the explanation of this designation], *ibid.* 36–37, and also in the Editorial AfterWord, pp. 408–411.)

It should be plain, even to those who would prefer to read history otherwise, that to *replace entirely* the traditional commentary with a treatise on signs is radically different from making the treatment of signs *a part of* or *an introduction to* a traditional commentary focused on logical interpretation. See Deely 1988: 55–56.

This solution is brilliant as far as it goes. "One sees there quite clearly the eye and hand of an exceptional artist", as Simonin says of Poinsot's treatment of logic in general (1930: 145). But, "whatever sympathy one may have for the attempt, it seems equally clear that it was not destined to develop and fulfill itself normally."

Why not? Because more is at stake than a mere question of respecting the pattern of long-standing tradition. The very determination to let no new achievements be lost itself *guarantees* that the pattern will have to be modified. It is only a question of how far one is to go with such modification. By insisting on *the minimal modification of tradition possible consistent with what has been newly achieved*, Poinsot no doubt achieves at the same time the maximum emphasis on the already achieved, which was his set and constant purpose. Whereas Descartes embodied in his work the modern spirit loving novelty for its own sake and valuing the newly discovered in principle over the already known, Poinsot embodied in his work exactly the opposite spirit of valuing the integrity of established truths equally with the importance of new discovery. Consequently, he paid heed to the importance of relating newly discovered truths to what has been established over against pursuing the lead of new consequences without regard for past connections.

It is here, I think, that Simonin (1930: 145) rightly sees in Poinsot "a synthesis of irreconcilables". The consequences of new truths inevitably lead beyond, as well as bear relations to, the boundaries of what has already been discovered. By emphasizing the boundaries of the already discovered, Poinsot risked having newly discovered truth, in effect, become camouflaged in the landscape of the already known. This, in fact, is exactly what happened with his *Treatise on Signs* (see Deely 1985: 447n76 and esp. 461n97). Moreover, the fixity of the pattern itself of long-standing tradition is not something given once and for all. The "most natural place" for the treatment of signs at the time of Poinsot's confrontation of the problem generated by Soto's *Summulae* vis-à-vis Latin philosophical tradition in general and Thomistic tradition in particular would not remain the "most natural place" after his separate publication of a foundational *Treatise on Signs* successfully reducing the doctrine newly established to its proper perspective and unity. For such a treatise, if successful, would inevitably alter this situation. What in Poinsot's time was disruptive of tradition would become, through Poinsot's creative work, integrated into tradition and, once integrated, would call for a further development according to the new requirements generated as a consequence of that very integration.

In fact, as we saw at the end of Chapter 3, exactly this is what happened with the logic by Michael Comas published at Barcelona in 1661. Basing his treatment not on questions of pedagogical preparedness but on the requirements proper to the order of doctrine expressly as clarified by Poinsot's work in this area, Comas provided a kind of anticipation of the Peircean project of deriving even the traditional concerns of formal logic and syllogistic directly from the prior consideration of the sign in its proper being (further specified as this and that kind of sign—in the case of logic as then conceived, "second intentions"). In other words, Comas used Poinsot's arguments on the nature of signs in relation to traditional logic to begin the treatment of that very logic, especially for beginners, with the discussion of signs; and Comas does this in a way systematically derived from Poinsot's *Tractatus de Signis*. Comas's derived way offered an alternative both to the way that Poinsot had chosen, following his teachers, and to the way that Poinsot had criticized, chosen by Soto.

If Poinsot's concern for integrating new achievements according to the pattern and methods of long-standing tradition represents a synthesis of irreconcilables in this sense, this is precisely because, as Simonin also notes (1930: 145), "Poinsot's work reveals itself as a work of transition". There are ample reasons for suspecting that Poinsot realized he stood at some kind of boundary of the Latin development, and felt charged with the task of preserving a record of its integrity down to the utmost refinement of its developments. He perhaps made a conscious choice to sacrifice the natural development of his own work in favor of preserving for future generations the landscape and organic texture of philosophy in the Latin Age. "Understood in this way", as Simonin suggests (1930: 146), "and given its place in the development of history, the work of Poinsot acquires a particular significance, and perhaps an especial interest, at a time when one rediscovers the flavor of an ancient style."

B. Adjusting the Focus: Understanding What We Have Found

Be that as it may, there remains a special problem with regard to the place of Poinsot's treatise on signs with relation to the *Cursus Philosophicus*

Thomisticus overall. While there is no doubt that the treatise on signs stands as a new achievement in one of the final developments of the plenitude of refinements of Latin scholasticism, there is also no doubt that this treatise proves, on Poinsot's handling, to stand also as a definitive fulfillment of Descartes' proposal (1628: 31) that we must "seek to encompass in thought everything in the universe, with a view to learning in what way particular things may be susceptible of investigation by the human mind" in order to answer that "most useful inquiry we can make at this stage", namely, "what is human knowledge and what is its scope?" For, as Locke would later agree (1690: 30), "we shall then use our understandings right, when we entertain all objects in that way and proportion that they are suited to our faculties, and upon those grounds they are capable of being proposed to us". In other words, Poinsot found within the resources of Latin tradition an answer to the modern question concerning "in what way particular things are susceptible of investigation by the human mind". The answer lay in the doctrine of signs.

There are two ways we can look at Poinsot's achievement on this point. We can consider his doctrine of signs specifically within the context of his *Cursus Philosophicus Thomisticus*, or we can consider the *Tractatus de Signis* as a virtually autonomous treatment that can be evaluated on its own terms as an independent whole establishing the sign as the key to a philosophy of experience. Looked at either way, even though his treatment of the sign was so skillfully balanced and qualified by his artistic integration of it into the traditional treatment of logic that this deep tendency escaped the notice of his contemporary readers, Poinsot turns out to have provided us with nothing less than a new starting point for the philosophical enterprise as a whole.

1. *The* Tractatus de Signis
Viewed from Within the Cursus Philosophicus Thomisticus

Let us consider the novelty of Poinsot's work within the context of his *Cursus Philosophicus* as a whole. The first part of the *Cursus* consists of the treatment of logic, first according to its form (the *Artis Logicae Prima Pars* or *Summulae*), then according to its informing an actual subject matter by way of providing proofs and establishing probabilities (the *Artis Logicae*

Secunda Pars or *De instrumentis logicalibus ex parte materiae*). True to his admission that the question of the sign goes to the foundations of the subject matter of logic, we find that the opening two and a half chapters of the first of the introductory logic or *Summulae* books introduce definitions and divisions of all the terms that will form the subject of the discussion in the *Treatise on Signs*. This discussion, concerning as it does the matter of interpretation throughout its scope, Poinsot sees as supplanting by right the traditional Perihermenias Commentary (the commentary on Aristotle's *De Interpretatione*) in the Second Part of the Logic. Here, in these opening two and half pages of the *Cursus Philosophicus*, Poinsot manages to list, without discussion, all the terms and distinctions originally used by Soto to introduce into the Spanish and Portuguese university world the substance as well as the fruits of the Parisian controversy whereby the definition of the sign proposed by Augustine in the fifth century (as something perceived by the senses) and used ever since among the Latins is relegated to the subdivision of signs as "instrumental", and a broader definition of sign (as whatever—whether perceived by sense or not—brings something other than itself into awareness) is proposed in its place as a definition comprehensive enough to cover "formal" signs as well. Thus the doctrine of signs, to be established on its own grounds, will cover the same materials as the opening chapters of the traditional introductory logic text, but at a deeper level and reorganized according to a different point of view, one that transcends the traditional division of being into *ens reale* and *ens rationis*. Poinsot calls this revolutionary point of view simply that of a *doctrina signorum*.

Nor is this all. Remember that Poinsot spoke of "the metaphysical and other difficulties from the books On the Soul" as those needing special resolution from the systematic perspective of the *doctrina signorum*. In my edition of Poinsot's *Tractatus de Signis* as an independent work, I included as Appendix B the complete Table of Contents from the *Cursus Philosophicus*, both as it appears in Reiser's edition and in the form of a Synoptic Table displaying the whole in an organizational chart. If one glances at that Appendix, one finds that nothing less than the final conclusions of Natural Philosophy traditionally viewed become the starting point of the newly demanded *doctrina signorum*. The reason for that is that the formal sign, which, remember, is identified with the products of perceptual and/or conceptual cognitive acts, usually called *species expressae* by the natural philosophers, does not come up for discussion in the traditional natural philosophy until the treatment of material being which is both living and cognizant is reached, and this is at the very end of the order of exposition. What is last in exposition, however, is first in discovery: with the *doctrina signorum* Poinsot professes to have discovered the means of accounting for the origins and structure of experience as irreducible to subjective being, whether physical or psychical.

Dramatically enough, he traces the basic insight of the *doctrina signorum* to Aquinas' treatment of the Trinity as a community of persons, and to Cajetan's interpretation in particular of the notoriously difficult text in his *Summa Theologiae* wherein St. Thomas says that the Persons of the Trinity are able to subsist as purely relational beings because of what is unique to relation among all the modes of physical being, namely, that it exists intersubjectively according to a rationale—the rationale of "being toward"—which is indifferent to the fact of being exercised independently of being cognized or known. In other words, every physical being which exists either in itself or in another exists subjectively and must, as such, exist whether or not it is known to exist by some finite mind, that is to say, whether or not it exists objectively as well as physically. But relation, in order to be what it is, exists not subjectively but as an intersubjective nexus or mode, and for this it *makes no difference* whether *the relation* obtains physically as well as objectively or only in the community of knowledge. In either case, whether it exists only as known or physically as well as objectively, it exists in exactly the same way: intersubjectively. By contrast, substance and accidents exist subjectively only when they are not pure objects of apprehension. Indeed, purely as objects apprehended, they are not subjective existents but relative objects *patterned after* what are not relative, namely, physically existent substances with their accidents, which, Poinsot points out, is precisely why there are mind-dependent relations but not mind-dependent substances or mind-dependent accidents other than relations.[20]

---

[20] Poinsot, *Artis Logicae Secunda Pars*, Q. 17 "De Praedicamento Relationis", Art. 2 "Quid requiratur, ut aliqua relatio sit praedicamentalis", 581b24–582a16 (= *Tractatus de Signis*, Second Preamble, Article 2, "What Is Required for a 'Categorial' Relation", 96/1–36): "When one insists that, as a matter of fact, other kinds of being too can in this way be said to be something mind-dependent—as a mind-dependent substance will be a chimera, a mind-dependent quantity an im-

In other words, as *isolated* in this or that respect, physical being is determinately subjective, but in whatever respect reality enjoys *communion*, in that respect it is determinately *intersubjective* and as such can be maintained in cognition alone, in physical being alone, or in physical being and in cognition alike. Hence in the case of the Trinity, Aquinas argues, a diversity of Persons subsistent as *relations* is consistent with the unity of God as pure existence subsistent in itself, *ipsum esse subsistens*; hence too, specifically as a development of St. Thomas, "it should be noted that Poinsot's location of the formal constitutive of deity in God's very self-understanding is a distinguishing feature of his thought".[21]

In the case of the *doctrina signorum*, the application of Aquinas' point about the being proper and unique to relation as a mode of being is much

aginary space, and so on for the other categories: *The response is* that, as was explained in our First Preamble on mind-dependent being [57/26–30], that on whose pattern a mind-dependent being is formed is not called mind-dependent; for mind-dependent being is formed on the pattern of mind-independent being, but that unreal being which is conceived on the pattern of a mind-independent being is called a mind-dependent being. There is not therefore mind-dependent substance nor mind-dependent quantity, because even though some non-being may be conceived on the pattern of a substance—for example, the chimera—and some on the pattern of quantity—for example, imaginary space—yet neither substance itself nor any rationale of subjectivity is conceived by the understanding and formed in being on the pattern of some *other* mind-independent being. And for this reason that negation or chimerical non-being and that non-being of an imaginary space will be said to be a mind-dependent being. But this [i.e., any unreal object whatever conceived as being a subject or a subjective modification of being] is the mind-dependent being which is called negation, yet it will not be a mind-dependent substance, because substance itself is not conceived as a mind-dependent being patterned after some mind-independent being—rather, negations or non-beings are conceived on the pattern of substance and quantity. But in the case of relatives, indeed, not only is there some non-being conceived on the pattern of relation, but also the very relation conceived on the part of the respect toward, while it does not exist in the mind-independent order, is conceived or formed on the pattern of a mind-independent relation, and so that which is formed in being, and not only that after whose pattern it is formed, is a relation, and by reason of this there are in fact mind-dependent relations, but not mind-dependent substances." (Latin cited in the Appendix of Longer Citations, p. 256 below.)

21 "Comme particularité de la doctrine de Jean de Saint-Thomas, il faut noter encore qu'il place le constitutif formel de la deité dans l'intellection actuelle de Dieu par lui-même" (Ramirez 1924: cols. 807–808).

humbler and, philosophically, quite independent of the theological doctrine that the interior life of God consists in a communion of three Persons.

By all accounts, Poinsot points out, signs are *relative* beings whose whole existence consists in the presentation within awareness of what they themselves are not. To function in this way the sign in its proper being must consist, precisely and in every case, in a relation uniting a cognitive being to an object known *on the basis of* some sign vehicle. What makes a sign formal or instrumental simply depends on the sign vehicle: if it is a psychological state, an idea or image, the sign is a formal sign; if the sign vehicle is a material object of any sort, a mark, sound or movement, the sign is an instrumental sign. But whether the sign is formal or instrumental is subordinate to the fact that, as a sign, the being whereby it exists is not the subjective being of its vehicle (psychological or material, as the case may be) but the intersubjective being of a relation irreducibly triadic[22] because tasked with presenting (1) an object signified (2) to a knowing subject (3) on the basis of a vehicle distinct from both.

Many centuries later, Peirce would resume this point under a clearer terminology: every sign, in order to function as a sign, requires an object and an interpretant, and hence consists in a triadic relation. But the point itself, that the *doctrina signorum* has for its subject matter a unified object of investigation in the being of relation as indifferent to provenating from nature or mind, debated intensely among the Latins, is found thematically established not in Soto, the Conimbriceneses, or Araújo (cf. Beuchot 1980), but in Poinsot. For the first time, a definitive resolution is effected of "the possibility", originally suggested by Augustine "of resolving" (as Eco and his collaborators put it) "the ancient dichotomy between the inferential relations linking natural signs to the things of which they are signs and relations of equivalence linking linguistic terms to the concept(s) on the basis of which some thing 'is'—singly or

---

[22] Artis Logicae Secunda Pars, Q. XXI, Art. 3, "Utrum sit eadem relatio signi ad signatum et potentiam", 664a49–b2 (= *Tractatus de Signis*, Book I, Question 3, 154/28–30): "by one same sign-relation is attained cognitive power and signified object, and this single relation is the proper and formal rationale of a sign"—"unica relatione signi attingitur signatum et potentia, et haec est propria et formalis ratio signi".

plurally—designated".[23] This definitive resolution is effected within
the *Cursus Philosophicus* of John Poinsot.[24]

[23] Eco *et al.* 1986: 65. Cf. Poinsot, *Artis Logicae Secunda Pars*, Q. XXII, Art. 5,
715b37–716a16; = *Tractatus de Signis*, Book II, Question 5, 270/38–271/12: "... the
conclusion [that natural and stipulated signs are univocal in their proper order] derives from that distinguished doctrine in Cajetan's *Commentary on the Summa theologica*, I, q. 1, art. 3, that the differences of things *as things* are quite other than the
differences of things *as objects* and in the being of an object; and things that differ
in kind or more than in kind in the one line, can differ in the other line not at all
or not in the same way. And so, seeing that the rationale of a sign pertains to the
rationale of the knowable [the line of thing as object], because it substitutes for the
object, it will well be the case that in the rationale of object a mind-independent natural sign and a stipulated mind-dependent sign are univocal signs; just as a mind-independent being and a mind-dependent being assume one rationale in their being as
object, since indeed they terminate the same power, namely, the power of understanding, and can be attained by the same habit, namely, by Metaphysics, or at
least specify two univocally coincident sciences, as, for example, Logic and Physics. Therefore in the being of an object specifying, stipulated and natural signs coincide univocally.

"So too a cognitive power is truly and univocally moved and led to a thing signified
by means of a stipulated sign and by means of a natural sign."—"... pars conclusionis [quod signa naturalia et ad placitum univoca sunt in genere repraesentativi]
pendet ex illa celebri doctrina apud Caietanum 1. p. q. 1. art. 3., quod aliae sunt dif-
ferentiae rerum ut res, aliae ut obiectum et in esse obiecti; et quae specie vel plus
quam specie differunt in una linea, possunt in alia non differe vel non ita differre. Et
sic cum ratio signi pertineat ad rationem cognoscibilis, cum sit vice obiectum, stabit
bene, quod in ratione obiecti signum naturale reale et ad placitum rationis sint signa
univoca; sicut ens reale et rationis in esse obiecti induunt unam rationem, siquidem
terminant eandem potentiam, scilicet intellectum, et ab eodem habitu possunt attin-
gi, scilicet a Metaphysica, vel saltem duas scientias univoce convenientes specificare,
v. g. Logicam et Physicam. Ergo in esse obiecti specificantis univoce conveniunt.

"Sic etiam per signum ad placitum et per signum naturale vere et univoce movetur
et deducitur potentia ad signatum."

[24] See the *Artis Logicae Secunda Pars* (1632), Quaestio XXI, "De Signo Secundum Se",
Articulus 3, "Utrum in signo naturali relatio sit realis vel rationis", 635b10–663b25,
esp. 658b30–659a39 (= *Tractatus de Signis*, Book I, "Concerning the Sign in Its Proper
Being", Question 2, "Whether the Sign-Relation in the Case of Natural Signs Is
Mind-Independent or Mind-Dependent", 135/1–152/7, esp. 141/12–142/13),
together with Quaestio XXII, "De Divisionibus Signi", Articulus 5, "Utrum sit
bona divisio in signum naturale et ad placitum et ex consuetudine", 715a33–719a15,
esp. 715b37–716a16, and Art. 6, "Utrum signum ex consuetudine sit vere signum",

In effecting his resolution, Poinsot writes in a typically "medieval" fashion. All the Latin scholastics of his time use the terminology of *relatio secundum esse* and *relatio secundum dici*, *relatio realis* and *relatio rationis*, *relatio praedicamentalis* and *relatio transcendentalis*,[25] confirming Eco's remark (ibid.: 64) that "medieval materials at first glance normally appear to be stubborn repetitions of a common archetype or model, differing not at all or at least not perceptibly". The forest stands out from the trees, but how make the trees stand out within the forest? Scholars skilled in the literal appearances have, on precisely literal ground, failed utterly to see the uniqueness of Poinsot's doctrine. Looking exclusively from the perspective of formal logic in the traditional Latin sense, Muñoz Delgado (1964: 14, 22) expressed a certain puzzlement or even exasperation over the preference among French and American researchers for the work of Poinsot over that of Soto, a view naturally enough echoed in students of Muñoz Delgado's work such as Ashworth and Angelelli.

Indeed, Ashworth (1988, 1990a) not only takes her orientation from Delgado's opinion, but seeks to establish it independently by appeal to literal appearances, proclaiming that she finds in Poinsot nothing which does not appear in Soto's texts. Ashworth tells us she is "one of the few philosophers who has actually read some of the sixteenth-century authors to whom Poinsot was indebted"; but her reading list at the time seems not to have included Araújo, nor the contemporary studies by Beuchot (1980, 1983, 1987: see Ashworth 1990b, and Ch. 5 below, pp. 124–125).

These scholars have failed to fathom the medieval adage that "the authorities have a nose of wax";[26] for as was said of the *topos* of *latratus canis* (Eco et al. 1986: 65), so must it be said of the *topos* of *signum*: "beneath

---

719a17–722a37, esp. 720a39–b26 (= *Tractatus de Signis*, Book II, "Concerning the Division of Signs", Question 5, "Whether the Division of Signs into Natural, Stipulated, and Customary Is a Sound Division", 269/1–277/12, esp. 270/37–271/12, and Question 6, "Whether a Sign Arising from Custom Is Truly a Sign", 278/1–283/32, esp. 280/15–43).

See the remarks in note 24 of Chapter 8, p 244 below.

25 See, for example, the analytically fragile but textually massive presentation of Krempel 1952, discussed in Appendix 1 of the present book.

26 No period verifies better than the Latin period Gracia's thesis (1992: 332) "that the history of philosophy must be done philosophically" in order to be intrinsically helpful to the philosopher.

literal appearances, every time the *topos* is cited, one has grounds for suspecting that a slight or more than slight shift of perspective has taken place''. Nowhere more than in the matter of the *doctrina signorum* do we find that, among the Latin authors, ''concealed differences stand out against the background of seeming repetitions—differences of the sort promising to reveal the heart of systems in reality very different.''[27]

27 This situation can lead even the most scholarly reader of the Latin text astray in various ways, as has happened with Poinsot's work on more than one occasion. Besides the example of Ashworth in the text above and the case of Simon and his collaborators who misconstrued Poinsot's opening gambit for locating signs in the order of relative being (see note 62 of this Chapter, p. 97 below), the example of Marmo 1967 stands as easily the most creatively misleading of the so far proposed readings of Poinsot's semiotic. It is perhaps not a coincidence that Marmo is a student of Eco who was also a collaborator in the original publication of the ''Latratus Canis'' (Eco *et al.* 1984 [see the discussion of ''Reading 6'' in Deely *et al.* 1986: xix]). The title of Marmo's essay, ''The Semiotics of John Poinsot'', is actually misleading, since the author discusses Poinsot only in view of theses of his own (particularly the recidivisticly idealist theory of ''meaning as content'') for which he mines Poinsot's texts selectively—as Marmo himself grants (1987: 118n12) concerning his attempt to locate sensation precisely where Poinsot denies it, namely, in the icon of a *species expressa*: ''My interpretation of the passage taken from the *Philosophia Naturalis* implies the attribution to Poinsot of a syntactical mistake in his use of reflexive pronouns. This would not be surprising in an author who writes in a rough medieval Latin. I think that a rather free use of reflexive pronouns ought to be found quite easily among Poinsot's works after a thorough analysis of them.'' Marmo hastens to add, without even hearing the odd ring of his words, ''*But this is not my aim here*'' (my italics). Perhaps, since it was not his aim, Marmo should not be criticized from the vantage of a thorough analysis of Poinsot's work. Nonetheless, a criticism from that vantage reveals that we have here an interpretation made of matchsticks. What are we to make of an interpretation which eschews thorough analysis?

The a-priori selectivity and eclectic character of Marmo's reading is exhibited through theses ascribed to Poinsot which are the opposite of what Poinsot actually holds. Poinsot's central thesis that all signs as signs pertain to the order of the knowable through the univocal rationale of means representative of an object (e.g., Poinsot 1632a: 236/15-16) becomes, in Marmo's hands, a thesis rather that signs are unified only by ''the weakest type of analogy''. This is something that Poinsot would grant when the relations constitutive of signs are viewed not in the order of cognoscibility proper to them as triadic but rather in the order of entitative being—that is, in the perspective proper to a purely traditional philosophy of nature or to a purely traditional logic, in contrast to the perspective required to understand the sign in its proper being. Similarly with Poinsot's fundamental position that, though

In the case of his *Tractatus de Signis* vis-à-vis the *Cursus Philosophicus* as a whole, at least two further points need to be noted if we are fully to appreciate in this context Poinsot's contribution to the seventeenth century search for a new beginning in philosophy.

a. From Sensation to Intellection: The Scope of the *Doctrina Signorum*

Poinsot's traditional *Cursus Philosophicus* as a whole begins with a treatment of logic under the established title of "Summulae books", and it is the very materials that make up the opening three chapters of this introduction to logic (the *Summulae* books) that is also covered in the *Tractatus de Signis*. Thus, the *Tractatus de Signis* reconsiders in a new light what was traditionally considered, not just in Poinsot's day but for the whole Aristotelian tradition both Greek and Latin, to be the proper starting point for philosophical study. Especially interesting, however, is the fact

in the order of physical being as such the entitative character of relations precludes this, in the objective order of being relations can found other relations, which is the reason why semiosis (anthroposemiosis: see Deely 1994: ¶138) is "unlimited", a *processus in infinitum*. On Marmo's reading (ibid.: 124) Poinsot's position is reduced to an unqualified assertion that "there are no relations of relations, i.e., relations on a level higher than the first one", despite Poinsot's express statements (e.g., 1632a: 60/7–62/18) contrary to what Marmo reports Poinsot's position to be. And so on throughout (see further discussion in note 35 of this Chapter, p. 80 below).

Can this all be a matter of misused reflexive pronouns? Marmo's essay says much that is interesting about medieval positions on semiotically related questions, but almost nothing reliable concerning semiotics in the work of Poinsot. The problem is threefold. The first and greatest part of the problem is that Marmo insists on reading Poinsot in the light of texts from earlier authors, Cajetan in particular, cast in terms of the traditional contrast between *ens reale* as the concern of philosophy and *ens rationis* as the concern of logic. But this is to read Poinsot not only extrinsically, but also reductively, failing to adopt the standpoint from which Poinsot identifies a unified subject-matter for semiotic inquiry—renvoi, as I will term it in Chapters 6 and 8—that transcends, while at the same time assimilating, the traditonal medieval perspectives on logic and ontology alike. A second part of the problem is that Marmo does not see that his conception of meaning as content belongs to the modern paradigm of idealism improperly imported into the perspective of semiotic (cf. Deely 1986e and 1990: Chapter 1). And a third part of the problem is that Marmo has ventured a public critique of one of the most subtle and difficult parts of Poinsot's thinking while eschewing the thorough textual analysis that makes that critique insupportable.

that these initial materials of traditional consideration as semiotically reconsidered bear on the experiential origins of cognition itself; for these opening materials of the *Summulae* books concern *the simplest elements of the primary form of cognitive life*, namely, concepts as the forms of, as providing the structure for, simple awareness. In Poinsot's *Libri Summularum* themselves, i.e., the *Artis Logicae Prima Pars* of 1631, concepts are envisioned primarily in the narrow sense as restricted to ideas in the understanding or intellect (*species expressae intellectus*). This point is perhaps not emphasized sufficiently in the Second Semiotic Marker[28] of the Deely edition of Poinsot 1632a (p. 19), since that "marker" was written mainly to help the reader anticipate the departure from the established tradition that Poinsot would make in returning to treat this matter of the concept more broadly from the standpoint of the *doctrina signorum* proper *in place of* the traditional Perihermenias commentary which restricts itself to the concept narrowly conceived, i.e., to ideas as opposed to images and as subserving intellectual judgment.[29] For in returning to treat this

---

28 "Semiotic Marker" is the name given to the device adopted in the Deely edition of Poinsot 1632a to bypass the need for lengthy introductory materials to enable readers to grasp the editorial structure of the whole. This device was explained in opening lines of the editor's "Word to the Reader" of the bilingual edition of Poinsot's *Tractatus*, p. 1: "Putting ourselves in the position of a reader coming to the *Ars Logica* for the first time and interested only in Poinsot's discussion of signs, we asked ourselves: What sections of the work would this hypothetical reader have to look at in order to appreciate that discussion both in its own terms and in terms of the whole of which it originally formed a part? To what extent are these separable philosophically?

"The pages that follow make up our solution to this problem. We have left Poinsot's text stand virtually entirely according to the order he proposed for it within the *Ars Logica* as a whole. To make this order clear, we have included title pages, and all general statements Poinsot set down concerning the whole (and therefore the *Treatise* as part), inserting where appropriate and to bridge necessary jumps a series of [six] brief comments designated 'semiotic markers', designed to show the reader how the rationale of all editing is derived from the original author's own intentions; and second, we have included all and only those sections of the whole which have a direct bearing on understanding the doctrine proposed in the *Treatise on Signs* proper, as the semiotic markers make clear."

29 *Artis Logicae Prima Pars* (1631), 6b2–13 (= 16/40–17/2 in the separate edition of the *Tractatus de Signis*): "Nor is it redundant for simple terms and what pertains to the first operation to be treated twice in Logic, because, as St. Thomas says in the first

matter from the standpoint of the *doctrina signorum* envisaged fully as such, Poinsot is at pains to establish with his opening sentence that it can no longer be concepts in the narrow sense that are at issue, but precisely concepts in the broadest sense as including the psychological life of animals as well, or, if one prefers, of human beings not only specifically as rational but generically as animals:

> The question holds as much for a concept of the understanding, which is called an expressed specifier and word, as for an expressed specifier of perception or imagination, which is called an icon or phantasm. How does the definition of a formal sign, which is a formal awareness and which of itself and immediately represents something, apply to these?[30]

However, seeing that the *doctrina signorum* resumes and recasts the whole doctrine of *phantasiari*[31] and *intelligere* from the natural philosophy

reading of his Commentary on the first book of Aristotle's On Interpretation, simple terms are treated from one point of view in the book of Categories, namely, as signifying simple essences, from another point of view in the book On Interpretation, namely, as they are parts of an enunciation, and from yet another viewpoint in the books of Prior Analytics, namely, as they constitute a syllogistic order. "—"Nec est inconveniens, quod de simplicibus et his, quae pertinent ad primam operationem, agatur in Logica bis, quia, ut notat S. Thomas 1. Periherm. lect. 1., de dictionibus simplicibus sub alia consideratione agitur in Praedicamentis, scilicet ut significant simplices essentias, sub alia in libro Perihermenias, scilicet ut sunt partes enuntiationis, sub alia in libris Priorum, scilicet ut constituunt ordinem syllogisticum." See following note.

30 *Artis Logicae Secunda Pars* (1632), Q. XXII, Art. 2, "*Utrum Conceptus Sit Signum Formale*", 702a44–b4 (= *Tractatus de Signis*, Book II, Question 2, "Whether a Concept is a Formal Sign", 240/1–242/2, where the passage is extensively annotated): "Procedit quaestio tam de conceptu intellectus, qui vocatur species expressa et verbum, quam de specie expressa phantasiae seu imaginativae, quae dicitur idolum vel phantasma, quomodo illis conveniat definitio signi formalis, quod sit formalis notitia, et quod seipso et immediate aliquid repraesentet."

In the face of such a text, even apart from the Poinsot's further discussion of the role of signs in external sensation and the life of brute animals which we shall consider shortly, it is fatuous to conjecture (Ashworth 1988: 132) "that Poinsot would not have gone beyond the standard debate as to whether *interpretatio* meant an utterance or an assertion".

31 I.e., the genus of knowing common to brute and rational animals over and above sensation: see Poinsot, *Philosophia Naturalis Quarta Pars in Tres Libros de Anima*, Quaestio

of cognitive organisms in reshaping the foundations of logic as such still does not reveal the full scope of the *doctrina signorum* as it bears on the understanding of experience. Not only intellection and perception are dependent on signs for the total structure of their objective apprehensions but sensation as well.

As if to emphasize the role of signs in cognitive life, not merely according to the narrow conception of interpretation worked out in the traditional commentaries on the *De Interpretatione*, but according to the broadest and fullest conception of cognition established in the traditional commentaries on the *De Anima*, Poinsot expressly frames his concluding question ''Concerning the Sign in Its Proper Being''[32] to establish ''Whether the True Rationale of Sign is Present in the Behavior of Brute Animals and in the Operation of the External Senses''.[33] The importance of such a question for the extra-Iberian context of the seventeenth century modern search for a new beginning in philosophy—whether we think of Descartes or of Locke—would be difficult to overemphasize. For even though Descartes turned radically away from sensation in his attempt to re-establish a foundation for philosophy, his attempt was soon countered in the work of John Locke and the empiricists after him who turned precisely to external sense in *their* attempt to renew philosophy's foundation. Thus, whether we regard sensation as the foundation of knowledge and core of experience or merely as a superficial point of departure from which to turn to inner experience, the matter of sensation became central to the modern search for a new beginning in philosophy and to the establishment of modern thought in its distinctive character.

VIII, ''De Sensibus Internis'', Art. 2, ''Quid sint phantasia et reliquiae potentiae interiores, et in quibus subiectis sint'', 252a38–265a46, discussed in editor's note 2 at 240/4 in the *Tractatus de Signis*. See also Deely 1971a: 55–83, for a detailed analysis of the scholastic discussion of internal sense powers.

32 *Artis Logicae Secunda Pars*, Q. XXI, ''De Signum Secundum Se'' (= *Tractatus de Signis*, Book I, ''Concerning the Sign in Its Proper Being'').

33 *Artis Logicae Secunda Pars*, Q. XXI, Art. 6, ''Utrum in brutis et sensibus externis sit vera ratio signi'' (= *Tractatus de Signis*, Book I, Question 6, ''Whether the True Rationale of Sign Is Present in the Behavior of Brute Animals and in the Operation of the External Senses'').

Given the biological constitution of *Homo sapiens sapiens*, it is not surprising that philosophers across the ages have been able to agree on a basic list of sensible characteristics or qualities presented objectively in experience: color, shape, size, temperature, solidity, texture, rest or motion, position, number or plurality, odor, flavor or taste, sound, warm or cool. But when it comes to assessing the epistemological or ontological status of items on the list, agreement rapidly dissolves in controversy. Modern philosophers distinguished within the list between primary and secondary qualities of objects, meaning by the latter color, odor, taste, sound, and warmth or coolness in particular; Greek and Latin philosophers distinguished rather between proper (or 'special') and common sensibles, meaning by the former color, odor, taste, sound, and texture or relative warmth. Of course it is the latter—the traditional—viewpoint that Poinsot works with in his *Cursus Philosophicus*.

Bearing on the same subject matter, the two viewpoints are not unrelated, even though, as Wilson has pointed out (1992: 210n42), "early modern figures" who were key to the emergence of Rationalism and Empiricism as the modern mainstream developments "did not put much weight on the special/common sensible issue in maintaining that only a subset of the apparent qualities are, as we perceive them, really in the objects". It remains that "the relation between the common/special sensible distinction and the objective/subjective [i.e., primary/secondary] quality distinction is," as Wilson notes without developing the point, "a complex and interesting one". Just this relation and contrast of the two sets of distinctions is what I want to explore here in the context of the nascent doctrine of signs.

In fact, the two distinctions—proper/common sensibles vis-à-vis primary/secondary qualities—are in one sense parallel, in another inverse. They are parallel, in that the modern list of qualities taken collectively matches the Latin scholastic list of qualities. They are inverse, however, in that the qualities listed as primary in the modern list match the common sensibles, which, in the scholastic list, are dependent on the proper sensibles and so are secondary; while the proper sensibles, which are primary in the scholastic list, match the qualities listed as secondary in the modern list. The inversion results from the standpoint according to which the two traditions distinguish the sensible characteristics or qualities of objects given in perception. The scholastics drew their distinction, as it were, unselfconsciously, from a point of view that is closest to what we would today call "phenomenological", but which they simply considered experiential. The moderns (ironically, set as they are on a path which leads inexorably to idealism) at first drew their distinction from an adamantly realist point of view: the primary qualities are those which hopefully will prove to be mind-independently present in objects, while the secondary qualities are those supposed easily constructed and inscribed in objects by the mental activity of the perceiver. Of course, as has long become evident, the hopeful realism of the modern distinction was hopelessly misguided. Nor was it long before Bishop Berkeley explicitly pointed out that the two kinds of qualities are interdependent in experience in such a way that there is little ground for alleging a difference in status for the two vis-à-vis a supposed order of mind-independent being (1710: Part I, Section 10, p. 45):

They who assert that figure, motion, and the rest of the primary or original qualities, do exist without the mind, in unthinking substances, do at the same time acknowledge that colours, sounds, heat, cold, and such like secondary qualities, do not, which they tell us are sensations existing **in the mind alone,** that depend on and are occasioned by the different size, texture, and motion of the minute particles of matter. This they take for an undoubted truth, which they can demonstrate beyond all exception. Now if it be certain, that those original qualities **are inseparably united with the other sensible qualities,** and not, even in thought, capable of being abstracted from them, it plainly follows that they exist only in the mind. But I desire any one to reflect and try, whether he can, by any abstraction of thought, conceive the extension and motion of a body, without all other sensible qualities. For my own part, I see evidently that it is not in my power to frame an idea of a body extended and moved, but I must withal give it some colour or other sensible quality which is **acknowledged** to exist only in the mind. In short, extension, figure, and motion, abstracted from all other qualities, are inconceivable. Where therefore the other sensible qualities are, there must these be also, to wit, in the mind and nowhere else.

If we employ the terminology of the moderns from the standpoint the scholastics developed from Aristotle, Berkeley's argument can be much more forcefully stated: the sensible qualities of the objects of experience are so linked in experience that the supposed primary qualities are only known and attained through and on the basis of the qualities supposed secondary. Hence, if the latter are constructed by the mind, there is no basis left for alleging the former not to be. The point was not lost on Hume, who makes it exactly in his own way (1748: 154 par. 15):

It is universally allowed by modern enquirers, that all the sensible qualities of objects, such as hard, soft, hot, cold, white, black, &c. are merely secondary, and exist not in the objects themselves, but are perceptions of the mind, without any external archetype or model, which they represent. If this be allowed, with regard to secondary qualities, it must also follow, with regard to the supposed primary qualities of extension and solidity; nor can the latter be any more entitled to that denomination than the former. The idea of extension is entirely acquired from the senses of sight and feeling; and if all the qualities, perceived by the senses, be in the mind, not in the object, the same conclusion must reach the idea of extension, which is wholly dependent on the sensible ideas or the ideas of secondary qualities.[34]

Poinsot, in his *Cursus Philosophicus*, takes up the standpoint on sensation of the Latin scholastics, and reshapes it according to the require-

---

[34] By this point of *An Enquiry Concerning Human Understanding* of 1748, Hume had already given us in its explicit thematic form the famous "problem of the external world" (*ibid.*, Sect. 12, Part 1, p. 152, pars. 11-13): "By what argument can it be proved, that the perceptions of the mind must be caused by external objects, entirely different from them, though resembling them (if that be possible) and could not arise either from the energy of the mind itself, or from the suggestion of some invisible and unknown spirit, or from some other cause still more unknown to us? ...

"It is a question of fact, whether the perceptions of the senses be produced by external objects, resembling them: how shall this question be determined? By experience surely; as all other questions of a like nature. But here experience is, and must be entirely silent. The mind has never any thing present to it but the perceptions, and cannot possibly reach any experience of their connexion with objects. The supposition of such a connexion is, therefore, without any foundation in reasoning.

"To have recourse to the veracity of the supreme Being, in order to prove the veracity of our senses, is surely making a very unexpected circuit. If his veracity were at all concerned in this matter, our senses would be entirely infallible; because it is not possible that he can ever deceive. Not to mention, that, if the external world be once called in question, we shall be at a loss to find arguments, by which we may prove the existence of that Being or any of his attributes.'

Whence "reason", Hume concludes (*ibid.*: par. 16), "can never find any convincing argument from experience to prove, that the perceptions are connected with any external objects."

ments of the *doctrina signorum*. The standpoint in question distinguishes among two types of sense data in a way that is neither realist nor idealist in the modern sense. In contemporary terms, this standpoint is not in the first place ontological nor even gnoseological, as Marmo is led to suggest,[35] but rather experiential in the sense that late modern philoso-

35 Marmo (1987: 122) considers that Poinsot is "not fully consistent in his application of the theoretical tool of analogy", by which Marmo means that Poinsot's semiotic is based specifically upon Cajetan's "analogy of inequality" ("analogia secundum inaequalitatem"), since it was through this analogy that Cajetan (1506, 1511) applied the term "being" to objects that have been identified as in one case *entia realia* and in another case as *entia rationis*. As an extrinsic interpretive strategy (an a-priori approach to the reading of a text) Marmo's approach demonstrates considerable scholarly cleverness. For a reader steeped in the general milieu of Latin philosophical texts the approach has a prima facie historical plausibility which only a careful and detailed internal reading of Poinsot's specific text, which Marmo unfortunately neglected, could gainsay. For, as a matter of fact, Poinsot's doctrine of the univocity of signs as providing the subject of a prospective discipline was neither conceived nor intended to be an application of that analogy or any other, but the identification of a unique standpoint, one proportioned to experience in *its* proper being (see Deely 1992), *out of which* doctrines of analogy of whatever sort would have to be critically derived. The semiotic standpoint Poinsot identifies, as experientially prior to the division of being into *ens reale* and *ens rationis*, is also prior to any doctrine analogizing the poles of that contrast in terms of one another. Moreover, since Cajetan is one of the few authors Poinsot customarily identifies and credits on any given point, it would be odd indeed if his whole *Treatise on Signs* which never once mentions Cajetan's *analogia secundum inaequalitatem* were intended to be nothing more than an application of that doctrine, particularly inasmuch as the particular doctrine in question expressly *presupposes* and rests upon the very division of being into *ens rationis* and *ens reale* which Poinsot expressly removes from the foundation of semiotic. This is a contradiction in his own interpretation that escapes Marmo; yet it remains that to see in Poinsot's semiotic an application of *analogia secundum inaequalitatem*, as Marmo does, requires that semiotic be treated not according to what is proper to it but from the external standpoint of a doctrine aimed at explicating a presupposed distinction between *ens reale* and *ens rationis*—that is to say, as presupposing the very distinction of traditional standpoints which the doctrine of signs begins by transcending. The inconsistency which Marmo fancies himeslf to uncover in Poinsot is thus a case of "seeing in the destination what has originated with the source" or the Clever Hans Fallacy (Sebeok 1989a: 85–106). When Marmo says that "one cannot understand why he [Poinsot] (and Deely with him) thinks that the ontologically oriented question of what sign is should have priority" when "the gnoseological one" is more consistent with "his definition of sign as a mean of representation of objects to a cog-

phers, after Husserl, have come to thematize as "phenomenological". The question answered in their distinction between proper and common sensibles concerns the relation of environmental things to the channels of sense through which and on the basis of which these things become aspectually and in part objectified: some aspects of the physical environment, namely, the proper sensibles, are objectified, cognized, or known through a single channel of sense only, while other aspects are assimilated to experience through more channels than one, namely, the common sensibles. Far from begging the question as the modern distinction between secondary and primary qualities did, the Latin scholastic distinction among sense qualities is drawn in a way—the *only* way, Poinsot thought, on this point following Aquinas—that allows for a rational decision concerning the ontological status of objects experienced in terms of the physical aspects of their being.

From the standpoint of contemporary consciousness, what Poinsot in his *Cursus Philosophicus* is able to demonstrate, in effect, is that the requirements of a doctrine of signs are consonant with the nascently phenomenological standpoint of the scholastics, but definitely incompatible with the would-be realist stance of the moderns. For this latter stance begs the question of the physical status of sensed things which experience must rather provide the basis for deciding, if decided it can be, and leads, in spite of itself, to idealism.

It is instructive to compare Poinsot with Hume in this area. To

---

nitive power" (*ibid.*: 122), one fears that he has been led by the proposed translation of "*relatio secundum esse*" as "ontological relation" (see Deely 1985: 463–465, 472–479) to miss the irreducible novelty of the standpoint Poinsot proposes as required to understand the being proper to signs, which is not that of two sorts of relations but only one sort of relation, *relatio secundum esse*, considered here in the perspective of the doctrine of signs in a way that it had not heretofore generally been considered, namely, as providing the ground upon which *one and the same sign* can be realized now through a physical relation that is *also* objective and now through a purely objective relation that is *only* such according as the external circumstances of its realization in semiosis vary. Since he has thus utterly failed to grasp the role of relation in the constitution of the sign in its proper being, it is not surprising but only disappointing to find Marmo (1987: 124–126) asserting that the insertion of signs operative through custom and at the level of external sense among animals other than human "should then be considered a theoretical mistake", on the ground that Poinsot's theory presupposes (which it does not) "an absolute distinction between *sign* and meaning".

Hume's claim (1748: 152 par. 9) that "no man, who reflects, ever doubted, that the existences, which we consider, when we say, **this house** and **that tree**, are nothing but perceptions in the mind", Poinsot answers, to the contrary,[36] that the view that external sense (as distinguished from perception as the further work of internal sense—*phantasiari*—and of understanding) attains as its object an image produced by the mind is more than merely subject to doubt. A sufficiently thorough analysis proves the view in question to be finally incoherent (*"implicat"*) in terms of sense experience as such (*"probatur a posteriori"*) as well as in terms of the rational analysis of sense experience (*"probatur etiam a priori"*) (see *Tractatus de Signis*, Book III, Question 2, 310/37–312/6).

Sense experience is defined by contact with physically present aspects of objects. We can imagine or remember an absent object, but we can feel the resistance only of what is present here and now. Between an object acting physically on an organ of external sense and that organ itself as a physical attribute of the organism there is no disproportion, as there is between a perceived object and the sensory stimuli taken as basis for the perception. Yet ideas or images are required only to supply presence for an object otherwise absent, or to supply the proportion between what is perceived and what is sensed. Neither of these reasons for supposing an image at work within cognition apply to the case of external sensation. Hence the supposition of images in the case of external sense is gratuitous, simply without warrant. Rational analysis of sense experience thus confirms what brute experience seems to testify: sensation is concerned with physical aspects of objects present here and now in the en-

---

36 *Tractatus de Signis*, Book III, Question 2, "Whether a Concept Is a Formal Sign", esp. pp. 309/47–312/6 (= *Artis Logicae Secunda Pars*, Q. XXIII, Art. 2, "Utrum Conceptus Sit Signum Formale", 734a37–735a36), with cross-references to the books commenting on the *De Anima*, namely, Poinsot's *Philosophia Naturalis Quarta Pars* of 1635, Q. 6, Art. 1, "Utrum requiratur necessario, quod obiectum exterius sit praesens, ut sentiri potest" ("Whether It Is Necessarily the Case That an Exterior Object Be Present Physically In Order To Be Sensed"), 170a38–177a47, esp. 172b13–173a30, and Art. 4, "Utrum sensus externi forment idolum seu speciem expressam, ut cognoscant" ("Whether the External Senses Form an Icon or Expressed Specifying Form In Order To Cognize"), 192a18–198a16, esp. 195a5–46. Lengthy citations from these cross-referenced texts are incorporated in the critical apparatus of the 1985 Deely edition, q.v.

vironment. There are simply no grounds for holding that external sense, prescisively distinguished as such within perception and understanding, attains as its proper object an image produced by the mind itself. How far apart the Latin and the modern mainstreams had drifted in this area is apparent from Poinsot's further remark that his conclusion on this matter (which we may note was at variance with Suárez no less than with Hume) "is the more common one among those competent to treat of the question" (1632a: 310/8-9).[37] So much for Hume's "no man who reflects has ever doubted".

The whole of Book III of the *Tractatus de Signis* is devoted to these and related issues concerning experience of physical aspects of objects, insofar as our perceptions and conceptions involve sensation. Notice in particular, at the present juncture, that Poinsot grants that *if* sense were to know in an image, then indeed would there be an insoluble "problem of the external world". And he grants this, as it were, anticipating Hume's very terms:

But if the object exists in something produced by itself as in an image or effect, it will not be seen immediately, but as contained in the image, while the image itself is that which is seen.[38]

Hume argues in his *Enquiry* (1748: Sect. 12, Part 1, p. 152 pars. 11-13) that *since* "the mind has never any thing present to it but the perceptions,"

---

[37] *Artis Logicae Secunda Pars*, Q. XXIII, Art. 2, 734a48-b1: "nostra conclusio communior est inter auctores".

[38] "Quodsi existat in aliquo sui ut in imagine vel effectu, non immediate videbitur, sed ut contentum in imagine, ipsa vero imago est, quae videtur."—*Artis Logicae Secunda Pars*, Q. XXIII, "De Notitiis et Conceptibus", Art. 2, "Utrum Possit Dari Cognitio Intuitiva de Re Physice Absenti, sive in Intellectu sive in Sensu Exteriori", 735a32-36 (= *Tractatus de Signis*, Book III, "Concerning Modes of Awareness and Concepts", Question 2, "Whether There Can Be an Intuitive Cognition, either in the Understanding or in Exterior Sense, of a Thing Physically Absent", 312/2-6).

This text makes an extemely fundamental point which those who have tried to hijack the notion of formal sign (see Deely 1978a: 22n10, last two paragraphs) in a single-minded obsession with "realism" ought to attend to. What Poinsot has told us here, quite plainly, is that the doctrine of the formal sign as such and by itself is not what "grounds" thought in the "real" in the sense of *ens reale*. The best that an analysis of formal signs can do is to show how concepts—mental images as well as ideas—so function as to be *open* to such a grounding *in the right circumstances*. The

i.e., the images the mind itself makes, "and cannot possibly reach any experience of their connection with objects," *therefore* "the supposition of such a connexion is without any foundation in reasoning." Poinsot

"grounding in the real" in the sense indicated, Poinsot shows, can be explained in only one way: through the *absence* of formal signs (*species expressae*) in the cognitive actions of external sense prescisively considered as such. Indeed, a careful look at the text at 311/23–312/6, esp. the passage at 312/2–6 just cited, reveals that Poinsot has in effect remarked that if sensation as well as perception and intellection were by way of formal signs, there could and would be no critically verifiabe direct contact of the mind with so-called external reality, no such thing as what Powell calls the "critical control of objectification" in which distinctively human understanding takes place among the animals. Because there are no reasons justifying the supposition of formal signs in external sense, however, and because every sign as such, including the formal sign, is, as an ontological relation, experientially indifferent to the distinction of *relatio realis* from *relatio rationis*, the formal sign *can* but certainly does not always realize in its own way (through the aspect of the sign relation which happens to be categorial) a contact with *ens reale*. In other words, the indifference of relation to mind-dependent and mind-independent provenance combined with the unique status of sensation as such (in contrast with perception and understanding) in involving specification but not termination in an icon is required for an any defense of "realism" worth taking into account. For "in the object of a cognitive power the focus of attention is not reality as formally mind-independent or entitative, according as the object has being in itself, but the proportion and adaptation to the power. This proportion indeed as it subjectively exists in a thing must be mind-independent; but in terms of the relation to the power, that it exists subjectively in an actual thing is not what is regarded, but rather that it exists objectively relative to the power in question—although on other grounds, if the power itself respects only mind-independent being [as is the case with external senses prescisively taken], that power will also require a mind-independent being in the object, not as existing, but as related to the power. For existence is always in an order to itself and subjectively, whereas to a power it always pertains objectively" (John Poinsot, *Quarta Pars Philosophiae Naturalis, De Ente Animato*, Quaest. II, "De Proprietatibus Animae in Communi", Art. 3, "Utrum Potentiae Specificentur et Distinguantur per Actus et Obiecta", Reiser ed. Vol. 3, 77b26–44, cited in the *Tractatus de Signis* p. 190–191, note 35: "... non attendi formaliter in obiecto potentiae realitatem seu entitatem, prout habet esse in se, sed proportionem et coaptationem ad potentiam. Quae quidem proportio, ut subiective existat in re, debet esse realis, sed secundum comparationem ad potentiam non consideratur formaliter, quod sit subiective in ipsa re, sed quod se habet obiective ad talem potentiam, licet aliunde, si potentia ipsa solum respiciat ens reale, etiam in ratione obiecti realitatem petat non prout existentem, sed prout comparatam ad potentiam. Existentia enim semper est in ordine ad se et subiective, ad potentiam autem semper se habet obiective").

argues that *since* the mind deals in sensation not with images but with physical relations grounded in physical interactions of brute force, *therefore* the supposition of images at the sensory core of experience is without any foundation in reasoning. The hypothetical consequence that *if* sensation were of images *then* we would have no experience of a connection with external objects, which Hume considers a conclusive direct proof of the insolubility of the ''problem of the external world'', Poinsot takes as an indirect dialectical proof (a *reductio ad absurdum*) of what Latin tradition had established along several independent lines of direct argument, namely, the superfluousness of *species expressae* (ideas or images) in external sense (sensation) as such, and the gratuitousness of supposing or positing them there in the first place. Thus, the very basis from which Hume concludes, in his *Enquiry concerning Human Understanding* (1748: par. 14), that reason ''can never find any convincing argument from experience to prove, that the perceptions are connected with any external objects'', is the basis from which Poinsot developed rather convincing proofs that perceptions are connected with external objects precisely through the action of external sense analytically distinguished and taken as such within the activity of perception and understanding as a global whole.

We find here an interesting and particularly instructive illustration of how the same material of experience, even while providing in its sensory component something of a common measure for the comparative soundness of differing views, can be transformed differently in the hands of different philosophers.[39] This is a point poorly understood by those who criticize philosophical theories without understanding that sensation, to the extent that it provides a common measure within perception for the evaluation of philosophical doctrine, does not function in the direct way that experimentation does in the testing of a scientific theory. Samuel Johnson, for example, confronted with the problem of

---

39 See ''A Maxim for Semiotics'' (*Nil est in intellectum nec in sensum quod non prius habeatur in signum*, i.e., ''There is nothing in thought or in sensation which was not first in a sign'') in the *Semiotics 1987* volume ed. John Deely (Lanham, MD: University Press of America, 1988), pp. iii–v, for a general discussion of the different ways in which the maxim ''nil est in intellectu quod non prius fuerat in sensibus'' has been understood in ancient, medieval, and modern thought, including a reinterpretation in the line of the present discussion.

responding to Berkeley's view that matter does not exist because "everything in the universe is ideal", reacted with unforgettable alacrity. According to Boswell's report (1793: entry for August 6, 1763), Johnson, "striking his foot with mighty force against a large stone, till he rebounded from it," said of Berkeley's view: "'I refute it thus'." That would be fine had it been a question of scientific theory, but for a philosophical doctrine Johnson quite missed the point. Rocks, trees, houses, and stars remain just what they are in common experience for any philosophical theory. What changes is not what is given in sensation, but how that given is to be understood. No kicking of stones, or throwing stones, or even hitting Berkeley—or Hume—over the head with a stone, will serve to disprove the theory of sensation as terminating in mental constructions as such. It is not a question of whether there *is* brute secondness, but of *how* brute secondness is to be interpreted, and for this discourse is necessary, not physical blows.

Crucial to Poinsot's discussion of sensation is his demonstration of how the Latin scholastic standpoint assimilates to the *doctrina signorum:* the scholastic way of distinguishing sensible qualities provides in this instance the materials for an analysis which results in the conclusion that the manner in which the common sensibles presuppose the proper sensibles is in strict accordance with the defining characteristics of the type of relation in which signification consists. I cite the most trenchant passage:

Wherefore we respond simply that sense cognizes the significate in a sign in the way in which that significate is present in the sign, but not only in the way in which it is the same as the sign. For example, when a proper sensible such as a color is seen together with a common sensible, such as a profile and movement, the profile is not seen as the same as the color, but as conjoined to the color, and rendered visible through that color, nor is the color seen separately and the profile separately; so when a sign is seen and a significate is rendered present in it, the significate is attained there as conjoined to the sign and contained in it, not as existing separately and as absent.[40]

---

40 Poinsot, *Tractatus de Signis*, Book I, Question 6, "Whether the true rationale of sign is present in the behavior of brute animals and in the operation of the external senses", p. 208/34–47 (= *Artis Logicae Secunda Pars*, Q. XXI, Art. 6, "Utrum in brutis et sensibus externis sit vera ratio signi', 687b27–42): "Quare simpliciter respondemus, quod sensus cognoscit signatum in signo eo modo, quo in signo

The importance of the point that the analysis of sensation establishes a grounding of cognition in real relations which are at the same time sign relations emerges from the following considerations. If indeed experience begins with sensations, as empiricists claim, and sensations are an irreducible mixture of common with proper sensibles, the latter of which are related to the former as sign to signified; and if the elaboration of sensations as perceptions requires, as all agree, the elaboration of images by the mind on the basis of which the sensible qualities are further presented *as* this or that; and if the understanding of what is perceived[41] also requires the elaboration by the mind of ideas or concepts in order for what is objectively perceived to be understood in this rather than that manner (not to mention understood at all); and if, in Peirce's formula (1868: 208), as Poinsot and others of the Latin milieu had argued, "all thought is in signs", meaning that all concepts—all images and all ideas—are related to their objects as signs to significates, and every thought must be interpreted in another thought; then indeed the whole of experience, the being proper to it, from its primitive origins in sensation to its elaboration in perception and further development in understanding, all experience from its lowliest origins in sense to its highest attainments in theoretical understanding, is a continuous network, tissue, or web of sign relations. If that be so, then the doctrine of signs—the thematic elaboration of the role of signs in the constitution of knowledge and experience as the only path we have to the apprehension of objects and the truth about things—is not something peculiar or marginal to the philosophical enterprise but rather something cen-

---

praesens est, sed non eo solum modo, quo cum signo idem est. Sicut cum videtur sensibile proprium, v. g. color, et sensibile commune, ut figura et motus, non videtur figura ut idem cum colore, sed ut coniuncta colori, et per illum visibilis reddita, nec videtur seorsum color et seorsum figura; sic cum videtur signum et in eo praesens redditur signatum, ibi signatum attingitur ut coniunctum signo et contentum in eo, non ut seorsum se habens et ut absens.'' The full context of this text, 205/34–209/32 (= 686a13–688a28), is worth looking at.

[41] Motion, say, as a point of departure for considering the question of whether a being transcendent to the material order might not be required in order for the perceived fact of physical motion to be possible in the first place (cf. Deely 1994: Gloss 33, esp p. 155); or as a point of departure for differentiating between projectiles and falling bodies, etc.

tral to it and at its core, however long it takes for individual philosophers and philosophy itself to reach that realization.

In other words, even viewed strictly within the traditional confines of the *Cursus Philosophicus*, Poinsot's *Tractatus de Signis* establishes nothing less than a comprehensive role according to which signs weave the fabric and provide the structure for experience as a whole, and for the acts of understanding as well in the full range of their theoretical postulations. The role of the sign at the origins and foundations of awareness as well as in its perceptual and intellectual superstructures is what Poinsot undertakes to envisage in removing the discussion of *signum* from the traditional terminist perspective and recasting it in a unity and perspective proper to itself.

The *Treatise on Signs*, then, for all Poinsot's conservative concerns and commitment to tradition in the very sense that post-Cartesian Europe will reject, is of its very nature a radical work: it takes up again the then-traditional point of entry into philosophical study, and reshapes that point of departure according to an understanding of the fundamental activity of mind—namely, awareness as such—which makes of that activity a branch of the doctrine of signs. We have here, in the heart of Poinsot's determinedly traditional *Cursus Philosophicus Thomisticus*, nothing less than the doctrinal beginnings of a revolution in philosophy, a revolution profoundly in sympathy and tune with the modern search for a new beginning in philosophy. Even from within his tradition, Poinsot's *Tractatus de Signis* constitutes just such a new beginning in philosophy, where the concerns of logic and the concerns of natural philosophy, of epistemology and ontology, are joined through their common origin in the action of signs within intellection and, more generally, within experience.

b. The Foundation of the Perspective Proper to the *Doctrina Signorum*,
    i.e., Its Point of Departure

The philosophical tradition indigenous to the Latin Age as it culminated in the work of Aquinas and the school that developed after him down to the end of the Latin epoch had a very clear focus: being. If there is one name that exactly characterizes that development overall it is surely the philosophy of being.[42] Being, the proper object of intellect as sound is of hearing or color of sight, is that with the grasp of which understanding begins, and being as first known (*ens ut primum cognitum*), in order that judgment might become possible in the first place, divides first into *ens reale* and *ens rationis*.[43] Each of these further divides into substance and accident, on the one hand, and negation and relation,

---

[42] But not "comme si une philosophie de l'être ne pouvait être aussi une philosophie de l'esprit", not "as though a philosophy of being could not also be a philosophy of mind", as Maritain put it (1963: 388); *une philosophie véritable épistemologique*, as we might also say (see note 6 of Chapter 6 below, p. 161). To appreciate what is at stake here, see Vincent Guagliardo 1989, but especially his "Being-as-First-Known in Poinsot: A-Priori or Aporia?", in the *ACPQ* Poinsot Special Issue, Vol. LXVIII, No. 3 (Summer, 1994), pp. 375-404.

[43] Aquinas, *In duodecim libros metaphysicorum Aristotelis expositio* (c.1268-1272), Liber IV, lectio 6, n. 10: "Since the activity of understanding is twofold: one wherein it grasps what something is, which is called the grasp of indivisibles: another wherein it composes and divides: in both phases there is something foundational: in the first activity there is something which first falls in the grasp of understanding, namely, this which I call being; nor can anything be conceived by this operation of the mind unless being be understood. And because this principle that it is impossible to be and not be simultaneously in a given respect depends on the understanding of being ..: for this reason is this principle naturally the foundation in the second activity of the intellect, namely, that of composing and dividing. Nor can anyone understand anything according to this second activity unless this principle be understood."—"Cum duplex sit operatio intellectus: una, qua cognoscit quod quid est, quae vocatur indivisibilium intelligentia: alia, qua componit et dividit: in utroque est aliquod primum: in prima quidem operatione est aliquod primum, quod cadit in conceptione intellectus, scilicet hoc quod dico ens; nec aliquid hac operatione potest mente concipi, nisi intelligatur ens. Et quia hoc principium, impossibile est esse et non esse simul, dependet ex intellectu entis ..: ideo hoc etiam principium est naturaliter primum in secunda operatione intellectus, scilicet componentis et dividentis. Nec aliquis potest secundum hanc operationem intellectus aliquid intelligere, nisi hoc principio intellecto."

Peirce puts the matter this way (1868a: CP 5.311): "What do we mean by the real? It is a conception which we must first have had when we discovered that there was an unreal, an illusion; that is, when we first corrected ourselves. Now the distinction for which alone this fact logically called, was between an *ens* relative to private inward determinations, to the negations belonging to idiosyncrasy, and an *ens* such as would stand in the long run. The real, then, is that which, sooner or later, information and reasoning would finally result in, and which is therefore independent of the vagaries of me and you."

On the order of primitive concepts from being as first known to the point where correspondence truth can be asserted, see Deely 1982: note 1, pp. 153-155. See also

on the other hand.[44] The study of substance and accident, as including the accident of mind-independent relation as a physical mode, was the work of natural philosophy. But the study of negation and relation as mind-dependent objective modes had no comprehensive study (still less was there any study of relation as precisely indifferent to the mode of its realization, such as a doctrine of signs requires).

Poinsot was able to show that both negations and relations as mind-dependent beings share with mind-independent relation the common rationale of a "being toward", in contrast with all other modes of mind-independent being which share as such the rationale of subjectivity or "being in" (*esse in se* in the case of substance, *esse in alio* in the case of accidents other than relation formally considered). But, in the main, the only focus in the study of *ens rationis* as such was established in the distinction between "first" and "second intentions", inasmuch as the latter relations—second intentions—were taken to provide the subject matter for formal logic,[45] along the following lines.

the general discussion of "Otherness" in Deely 1994: 121–133. And see Guagliardo 1993.

[44] Just as a passing technical point, in my article on First Philosophy (Deely 1987: 8) the text on this point erroneously is printed as "negation and privation" instead of "negation and relation".

[45] *Artis Logicae Secunda Pars*, Q. II, Art. 2, 291a26–48 (= *Tractatus de Signis*, First Preamble, Article 2, 59/19–6): "But this formality of a second intention is called 'second intention' according to the difference from a first intention, as if a second state or condition of an object were being expressed. For an object can be considered in two states: *First*, as it is in itself, whether as regards existence or as regards definable structure. *Second*, as it is in apprehension, and this state of existing in cognition is second in respect of the state of existing in itself, which is first, because just as knowability follows on entity, so being known follows on that being which an object has in itself. Those affections or formalities, therefore, belonging to a thing according as it is in itself, are called first intentions; those belonging to the thing according as it is known are called second intentions. And because it is the task of Logic to order things as they exist in apprehension, therefore of itself Logic considers second intentions, the intentions which coincide with things as known."—"Vocatur vero secunda intentio ista secundum differentiam a prima, quasi dicatur secundus status seu conditio obiecti. Potest enim obiectum considerari in duplici statu: Primo, secundum quod est in se, sive quantum ad existentiam sive quantum ad quidditatem. Secundo, ut est in apprehensione, et status iste essendi in cognitione est secundus

Scholastics distinguished. Those properties which belong to an object of apprehension as existing in itself prior to and independently of its being apprehended they called "first intentions": "first" because they belonged to an object insofar as it was a thing of the physical world before it became an object known, but "intentions" because they yet pertain (insofar as it is indeed the thing that is now known) to the relationship or set of relationships whereby what formerly *only* existed now *also* is known. Those properties which belong to an object *precisely and only* as it exists objectively, i.e., dependently on being apprehended, they called "second intentions": "second" because they did not characterize the object according to any prior being or state of being other than that of being known, i.e., they belonged to an object *only* insofar as it is part of a network of thought relations able to obtain whether or not the object they characterize is also a thing of the physical world.[46] Second intentions, thus, are mind-dependent relations, but not all mind-dependent relations, by any means, are second intentions. Many mind-dependent relations, indeed, come to characterize objects in their *physical* reality as such, as when a human being, through long training, becomes a doctor, scientist, or judge. These relations thus pertain to the order of first intentions. Only those mind-dependent relations pertaining to the *intellectual* grasp of objects as objects, and as distinguished from whatever percep-

respectu status essendi in se, qui est primus, quia sicut cognoscibilitas sequitur ad entitatem, ita esse cognitum est post illud esse, quod habet in se. Illae ergo affectiones seu formalitates, quae conveniunt rei prout in se, vocantur primae intentiones, quae conveniunt rei prout cognita, vocantur secundae. Et quia pertinet ad Logicam dirigere res, secundum quod sunt in apprehensione, ideo per se considerat Logica intentiones secundas, quae conveniunt rebus ut cognitis."

46 Thus, a human being, even if there were no human beings alive, would still be a rational animal, such that, were there to be a human being, it could not be human and not be both animal and rational; or a plant, even if there were no plants, would still be a living substance, such that, were there to be a plant, it could not be a plant and not be both a substance and living; etc. This was essentially the so-called doctrine of "the predicables"—genus, species, difference, property, accident—developed by the scholastics in fleshing out Aristotle's theory of logical definitions on the basis of the c.271 work of Porphyry, q.v. See the "Explicatio Textus Isgagis Porphyrii" in Poinsot's *Artis Logicae Secunda Pars* of 1632: 376-378, and Qq. 6-12, pp. 378a32-472b48. (A Spanish translation of this portion of Poinsot's *Cursus Philosophicus* is available in Ferrer 1990).

tual or sensory elements are involved in the apprehension of objects or whatever subjective habits are formed in beings as a consequence of cognitions, belong to the narrow class of second intentions.

Second intentions, thus, comprising the set of intellectual relations according to which things are *thought to be* this or that way (second intentions), in counterdistinction to the way in which they *in fact are* (first intentions), provide the subject-matter for logic as a science distinct from the science of nature which studies being (or tries to) in its mind-independent dimension taken as such.

The distinction appears so straightforward that only the best of the Latin logicians saw much need to make their students aware of the considerable subtleties required to understand its full implications and the considerable complexity glossed over in the order of *ens rationis* by the narrow focus of logicians on second intentions as such. Beyond this narrow focus, the order of *ens rationis* consists of far more and more complex relations than those classed as second intentions by logicians, including the whole realm of social interactions and cultural roles. These relationships have come to provide, toward the end of modern times, the subject matter of sociology and anthropology and the social sciences generally—a development undreamed of in the Latin Age. And it is just these neglected complexities that are of much greater importance to the *doctrina signorum* than the distinction itself of second from first intentions as taken to provide the focus for formal logic, as Poinsot seems well to have realized.

For example, Poinsot notes that "'a first intention can also be found in the case of mind-dependent beings, such as are many negations and privations and extrinsic denominations'",[47] for which last he gives the examples of being a doctor, judge, or teacher, etc.[48] This is a seminal

---

[47] *Artis Logicae Secunda Pars*, Q. XII, Art. 1., 464b24–28 (= *Tractatus de Signis*, First Preamble, Article 2, 58n2): "etiam in entibus rationis potest inveniri prima intentio, sicut sunt multae negationes et privationes et denominationes extrinsecae".

[48] Poinsot 1632, *Artis Logicae Secunda Pars*, Q. 2, "De Ente Rationis Logico, Quod Est Secunda Intentio", 291b2–46 (= *Treatise on Signs*, "First Preamble: On Mind-Dependent Being", Article 2, "What Is the Second Intention and Logical Mind-Dependent Relation and How Many Kinds Are There", 60/7–44, bold emphasis in original): "**not every mind-dependent objective relation is a second intention, but, nevertheless, every second intention taken formally, and not only fundamentally,**

point which the Latin Age died without seriously exploring, as I have had occasion to note at length elsewhere.[49] Thus, as I mentioned above, social and cultural roles and personality structure, though mind-dependent creations, *yet belong to the order of first intention*.[50] Again, "One second intention can even be materially subtended and accidentally denominated by another second intention, and so a second intention assumes the manner of a first intention in respect of the second intention to which it is subtended."[51] Whence a *processus in infinitum*, useless

is a mind-dependent objective relation, not a mind-independent form, nor an extrinsic denomination, as some erroneously think.

"The first part of this conclusion is manifestly the case, because even though every mind-dependent relation results from cognition, yet not every such relation denominates a thing only in the state of a cognized being, which is a second state, but some also do so in the state of an existence independent of cognition, as, for example, the relations of Creator and Lord do not denominate God known in himself, but God existing, and similarly being a doctor, being a judge. *For the existing man, not the man as cognized, is a doctor or a judge, and so those mind-dependent relations* [being a doctor, judge, teacher, etc.] denominate a state of existence [italic added; cf. Book I, Question 2, 141/12–142/13, esp. 141/37–142/8].

"Here note this difference: even though cognition is the cause from which a mind-dependent relation results (as it is the cause of all mind-dependent being), and thus, as the mind-dependent relation belongs to and denominates some subject, it necessarily requires cognition, yet cognition does not always render *the object itself apt* and congruous for the reception of such a denomination, so that the denomination belongs to that object only *in cognized being*, for this happens only in second intentions. And thus the relations of Creator and Lord, judge and doctor, as they denominate a subject, require cognition, which causes such relations but does not render the subject capable in cognized or known being of receiving that denomination. But indeed the being of a genus or species not only supposes cognition causing such relations, but also supposes a cognition which renders the subject abstracted from individuals, and upon the thing so abstracted falls that denomination [i.e., the denomination by a second intention]." (Latin cited in the Appendix of Longer Latin Citations, p. 256–257 below.)

49 See the discussion of "The Indigenous Latin Development" in *Introducing Semiotic* (Deely 1982), pp. 23–26, esp. the diagram on p. 26, "Divisions of being in the structure of experience".

50 In the *Tractatus de Signis*, see the First Preamble, Article 2, 60/15–35; and Book I, Question 2, 141/28–142/13, and note 32 p. 150, at the end.

51 Ibid., 464b28–33: "Potest etiam una secunda intentio materialiter substerni et denominari accidentaliter ab alia secunda intentione, et sic induit quasi modum

in principle for explaining things at the level of physical causality,[52] is perfectly possible within the objective order,[53] and is also, as Peirce best pointed out, the normal condition in the action of signs within cognition—normal, because, as Peirce observes (1902: 2.303), it is a consequence of the very nature of a sign as "anything which determines some-

primae intentionis respectu eius, cui substernitur." Indeed, it is just this fact that underlies the "unlimited" or "infinite" character of semiosis in the species-specifically human case, wherein one relation is founded on another in the constitution of discourse. See Deely 1990: 62n23; and Deely 1994: *passim*.

52 Such is the classical foundation for the rational demonstration of the existence of God from our experience of the world in Aquinas c.1266: *Summa Theologiae Prima Pars*, Q. 3, Art. 3. Cf. *Artis Logicae Secunda Pars*, Q. 17, Art. 2, 584b40–586a48, esp. 585a24–b11 (= *Tractatus de Signis*, Second Preamble, Article 3, "First Difficulty", 102/37–105/13, esp. 103/12–39); and Deely 1994: 152–155, Gloss 33.

53 *Artis Logicae Secunda Pars*, Q. II, Art. 2, 292a33–293b12 (= *Tractatus de Signis*, First Preamble, Article 2, 61/31–62/18, bold in original): "It follows secondly that although a first intention absolutely taken must be something mind-independent or belonging to something in the state of being independent of objective apprehension (for otherwise it would not be simply first, because that which is mind-independent always precedes and is prior to that which is mind-dependent), yet nevertheless **it is not contradictory that one second intention should be founded on another. In such a case, the founding second intention takes on as it were the condition of a first intention in respect of the other or founded intention, not because it is simply first, but because it is prior to that intention which it founds.**

"For since the understanding is reflexive upon its own acts, it can know reflexively the second intention itself and found upon that cognized intention another second intention; for example, the intention of a genus which is attributed to animal, can, as cognized, again found the second intention of species, inasmuch as the intention of genus is a kind of predicable species. And then this founded second intention denominates the founding second intention as prior, by reason of which circumstance it is said that the genus formally is a genus and denominatively is a species. This is something that frequently happens in these second intentions, to wit, that one of them is in itself formally of a certain type, but is of another type as known denominatively. Nevertheless these are all said to be second intentions, even though the one second intention is founded on another second intention, and there is not said to be a third or a fourth intention, because they all belong to (or coincide with) the object as known, but being known is always a second state for a thing. And because one second intention as it founds another takes on as it were the condition of a first intention in respect of that other founded on it, so even that intention which is founded is always said to be second." (Latin cited in the Appendix of Longer Citations, pp. 257–258 below.)

thing else (its *interpretant*) to refer to an object to which itself refers (its *object*) in the same way, the interpretant becoming in turn a sign, and so on *ad infinitum*".[54]

In view of this situation, it is not surprising that Poinsot devotes one of the longest questions in his *Tractatus de Signis*[55] to showing that the action of signs requires for its explanation the extrinsic formal causality of objective interaction —what Peirce calls "ideal" causality (but also confuses with final causality)[56]— which can be found in nature wherever there is an assimilation through representation of one thing to another in guiding future outcomes.[57] And, as if to underscore the point, Poinsot devotes the following question[58] to showing why the Aristotelian four causes of material interaction do not explain the action of signs.

Equally fascinating is Poinsot's demonstration that brute animals as well as rational animals fashion and deploy mind-dependent struc-

---

[54] Eco (1990: 28 and 38) makes two important glosses regarding "infinite semiosis". First, "In structuralistic terms, one could say that for Peirce semiosis is potentially unlimited from the point of view of the system but is not unlimited from the point of view of the process. In the course of a semiosic process we want to know only what is relevant according to a given *universe of discourse*." Second, "Semiosis is unlimited and, through the series of interpretants, explains itself by itself, but there are at least two cases in which semiosis is confronted with something external to it. The first case is that of indices.... indices are in some way linked to an item of the extralinguistic or extrasemiosic world. The second case is due to the fact that every semiosic act is determined by a Dynamic Object.... We produce representamens because we are compelled by something external to the circle of semiosis."

[55] *Artis Logicae Secunda Pars*, Q. XXI, Art. 4, "Qualiter dividatur obiectum in motivum et terminativum", 670a18–679b53 (= *Tractatus de Signis*, Book I, Question 4, "In What Way Are Objects Divided into Stimulus Objects and Terminative Objects", 166/1–192/14).

[56] See the "Excursus on Peirce and Poinsot" in the Editorial AfterWord to the *Tractatus de Signis*, 492–498, esp. 493–494; and Chapters 6 and 7 below, esp. pp. 158–162, 168–178, 191–192, and 194ff.

[57] See Chapter 6 below, and also Chapter 6 of *Basics of Semiotics* (Deely 1990), 83–104.

[58] *Artis Logicae Secunda Pars*, Q. XXI, Art. 5, "Utrum significare sit formaliter causare aliquid in genere efficiendi", 679b14–685a33 (= *Tractatus de Signis*, Book I, Question 5, "Whether To Signify, Formally Considered, Is To Cause Something in the Order of Productive Causality", 193/1–203/32). Detailed discussion in Chap. 6 below.

tures of objectivity which they make use of in adapting the world to their own interests and needs. This analysis of so-called *entia rationis* materially formed and employed in the use of signs by animals is one of the most important elements in the preambles to Poinsot's *Tractatus de Signis*, bound up with his argument that percepts as well as concepts are formal signs. Animals, remarked Maritain (1957: 53), make use of signs without knowing that there are signs; Poinsot shows further that animals make use of mind-dependent relations without knowing that there are mind-dependent relations.[59]

My concern here, however, is not to show how the *doctrina signorum* brings into a more comprehensive focus the many complexities of the problematic of mind-dependent being which were left in the background and on the margins of traditional logical and ontological analysis. My concern rather is to show exactly how the *doctrina signorum* within Poinsot's *Cursus Philosophicus Thomisticus* relates to *ens reale* and *ens rationis* as terms distinguished within the intellectual grasp of *ens ut primum cognitum*. As Poinsot himself remarks,[60] the doctrine of signs begins with the establishment of the notion of relation as transcending our experience of the objective contrast between *ens reale* and *ens rationis*.

The point is simple; the move based on it is dramatic. Yet the text conveying this feat[61] is framed with so many technical complexities

---

59 See Poinsot, *Artis Logicae Secunda Pars*, Q. II, Art. 4, "Per quam potentiam et per quos actus fiant entia rationis", 301a1–306b45, esp. 301b33–302b4, where he explains precisely that "sensus interni ... repraesentare possint id, ad cuius instar formatur aliquod ens fictum, quod est materialiter formare entia rationis", and 305b19–28 (= *Tractatus de Signis*, First Preamble, Article 3, "By What Powers and through Which Acts Do Mind-Dependent Beings Come About", 65/1–76/45, esp. 66/47–68/31, and 74/39–48); Q. XXII, Art.2, "Utrum conceptus sit signum formale", 704a11–41 (= Book II, Question 2, "Whether a Concept Is a Formal Sign", 246/13–247/21). Cf. "Idolum. Archeology and Ontology of the Iconic Sign" (Deely 1986d).

60 *Treatise on Signs*, Book I, Question 1, 117/28–118/6, included in the quotation in the following note.

61 *Artis Logicae Secunda Pars*, Q. XXI, "De Signo Secundum Se", Art. 1, "Utrum signum sit in genere relationis", 646b16–45 (= *Tractatus de Signis*, Book I, "Concerning the Sign in Its Proper Being", Question 1, "Whether a Sign Is in the Order of Relation", 117/18–118/18): **"We ask therefore whether this formal rationale of a sign consists, primarily and essentially, in a relation according to the way**

from the analysis of relation as a mode of being, presupposed to the discussion of *signum* as Poinsot is concerned to situate it, that Poinsot's best modern students have missed its thrust,[62] although once just bare-

it has being (*an ontological relation*) **or in a relation according to the way being must be expressed in discourse** (*a transcendental relation*), *that is to say*, **in something subjective which founds an ontological relation.**

"What a relation is according to the way being must be expressed in discourse and according to the way it has being, what a transcendental relation is and what a categorial relation is, has been explained in our Second Preamble concerning Relation. And we speak here of ontological relation—of relation according to the way it has being—not of categorial relation, because we are discussing the sign in general, as it includes equally the natural and the social sign, in which general discussion even the signs which are mental artifacts—namely, stipulated signs as such—are involved. And for this reason, the rationale common to signs cannot be that of a categorial being, nor a categorial relation, although it could be an ontological relation, according to the point made by St. Thomas in the *Summa theologica*, I, q. 28, art. 1, and explained in our Preamble on Relation—to wit, that only in the case of these things which exist toward another is found some mind-independent relation and some mind-dependent relation, which latter relation plainly is not categorial, but is called a relation according to the way relation has being (an ontological relation), because it is purely a relation and does not import anything absolute."—"Quaerimus ergo, an formalis ista ratio signi consistat in relatione secundum esse primo et per se, an in relatione secundum dici seu [see following note] in aliquo absoluto, quod fundet talem relationem.

"Quid sit autem relatio secundum dici et secundum esse, relatio transcendentalis et praedicamentalis, dictum est in q. 17. de Relatione [art. 1. et 2., = *Tractatus de Signis*, Second Preamble, Articles 1 and 2, 80/1–99/42]. Et loquimur hic de relatione secundum esse, non de relatione praedicamentali, quia loquimur de signo in communi, prout includit tam signum naturale quam ad placitum, in quo involvitur etiam signum, quod est aliquid rationis, scilicet signum ad placitum. Et ideo praedicamentale ens esse non potest nec relatio praedicamentalis, licet possit esse relatio secundum esse iuxta doctrinam D. Thomae 1. p. q. 28. art. 1. explicatam eadem q. 17 [esp. 580a32–582a16, = *Tractatus de Signis*, 93/17–97/36], quod solum in his, quae sunt ad aliquid, invenitur aliqua relatio realis et aliqua rationis, quae relatio manifestum est, quod non sit praedicamentalis, sed vocatur relatio secundum esse, quia pure relatio est et non aliquid absolutum importat."

[62] Editor's note on the text of the *Tractatus de Signis*, Book I, Question 1, at 117/22: "*Seu* in classical Latin usage introduces an alternative condition or a disjunction. This has led even careful scholars (e.g., Yves R. Simon, John J. Glanville, and G. Donald Hollenhorst, *The Material Logic of John of St. Thomas* [Chicago: The University of Chicago Press, 1955], p. 389) into a most serious misreading of Poinsot at

ly.[63] Let me extract from the tangle the key assertion, and then try to explain its import (Poinsot 1632a: 117/28-118/18):

we speak here of ontological relation (relation according to the way it has being), not of categorial relation, because we are discussing the sign in general, as it includes equally the natural and the social sign, in which general discussion even the signs which are as artifacts mind-dependent—namely, stipulated signs as such—are involved.[64] And for this reason, the rationale *common* to signs cannot be that of any categorial being as such, including a categorial rela-

> this point—most serious, because it involves as a consequence nothing less than total misunderstanding of the point of departure for the doctrine of signs. Their rendering of this passage reads: 'We propose to determine whether the formal notion of the sign consists, primarily and essentially, (a) in a relation according to existence or (b) in a relation according to expression or (c) in a thing absolute which would ground the relation that the sign implies'. This is not a correct reading of the text.
>
> "What Poinsot envisages here, as Ralph Powell has shown (see my 'What's in a Name?' *Semiotica* 22:1-2 [1978], 159-163, esp. note 8, pp. 175-176), and as is clear from the first two Articles of the Second Preamble above, are not three alternatives for the being proper to signs, but only two. The *seu* here, thus, expresses neither an alternative condition nor a disjunction, but an *explication only*. Poinsot is using '*seu*' not in the classical but rather in line with the novel medieval sense cited by Du Cange, *Glossarium Mediae et Infimae Latinitatis* (orig. publ. 1883-1887; Graz, Austria: Akademische Druck- u. Verlagsanstalt, 1954, VII: 461: 'Seu, pro *Et*, conjunctiva. Occurrit passim' (see also the entry for *sive*, p. 499). In other words, the *seu* here adds something further but not opposed to the preceding *secundum dici*, namely, its explication *aliis verbis*. *Secundum esse* and *secundum dici* are exclusive and exhaustive *secundum rem*, so that the *seu* here adds to *secundum dici* something *secundum verba tantum*—a *verbal* alternative that is *conceptually equivalent*. Note the parallel construction in Poinsot's text shortly below at 118/21-24; and see the Second Preamble, Article 1, note 16, p. 86 above, and Article 2, 89/21-91/29, esp. 90/15-37." Note that there are also passages in which Poinsot does use "*seu*" in the classical manner (see the discussion in the first par. of note 2 to Book II, Question 2, at 240/4).

63 Maritain alone in recent times begins to penetrate Poinsot's foundational doctrine in what is original to it, yet never quite cuts fully to its core: see Deely 1986c, esp. 120-122.

64 See the extended discussion of this point at *Artis Logicae Secunda Pars*, Q. XXI, Art. 2, "Utrum in signo naturale relatio sit realis vel rationis", 658b30-659a39 (= *Tractatus de Signis*, Book I, Question 2, "Whether the Sign-Relation in the Case of Natural Signs Is Mind-Independent or Mind-Dependent", 141/12-142/13.

tion,[65] although it *could* be an ontological relation, according to the point made by St. Thomas in the *Summa theologiae*, I, q. 28, art. 1, and explained in our Preamble on Relation—to wit, that only in the case of these things which exist toward another is found some mind-independent relation and some mind-dependent relation,[66] which latter plainly is not categorial, but is called a relation according to the way it has being (an ontological relation), because it is purely a relation and does not import anything absolute.[67]

---

[65] The editor's note (note 10 on p. 118, at line 8) in the *Tractatus de Signis* at this point reads as follows: "See Logica 2. p. q. 14. art. 1., '*Quid sit praedicamentum et quid requiratur ut aliquid sit in praedicamento*' ('What a category is and what are the conditions for anything's belonging to a category'), Reiser ed., 500b36–501a2: '*Et quia praedicamentorum distinctio ad hoc introducta est, ut diversarum naturarum ordines et classes proponerentur, ad quae omnia, quae naturam aliquam participant, reducerentur, ideo imprimis secludendum est ab omni praedicamento ens rationis, quia non habet naturam neque entitatem veram, sed fictam, ideoque neque ad praedicamentum verum, sed fictum reici debet. Unde D. Thomas q. 7. de Potentia art. 9. tantum res extra animam dicit pertinere ad praedicamenta.*' — 'Since the distinction of the categories was introduced for this, that the orders and classes of diverse natures might be set forth, to which all the things that participate some nature might be reduced, the very first thing to be excluded from *every* category is mind-dependent being, for being that depends for its existence on being cognized (mind-dependent being) has not a nature nor a true entity, but a constructed one, and therefore must be relegated not to a true category, but to a constructed one. Whence St. Thomas says (in q. 7, art. 9 of his *Disputed Questions on the Power of God*) that only a thing independent of the mind pertains to the categories.'"

[66] See the *Artis Logicae Secunda Pars*, Q. 17, "De Praedicamento Relationis", Art. 2, esp. 580a30–582a16, but also 578a24–579a34 (= *Tractatus de Signis*, Second Preamble, "On Relation", Article 2, "esp. 93/17–96/36, but also 89/21–91/28). See further Q. II, "De Ente Rationis Logico", Art. 1, "Quid sit ens rationis in communi et quotuplex", 287a10–32, 288a25–39; Art. 2, "Quid sit secunda intentio et relatio rationis logica et quotuplex", 291b1–46; Art. 4, 303b8–304a5 (= *Tractatus de Signis*, First Preamble, "On Mind-Dependent Being", Article 1, "What in General a Mind-Dependent Being Is, and How Many Kinds of Mind-Dependent Being There Are", 51/37–52/5, 53/32–45; Article 2, "What is the Second Intention and Logical Mind-Dependent Relation, and How Many Are There", 60/7–44; Article 3] = Art. 4 in Reiser], 70/24–71/19).

[67] *Artis Logicae Secunda Pars*, Q. XXI, Art. 1, "Utrum signum sit in genere relationis", 646b26–45 (= *Tractatus de Signis*, Book I, Question 1, "Whether a Sign Is in the Order of Relation", 117/28–18).

Put as simply and straightforwardly as possible, Poinsot is saying here that the *doctrina signorum* must take its departure from a standpoint which transcends the division of being into *ens reale* and *ens rationis*.[68] This explicit realization is what sets his *Tractatus de Signis* apart within the *Cursus Philosophicus* and Latin tradition as a whole as a virtual demand for a new beginning in philosophy, a beginning in terms of which the division of being into categories, for example, needs to be justified anew in terms of an experiential starting point.[69]

To begin with, what is called *ontological relation* or *relation according to the way it has being* in my translation is called, in Poinsot's Latin, *relatio secundum esse*. Within the Thomistic tradition, the *secundum esse* relative had become a technical term of exceptional precision thanks to the commentaries of Cajetan, Soto, and Araújo, among others, a classical example of new wine in an old bottle. Categorial or physical relation, *relatio praedicamentalis seu relatio realis*,[70] fits the definition of *relatio secun-*

---

68 See Deely 1977b, and 1980: 82–86.

69 Note 16 to 86/22 in the 1985 publication of Poinsot's *Tractatus de Signis* was intended to clarify this implication of Poinsot's work, but proved instead to be the single greatest occasion of misunderstanding in the contemporary discussion of Poinsot (Bird 1987: 106–107, followed by Ashworth 1988: 134–136). Accordingly, I found it necessary further to develop the point at some length (Deely 1988: 56–87, esp. 56–69), and this clarification has been incorporated into a much expanded version of note 16 for the electronic version of the *Tractatus de Signis* released by Intelex Corporation in 1992. See the Epilogue to Part I below, esp. p. 146; and Chapter 8 note 4, pp. 208–9 below.

70 The translation of *relatio realis* as ''physical relation'' has been the second greatest occasion of misunderstanding in contemporary discussion of the 1985 edition of Poinsot's *Tractatus de Signis*. '''Physical beings' will not do for *entia realia*'', D. P. Henry states (1987: 1201), ''since theological entities are for Poinsot non-physical (indeed meta-physical) but nevertheless real''; whence Henry deems this a ''quite inappropriate'' translation of a key term, a criticism in which he is joined by Furton (1987: 767) and Ashworth (1988: 145), who also objects on the ground that ''there are places in which the type of real being picked out may well include spiritual beings''.

The objection stems from ignorance of the details of the philosophical vocabulary in Poinsot's tradition, to be sure, but it also serves to emphasize the need mentioned above to go beyond the literal appearances in reading the authors of mainstream Latin tradition. In this particular, nonetheless, I am surprised to learn that it is apparently little known among contemporary renaissance Latin scholars that, beginning with Aquinas himself (e.g., c.1269: liber I, lect. 1, n. 1), the term ''physical'' extends equally to material and spiritual substances, including the *esse divinum* (''Es-

dum esse, but so does mind-dependent relation or *relatio rationis* fit the definition.

Now the sign is a peculiar being because our experience of it cannot be reduced to the categories of *ens reale* and *ens rationis*. Our experience and use of *signum* conveys with equal facility phenomena of nature, such as lead us to anticipate a storm, and phenomena of culture, such as lead us to respect a flag for what it symbolizes.

Poinsot emphasizes a twofold point which sets the Thomistic development of *signum* apart within Latin tradition.[71] The reason that *signum* must be identified with *relatio secundum esse* is, first of all, because relation in this precise sense designates the only ontological rationale (*ratio entitatis*) which can be found verified in each of the opposed orders of *ens reale* and *ens rationis*: this much is already clear in the cited text, with

sentia Dei physica consistit in cumulo omnium perfectionum in gradu infinito et in summa simplicitate, ita ut, quamquam perfectio a perfectione differt plus quam ratione ratiocinante, non distinguantur tamen inter se nisi ratione ratiocinata cum fundamento in re imperfecto''—Gredt 1936: vol. II, Thesis XXXII). Thus Poinsot, in his theological *Cursus* (1643a: 38 n.8), speaks of divine grace as producing a ''specialem modum praesentiae realis et physicae respectu Dei'', flatly contradicting Henry's assertion that theological entities for Poinsot are non-physical.

The division of *ens reale* into spiritual and material substances, in the Thomistic tradition, is precisely a division in the order of physical being—the order, that is to say, of being as existing independently of objectification in finite cognition. ''Ens physicum'' and ''ens reale'' alike designate this order of being throughout its extent, whence the synonymy drawn upon in the 1985 *Tractatus de Signis* translation is inaptly singled out by the reviewers for criticism. A reliable modern guide to the technical Latin usages in Poinsot's tradition can be found in the two-volume text entitled *Elementa Philosophiae Aristotelico-Thomisticae*, written by the learned Benedictine philosopher-scientist, Joseph Gredt, exactly according to the traditional plan of Poinsot's *Cursus Philosophicus*, but updating the material of natural philosophy pertaining to experimental science (psychology, biology, physics, etc.) and addressing the problems under more current headings: see the Editorial AfterWord to the *Tractatus de Signis* (Deely 1985), p. 461n97. Originally published in 1899, Gredt's *Elementa Philosophiae* went through seven editions in the author's lifetime, and there have been at least five posthumous editions, of which I have relied primarily on the 1961 edition by Zenzen.

[71] I am indebted to Mauricio Beuchot (1980) for learning that Francisco Araújo's *Commentariorum in Universam Aristotelis Metaphysicam* of 1617 provides a direct link in the development from Soto's *Summulae* to Poinsot's *Tractatus de Signis*.

its explicit demand that the *doctrina signorum* begin at a point beyond, or prior to, the distinction between *ens reale* and *ens rationis*. The uniqueness of the action of signs that follows from this, however, Poinsot uniquely developed.

Even though others in Poinsot's tradition had identified the sign-relation with *relatio secundum esse*, they had not seen how this identification implied a unified subject matter for the *doctrina signorum*. Sometimes relations are mind-independent, as in the case of natural signs, sometimes relations are mind-dependent, as in the case of conventional signs: this much everyone saw. What Poinsot further saw was that this opposition of natural to conventional signs does not preclude the relation constituting *either* type of sign from being sometimes mind-dependent and sometimes mind-independent.

In the case of natural signs, a natural sign functioning formally as a sign here and now is "mind-dependent"—that is to say, objective only (i.e., consisting in a cognized relation which is not also physical)—when the conditions required for the relation to be physical or "mind-independent" as well are not realized. As Poinsot put it, "the relation of a natural sign to its significate is mind-independent supposing the conditions requisite for such a relation are prevailing."[72]

In the case of conventional signs, the foundation for the sign-relation consists "in the extrinsic denomination whereby it is rendered imposed or appointed for signifying by common usage", inasmuch as "it is through this imposition that something is habilitated and appointed to be a stipulated sign, just as it is through some natural sign's being proportioned and connected with a given significate that there is founded a relation of the sign to that significate."[73] But this original foundation in stipulation does not prevent that same conventional sign from becoming habituated within a population, and by this means becoming transformed into a sign relatively natural, signifying as such by

---

72 *Tractatus de Signis*, Book I, Question 2, 137/9–15: "relatio signi naturalis ad suum signatum ... realis est ... supponendo ... conditiones relationis realis", alias rationis (i.e., otherwise it becomes a mind-dependent relation). Araújo, as reported in Beuchot 1980: 52–53, is even more explicit on the point.

73 *Tractatus de Signis*, Book I, Question 2, "Utrum in Signo Naturali Relatio Sit Realis vel Rationis" ("Whether the Sign-Relation in the Case of Natural Signs is Mind-Independent or Mind-Dependent"), 141/16–18, 23–27.

a triadic relation grounded now in the habit structures of a community and no longer merely mind-dependently in the explicit cognitions of a few.[74]

Thus, just as circumstances can dictate that a natural sign be realized as such through a mind-dependent relation, so circumstances can bring it about conversely that a conventional sign be realized through participation in a physical relation. And physical relations based on habit constitute signs not only in the order of conventions among human animals, but also in the order of interactions between human beings and other animals or among animals themselves. In Poinsot's terse summary, "not all custom is a human act, but all custom can found a natural sign".[75]

[74] *Tractatus de Signis*, Book II, Question 6, "Whether the Division of Signs into Natural, Stipulated, and Customary Is Sound" ("Utrum Sit Univoca et Bona Divisio Signi in Formale et Instrumentale"), 280/26–43: "When speaking of human custom, even though it proceeds from a free cause and so is denominated a free effect, nevertheless, the formal rationale of signifying is not any free deputation, but the very frequency and repetition of acts, and this signifies naturally, because it is not a moral deputation, that is to say, it is not an extrinsic deputation which denominates only morally, but the intrinsic performance of acts and their frequency and multiplication constitutes the customary sign. Therefore a signification attaches to that sign naturally, even as multiplied free acts generate a habit as a natural and not as a free effect, because the very multiplication of the acts does not function freely relative to generating the habit, so neither to the signifying resulting from the force of the repetition of the acts, even though these acts in themselves [i.e., singly taken] may be free."—"Secundo respondetur loquendo de consuetudine humana, quod licet a sua causa libera procedat et sic denominetur effectus liber, tamen ratio formalis significandi non est aliqua libera deputatio, sed ipsa frequentia et repetitio actuum, et haec naturaliter significat, quia non moralis, id est extrinseca deputatio, quae solum moraliter denominat, sed intrinseca processio actuum eorumque frequentatio et multiplicatio constituit signum ex consuetudine. Ergo naturaliter convenit illi significatio, sicut etiam actus liberi multiplicati generant habitum tamquam naturalem effectum et non liberum, quia multiplicatio ipsa actuum non se habet libere ad generandum habitum, sic neque ad significandum ex vi repetitionis actuum, licet ipsi in se liberi sint." Commentary in Deely 1978a

[75] *Tractatus de Signis*, Book II, Question 6, 280/15–23: "Generally speaking custom is found not only in the case of human animals, but also in brute animals acting from natural instinct. Whence ... also though not every custom is a human act, every custom is able to found a natural sign."—"Generaliter loquendo consuetudo non solum invenitur in hominibus, sed etiam in brutis naturali instinctu operanti-

In other words, the status of sign as ontologically relative is not that of a genus respecting natural and conventional signs as its determinate species. The status is, rather, an existential condition which can be physically realized in the natural and cultural orders indifferently according to the role of the fundament (the foundation of the sign-relation, the sign-vehicle) together with the circumstances which surround it but do not constitute it within cognition as a sign. For only a triadic relation can constitute a sign as such. Whether this relation will be objective only or will include a physical intersubjectivity as well is determined not only by the role of the fundament engendering the sign relation, but also by the circumstances under which that fundament operates in generating the relation.

Thus, if the fundament of a sign-relation is a pure stipulation taken as such *prescinding from any custom which has grown up around the stipulation*, the resulting sign will be a conventional sign constituted by a mind-dependent relation. If the fundament of a sign-relation is a natural feature or characteristic of an object, or a psychological condition or state (a concept, be it an idea or an image), *and the terminus of the sign-relation (the object signified) also exists physically*, then the resulting sign will be a natural sign constituted by a mind-independent relation. But the *sign*, whether here and now verified physically under a determinately mind-independent relation or under a purely objective determinately mind-dependent relation, is realized according to the same rationale in either case: the rationale of a triadic "being toward" which as such transcends subjectivity in every case and renders objects signified univocal in their being as objects regardless of differences in their status as things physically existing.

This singular ability of the sign to pass back and forth between the orders of natural and cultural being with rationale unchanged gives the *doctrina signorum* the unique capacity to explain both the possibility of correspondence truth and the reason why truth as correspondence is needed as a critical check upon truth as coherence, the truth of experience as constituted from within by a texture of relations commingling real and unreal objects, natural and conventional signs, deceits as well as

bus. Unde ... et ita non omnis consuetudo est actus humanus et [omnis consuetudo] fundare potest signum naturale''.

wisdom. The doctrine of signs has a unified subject matter to investigate precisely because the rationale which constitutes any given sign is the same regardless of the circumstances of its occurrence, even though the circumstances of its occurrence will locate the sameness now as resulting primarily from nature, now as primarily from cognition, usually as an admixture of the two orders as together constituting experience. The very fact that the same being of the *intersubjectively relative* is realized in the diversity of all signs as the common ground of the action proper to signs explains the difference between the objective order as such and the subjective order of physical being, including psychological subjectivity.

Poinsot is not only re-explaining the opening chapters of his traditional *Cursus Philosophicus* in terms of the bearing thereon of the later chapters which conclude the traditional *Cursus Artium*, chapters from the tradition of commentary on the *De Anima*; he is also explaining the nature of experience and the experiential origins of the traditional doctrines of logic and the categories of natural philosophy. But his concern is not to emphasize all this inasmuch as it is assuredly new. On the contrary, his concern is to control, balance, qualify, and restrict by the total concerns of Latin tradition the *doctrina signorum* that more recent concerns and refinements of Latin tradition had forced to the foreground.

The question we have now to ask is what would have to be made of this doctrine newly systematized were it free to follow on its own terms its deep tendency and enter history on its own terms, rather than in terms imposed upon it by a traditional superstructure developed largely oblivious to its own foundations as a sign-dependent structure. In other words, how does the *doctrina signorum* appear when viewed no longer in the context of Poinsot's *Cursus Philosophicus Thomisticus* (and hence, indirectly, as a commentary on Thomas Aquinas), but rather as a pure philosophical possibility in its own right?[76]

---

[76] In other words, what would happen were we to put to the *Cursus Philosophicus* and existing tradition as a whole the proposal Poinsot put to the logicians of his day? I paraphrase 38/11–19:

> Nevertheless, because these matters are all treated in those books by way of interpretation and signification, since indeed the universal instrument of awareness is the *sign*, from which all its instruments are constituted, therefore, lest the foundation of the expositions of philosophy itself go unexamined, the project of the present work is to treat of those things concerning the nature and divisions of signs

2. *The* Tractatus de Signis
Viewed In Terms of Its Own Requirements for Philosophy

The first thing to be said about Poinsot's *Treatise on Signs* viewed on its own has been said by the grand old man of Peirce scholarship, Max H. Fisch (1986a: 180): "it is the most *systematic* treatise on signs that has ever been written". What Poinsot has presented in his thematization of the sign is a thoroughgoing demonstration that the action of signs is what gives structure to our sensations, perceptions, and understanding, both practical and theoretical—in a word, to our experience as a whole. If this is true, a philosophy based on experience must be based on the sign, and a philosophy of signs must be a philosophy of experience. If philosophy begins with experience, then philosophy begins with signs and remains dependent upon signs in its farthest developments. Philosophy can know objects which are more than signs and, through such objects, something of things as well in their own being, as can science; but nothing of this can come about without signs or other than through the action of signs, albeit critically controlled and adjusted by understanding, both comparative and reflexive.

Viewed in terms of its own requirements for philosophy, therefore, Poinsot's *Tractatus de Signis* has the same consequences that we have seen it to have for tradition: it requires a re-examination of philosophy's starting point, and an admission that that starting point is rooted in the action of signs which determine the nature and extent of our knowledge. "Poinsot's semiotics", wrote Sebeok (1986: 15), "not only expands our comprehension of communication, but in countless ways of what is communicated, and it suggests possibilities for finding a unity for knowledge that may have seemed lost forever after Descartes."

In the end, once the traditional terms of its discussion have finally been understood, the most surprising thing about Poinsot's *Tractatus de*

---

insinuated in the works of traditional philosophy, but which have been reserved for special treatment here.

(This paraphrase would read, in Latin: *Sed tamen, quia haec omnia tractantur in his libris per modum interpretationis et significationis, commune siquidem cognitionis instrumentum est signum, quo omnia eius instrumenta constant, idcirco visum est in praesenti pro doctrina horum librorum ea tradere, quae ad explicandam naturam et divisiones signorum in libris traditionalibus insinuata, huc vero reservata sunt.*)

Signis is how modern it clearly is. History has its accidents, but in this case it has also its confluences. The year in which Poinsot brought his *Tractatus* to publication was the year in which John Locke was born. At the age of fifty-eight, Locke, in fathering the second of the two great traditions which defined the development of modern philosophy, concluded his famous *Essay Concerning Humane Understanding* by proposing that the answer to the modern question posed by Descartes in launching the rationalist tradition, and posed anew by Locke himself in launching the empiricist tradition, should perhaps be sought instead by launching another tradition, a line of reflection based on *"semiotic or the doctrine of signs"*.

This is a remarkable proposal, one that deserves a closer look. Locke's concluding chapter, anomalous vis-à-vis the opening and body of the *Essay* as a whole, in effect announces the prospective end of modern thought in favor of a development today quintessentially postmodern, but in Locke's day already adumbrated in the context of late Latin Iberian thought beyond the confines of either Locke's or Descartes' familiarity. The saying that "the end lies in the beginning" knows no more unusual illustration than this peculiar case provided by the last chapter of Locke's essay, to which we now turn.

5

Locke's Proposal for Semiotic:
What Was New and What Was Not

To be sure, one of the promising developments in philosophy today is the expanding body of research dedicated to the exploration and analysis of the role of signs in the structuring of experience and knowledge. This development traces in large part, though not entirely, to the influence of Charles Sanders Peirce's decision to take seriously John Locke's previously ignored or disparaged proposal to divide the sciences into speculative, practical, and semiotic,[1] i.e., into the knowledge that results from the study of nature, the study of human affairs, and the study of the means whereby knowledge itself is acquired, developed and communicated. Locke also called his proposed third branch (1690: 361, original italics) *"the Doctrine of Signs"*, echoing a Renaissance development of Latin scholasticism (especially, but not exclusively) in Iberia. Locke himself, as we saw earlier, appears to have been wholly ignorant of this development, even though its culmination preceded his *Essay Concerning Humane Understanding* by just fifty-eight years. In this chapter, we will analyze first the principal synecdoches that can be found embedded in Locke's text. After that we will make an analysis of the scholastic doctrine of "species" or "ideas" as that was developed by the Iberians' de facto anticipation of Locke's proposed semiotic sense of ideas as the principal of the two great instruments—words and ideas—demanding the contemplation of those "who would take a view of humane knowledge in the whole extent of it."

---

[1]   The main discussions of this coinage to date are Russell 1939, Sebeok 1971, Romeo 1977, and Deely 1985a, 1986.

By way of preamble, let us briefly recapitulate our discussions so far.

In the university world of the Iberian peninsula, beginning at least from 1529 with the first publication of Domingo de Soto's *Summulae* logic, issues in what the Iberians too called the *doctrina signorum* became matters of "almost daily dispute", as a principal author of the region testified at the time ('quotidianis disputationibus agitare solent"[2]). The purest line of development among these late scholastics, listed "in order of succession and importance" (Beuchot 1980: 59), ran from Domingo de Soto (1529, 1554) through Francisco de Araújo (1617) to John Poinsot, who published (at the University of Alcalá) his synthesis of the development in the very year of Locke's birth, 1632, as a part of the second of the five original volumes of his *Cursus Philosophicus* (1631, 1632, 1633, 1634, 1635).

If we consider, *in the light of this Iberian development*, Locke's closing conjecture (1690: 362) that, were words and ideas to be "distinctly weighed and duly considered" in the perspective of a doctrine of signs, the result would perhaps be "another sort of Logick and Critick, than what we have been hitherto acquainted with", we find that the conjecture is amply confirmed. For one of the results in common of the work of Soto, Araújo, and Poinsot, is an analysis showing that the view of ideas as signs is incompatible with the common modern doctrine that ideas are objects of the understanding. Poinsot in particular takes pains to point out that the demonstration in this regard holds for ideas equally at the level of perception and at the level of intellection or "understanding".[3]

The purpose of the second half of this Chapter is to give some notion of how the *doctrina signorum* resumes and recasts in this way the whole doctrine of *phantasiari*[4] and *intelligere* from the natural philosophy

---

2 Poinsot, in his *Artis Logicae Secunda Pars*, Q. XXI, Art. 5, 680a38–39 (1632; = *Tractatus de Signis*, Book I, Question 5, p. 194/38–39).

3 Poinsot, *Artis Logicae Secunda Pars*, Q. XXII, Art. 2, 702a39–707b23, esp. 703b4–704a1 and 704a42–b39 (= *Tractatus de Signis*, Book II, Question 2, pp. 240/1–253/37, esp. 245/5–246/1 and 247/22–248/21).

4 I.e., as we saw earlier, the genus of knowing common to brute and rational animals over and above sensation: see Poinsot, *Philosophia Naturalis Quarta Pars in Tres Libros de Anima*, Quaestio VIII, "De Sensibus Internis" ("On the Internal Senses"), Art. 2, "Quid sint phantasia et reliquiae potentiae interiores, et in quibus subiectis sint" ("What Is the Imagination and the Other Interior Cognitive Powers, and in What

of cognitive organisms as appealed to by Locke (under the misnomer "idea") in opening his *Essay*. To be especially borne in mind, however, is the crucial detail of the *doctrina signorum* developed in the mainstream school of Latin thought to which Soto, Araújo, and Poinsot alike belonged (namely, the school derived from Aquinas), to wit, the detail of the uniqueness of *sentire* or sensation itself in forming no image within which the sensed aspects of objects are conveyed, even though sensation has a semiotic structure through and through in the interplay of proper and common sensibles, the "appearances" of objects as sensed. For if we presume for the present discussion the late scholastic doctrine that intellection and perception are dependent on signs for the total structure of their objective apprehensions, it will be evident that, given the same claim established for sensation as well (as we saw in Chapter 4 above), notwithstanding the uniqueness of sensation prescisively considered, we are confronting a philosophical issue with implications for philosophy of knowledge and mind at least as radical as Locke hinted they might be.

A. The Text Itself of Locke's Proposal for Semiotic

For our purposes here, the first actual publication of Locke's *Essay Concerning Humane Understanding* is the crucial referent, as it is there that the ostensibly Greek term σημιωτική appears (see Figure 1, page 112), and it is mainly thence that the contemporary English terms "semiotic" and "semiotics" derive, with their many congeners (see Sebeok 1971).

I call the term in question "ostensibly Greek", for in fact it seems to be a neologism on Locke's part. According to the best evidence adduced so far, this template for our current notion of "semiotics" was not only a neologism, but one cast somewhat incorrectly from a strictly grammatical point of view, on the basis of 1605 and 1663 editions in Locke's private library of Scapula's 1579 pirated abridgment of the

Organs Do They Reside"), 252a38–265a46, discussed in editor's note 2 at p. 240/4 in the 1985 Deely edition of Poinsot's *Tractatus de Signis* (Poinsot 1632a). See also Deely 1971a: 55–83 for an extended discussion of internal sense (the idea of a purely perceptual intelligence).

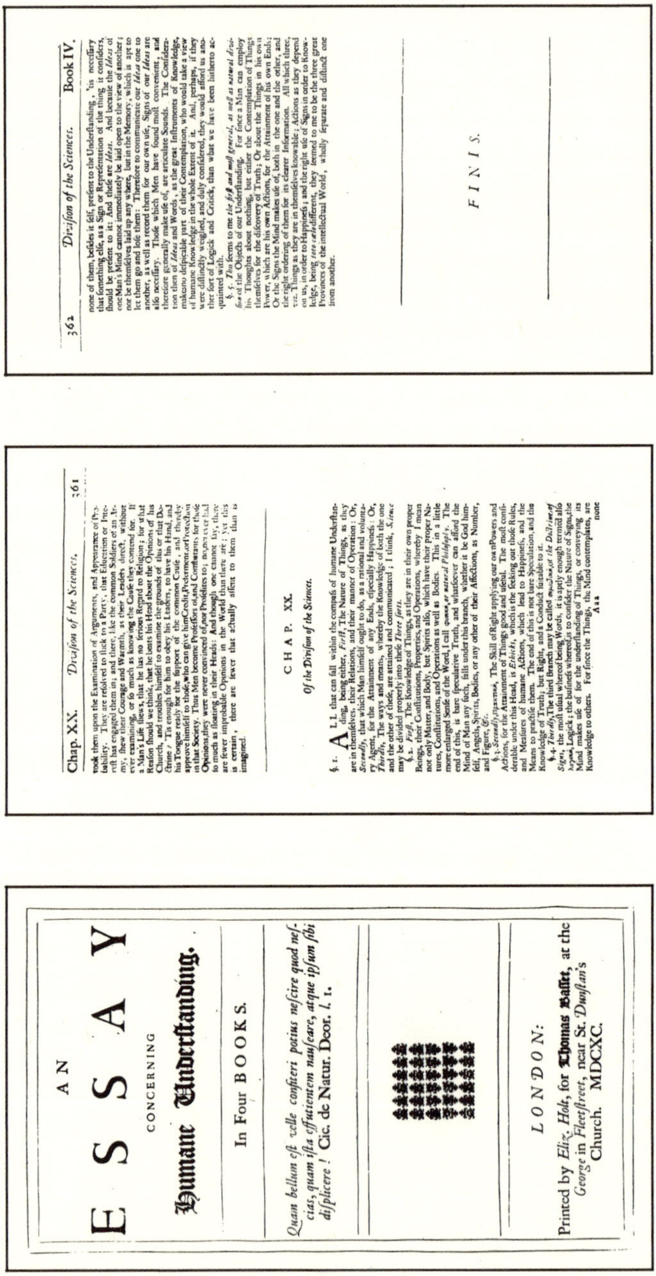
AN
ESSAY
CONCERNING
Humane Understanding.
In Four BOOKS.
Quam bellum est velle confiteri potius nescire quod nescias, quam ista effutientem nauseare, atque ipsum sibi displicere! Cic. de Natur. Deor. l. 1.
LONDON:
Printed by Eliz. Holt, for Thomas Basset, at the George in Fleetstreet, near St. Dunstan's Church. MDCXC.

Figure 1. *Title Page from the 1690 Original Edition of Locke's* Essay Concerning Humane Understanding, *along with the Concluding Chapter introducing the term ''semiotic'' into philosophy, courtesy of reproduction from the Lilly Library in Deely, Williams, and Kruse 1986: 2–4.*

1572–1573 *Thesaurus Graecae linguae* of Henricus Stephanus. There in the Stephanus work is where the term Σημειωτική appears for what is, according to present knowledge (Romeo 1977), the first time historically. Notice, then, that the Stephanus term is also a neologism of Latin times, very close to Locke's own, differing, as a matter of fact, only in its being correctly formed according to the word-formation rules of classical Greek. These rules call for the epsilon which is added after the mu in Stephanus' *Thesaurus*. Perhaps Locke wanted to introduce a term specific to philosophy, Σημιωτικέ, since, as he would well know, the "semeiotic" variant had been appropriated by diagnosticians to name their branch of medical science (the *OED* cites such a usage in English as early as 1625).

Be that as it may, there are many curiosities surrounding these facts which call for extended investigations, as is especially clear from a reading of the most detailed investigation of Locke's coinage that has up to now been made, Luigi Romeo's 1977 "Derivation of 'Semiotics' through the History of the Discipline". This study supersedes in this particular the two previous studies of the matter by Russell in 1939 and Sebeok in 1971 (the latter study, moreover, is completely dependent on Russell in its speculations as to Locke's sources for his term).

Although both variants at the Latin base of semiotic consciousness— that of Stephanus and that of Locke—are clearly derived from the σημ- root of the ancient Greek word for sign, σημεῖοω ("semeion"), we have seen that neither of them are actually ancient terms. They belong to the Renaissance, that is, to the late Latin phase of Western development. Locke provides no transliteration for his quasi-Greek neologism, but only an English translation of it as "the Doctrine of Signs". This "doctrine of signs", he tells us, is to have as its province the investigation of the means whereby knowledge of whatsoever kind is acquired, developed, and communicated.

After Locke, the coinage he introduced begins to appear here and there in a transliterated form, now as "semiotic", again as "semeiotic" (as in the medical usage). Both variants appear in the work of Peirce, with a preference usually given to the more philologically correct transliteration mirroring the Stephanus coinage. As late as c.1906 (CP 5.488), explicitly on the basis of his reading of the conclusion to Locke's *Essay*, Peirce described himself as "a pioneer, or rather, a backwoodsman, in the work of clearing and opening up … *semiotic*, that is, the doctrine of the essential nature and fundamental varieties of possible semiosis''. This last term, ''semiosis'' (sometimes ''semeiosis'' or ''semeiosy''), is Peirce's own neologistic adaptation of the Greek term σημείῶσις, which occurs at least thirty times in the Herculanean papyrus *On Signs* authored in 54BC by Philodemus. In Philodemus' work, the term represents a type of reasoning or inference from signs. But Peirce uses the English transliteration to mean the more basic action of signs which itself underlies any and all inference, and indeed occurs objectively even when no inference happens to be made or when an inference is made incorrectly. Indeed, the action of signs as underlying and guiding, or at least as *able to guide*, actual acts of inference of various kinds is taken today as the basis for semiotics as a form or body of knowledge. As biology is that complex of knowledge which results from analysis and study of the realm of living things, as physics is knowledge that results from the study and analysis of the action of bodies and their constituents in space, so semiotics is knowledge that results from analysis and study of the realm and action of signs.

Who was actually the first to transliterate Locke's bastard Greek coinage, and thus actually to introduce either the term ''semiotic'' or ''semiotics'' into modern English literature? There is at present no known answer to this question. Much original research with many new clues has recently been provided by Sebeok's survey of *Semiotics in the United States* (1991), a book which has been made the basis of an international seminar at the Centro Internazionale di Semiotica e di Linguistica of the University of Urbino, Italy, July 6–9, 1992, with results reported in a Special Issue of the international journal, *Semiotica* (Deely and Petrilli, Eds. 1993). Perhaps it is not too much to hope that some eager student will have the distinction of providing an answer to this curiosity as part of a doctoral dissertation one day soon to be written.

Our immediate concern in this chapter is with Locke's definition of the new term and with the main implications of that definition for philosophy. That is to say, we are concerned, first, with the typology rather than the etymology, with the conceptual architecture rather than the philological derivation, of Locke's proposal for a *doctrine of signs* to take its place among the sciences; and then with the conceptual connections this proposal has with earlier developments in the Latin Age, particularly in the closing Latin centuries most commonly referred to to-day under the rubric of "the Renaissance".[5]

Considering Locke's proposal directly, what are we to understand the doctrine of signs to comprise? At the outset, the understanding of Locke's text demands a particularly careful interpretation, on two counts, the reception of the text by those who came after Locke, and the subtle architecture, so to speak, according to which the proposal is laid out.

1. The Impact of the Proposal

One looking at the text of Locke's proposal for the first time is likely to be struck most by the very brevity of the text, a scant five paragraphs barely exceeding a page in length. The casual observer might be inclined to think we are making much out of little, particularly in view of the fate of Locke's proposal among the principal authors of classical modern philo-

---

[5] As we have already seen, so far as the question of semiotic is concerned, "early modern philosophy" and "Latin renaissance philosophy" are synonymous terms at least in one region of the late Latin world, namely, the Iberian peninsula. And, as we also saw in Chapter 4, a decisive influence upon this renaissance development took shape in late medieval times, at the University of Paris: there Thomas Aquinas taught in the high middle ages; and there, in the 14th century, William of Ockham inspired the turmoil of questions that migrated to Spain and gestated, unknown to Locke, the first full-blown *doctrina signorum* essayed in the philosophical literature, the *Treatise on Signs* of John Poinsot published at Alcalá in the year of Locke's birth, 1632.

Indeed, though nothing like the full-blown Iberian move toward a semiotic consciousness seems to have taken place in Continental or English circles of early modern philosophy, surely it is echoes of the Parisian Masters from Soto's student days that we hear in the Arnauld-Malebranche debate over intentionality "considered by everyone who was anyone in late seventeenth century intellectual circles to be *the* philosophical event of the times", but "today, however, largely ignored or misunderstood by philosophers and historians alike" (Nadler 1992a: 73). Once we widen the discussion of early modernity to include the Iberians and begin looking to the late Latin context as the *terminus a quo relictus* rather than to Kant as the *terminus ad quem* of the classical modern development, as we must if we are to get beyond the intellectually crippling confines of the "standard history", it will not be surprising to discover, even in the classical circles, lines of discussion that only make full sense against this expanded horizon which is, after all, the one actually proper to the historical emergence of modern philosophy even in its most narrow classical sense. Cf. Beuchot 1994 ("Intentionality in John Poinsot").

sophy. The proposal actually meets the fate that Hume (1776: 4) feared had befallen his *Treatise of Human Nature* (1739-1740), namely, the fate of falling "deadborn from the press".

Such a judgment, however, would be hasty as well as casual. Leibniz's glosses on Locke's proposal in his *New Essays concerning Human Understanding* of 1704 are of a sophistic and relatively superficial character (this is said to goad the Leibnizians into rebuttal, the consequences of which would benefit our understanding of the history of early modern philosophy). But the same can hardly be said of Berkeley's provocative and numerous remarks sprinkled throughout his 1732 work, *Alciphron*, wherein he opines (1732: 307) that "the doctrine of signs" is "a point of great importance and general extent, which, if duly considered, would cast no small light upon things, and afford a just and genuine solution of many problems". And of course there is the decisive taking up of Locke's term and proposal by Peirce beginning in 1867, whence principally results the international movement known today as "semiotics".

2. The Synecdochic Structure of the Proposal

The second count on which Locke's text calls for a particularly careful interpretation is related to its brevity, and, indeed, may be said both to underlie that brevity and to belie it. This second point is the matter of Locke's complete reliance in structuring the text of his "division of the sciences" around the literary device of synecdoche. The thoroughgoing use of this device is mainly responsible for the concluding chapter's misleading appearance of great brevity; for there is considerably more here, intellectually speaking, than meets the eye of quantitative measure or "word count". Each of the key terms introduced in this chapter—physics, ethics, logic, word, idea—has to be understood in two senses, one narrow and one broad, and, in each case, the narrow sense provides the synecdoche connecting the larger sense with the narrower and specific one. In the case of "words" and "ideas" particularly, the narrow sense is so obvious and dominant that most readers tend to miss the underlying thrust to the proposal of semiotic, or at least so we must suspect from the history of the proposal in the classical modern development that culminated in the Kantian critiques of judgment and reason.

To grasp the thrust of Locke's original proposal, notice that Locke begins, in effect, with Aristotle's distinction (cf. *Metaphysics* c.348-330BC:

Book II, Ch. 1, 993b19–23; and esp. *Ethics* c.335–4BC: Book VI, Chs. 3–8, 1139b14–1142a31) between knowledge we acquire of objects having as part of their objectivity an existence that obtains independently of, and extending outside of, our thinking ("speculative" thought), on one hand, and, on the other, knowledge of objects that precisely come into being as a result of human thought and action and would not exist as such apart from the context of human interaction ("practical" thought).

Drawing on classical terminology, Locke uses "Physics" as a synecdoche for the knowledge of mind-independent being, and "Ethics" as a synecdoche for the knowledge of mind-dependent being. "Logic" he then uses in a synecdochic way to name the study of the means whereby all knowledge—whether speculative or practical—is acquired, developed, and communicated. Thus, in each part of his main division of knowledge into Physics, Ethics, and Logic, Locke assigns a name to the whole which is also the name for a specific part within that whole.

In each of the three cases, besides the synecdochal name, he gives an alternative name for the whole area of knowledge (or "science") identified: "praktica" in the case of ethics, "natural philosophy" in the case of physics, "semiotica"[6] in the case of logic. There are critical details of this terminology that bear noting.

In the first place, "natural philosophy" as a synonym for physics in the synecdochal sense of speculative knowledge *tout court* (unlike "prac-

---

6   This is my transliteration of Locke's Σημιωτική, which is the form that Locke uses in his original Essay of 1690 (unlike his modern editors, Fraser 1894 and Nidditch 1975, who introduce without discussion—perhaps because they work mainly from later editions of Locke's essay?—an epsilon between the mu and the iota to get "semeiotic", the spelling preferred by purist Peirceans and pronounced by them "see-my-oh-tick"—see Fisch 1978: 32 and 66, notes 1–4). My transcription is idiosyncratic inasmuch as the final eta is customarily ignored in contemporary derivations from Locke's text, leaving the familiar "semiotic", but justified, I think, by the immediate Latin background and context against which Locke wrote as a thinker of the seventeenth century. This context and background provides a crucial interpretant for understanding Locke's choice of the term "doctrine" (Deely 1978: 152–157, 1982: 127–130, 1986: 214, 1986a: 408), and here guides my transcription of his Greek term. Perhaps a similar interpretant was at work culturally, not as a component of any individual consciousness as such, but as operative within the relevant linguistic traditions bearing on the choice (as operative within the heritage) of the individuals involved in the selection of the name *Semiotica* for the official journal of the International Association for Semiotic Studies.

tica'' as a synonym for ethics in the synecdochal sense of practical knowledge *tout court*) was itself already a synecdoche for speculative knowledge. This point was expressly made by Aquinas (c.1269: Book I, lectio 1, n. 2) as a gloss on the Stoic use of the term ''philosophia naturalis''.[7] The Stoic use, thus, appears to us in retrospect as anticipatory of Locke's usage in this particular. For our purposes, then, this second, embedded synecdoche says nothing new, but must be regarded rather as an already established and traditional usage. It has no bearing on what is novel in Locke's proposal for semiotics. All of the terms pertaining to the division of knowledge into physics and ethics, in whatever sense they are taken, are traditional terms to which Locke adds no distinctively different sense.

By contrast, in the case of synecdochically so-called ''Logic'', he is not merely repeating a traditionally established distinction. That he is saying something new is keyed by the fact that the alternative name he gives for the whole alongside the synecdochical one is anything but traditional. In fact, as we have seen, the alternative name is a neologism. According to Locke, ''Logic'' properly—that is, in the then-established, traditional sense—names the study of conceptual relations among linguistic signs. Synecdochically, however, it names the study of sign relations in their totality (as including linguistic signs) only by way of a neologism. Hence, in its total sense as the doctrine of signs, ''Logic'' is not just alternatively but *better* called ''Semiotica''.

---

7   Taking the fourfold Stoic division of the sciences as his vehicle, Aquinas makes the following remarks in his *Commentary* on Aristotle's *Nichomachean Ethics* (*Sententia Libri Ethicorum*, c.1269: Book I, lectio 1, n. 2): ''Since the human mind develops through disciplined exercise, there are as many kinds of knowledge as there are respects in which reason can be methodically employed. The first respect in which reason can be methodically and systematically employed concerns the *universe of nature* [ad philosophiam naturalem pertinet], to which pertains all deliberation about the order which the mind discerns as obtaining or able to obtain in things independently of the activity of our thinking. 'Nature' here must be understood in such a way as to include whatever there is of being.''—''Et quia consideratio rationis per habitum scientiae perficitur, secundum hos diversos ordines quos proprie ratio considerat, sunt diversae scientiae. Nam ad philosophiam naturalem pertinet considerare ordinem rerum quem ratio humana considerat sed non facit; ita quod sub naturali philosophia comprehendamus et mathematicam et metaphysicam.''

This reconceptualization may be represented in a schema, exhibiting both the generic or novel synecdochic sense of "logic", and "logic" in its specific traditional sense, yet as now transformed to be seen as a part of semiotic. This schema embodies what I have called Locke's "initial proposal or sketch" for the doctrine of signs (see Figure 2, following).

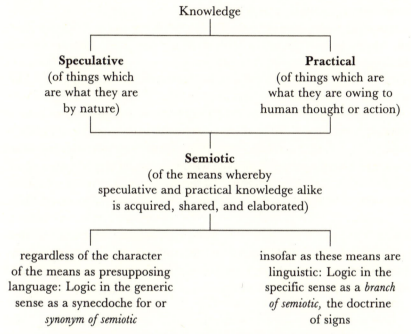

Figure 2. *Locke's "Initial Sketch" for the Doctrine of Signs*

Just as the order of what exists independently of our thought and action is considerably wider than what we learn from physics as a specific science, and just as the order of what comes about as a result of what we do and make is considerably broader than what we learn from ethics, so the study of the means whereby knowledge develops is considerably broader than the study of logical forms within language.

Within this realm wherein knowledge develops, accordingly, the terms "word" and "idea" take on a startlingly expansive sense, even though it is an open question to what extent Locke was aware of the full expansion. In the ordinary and obvious sense, words mean words, the specifically human sub-units of linguistic communication orally and graphically articulable. Similarly, ideas mean what words stand for in linguistic exchanges among human beings, in the ordinary and obvious sense that Locke invokes when he says that "since the things the mind contemplates are none of them, besides itself, present to the understanding, 'tis necessary that something else, as a sign or representation of the thing it considers should be present to it".

These ordinary and obvious senses, however, are not the newly acquired semiotic sense of the terms in question. Chosen on the basis of their traditional sense in view of a new proposal, the further semiotic sense accrues to the key terms from their play within the proposal . That is to say, the terms in question take on their semiotic sense by becoming, in context, each in their own turn synecdoches. In the case of "words", the sense of the term is expanded to represent that whole panoply of gestures, marks, and movements whereby one organism signals another or provides signals (wittingly or unwittingly) to another. In the case of "ideas", the sense of the term is expanded to represent that whole panoply of interior or psychological states thanks to which one organism has "something to say" to another (again, wittingly or unwittingly)—its mood, "state of mind", attitudes, or intentions. Ideas and words taken semiotically become markers for the more general distinction between "inner" and "outer" as it applies especially to the cognitive activity of organisms.

We see thus plainly that "words" and "ideas" as semiotic is concerned with them go well beyond the boundaries of the ordinary and obvious sense the reader of the *Essay* casually and customarily attaches to these expressions. We have also seen that the semiotic sense of words and ideas is not only larger than, but actually at odds with, the specifically philosophical understanding of the terms Locke has developed in the main body of his *Essay*. But what is to be immediately noted here is that the "semiotics" of which logic forms a part has to interpret much more than merely intellectual discourse. Semiotics has to make sense of experience as a whole, in all of its parts, and, ideally, in all of its biological manifestations. It has to deal with all those inner states on the basis of which the living, feeling, knowing being orients itself within the physical environment and interacts within and across species lines. And it has to deal with all those outer manifestations on the basis of which inner states are interpreted and clues are taken as to the nature and activity generally of a living being as a part of the physical world.

Taking but one baby-step beyond Locke, we can now contrast *semiotics*, as a form of knowledge, to *the action of signs*, from the study of which action that knowledge specifically derives. For making this contrast Peirce's term, "semeiosis"—adapted, as we saw above, from Philodemus (see Fisch 1978: 40–41)—to name the action of signs (and omitting the superfluous second "e"), is exactly suited (see Figure 3):

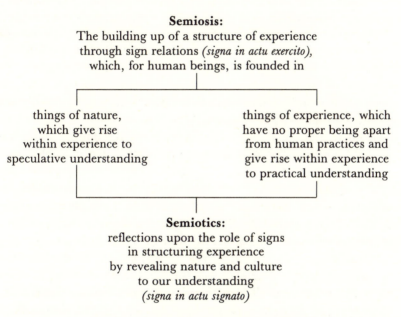

Semiosis:
The building up of a structure of experience
through sign relations *(signa in actu exercito)*,
which, for human beings, is founded in

things of nature,
which give rise
within experience to
speculative understanding

things of experience, which
have no proper being apart
from human practices and
give rise within experience
to practical understanding

Semiotics:
reflections upon the role of signs
in structuring experience
by revealing nature and culture
to our understanding
(signa in actu signato)

Figure 3. *Semiosis and Semiotics Distinguished*

Seeing how little further effort of thought is required to make explicit the scope of the vistas implicit in Locke's original proposal, we may consider it a pity that Locke himself did not develop his own proposal. That the principal modern authors did not see fit to develop the proposal themselves is perhaps even more a pity. No doubt the history of classical modern philosophy, the period from Descartes to Kant, would have been strikingly different in all that concerns what we now call epistemology.

Be that as it may, given that Locke himself neither undertakes exposition of his synechdoches nor makes any particular adversion to their purport, he left his readers to fall back mainly upon the obvious and ordinary sense of "words" and "ideas" as specifically developed earlier throughout the *Essay*, and thus to blind themselves (e.g., Messenger 1974) to the full extent of what was being proposed when he wrote (concluding par. 4):

The consideration then of *Ideas* and Words as the great instruments of knowledge, makes no despicable part of their contemplation, who would take a view of human knowledge in the whole extent of it. And, perhaps, if they were distinctly weighed and duly considered, they would afford us another sort of Logic and Critic than what we have been hitherto acquainted with.

We can only wonder whether, or to what extent, Locke himself realized what he was actually proposing.

I think it is not too much to say that Locke's initial proposal for semiotic held the potential for a threefold revolution in philosophy. First, it would have been a revolution against modern philosophy as it was to develop after him in both its rationalist and empiricist strains. Second, at the same time it would have joined the modern development in mounting a revolution against the reliance upon authority in philosophy: the proposal of semiotic pointed the way to what has become a fully explicit goal of philosophy only in most recent times, namely, the goal of resting at every point upon experience broadly but integrally conceived. (This goal has become especially associated in our day with the movement of Pragmatism in American philosophy, but wrongly so associated, as Peirce pointed out—e.g., 1904a, 1905a—in dissociating himself from that movement in order to speak rather of "pragmaticism".) Third, taking up the proposal would have avoided a major disruption of the historical continuity of philosophy. For semiotics points exactly down one of the main historical paths along which the last century of Latin speculation had already been moving when Descartes substituted the Cogito for being as the heart of the philosophical enterprise. Hence it is that, at the level of speculative concerns, the semiotic revolution today rejoins contemporary philosophy in its postmodern phase to the medieval and renaissance development of philosophy, and thereby puts an end to the Cartesian idea that with the advent of modern thought the preceding Latin centuries could be ignored without loss.

This third point is the one most pregnant with import for a renewed understanding of early modern philosophy as that history bears most directly upon the further development of philosophy today: not in its mainstream development, but in the Latin matrix from which that development selectively—overselectively, as would now appear—took rise. For neither Locke himself nor any of his successors in the modern period tried out this "way of signs". Instead, as history amply record-ed, the "way of ideas" was pursued by modern philosophy down to its classical systematization in the *Critiques* of Immanuel Kant. Yet the very idea of idea was something taken for granted, rather than examined in its own right, from the outset of the classical modern development. By this singular oversight, the modern "way of ideas" was destined to come a cropper eventually over the alternative "way of signs". That is the defining event for what postmodernism portends of a positive nature.

B. Semiotic and the Scholastic Doctrine of Species

Let us go back to Locke's *Essay*, considering now not its concluding chapter but rather its Introduction (§ 8), where Locke claims to mean by idea "whatever is meant by the term phantasm, notion, species, or whatever it is which the mind can be employed about in thinking":

I must here in the Entrance beg pardon of my Reader, for the frequent use of the Word *Idea*, which he will find in the following Treatise. It being that Term, which, I think, serves best to stand for whatsoever is the Object of the Understanding when a Man thinks, I have used it to express whatever is meant by *Phantasm, Notion, Species,* or whatever it is which the Mind can be employ'd about in thinking.

The Latins had, by Locke's time, about a dozen synonyms for "whatever it is which the mind can be employed about in thinking", each with its own nuances and overtones of analysis, as exemplified in the following list (which is not exhaustive): "repraesentatio", "species", "concep-tus", "idea", "notitia", "intentio", "verbum", "idolum", "phan-tasma", "phantasia", "imago", "proles mentis". Thus there is a prima facie plausibility to the claim that Locke's intention in this passage was "to replace the theory-loaded terms of the schools" (Tipton 1992: 97). But I think that intention was less to provide "a more or less theory-neutral" term than a single-theory-specific one to supplant the all too poly-theory-laden scholastic usage; and even were we to prefer the theory-specific usage of Locke, to justify that preference we would of course need to understand what was being supplanted from the older usages.

Although several of the terms on the scholastic list were applied most specifically to the analysis of intellectual cognition, in the mainstream Latin renaissance traditions of natural philosophy all of these terms would apply, in modern parlance, to the psychological states involved in the cognitive behavior of any biological organism, any animal.

It is important to understand that, by the fifteenth century, the mainstream philosophical schools of university life had tended to group in three main currents: those who took chief inspiration from Thomas Aquinas, those who took chief inspiration from William of Ockham, and those who took chief inspiration from Duns Scotus. Further complicating the scene was the split between Catholics and Protestants. Some of the most interesting work in the philosophical region adjacent to Locke's proposal was in fact done in a series of late works by Protestant authors— Timpler (1604, 1612), Keckermann (1614), Scheibler (1617), among others—which are deserving of careful study.

To achieve even a preliminary survey of so vast and complicated a landscape we need a mountain peak to look from. Later it will be necessary of course to verify and correct what we seem to see from thence in detail; but even for that we need to have some overall sense of which details are crucial, else we will have no idea when we encounter verification or when we need to make a correction.

For this purpose, on two grounds, we will avail ourselves of the semiotic of John Poinsot. First, of all the Latin authors who participated in the Iberian development of the *doctrina signorum* in the closing Latin centuries, Poinsot provided by far the most systematic treatment of the subject, as Beuchot (1980: 59) and Fisch (1986: 180) have pointed out.[8]

---

8   Beuchot's work (1980, 1983, 1987, and forthcoming) in bringing to light Araújo's work, particularly his treatment of the sign as intermediate between Soto and Poinsot, is an especially important contribution; for while it is possible to find Araújo in com-

Second, Poinsot's treatment of signs, precisely as a result of its having been written with a systematic character both after and in full cognizance of the work of Soto and Araújo, has greater heuristic value respecting Locke's prognostication of what could result in philosophy from a full exploration of the way of signs. This historically pregnant work came to publication in the very year of Locke's birth, from the pen of an author intimately familiar with the family of terms with which Locke equivalated his use of "idea" in the *Essay*. This family of terms Poinsot had uniquely "distinctly weighed and duly considered", just as Locke would propose, in the light of a doctrine of signs. Thus a study of Poinsot's work is well calculated to see whether indeed, as Locke professed to suspect, the notion of idea, along with the notion of word, rethought under the rubric of semiotic, would lead to "another sort of Logick and Critick" than what was familiar in either the Rationalist or nascent Empiricist traditions of modern philosophy as such.[9]

prehensive scholarly indices, he does not appear in such standard works as *The Cambridge History of Renaissance Philosophy* edited by Schmitt *et al.* (1988), or *Renaissance Philosophy* edited by Copenhaver and Schmitt (1992), an absence underscoring the point often made that semiotics calls for an unusual degree of revision of the currently standard histories of philosophy.

9 Indeed, we have already seen in Chapter 4 that, so far as can be judged from Poinsot's *Treatise on Signs* as the earliest systematic instantiation of the project of a doctrine of signs, it appears that Locke rightly suspected that the project is of its very nature a radical enterprise. In Poinsot's version of the enterprise, the logic of terms and concepts as the then-traditional point of entry into philosophical study is taken up anew and reshaped according to an understanding of the fundamental activity of mind—awareness as such—which makes of that activity a branch of the doctrine of signs. It is thus that we have found, in the heart of Poinsot's determinedly traditional *Cursus Philosophicus Thomisticus*, nothing less than the doctrinal components of a veritable revolution in philosophy, but one which follows the way of signs rather than the modern way of ideas. Poinsot's *Tractatus de Signis* establishes nothing less than a *doctrina signorum*, or "semiotic" in Locke's sense. This doctrine reveals a comprehensive role for the sign in weaving the fabric and providing the structure for experience as a whole, inclusive of the acts of sensation as well as of perception and understanding (this last in the full range of its theoretical postulations). The role of the sign at the sensory origins and foundations of awareness, as well as in its perceptual and intellectual superstructures, is exactly what Poinsot envisaged in removing the discussion of *signum* among the Latins from the terminist perspective of (then)

Within the family of notions covered by the term ''idea'' in Locke's sense of the intraorganismic factor enabling awareness of whatever object we experience or know, it strikes me that two in particular are the most fundamental: *repraesentatio* and *species*. ''Repraesentatio'' is fundamental because it designates the fundamental function of every idea in making present within awareness objects regardless of their proximity within the environment. This is the main function of idea, certainly, that Locke had in mind, as also Descartes, and it is perhaps not too much to say that this is the principal notion of idea throughout the period of modern philosophy.

With respect to this notion, Poinsot will introduce a basic distinction. Representation, he will say, is indeed fundamental to the idea, but it does not constitute the idea in what is formal to it as idea (1632: Book I, Question 1; Book II, Questions 1 and 2). I will come back to this point. First let us take up the other basic term applicable to the idea, *species*.

1. Nominal Usage

The term ''species'' in English today has become primarily a biological term, although it has remained also a logical term, and retains a tertiary sense of ''mental image''. As a Latin term in the context of what we today call epistemological discussions, by contrast, the term *species* derives from Greek to designate especially the outward appearance or form of something, especially as constituting the immediate object of vision (cf. Tachau 1988). In this context, moreover, ''species'' represents not so much what we would ordinarily think of today in speaking of a ''mental image'' as it does a detailed, precise presentation of a plan or proposal for something *to be known*, i.e., to be grasped or formed by the mind as its object of apprehension. Thus a ''species'', in the Latin context already well established by the time, say, Thomas Aquinas began to treat of epistemological issues, stands for a determinate character or quality *according to which* the mind must function *in order to* arrive at the apprehen-

traditional logic and recasting that discussion in a unity and perspective proper to itself. See especially the ''Third Semiotic Marker'' in the Deely edition of Poinsot 1632a: 30.

sion of this specific object rather than some other one. Whence Ockham, for example, went so far as to propose doing away with the notion and term entirely in favor rather of talk simply about the "qualities" of individual things.

Tachau has shown (1988) that most of the better Latin authors in fact would have no use for Ockham's attempt to dispense with the very term "species" in epistemological discussions of how cognitive powers are specified to form particular cognitions of objects within their range of possible apprehensions. Poinsot spoke for this Latin majority in further holding as central to the discussion of specifying forms the distinction between specifying forms as principles and as terms in cognition, i.e., the distinction between *species impressae* and *expressae* (cf. Doyle 1990).

But the immediate point to be made here is that the contemporary term "species" in English is not in any way helpful for understanding the Latin epistemological discussions of *species*. In fact, the main sense of the epistemological Latin term *species*, namely, the sense of *giving specification* or *specifying form*, is one that has never been really brought out in modern English discussions or translations of relevant Latin texts prior to the 1985 edition of Poinsot's *Treatise on Signs*. One of the few modern philosophers seriously to investigate the notion (Maritain 1959: 115) made the point, many decades before the English-Latin edition of the Poinsot *Treatise* appeared, that "The word 'species' has no equivalent in our modern languages." But Maritain did not go on to clarify the *specificative character as such* assigned to the *species* of Latin tradition.

Maritain noted only that the "species" of which the Latins speak is a representative quality that provides the basis on which a cognitive power is determined to form a cognition of *this* rather than *that* or *some other* object within its range of possibilities. It is a "presentative or objectifying form", says Maritain (ibid.), if we want to have a "suitable expression to render it". The notion of "species" for the Latin philosophers, he continues, is not "an explanatory factor already known and already clarified by some other means." On the contrary:

Species are, as it were, the abutments upon which an analysis of the given leans for support, the reality of which the mind, by that very analysis, is compelled to recognize—with certainty, if the analysis itself has proceeded correctly and under the constant pressure of intelligible necessities. Some determination must, of necessity, actually supervene upon the knower.... *The species is nothing but that internal determination.*[10]

In the context of the analysis of sensation and perception, the argument is that any given physical entity modifies its surroundings up to a point in such a way that a cognitive organism in contact with that sphere of influence will be keyed to respond by becoming aware of the source of the modifications as *object* (a term best reserved, in this same context, to anything as and only insofar as cognized or "known"). The "species" of Latin scholasticism, thus, are precisely *specifiers* or *specifications* of the milieu ("specifying forms"), modalities thereof transcendentally relative in Aquinas's or Poinsot's sense to their source (and insofar representative). This source *as thus represented, in conjunction with cognitive powers,* enables those powers to know specific objects within their generic range—much the way in which, to introduce a contemporary analogy, the surface of a disk (an old-time record or a more recent CD-ROM) has been modified determines whether it will play Bach or Beethoven or something else (perhaps Elvis).

2. Ontological Application

In the Latin tradition as Poinsot represents it, species is probably the most fundamental of all the epistemological terms.[11] Somewhat analo-

---

10 If the reader looks at Maritain's full context from which citation here is made, the quotation will be found tangled together with many remarks on the notion of *esse intentionale* which, despite my own reliance on those additional remarks in my original work on Heidegger (Deely 1971), and without repudiating that earlier analysis, do not carry equal force—either historically or philosophically, for the reasons I have outlined elsewhere in discussing the problematic notion of "postmodernism" (Deely 1995)—with what has been here quoted. In fact, for reasons that I hope are clear in the text following, tying the notion of *species* directly to the notion of *esse intentionale* may obscure more than it clarifies because it puts a secondary explanatory notion on a par with a primary one.

11 Like Ockham (cf. Tachau 1988: 115) and, indeed, all the Latins, Poinsot "adopted a dichotomy between sensation and intellection, and posited for each intuitive and abstractive modes of cognition", i.e., cognition based on physically present aspects of objects as physically present *versus* cognition attaining aspects of objects physically absent from the immediate environment ("*intentiones insensatae*", qualities perceived

gous to Hume's "impressions of sense" and "recollections", but with more difference than similarity (since for the Latins cognition was a progressive notion involving basic levels or stages wherein what was an expression of an earlier stage could become the impression for a later stage), the Latins had early distinguished *species* as *impressa* and *expressa*. At the level of sensory impressions considered as such, the Latins were divided over the question of whether these impression were: (1) already images formed by the mind under the influence of things and known as such, (2) simply the very qualities inherent in the material objects acting on the senses now made present in awareness through that action, or indeed (3) relative qualities formed neither by the cognitive power as such nor inherent in the physical object as such but merely revelative of the physically acting thing as here and now impacting upon a cognitive power or disposition of this biological type (the eye of a frog vs. the eye of a leopard, for example, or the acoustical sensitivity of a whale vs. the human ear, etc.). In schema:

but not sensed) or even objects nonexistent in the physical environment. The distinction between sense and intellect was as old as Plato and Aristotle, whence the Latins took it; but the distinction between so-called intuitive and abstractive awareness of objects was first stabilized in the writing of John Duns Scotus, the *"Doctor Subtilis"*, 1266–1308 (Tachau 1988: 70). Yet no less than Ockham, and probably more so, this "aspect of being another modification of the Subtle Doctor's" distinction is superficial. For where Ockham took as his principal distinction that between apprehensive and adjudicative acts of the cognitive powers (Tachau 1988: 116), Poinsot, at least in this area, takes as his principal distinction (in which he no more than follows Aquinas) that between cognitive powers which depend on forms of specification ("species") *only* at the level of seminal principle and those which so depend *also* at the level of termination in the object as such. This is for Poinsot, as we saw above in Chapter 4, the distinction between external sense, on the one hand, and internal sense *together with intellect*, on the other hand (see especially Book III, Questions 1 and 2 of Poinsot's *Treatise on Signs*). Whence perception ("phantasiari") and intellection ("intelligere") participate in "intuitive" awareness—the awareness of physically present aspects of objects as physically present—through their dependence upon and continuity with sensation ("actio sensibilis in sensu"), on one side, while, on another side, being open to (while being *also capable of*) "abstractive" awareness—the awareness of physically absent or nonexistent objects—as external sense is not. In other words, alike for the distinction between sense and intellect and for the distinction between intuitive and abstractive awareness, Poinsot posits the notion of *species* or "specifying form" as an interpretant.

Figure 4. *Latin Positions regarding the Ontological Status of Sense Qualities:*

the qualities are images formed by the mind under the influence of things and known as such (Suárez)	the qualities as such inhere in the material objects acting on the senses and are made present as such through that action (Ockham)	the qualities have a status birelative to the structure of the entity acting upon a sense organ and the structure of the sense organ itself as a biological disposition (Aquinas, Scotus, Poinsot)

There is an immense theoretical difference between these three positions. The first of the three positions became the standard one for Descartes and Locke. The Latin author chiefly responsible for this was Francis Suárez, through the filter of whose 1597 *Disputationes Metaphysicae* Latin philosophy made its way into the national language traditions.

The second position was also a common one, and familiar to the principal figures of modern philosophy. The position is indeed a *realism*, but a decidedly naïve one at that. This is the position perhaps most commonly ascribed to medieval philosophy, but the ascription is an oversimplification that distorts the actual epistemological situation even of the high middle ages.

The third position is clearly the most sophisticated of the three. The doctrine of species can be most fully understood in relation to this position, which was the position of the tradition in which Poinsot wrote. Certainly, without a clear understanding of the doctrine of *species*, the third position cannot be understood, for the third position requires us to understand that the *species* as such is postulated to account for the precise aspect of specification in relation to cognition, and the circumstances under which that aspect is realized and the function of specification fulfilled are what determine whether the *species* is or is not a representative image (*imago seu idolum seu idea vel conceptus*), that is to say, an "idea" in Locke's sense. This is the point of the difference between *species* as *impressa* and *species* as *expressa*,[12] and this is the point I want to explore now.

In Poinsot's tradition, from as early as before Aquinas, the question as to what an idea is and why ideas are posited had been squarely faced. In that line of philosophical speculation, several reasons for the positing of ideas had been recognized (see Poinsot 1632: Book II, Question 2, 242/3–245/3, esp. 243/19ff., text and notes). A first reason for positing ideas is to supply for the presence of an object in awareness when that object is not present in the physical environment, either because the object is too far away to be perceived here and now, or because it no longer exists as a physical entity, or indeed because it is a fiction that never existed in the first place.

A second ground in Poinsot's tradition for acknowledging the reality of ideas is far more fundamental, subtle, and interesting, although the reasoning involved is not usually discussed in the historical literature, at least not as far as common classroom presentations go (Deely 1985). Ideas are necessary, these Latins argued, in order to establish and maintain the proportion between objects as we experience them and bare impressions of sense which alone are directly given in experience. A sound wave impinges on our ear, and we hear not merely a sound, but one we recognize to be a symphony of Beethoven, or a sound we recognize to be the whistle of a train, or a sound we recognize to be the wind in the pines below the cabin. We see not merely patches of color, but the uniform of the royal palace guard, or the flag of the United States. And so on for each of the so-called external senses: the objects we experience through them are not given as such through those senses, but what is given as such through the sense is worked up and organized—

---

12 I.e., cognitive stimulus as such and cognitive response: cf. Poinsot's *Artis Logicae Secunda Pars* (1632), Q. 21, *De Signo Secundum Se*, Art. 4, "Qualiter Dividatur Obiectum in Motivum et Terminativum"; Q. 22, *De Divisionibus Signi*, praecip. Art. 2, "Utrum Conceptus]i.e., Species Expressa[Sit Signum Formale", et Art. 4, "Utrum Species Impressa Sit Signum Formale" (= *Treatise on Signs*, Book I, "Concerning the Sign in Its Proper Being", Question 4, "In What Way Are Objects Divided into Stimulus Objects and Terminative Objects"; also Book II, "Concerning the Division of Signs", esp. Question 2, "Whether a Concept [that is to say, an Expressed Specifying Form] Is a Formal Sign", and Question 3, "Whether an Impressed Specification Is a Formal Sign").

proportioned, in a word—so as to constitute the objects we experience as houses, carts, trees, cobblestones, and the rest. This proportioning, according to Poinsot and his school, is the work of ideas, and the disproportion between what external sense gives us and what we actually perceive is what the idea is principally posited as overcoming.

Now, as far as the doctrine of species is concerned, here is the crucial step in the argument. The objects of external sense are, in every case, things which exist physically in the environment as here and now present and active upon the sensory power. Moreover, these objects as material things are directly proportioned to the physical, material organs in which the external sense powers reside. There is neither an absence to be supplied for nor a disproportion to be overcome. Therefore there is no reason for positing ideas at work in external sense as such, and to posit ideas at work there is gratuitous: *Gratis asseritur, gratis negatur.*

We confront here the most sophisticated epistemological tradition within the Latin mainstream. The *species impressae* as understood within this tradition were necessarily understood differently than in other Latin schools (see especially Poinsot 1632: Book II, Question 3).

To see this difference in understanding, let us first settle on what the basic notion of a *species* is supposed to convey. This is a Greek-derived term, meaning "form as related to appearance" in its etymology. And indeed, outward appearance is precisely what the *species impressae* were considered to convey. But the etymological component of a technical term is never a sufficient explanation of the term. Etymology chiefly conveys and rests on associations present in the culture at the time the term was coined, whereas the reason for the coining, the stipulation as such, and not merely the associations contributing to its motivation, is what gives the term its technical meaning. In the case of *species*, the technical point of the term (Poinsot 1632: Book I, Question 4) was to indicate the need of cognitive powers to be specified in order actually to know any particular object.

The eye as such is proportioned to a certain range of colors, above and below which it is unable to see. The ear as such is proportioned to a certain range of sound, below or above which it hears nothing, and so on for each of the other sensory capacities excitable by environmental influences. Each sensory power is generically proportioned to a specific range of possible apprehensions. But what determines, within that generic range, which specific sensations will be experienced through the power is not explicable by the power alone. What is required is a collusion between particular objects and generic powers, a collusion whereby the generic capacity is, literally, *specified* and determined to *this* rather than to *that* possible object. At that moment, a capacity to sense does actually sense; a possible sensation becomes an actual sensation. Neither the power by itself nor the stimulus by itself creates the sensation (hence the answer to the question of whether the tree falling which no one hears makes a noise: *distinguo: sensu stimulus, facit, sensu sensationis, non*). The sensation is a purely relative being suspended between the specific stimulus engendered by the action of a thing present in the environment and the generic capacity for sensation determined and specified through this action to engender an awareness of an influence at work here and now, whether audial, visual, tactual, gustual, or olfactual.

The species, then, is not merely a form, still less an apparent form. Indeed, at the level of impressions, the species itself does not appear at all. What appears, when anything does appear sensorially, is an environmental influence. Absent the power of sensation capable of detecting the influence, the influence is no less active and present in the environment, just as the fact that our bodies are not radios does not remove the radio waves filling this room. The *species* does not appear, it merely conveys the specific energy which determines that the power able to know becomes aware of the influence at work in the environment here and now.

The analogy to which this epistemological theory appeals is purely sexual, so it is perhaps surprising that the theory itself has not been better understood. The species is a seminal form, the sensory power a maternal womb. The power inseminated gives birth to the object apprehended.

But the sexual metaphor, apt as it is, is also misleading in one crucial particular. At the level of external sense, the object born has no existence apart from the interaction between thing and sense giving rise to it. Here is where the position of Poinsot and his school departs from the view of those who see in sensation a naïve realism, *and* of those who see in sensation already an image constructed by the mind and known as such.

The *species impressa*, in short, is indeed a specifying form, but it is not an idea. It does not make present something physically absent, and it does not elevate the objective sensation to the level of an object of perception. The *species impressa* merely enables the active influence of environmental aspects upon organs of external sense to become an apprehended influence, and merely provides in this way the sensory context on the basis on which perceptual elaboration and organization of objects takes place.

The idea enters in, that is to say (in the Latin terms), the *species expressa*, in contrast to the *species impressa* of external sensation as such, not necessarily later in time, but at a higher stage or level, as a further dimension, of cognitive organization. Sensation as such is explained adequately by the terms of the interaction between organism and environment: a present object proportioned to and active upon the organism in a specific respect is experienced by the organism as so acting. The organism, of course, responds to the sensory experience not purely passively but by situating the sensation(s) here and now experienced within the larger context of its immediate interests, needs, and past experiences. The organism presents to itself not merely a sensation, but an apprehensive complex which includes the sensation prospectively *of* some developed object of perception.

Precisely here, at the interface between the sensation and the response to the sensation, the idea enters in. The idea is the cognitive response of the organism to the cognitive experience of a stimulus. As such, the idea is itself and in turn a *form of specification*: if the sensation is experienced as a strain of country music, and the listener hates country music, the organism will initiate a motor response designed to change the source of the stimulus. At the level of cognition alone, however, the response of recognition wherein a sound becomes a country song is primarily active. The specification is no longer merely *impressed*, it is now something *expressed* and achieved by the organism at the level of perception and mayhap also intellection (if the organism is human).

Now this specifying form, dependent not merely on the dispositions of the organism and what influences are present in the environment, but further upon a capacity to synthesize those influences into a perception related to the organism's likes and dislikes, is the first specifying form that meets the criteria according to which we are entitled to posit ideas as theoretical entities required to account for experience. The *species expressa* integrates and elevates sensations to the level of perception, and supplies presence for objects independently of their environmental status as physical. In functioning thus, the formation of the *species expressa* is itself guided and determined by, or, perhaps better to say, formed and developed around, the objective sensation. *Impressa* and *expressa* alike are thus specifying forms, but only the *species expressa* is an idea (Poinsot 1632: Book II, Question 2). The *species impressa*, as a theoretical entity and technical term of philosophical vocabulary, is, at least in Poinsot's tradition, as far removed from Hume's impressions or Locke's "simple ideas of sense" as could be, for the *species impressae* as such are neither sensations nor ideas, but simply that specification according to which the power of sense forms a sensation under some environmental stimulus. There are no simple ideas of sense as distinct from the complex ideas of perception. At the level of sense, prescised and distinguished as such within perception, there are no ideas at all, but only aspectual manifestations of the environment as influencing some particular type of organism here and now.

The *species expressa* thus emerges as the basic scholastic notion—again, within one specific current of the late Latin mainstream—answering to Locke's notion of idea. But in its contrast with the prior notion of the *species impressa*, we also find in the notion of *species expressa* elements of analysis which have no counterpart or place within Locke's representationalist doctrine. Locke's position is rather that of Suárez, who held that external sense, no less than internal sense and understanding, required the formation of *species expressae* to provide its object of apprehension. Important to note here is that, through all the variant positions, the *species impressae* differ from the *expressae* in this: the *species expressae* are objective forms, that is, forms that belong to the formal constitution of knowledge or awareness as such, whereas the *impressae* as such belong rather to the subjective determination of nature and cognitive power prior to the actual emergence of an apprehension of whatever sort.

In Poinsot's tradition, the *species expressa*, whether formed by internal sense or by the understanding, was also called a concept, *conceptus*, because it is born or brought forth within the mind precisely as the mind is fecundated or specified through the action of a *species impressa*, as we have seen. At the level of the concept the sexual metaphor is both apt and no longer misleading: the concept gives birth to the object in its complete being, its being, that is, as independent of physical existence in the surrounding environment. Objects born of concepts, *conceived* objects as distinct from merely sensed aspects of objectivity (such as ex-

ternal sense provides), have indeed an existence apart from physical interactions. These objects can be completely unreal and fictive. But concept and object in every case differ as that which is known from that on
the basis of which it is known. In representational terms, object and concept differ as that which is represented from that which represents,
regardless of whether that which is represented has or ever had a mind-
independent physical existence.

This fundamental contrast and distinction between concept and object brings us close to the heart of the matter of semiotic. To get to the
heart of the matter, however, we need to introduce one more term from
late Latin scholasticism, *signum formale*, a term applicable to perception
and intellection alike. When we ask whether the concept is a formal sign,
Poinsot tells us (1632: 240/1–241/1): "the question holds as much for
a concept of the understanding, which is called an expressed specifier
and word, as for an expressed specifier of perception or imagination,
which is called an icon or phantasm".

When exactly the expression "*signum formale*" was introduced into
Latin remains so far undetermined. What is clear is the speculative
motivation behind the expression, namely, to reject the ancient Augusti-
nian definition of the sign (as something which, on being perceived,
makes something else besides come into awareness), in order to establish
that ideas, which are not perceptible, are nonetheless signs. The connection with Locke's proposal for semiotic is unmistakable. Williams
has summarized the situation thus (1985: xxxiii):

A major strand of semiotic reflection and controversy, beginning from at least
the fourteenth century and developing especially in the Iberian university world
of the sixteenth and seventeenth centuries, but involving also a wide
geographical area ... turned precisely on this question of whether the sign as
such involves a *per se* sensible half. The increasingly consistent answer was made
in the negative.

But what is of principal interest here is that, as it turns out, this point of
historical controversy is the central point thematically for the accomplishment
of the main task of semiotic as Locke proposed it, to wit, the bringing of ideas
as well as words into the perspective of a doctrine of signs.

By Poinsot's day, at least in the Iberian university world where questions of signs had become matters of "daily dispute" in the schools,

Augustine's question-begging definition of the sign as something per se sensible had been rejected in favor of the more neutral definition, "anything that represents something other than itself to a cognitive power". This definition, it was argued, would then apply both to sense-perceptible objects which function as signs (such as words and cultural artifacts generally, along with natural occurrences such as clouds and smoke), and to ideas and images in our minds. Signs were divided accordingly into so-called *instrumental* and *formal* signs.

But how exactly to explain the performance of either type of sign in situations where the supposed object of the signification was nonexistent was a vexing problem. Poinsot's proposed solution to the difficulty depended on a little-noticed and not generally understood fact about the category of relation as Aristotle had defined it and as the natural philosophers of Latin times had taken it over from Aristotle. This was the fact that relation, understood as an accident or characteristic of being which has its whole existence in a respect or bearing toward another, is the only form of being which is not determinately tied to the order of what is conceived as existing independently of human thought. By contrast, substance, and all the other accidents which inhere in substance, in order to be realized according to their proper definition, must be predicated of something which is or is supposed to exist independently of our minds. What makes a relation to be a relation, however, is that it be a reference toward another, regardless of whether it exist in the world of physical nature or only as the result of someone thinking. The being proper to relation, thus, is the only form of being indifferent to the distinction between what is and what is not independent of thought.

Passing over for now the details of the lengthy discussions Poinsot engages in to make this point (Poinsot 1632: First and Second Preamble, esp. 93/17–96/36), what I want to call attention to is that the point itself is what provides Poinsot with the means of explaining how ideas are pure signs even when the objects they represent in thought do not exist apart from thought. Ideas in our minds are representations, but representations of something besides themselves. This something besides the idea is the object of the representation. The connection between the two, concept and object, is a pure relation. In some cases, namely, when the object thought of is also a physical being and existing at the time that we think of it, the relation is also a physical relation (Poinsot 1632: Book

I, Question 2; see also notes 70 and 72 in Chapter 4, pp. 101 and 102 above). But it is not the fact of being physical that makes it be a relation. On the contrary, the relation need not be physical in order to be a relation, and it remains as a relation even when the conditions for physical existence do not obtain, as is notably the case when the terminus of the relation does not, or does no longer, exist.

In the case of a physical relation, the characteristic of an individual on the basis of which it is related to another individual—the foundation or fundament of the relation—is distinct *both* from the other individual which is the terminus of the relation *and* from the relation itself. The fundament exists within or as part of the individual related, whereas the relation itself is always something over and above the individual related and intersubjective between the individuals related. Just so, in the case of a mind-dependent relation, the idea as a representation provides but the fundament or foundation for the idea as a relation to its object. And, just as in the case of a physical relation it is the relation itself that makes the terminus be as a terminus (despite the fact that, in the supposed case, the terminus also has a further existence in its own right as a material object), so in the case of a mind-dependent relation what makes the terminus be as terminus is the relation itself (even though in this case the terminus has no further existence in its own right and is nothing material). Similarly, in the case of a photograph or a statue of a dead person, the photograph or statue in its own being is fundamentally a representation. But this representation, on being perceived, becomes the ground for a cognitive relation which goes beyond the physical photograph to the very nonexistent person of whom the photograph was taken. The sign formally consists in this relation, not in the representation that constitutes it only fundamentally.

The idea as a formal sign is thus conceived as always and necessarily, by virtue of its proper being, creating, as it were, a suprasubjective zone or objective realm around the individual thinking. This zone is always, at the same time, actually or virtually intersubjective. It is actually intersubjective whenever some object of thought is also being actually considered by another thinker. It is virtually intersubjective when the thought concerns a nonexistent object which, as object, could also be (but is not here and now) constituted as terminus of thought for another, should the requisite representation be formed fundamentally in that other's mind. The objects of thought, regardless of their status vis-à-vis the physical environment, always exist as objects at the terminus of an idea-based relation. Communication is possible in exactly the same way that any two things can be related to a common third.

C. Conclusions

The relation of Locke's concluding proposal to the substance and body of his *Essay* is somewhat mysterious. After all, words and ideas had been his subject throughout the work. So, when he concludes by proposing that ideas and words, distinctly weighed and duly considered in the perspective of the doctrine of signs, might afford us with another sort of Logick and Critick than what we have been hitherto acquainted with, one who has paid attention to the discourse as a whole can hardly avoid thinking that Locke may have had his own work in mind.

Be that as it may, the development of the doctrine of signs in the Iberian world as it culminated in the semiotic of John Poinsot presents us with a picture of Locke's work as being in its concluding proposal at odds with its starting point and main development. For the "idea of ideas" as being the very objects of which we are aware proves to be antinomic respecting the "idea of ideas" as signs.

Indeed, Poinsot explains the difference between signs and objects in terms of the difference between representations which are signs (and hence always of something other than themselves) and representations which are self-representations (and as such may be objects without being signs). A representation may be a thing or an object, but as an object, a representation always manifests itself, whether or not, over and above this self-manifestation, the object in question happens *also* and *further* to be a sign. It remains that an object as object is never a sign.[13]

---

[13] In my own work, it is the distinction between the manifestative as a self-representation (the manifestative element constituting the object as such) and the manifestative as an other-representation dependent upon the other represented (the manifestative element constituting the sign as such) that I have thematically focussed upon. But in Poinsot's text, in fact (e.g., at 1632a: 116/23-117/17, 122/17-49), the other-representation proper to the sign is distinguished *both* from the self-representation of an object *and* from a second form of manifestation, other-manifestation *without a dependence on the other* "but rather through a dependence of the other on the one manifesting",

Far from being equatable with objects, ideas as signs prove to be more fundamental than, and presupposed to, the existence of objects as distinct from things. In bare sensation analytically considered, the relations among proper and common sensibles is already a sign relation, regardless of the status of the qualities so presented objectively. In perception, as incorporating and going beyond sensation, the objects of experience are precisely given on the basis of a network of formal sign relationships. In understanding, as arising within perception, the same obtains.

The doctrine of signs as Locke sketched it was, therefore, all unwittingly, actually more than a bare proposal. It was at the same time a kind of archetypically unconscious summary of developments of the recent past achieved in the Iberian Latin world, and a harbinger of a contemporary development that would take place after Peirce.[14] Both of these developments, the past no less than the future one, were unbeknownst to Locke. Yet his proposal in concluding the *Essay* stands as a bridge between the two, a bridge under which run the waters of rationalism and empiricism alike.

For Locke's proposal, when it was directly considered within the classical modern development (with the exception of Berkeley noted above), tended to receive an out-of-hand rejection. For example, Leibniz rejected it in his *New Essays concerning Human Understanding* (1704), on

as when light manifests a color. Thus there is not only the question of self-representation and other-represenation (i.e., of objects distinguished from signs), but also the question of manifestation in general which includes, besides these two forms, a manifestation in some sense prior to signification (yet within objectification—or, rather, in the line of objectifiability) in which the manifested is causally produced by (or dependent upon) the manifesting factors. James Maroosis (1993) has recently brought to my attention an argument that this threefold notion of manifestation in Poinsot anticipates Peirce's 1867 (and after) analysis of Firstness, Secondness, and Thirdness as the irreducible categories of human experience, necessary and sufficient to account for its semiotic structure. Since I have never analyzed the text either of Poinsot or of Peirce in this light, I can do no more here than simply call attention to Maroosis' intriguing claim, the substantial development of which remains unpublished, though available through the University of Toronto (Maroosis 1981). The claim is important enough and well enough made, certainly, to warrant further study—yet one more doctoral dissertation waiting to be written as we open up the history of early modern philosophy in light of postmodernity.

14   See the "History of Semiotics" in Deely 1990: 108–124.

the ground that natural phenomena and conventional signs have no common denominator inasmuch as the latter are arbitrary and the former not, and because a distinction one of whose parts—semiotic—virtually absorbs the other two—physics and ethics—is defective. Fraser, in his 1894 edition of Locke's *Essay* (Vol. II, p. 463 note 1), has only disparagement for "this crude and superficial scheme of Locke" wherein it is proposed that the study of signs as providing the means for speculative and practical knowledge alike may hold the key to understanding aright the nature and extent of human knowledge.

Not until the modern period in philosophy neared its end was a more judicious assessment made by Charles Sanders Peirce. Directly inspired by a reading of Locke (Fisch 1978: 34) and thoroughly cognizant both of the modern period and of the Greek and Latin periods in philosophy (though not, unfortunately, of the Iberian development of the doctrine of signs except for the work of the Conimbricenses, who adopted all the positions concerning signs which, on Poinsot's demonstration, make a unified doctrine impossible[15]), Peirce was compelled to describe himself as "a pioneer, or rather, a backwoodsman, in the work of clearing and opening up ... the doctrine of the essential nature and fundamental varieties of possible semiosis". This last was Peirce's term for the action of signs, derived from a reading sometime around 1879[16] of the remains of an *ante* 79AD Herculaneum papyrus on the subject of signs by the Epicurean philosopher Philodemus.

Locke's proposal for semiotic, once seen against the backdrop of Poinsot's *Tractatus de Signis*, surely appears as one of history's confluences within the *Zeitgeist* of the seventeenth century,[17] revealing as it does that

---

15 A masterful preliminary investigation of the Latin sources drawn upon in common by Peirce and Poinsot has been made by Mauricio Beuchot (1993). One might quarrel with his interpretation of the Peircean notion of "final interpretant" which seems to rely on Eco in fact more than on Peirce, but this is peripheral to the main point and value of Beuchot's inquiry. To gain an idea of the extent to which Poinsot's doctrine of signs was developed in counterpoint to the Conimbricenses group Fonseca founded, see "The Conimbricenses on the Relations Involved in Signs" (Doyle 1984a).

16 See Fisch 1986a: 329–330.

17 See "John Locke's Place in the History of Semiotic Inquiry" (Deely 1986a).

the very problem exercising modern thought in its rejection of the Latin immersion in the Aristotelian philosophy of nature was the problem on which Poinsot brought all the resources of Latin tradition to bear. For Locke (1690: 30), it was a question of getting our understandings right, for which we must find out "the way and proportion that objects are suited to our faculties", and entertain them only "upon those grounds they are capable of being proposed to us". This task, in Descartes' words (1628: 31), is one which "everyone with the slightest love of truth ought to undertake at least once in his life, since the true instruments of knowledge and the entire method are involved in the investigation of the problem". That Peirce should have come to be regarded as the father of the semiotic tradition, as Descartes was of the rationalist and Locke of the empiricist tradition, is, by contrast, rather more of an accident, the historical accident whereby, in this area, the highest development of Latin thought after Ockham fell into oblivion, and the Iberian influence on university life, except as filtered through Suárez, became lost to modern times.

As the contemporary development enters a postmodern age, this particular accident of history, at least, is being redressed. And in this particular we have learned enough to see clearly now that, when it comes to the doctrine of signs, it is anything but the case that, as Whitehead could once credibly allege (1925: 39):

a brief, but sufficiently accurate, description of the intellectual life of the European races during the succeeding two centuries and a quarter up to our own times is that they have been living upon the accumulated capital of ideas provided for them by the genius of the seventeenth century.

The problem with Whitehead's assertion is that, in the area of the doctrine of signs, the accumulated capital of ideas provided by the genius of the seventeenth century was primarily Hispanic, and by dint of circumstance (not excluding some deep-rooted prejudices), was not available to the European races to draw upon. Whitehead's observation is, in equal parts, sufficiently accurate and sufficiently inaccurate. In this book we have been dealing with the part that is inaccurate, as will I hope the books of many investigators to follow. If the intellectual life of the European races during the past three centuries had been living upon the complete capital of ideas laid up in the seventeenth century, Peirce would not be the father of semiotic tradition but one of its late systematizers, perhaps in a position respecting semiotic tradition comparable to the position in which Poinsot found himself respecting Latin tradition in logic and natural philosophy.

What is certain is that philosophical doctrine as it developed in the later Latin centuries in the area of what we today call "epistemology", or the theory of knowledge, has an intrinsic relevance to the concern voiced by Locke under the name of semiotic. Locke's concern, anticipated by Poinsot, has been taken up today through the work of Charles Sanders Peirce, whence it bids fair to become the mainstream postmodern development as philosophy, along with the rest of civilization, moves toward the twenty-first century. At the very least, the evidence strongly indicates that a semiotic approach to the history of early modern philosophy provides, both as background for classical modern philosophy and as link between contemporary and high medieval thought, the best chance for achieving a living understanding of Latin Baroque and Renaissance thought, what Randall has described (1962: vi–viii) as the "least known period in the history of Western philosophy", that is, "the transition from the thirteenth to the seventeenth centuries, when modern philosophy is conventionally supposed to have begun". Despite the appearance in 1988 of *The Cambridge History of Renaissance Philosophy* (Schmitt and Skinner 1988), the understanding of this transition has not advanced much beyond Randall's aging description. The standard histories continue to want for a proper outline of Latinity, both in its own integrity and—especially—in its complex of relations to early modern philosophy.

Epilogue to Part I

Further Signs

The independent publication of Poinsot's *Tractatus de Signis* in 1985 indeed had the merit, among others, as Santaella-Braga said (1991: 155), "of making evident that the doctrine of signs proclaimed by Locke did not have to wait two hundred years to rise in the bosom of Peirce's complex and monumental work". Yet, as we enter a postmodern age, Peirce does not provide the only proof in contemporary philosophy of the value of Poinsot's work to philosophy's future. Jack Miles, in preparing copy for the release by the University of California Press of my 1985 autonomous edition of Poinsot's *Treatise on Signs*, wrote: "That Poinsot's diagnosis of the course of western philosophy was superior to—or at the very least clearly distinct from—the alternative diagnosis of Descartes and of all modern philosophy is proven, Deely argues, by the reemergence in our day of Poinsot's questions as semiotic." I would stand by Miles' formulation, but add in support of it here the following concluding observations for Part I.

If we put into modern terms Poinsot's claim that the doctrine of signs transcends in its starting point the division of being into *ens reale* and *ens rationis*, what is being asserted is that semiotic transcends the opposition of *realism* to *idealism*. Not until Heidegger in the contemporary period do we encounter such a claim among the philosophers. Heidegger at least recognized what the avatars of modernity still have no cognizance of, namely, that "this problem [of the unity of being prior to the categories] was widely discussed in medieval ontology especially in the Thomist and Scotist schools"; and although Heidegger did not think that the medieval discussion succeeded in "reaching clarity as to its principles", neither did he know of Poinsot's work in this particular.[1] Correspondence truth both Poinsot and Heidegger recognized, as Powell best brought out (1969). But with his doctrine of signs Poinsot was achieving within the Latin tradition the first systematic clarification of the ontological foundations in relation for the possibility of truth as a conformity knowable in the structures of objectivity between thought and things of the environment in their physical reality. Such a clarification Heidegger called for as late as 1943 in his essay *Vom Wesen der Wahrheit*.

The difficulty and originality alike of Poinsot's work derive, in short, from his recognition that *the first concern* of anyone who would seek to explain signs, the universal means of communication, must be precisely to pay heed "to Aristotle's *problem of the unity of Being* [as that which is experientially first in human understanding] as over against the multiplicity of 'categories' applicable to things".[2] The experience of signs and of the escape from the subjectivity of the here and now is as fundamental in its own way as is the experience of things in terms of the data which provide experimental justification for the scheme of the categories, as is clear from the fact that the derivation of the categories from experience is itself a function of the use we make of signs in developed discourse.[3]

---

1 "Die mittelalterliche Ontologie had dieses Problem vor allem in den thomistischen und skotistischen Schulrichtungen vielfältig diskutiert, ohne zu einer grundsätzlichen Klarheit zu kommen" (*Sein und Zeit* 1927: 3). The first serious investigation that I have seen of this point, either doctrinally or historically, is the major article by Vincent Guagliardo, "Being-as-First-Known in Poinsot: A-Priori or Aporia?" which he prepared for the *ACPQ* Special Issue on John Poinsot, Vol. LXVIII, No. 3 (Summer 1994), 375-404.

2 Martin Heidegger, *Sein und Zeit* (1927), p. 3: "Und wenn schliesslich *Hegel* das 'Sein' bestimmt als das 'unbestimmte Unmittelbare' und diese Bestimmung allen weiteren kategorialen Explikationen seiner 'Logik' zugrunde legt, so hält er sich in derselben Blickrichtung wie die antike Ontologie, nur dass er das von Aristoteles schon gestellte Problem der Einheit des Seins gegenber der Mannigfaltigkeit der sachhaltigen 'Kategorien' aus der Hand gibt".

3 See p. 86n10 in the 1985 *Tractatus de Signis*, Second Preamble, Article 1, "Whether There Exist on the Side of Mind-Dependent Being Intrinsic Forms Which Are Relations" (= *Artis Logicae Secunda Pars*, Q. 17, Art. 1, "Utrum a parte rei dentur relationes, quae sint formae intrinsecae"), which is a gloss especially on the passage at 86/9–22 (= 577a10–28). This gloss has been much expanded in the electronic edition

Poinsot's contribution to the seventeenth century search for a new beginning in philosophy was nothing less than to show in detail what that new beginning might best be, namely, a setting out in earnest along the way of signs. It was a contribution destined to be overlooked in its day, but privileged to enter into the history of semiotic development anew at a later time, the time when the exploration of the way of signs would be, for the first time, thematically undertaken. By this accident, history achieves another confluence, and the last of the Latins joins the last of the moderns to initiate a postmodern era in philosophy, where experience and the being proper to it become the central occupation of philosophy in exploring the way of signs.

on the basis of Deely 1988, in response to the misunderstandings mentioned in note 69 to Chapter 4 above, p. 100.

PART II

Expanding the Speculative Links

"What is 'old' (the sign) is still so new

(as a relation secundum esse*)*

that Jacques Derrida does not yet seem to have heard about it.

— Vincent Guagliardo 1992: 71 —

6

How Do Signs Work?

At the December 5, 1992 fifth gathering of The Midwest Seminar in the History of Early Modern Philosophy (the third such at the University of Chicago), Steven Nadler delivered a paper titled "Descartes and Occasional Causation". The concept of occasional causation, he emphasized, had nothing whatever to do with the modern philosophical doctrine of occasionalism. Occasional causation he set in contrast to "the standard model of transient efficient causation": the latter requires "a real action or influence", the former "exercises no efficiency" but brings about an effect by *occasioning another* to exercise its efficient causation—"A occasions B to cause E". "All that the claim amounts to", Nadler summarized, is that "there is an ontological relation with some foundation."

Despite showing a clear need for some such novel notion of causality in terms of his examples, in the end Nadler himself was not ready to stake his reputation on the claim that occasional causality could not be reduced to an equivocal way of speaking about indirect efficient causation in Descartes' text. In other words, regardless of the philosophical need for some such expansion of the notion of cause, as a textual exegete, Nadler professed only to find "some evidence" that such a notion could be legitimately drawn out of Descartes' writings, especially after 1647.

Nadler's discussion is interesting on a number of grounds, beyond its demonstration of how narrow the concept of causality had become in modern philosophy and how difficult it would be, right from the early days, to expand or diversify that narrow conception. Nevertheless, for Locke's proposal for semiotics to take hold, exactly such an expansion as Nadler indicated would, at the minimum, be necessary. For the action of signs is quite opaque on any attempt to explain it directly through efficient causation alone, while the triadic nature of the sign relation, on the face of it, is "an ontological relation with some foundation" which calls upon one thing to effect another.

Nonetheless, the terminology of "occasional cause" in Nadler's discussion, while justified by his narrow exegetical and textual concern, violates at least the third and sixth rules governing the ethics of terminology (Peirce 1903: 2.219–2.226) It violates the sixth because it interferes with an existing term, namely, occasionalism; and it violates the third by failing to use the applicable scholastic terms (*objective* or *extrinsic formal cause* in the case at hand) in their proper senses.

The subject of causality, in this particular instance and in general, provides one of the clearest illustrations of how much richer in philosophical conceptions and possibilities the Latin matrix of early modern philosophy was than can be gleaned from any study restricted to the mainstream national language development from that matrix of rationalism and empiricism, taken separately or together.

We have already seen, both from Locke's proposed schema and from Poinsot's foundational analysis, that our knowledge, whether of natural or of socio-cultural phenomena, is acquired, elaborated, and communicated through a network of sign relations, and that this network is by no means restricted to the realm of species-specifically human language and cognition, but extends to nonverbal communication as well and to affective life (therefore to unconscious structures) no less that to cognitive structures. But how do signs effect and sustain this vast network of experience joining us in a partially public world of objects over and above the subjectivity of environmentally existing things? And how far does this action of signs extend? In other words, when we say that semiotics is the study or doctrine of signs, what exactly are we saying as regards causality in particular?

There is, of course, little point to the inquiry if "what semiotics is" be taken as a matter of mere stipulation, as in the clever "semiotics is what semioticians do", a tired formula ever applicable to any area, with roughly equal theoretical illumination in each case. Not that it is easy to say what semiotics is (any more than it is easy to say what anything is). But difficulty is no excuse, in matters of thought, for recourse to shibboleths or lazy formulae of whatever kind.

The plain fact is that no one can say how semiosis works or how far semiotics extends who does not also say, explicitly or implicitly, what semiotics is. Thus, anyone denying that such or such a phenomenon is semiotic or has a semiotic aspect is necessarily, whether they want to admit it or not, whether they realize it or not, *also* saying, in an implicatory sub-text or meta-text, "because what semiotics is, is X, therefore semiotics does not extend to Y", or "Since semiotics is X, therefore it does not extend to Y", etc. Clarifying the concept of causality especially with the aid of the Latins from the gestation period of early modern philosophy is, we shall shortly see, of the greatest assistance in clarifying the notion of semiotics itself.

A. What Does Semiotics Study?

Semiotics can be said to be the study of signs, but I think this is a loose and casual way of speaking that needs considerable expansion in order to be correctly understood. A sign is anything that stands for something other than itself—"A", for example, stands for the first letter in our alphabet in capitalized form, or for an indefinite article opening a new sentence. But you see at once that a relation of "standing for" requires a specified context: one thing stands for another only in some respect or capacity. So the sign is not a thing as such, not a physical element merely existing in the environment, like a rock or a toad, but something as doubly related: A stands for B in context C. Yet to say "doubly related" is not to say "two relations", but to say rather that one "thing" is related to two other "things" at one and the same time by one single relation. It is not a question of two relations, one between A and B, and another between A and C, for, even supposing there to be such, neither such relation taken independently would constitute A as a sign. The relation constituting A as a sign is a single relation with three terms—sign, signified, and specified context or ground within and on the basis of which the sign signifies this signified rather than some other, or rather than not signifying at all. The physical mark A is constituted as sign not by its physical "reality" or being as such, but by its being the intermediate term in a triadic relation of the type Jakobson (1974; 1980) aptly named *renvoi*—a relation which has an intermediate term that sends the mind beyond itself to a signified according to a specific context. (After all, a thing may represent itself and nothing more, in which case it is an object rather than a sign.)

"According to a *specific* context": what makes the sign stand in this rather than that capacity or respect to what it signifies? What constitutes a specific "context" as specific? This third term in the sign-relationship Peirce called the *interpretant*.[1] Earlier thinkers had meticulously established that for one object of perception to function as sign relative to another object, a concept in the mind is necessarily presupposed to ground the relation of signification.[2] This they showed to be true

---

1 The interpretant thus is not merely the "context and circumstances" in which the sign occurs generically considered, but is rather something explicit within the sign itself, namely, that element or factor at work in the signifying which determines within the general "context and circumstances" what specifically is relevant to the signifying, or, as I put it above, what makes the context *specific* to what is signified. Cf. Deely 1990: Chapter 3. Using the example of a dicisign, Peirce (c.1907a: 5.473) says: "... anything belongs *to the interpretant* that describes the quality or character of the fact, anything *to the object* [signified] that, without doing that, distinguishes this fact from others like it".

2 Poinsot 1632a: 271/22–42: "Nor does it matter that a sound or name does not signify except by means of a concept, which is a natural sign. For this also holds for a natural instrumental sign, that it does not represent except by means of a concept making it an object of awareness, and yet the natural instrumental sign is not on this account a sign analogically, but truly and univocally [see Book I, Question 1, 236/46–237/15]. For the fact that [instrumental] signs depend on a concept in representing does not remove the univocal rationale of a sign, since indeed a concept and cognition is that to which the [instrumental] signs represent, not a means by which they represent as by a formal rationale, even though the instrumental signs [if they are stipulated or customary] may be produced from that concept and cognition. For not every dependence of one thing on another constitutes an analogy, but only that which is in an order to participating a general or common rationale; for unless that inequality [i.e., a given dependence] is partly the same [in rationale] and partly different, it does not destroy univocation, as St. Thomas best explains in his *Commentary* on the first book of Aristotle's treatise *On Interpretation*, in the opening paragraphs of the eighth reading."—"Nec obstat, quod vox seu nomen non significat nisi mediante conceptu, qui est signum naturale. Hoc enim etiam signo instrumentali naturali convenit, quod non nisi mediante conceptu et notitia sui repraesentat, et tamen non ob hoc est signum analogice, sed vere et univoce [vide 236/46–237/15]. Quod enim signa in repraesentando dependeant a conceptu, non tollit univocam rationem signi, siquidem conceptus et cognitio est, cui repraesentant, non mediante quo repraesentant tamquam formali ratione, licet effective possint ab eo esse. Non omnis autem dependentia unius ab alio constituit analogiam, sed solum illa, quae est in ordine ad participandam rationem communem; nisi enim illa inaequalis sit

even when, as in the case of so-called natural signs, a causal relation is also supposed to obtain between the sign (say, smoke or clouds) and the signified (say, fire or rain to come). In every case without exception, the relation of signification is other than any dyadic relation of cause-effect.[3] Earlier thinkers had likewise established firmly that the relationship in which a sign consists must be as such triaspectual (Araújo 1617, Poinsot 1632a; cfr. Beuchot 1980). But no thinker before Peirce, as far as I know, had gone so far as to assign a name to this silent partner or third term essential to the sign-signified linkage. The inclusion of the interpretant as a thematic factor in the analysis of signs was thus a major theoretical advance in the development of semiotics as a body

et partim eadem, partim diversa, non destruit univocationem, ut optime tradit S. Thomas 1. Periherm. lect. 8. in princ." The shallowness of contemporary objection to this point has been noted by both Beuchot (1994: 309) and Cahalan (1994 throughout)

[3] Poinsot 1632a: 137 n.4: "Similarly, those relations by which a sign can be proportioned to a signified are formally other than the sign-relation itself, e.g., the relation of effect to cause, of similitude or image, etc., even though some recent authors confound the sign-relation with these relations, but unwarrantably: because to signify or to be caused or to be similar are diverse exercises in a sign. For in signifying, a substitution for the principal significate is exercised, in order that that principal may be manifested to a power, but in the rationale of a cause or an effect is included nothing of an order to a cognitive power; wherefore they are distinct fundaments, and so postulate distinct relations. These relations, moreover, can be separated from the sign-relation, just as a son is similar to the father and his effect and image, but not a sign. The sign-relation therefore adds to these relations, which it supposes or prerequires in order to be habilitated and proportioned to this significate rather than to that one."—"Similiter relationes illae, quibus signum proportionare potest ad signatum, diversae sunt formaliter a relatione ipsa signi, e.g. relatio effectus vel causae, similitudinis vel imaginis etc., licet aliqui recentes confundant relationem signi cum istis relationibus, sed immerito: tum quia diversum exercitium est in signo significare vel causari aut similem esse. In significando enim exercetur substitutio principalis signati, ut manifestetur potentiae, in ratione vero causae aut effectus nihil de ordine ad potentiam includitur; quare distincta fundamenta sunt, et sic distinctas relationes postulant. Et praeterea separari possunt relationes istae a relatione signi, sicut filius est similis patri et effectus eius et imago, non tamen signum. Addit ergo relatio signi super illas relationes, quas supponit aut praerequirit, ut habilitetur et proportionetur huic signato potius quam illi."

See further Book I, Question 3, 160/10–21, esp. note 13, pp. 163–164.

of knowledge. Even though the essential clue that the interpretant need not be mental had already been uncovered prior to Peirce, as in Poinsot's formula (1632a: 126/3–5): "It suffices to be a sign virtually in order to signify in act", nonetheless, the role of the interpretant in the semiotic structuring experience had never, prior to Peirce, been analyzed in sufficient detail to appear as an instance of a more general phenomenon—as a species of thirdness.

What then is the sign? It is simply the element that is *playing the role* of a standing-for at any given time. Insofar as this element is something sensible—a red octagon, say, with a four character string on it in white—it is merely a physically instantiated object. What makes of that object, any such object, a sign is not that it is a sensible element as such, but only that it is a sensible element serving as the intermediate one of three terms in a relation of *renvoi*, a relation whereby an observer is made to attend to something other than the so-called "sign" identified with the sensible element (technically called properly a "sign-vehicle" rather than a "sign"). Were we from the wrong culture, the red octagonal white-marked thing would still exist as an object that could be ostended. Only after the requisite information had been gleaned, however, would the object in question reveal itself as also a sign regulating specific types of behavior, particularly as pertains to the operators of motor vehicles.

In recognition of this complexity within the sign, contemporary semioticians have learned to speak rather of "sign-vehicles" than of signs when intending physical entities—be they marks or sounds or cultural artifacts of whatever type—functioning in the role of signs. Signs, strictly speaking, that is to say, signs as signs, it is now recognized, are not as such perceptible entities at all. Signs are rather certain patterns of relationships—always triadic, as we have seen—into which perceptible entities as such enter upon actually being perceived or understood, that is to say (in either case), objectified. Semiotics is not the study of sign-vehicles: the physics of acoustical phenomena is not the science of spoken language for all that spoken language involves such physics, any more than the physics of light waves is the study of written language, for all that written language involves light waves; the physiology of optic nerves is not the study of reading, for all that reading normally involves optic nerves; and so on. Each science has its subject matter, the study of which gives rise to the knowledge typical of that science.

What then are we saying when we say that ''semiotics studies signs''? We are saying that, when objects of experience are looked at in a certain guise, we find that they relate to other objects in a distinctive way, specifically, in a way that leads to awareness of things other than themselves; and that when objects function in this way the analysis and study of them results in a distinctive kind or type of knowledge we call *semiotics*. Thus, semiotics names a prospective body of knowledge that results from the study of a distinctive subject matter, the behavior or action peculiar to signs. This action is distinguished by the causing of one thing to lead to an awareness of other things besides itself, and has been called *semiosis* in recent times in order to distinguish it from the many other types of activity in which perceptible objects engage, notably interactions of brute force which directly and immediately change the material structures involved. Semiosis, by contrast, is involved in such changes but does not consist in them.[4]

Semiotics, then, is the study or, rather, the knowledge gained by the study, of thirdness within experience as the manifestation or result of an action of signs. Semiotics extends as far as this action extends, no farther, and no less far. The question, then, is: How far does the action proper to signs extend? To answer this question with any reasonableness we must first determine how signs act. What is the action proper to signs? And how is this action accomplished?

B. How Does Semiosis Effect *Renvoi?*

Signs produce an effect proper to themselves: *renvoi*, as we have seen. And to speak of an effect is to speak of a cause. How are we to conceive of the sign as cause?

1. Cause in Greek and Latin Thought.

The notion of cause, of course, is an ancient one. The most comprehensive framework for the discussion of this notion dates back to the work

---

[4] Of course, it is generally known today that the contrast between these two types of action is the basis on which Peirce distinguished *secondness* from *thirdness*, and distinguished both of these alike from the realm of pure possibility and dream he called *firstness* in establishing the categories for the analysis of experience in its proper being.

of Aristotle, in the fourth century BC, as expanded in the later period
of Latin philosophy (c.1150–1650).[5] The central notion of causality,
according to this analysis, is the notion of a *dependency in being* of one thing
or aspect of a thing upon another thing or aspect of a thing. A dependency
in being can occur in four ways: either in respect of production, outcome, material, or form.

a. Dependency Respecting Production.

Dependency in production is the notion of *efficient cause*, the agent or agency bringing a change or an individual into being. Dependency in production is thus a common notion that pertains to all things in space-time:
all things depend on an agent or agencies for coming into being.

b. Dependency Respecting Outcome.

Dependency in outcome is twofold, intrinsic or extrinsic. An intrinsic
dependency obtains in the case of individuals which develop from an
initial primitive state to a mature adult state (Ashley 1952). This notion applies especially to living organisms. The course of growth and

---

[5] The best-informed contemporary discussion of this topic is Wallace 1972 and 1974.
   For a synoptic summary of the Latin discussions on efficient, material, intrinsic
   formal, and extrinsic exemplary formal causality, see Poinsot 1633: Questions 10–13,
   197a11–287b43, where, however, extrinsic specificative formal causality ("objective causality") is mentioned only in response to an objection confusing it with exemplary causality (245a24–43, 247a7–14).
   The discussion of formal causality as extrinsic specification is to be found rather
   in Poinsot 1632: Q. 17, Arts. 5–7, 595b25–608b7, Q. 21, Arts. 4 and 5,
   670a11–693a31, Q. 22, Arts. 1–4, 693a34–715a21, and Poinsot 1635—i.e., in the
   context of his discussion of cognitive organisms in the biological treatises—Q. 6.,
   Arts. 2–4, 177b1–198a16, Q. 8, Art. 4, 265b1–271b20, Q. 10, Arts. 1–5,
   295b1–339a45, Q. 11, Arts. 1 and 2, 344b1–366b34. Notice, therefore, the generally
   biological and epistemological contexts in which these questions mainly arise, not
   to mention the specifically semiotic ones (Poinsot 1632a: Book I, Questions 4 and
   5; Book II, Questions 1–4), where it is not too much to say that some of the most
   difficult and extended passages in Poinsot's attempt to systematize the foundations
   of semiotic inquiry arise from the need to make this heretofore peripheral topic of
   natural inquiry central to the establishment of semiotic.

development is plainly not random but follows a plan, and that plan is the mature state toward which the development tends at each stage. This inner-directed tendency is the notion of *teleology* or *final cause*, sometimes called also *teleonomy* in recent literature (Simpson, Pittendrigh, and Tiffany 1957; Pittendrigh 1958; Mayr 1974, 1983).

An extrinsic dependency in outcome obtains in the case of one individual using something else to achieve the user's ends. Thus the production of artifacts of whatever kind, all works of art or technology, exhibit a dependency of this kind: acorns grow on trees through a process of intrinsic final causality, but forks as eating implements come into being only through manufacture, an external agency which shapes them according to a plan of the agent.

c. Dependency Respecting Material

All spatio-temporal entities similarly have a material structure and formal architecture, that is, they are made out of something and made out of it in a definite way. Dependency in material structure is the notion of *material cause*: what something is made out of gives it definite properties affecting all that it is and can do. In the case of organisms, for example, what substances count as food and what as poison, what tissues or organs can be transplanted and what can not, etc., all this is determined by a material dependency or *dependency in type of matter*. Similarly in the case of artifacts: cardboard may be suitable for constructing a model of a building, but an actual building so constructed will fare ill in adverse weather, and so on. Aristotle called this aspect of dependency in being, accordingly, *material cause*. Note that, unlike a final cause which may be either extrinsic or intrinsic to the effect produced, efficient and material cause are, respectively and determinately, the one extrinsic and the other intrinsic: just as efficient or productive causality is always extrinsic to the effect as such produced, so material causality is always intrinsic to the effect and defines or limits the range of activity.

d. Dependency Respecting Formal Arrangement.

The activity or function of an effect, indeed, its very being as effect, is also limited by a second form of intrinsic dependency: the manner in which it is put together or composed of whatever material it may be that the effect is composed of. This intrinsic dependency upon the pattern or form exhibited in the effect as such is called the *formal cause*. When something is produced, when it has come into existence as something distinctly distinguishable from other factors surrounding it, whether as an individual in its own right or as a change within an existing individual (say, a rotten spot in the wood of a door frame, or a symptom of a malady in an organism), the effect as such exhibits a pattern or formal structure, an "architecture", as it were, according to which it holds together and functions as a distinct effect. When this pattern dissolves, for whatever reason and in whatever way, the effect ceases to be in its own right. The formal cause, thus, in one respect is always embodied in the effect, specifically, as constituting the being of the effect correlative with the material cause. In this respect the formal cause is unlike the final cause which has no internal correlate constituting the being of the effect, and hence can fail while the effect survives as a physical entity. But the formal cause is somewhat like the final cause in that, even though the embodiment of the formal cause is itself an intrinsic dependency, formal causality can also be exercised according to an extrinsic source, and this in two ways.

(1) Formal Causality as Exemplar   The first and obvious way in which a formal cause can be extrinsic to an effect, and the way which was principally considered in the history of the discussion of these questions, is again in the case of artifacts: the architect constructs a building out of materials and according to a plan which he has drawn up, and this plan is then embodied in the building, so that it becomes a "Mies van der Rohe building", for example, an instance and illustration of a definite architectural style and school; the artist creates a painting as an expression of something within the artist, or models a work, such as a statue or a portrait, on something external which the artist nonetheless wishes to represent. Even when the work is called "non-representative" and so strives to be a mere object with no significant power, as an expression it fails, in spite of itself, to be without significance. Extrinsic formal causality in this first sense came to be called *ideal* or *exemplary causality* among the Latins.

(2) Formal Causality as Specificative.   The second way in which a formal cause can be extrinsic to its effect is much more interesting, and actually much more important for science and philosophy, despite its comparative neglect in the history of these questions. As a matter of fact, historically speaking, it appears that, among the Latins, the variety of formal causality I am here trying to describe received attention thematically only in the context of epistemological questions (the term "epistemology", of course, is a much later coinage[6]), that is to say, in proximately semiotic context, where it received the name of *specifying* or *objective causality*. This is the "causality", that is to say, the dependency in being, that knowledge as such has upon the object known. The object *specifies* the knowledge as being of this rather than of that. "Object", in this sense, of course, means the *subject matter* or *content* of the knowledge: biology as distinct from psychology (or psychology as a subdivision of biology), physics as distinct from chemistry, history as distinct from political science, etc.

Extrinsic formal causality of this second type is far removed from considerations of art or artifact, even though it pertains to such considerations insofar as they involve questions of knowledge. Objective causality occurs in nature itself wherever there are instances of relationship— that is to say, it occurs everywhere in nature. The dinosaur, long dead, is present in the fossil bone as its extrinsic specifier, enabling the scientist—paleontologist, in this case—definitely to classify a bone as belonging to a brontosaurus rather than a pterodactyl, etc.

Objective causality occurs equally throughout culture, again wherever there is a question of relationships, which (again) is everywhere. The question of "style" is a matter of extrinsic formal causality in the objective sense; deconstruction is an exercise in tracing patterns of extrinsic formal cause relative to a text; detective work is a matter of determining the extrinsic formal patterns which clues provide for the detective

---

6   And I would note in this etymological context the remark of Sebeok (1991: 2): "In my view, the midmost target of semiotics is indeed, as Rey so persuasively argued [1984], *epistemology*, understood in the broad sense of the cognitive constitution of living entities, comprehending the physiological and psychological make-up of each in their interaction. In semiotics, we must in any case think of ourselves as both working within a tradition that changes over time and trying to grasp things as they 'really are'." Cf. note 42 of Ch. 4, p. 89 above.

(and which patterns, by including this or that sensible element, constitute a clue—a sign-vehicle—in the first place).

Such then, in outline, is the result of the historical analysis of causation up to the end of the Latin Age, effectively in the seventeenth century. In the world of ancient Greece, Aristotle introduced the notion of cause as dependency in being, and showed that this notion is basically[7] fourfold: efficient, final, material, and formal. In the Latin world of Medieval and, especially, Baroque and Renaissance times, the basic fourfold scheme was developed and refined by the demonstration that some causes are always extrinsic to the effect produced (efficient causes), others are always intrinsic to, in the sense of being constitutive of the being proper of, the effect (material causes), and yet other causes (final and formal causes) are sometimes extrinsic as well as always intrinsic to—in the sense of being embodied within (final cause) or of being constitutive of the being proper to (formal cause)—the effect.[8]

---

[7] ''Basically'', that is, there are further distinctions to be made within the fourfold scheme, as the Latins especially showed, but of the further distinctions all reduce to one of the four basic categories (Poinsot 1633: Phil. nat. 1. p. q. 10. art. 2, 200b38ff.).

[8] The classical analyses emphasized the extrinsicality of the final cause to the effect and the intrinsicality of the formal cause to the effect, because the formal cause together with the material cause constitutes the being of the effect as an entity in its own right, whereas the efficient cause and the final cause alike are extrinsic to that entitative reality, in the sense that the effect often remains when the productive cause ceases and remains when the final cause fails (the effect may fall short of the final state while still existing in its own right). Nonetheless, the final cause is intrinsic to a natural effect, in the case of organisms, as an embodied tendency, and, in the case of an artifact, is identical with the embodied form as that which makes the artifact suitable for this or that function, regardless of whether it is actually so used or not. Thus matter and form were considered *principles* as well as *causes* of natural things, whereas efficient and final factors were considered *causes* but not principles, because their absence left the entity in being as an effect. A principle of natural being, Poinsot writes (1633: 41a38–b11), ''conveys only whatever it may be that a thing essentially depends upon, whether in being or in becoming, as upon component or inchoative factors, from the fact that a principle and the principled thing are so related to one another that the thing principled is resolved into the principle. But a principle insofar as it is such is not resolved into something else, unless it too be something principled; and so, insofar as it is a principle, it is not from another. But an efficient cause [a cause of production] and whatever other extrinsic factor is not included

2. Cause in Modern Thought

In modern times, that is to say, in the traditions of science and philosophy as they developed in the national languages from the seventeenth century onwards, the discussion of the notion of cause is greatly simplified, not to say oversimplified.

To begin with, as far as the scientists were naively concerned, only efficient causality deserved the name "cause". But, at the same time, among the philosophers, even this notion of producing something was eviscerated by their postulate that the objects of experience, as known objects, are thoroughly constructs of the mind. Locke, who also coined the name "semiotics", helped to prepare the way for this evisceration of causality with his notion of ideas in the mind being the objects of direct experience. (Of course, in the realm of physical nature, efficient causes were not blocked from operating by the epistemological presuppositions of the modern philosophers; hence the regnant paradigm of "transient

in this definition of natural principles ... For extrinsic causes are not principles from which the very nature of things is established whether in becoming or in mature being, but a producing cause is called 'that by which a change is initiated', a final cause that on account of which it begins [i.e., the direction of the change]', an exemplar that in imitation of which a change comes about, but no extrinsic cause is said to be that out of which anything comes" ("solum importat ea, a quibus res essentialiter pendet, sive in facto esse sive in fieri, ut a componentibus vel inchoantibus, eo quod principium et principiatum ita se habent, quod principiatum resolvitur in principium. Principium autem in quantum tale non resolvitur in aliud, nisi etiam sit principiatum; et ita in quantum principium, non est ex alio. Causa autem efficiens et quaecumque alia extrinseca non includitur in definitione ista principiorum naturalium.... Nec enim causae extrinsecae sunt principia, ex quibus natura ipsa rerum constat sive in fieri sive in facto esse, sed efficiens dicitur 'id, a quo incipit motus', finis, propter quem incipit, exemplar, ad cuius imitationem fit, nulla vero causa extrinseca dicitur, ex quo aliquid fit").

The fact that the formal cause is always intrinsic to effects in a proper and direct way, while the final cause is not, is important for the case of extrinsic formal causality as *objective* (not as *exemplary*, however), because it ties intelligibility to the intrinsic constitution and being of an entity, whether the entity be natural or artifactual, material (a *forma naturalis*) or mental (a *species* or "intentional form"). As we will see, for this very reason semiotics cannot be confined to the order of culture alone, but, like semiosis itself, constitutes an interface between the two orders of nature and culture.

efficient causation'' could continue to be clung to, despite its theoretical antinomies as presumed to be actually known.) The definitive diminution of the idea of causality in modern philosophy did not occur, however, until David Hume systematized the consequences of Locke's and Descartes' common assumption that the mind's own ideas are the complete objects of direct experience and sensation (cf. Miller 1979). Here, not only was causality conceived exclusively in terms of efficient causality, but the notion of efficient causality itself was transformed from the idea of one being depending on another being in its production to the idea of one being accompanying or following upon another being in our experience—that is to say, to an association of ideas in the mind.

3. Cause in Semiosis

If, now, we return to our question, How are we to conceive of the sign as cause?, we see that, at least in the terms of previous analyses, we have a considerable number of choices to make before deciding if it may not be necessary to introduce new terms into the analysis.

To begin with, we can rule out as proper to the sign all those forms of causality which are intrinsic to an effect as an entity in its own right (material cause and intrinsic formal cause[9]), for the causality of the sign

---

9 ''Parts are said to cause a whole by a causality that is intrinsic and constituting of the whole itself, not by one that is extrinsically related to the whole, just as essential predicates are said to constitute what something is. But intrinsic causes are not distinguished from something caused entitatively, because they do not cause through an emission of some entity other than themselves but through a communication of themselves in the entity which they constitute, just as form informs matter by communicating itself thereto. And this is the formal effect of a form, namely, the passive communication of itself which is entitatively not distinguished from the form communicating itself, and so is a physical effect insofar as it is a physical communication of itself. *Or it can also be said* that in this causation of the whole there also occurs a physical and proper causation of the very parts among themselves. For matter and form are reciprocally causes [or causes each to the other] ... and are distinguished from one another, and out of this physical causation there results a whole physically indistinct from the very parts not as something immediately caused but as resulting out of that prior causation of the parts among themselves; and this suffices for preserving physical causation, to wit, that it occur mediately'' (Poinsot 1633: 107b35–108a15: ''Partes dicuntur causare totum causalitate intrinseca et constituente

produces *renvoi*, something beyond the entity serving as sign-vehicle. We can also rule out efficient cause, for efficient causality pertains, in semiotic terms, to the realm of brute secondness and dyadic interaction, and so is certainly and definitively not the causality proper to the sign as such. This leaves us with three candidates: association of ideas, extrinsic formal causality, and final causality.

a. Associative Drift

Certainly, in association of ideas, "one thing leads to another", "one thing makes us think of something else besides", as is required for a sign. Like semiosis, associationism knows no bounds.

Without question, association is a factor in semiosis. But can the two be identified? As an interpretive habit, Eco has recently pointed out (1990: 24), associationism—which Eco calls "Hermetic drift"—"is based on the principles of universal analogy and sympathy":

The basic principle is not only that the similar can be known through the similar but also that from similarity to similarity everything can be connected with everything else, so that everything can be in turn either the expression or the content of any other thing.

Such a process, Eco suggests (ibid.: 29–30), "could be defined as an instance of connotative neoplasm", inasmuch as "in cases of neoplastic growth ... no contextual stricture holds any longer". Eco goes on to

---

ipsum totum, non extrinsece se habente, sicut etiam praedicata essentialia dicuntur constituere quidditatem. Causae autem intrinsecae non distinguuntur a causato entitative, quia non causant per emissionem alterius entitatis a se, sed per communicationem sui in entitate, quam constituunt, sicut forma materiam informat communicando se illi. Et iste est effectus formalis formae, communicatio sui passiva, quae entitative non distinguitur a forma se communicante, et sic est effectus realis, quatenus est realis communicatio sui. *Vel etiam dicitur*, quod in ista causatione totius etiam intercedit realis et propria causatio ipsarum partium inter se. Materia enim et forma ad invicem sunt causae ... et distinguuntur inter se, et ex ista causatione reali resultat totum indistinctum realiter ab ipsis partibus, non tamquam immediate causatum, sed ut ex illa priori causatione partium inter se resultans; et hoc sufficit ad salvandam causationem realem, scilicet mediate").

discuss also Derridean or deconstructive drift, in which likewise we confront a process which knows no limits outside itself.

But this absence of external check is precisely why associationism or "drift", in whatever form, cannot by itself constitute the process of semiosis. Proceeding toward the infinite is not the only characteristic of semiosis, and not the defining one.[10] What defines semiosis is not *how far* it proceeds in any given case or *how far* it proceeds from the point of view of the individual and the community of inquirers, but *how* it proceeds in each case. Assuming the pragmatic maxim that a conception is defined accurately by all the conceivable experimental phenomena which it implies, Eco observes (ibid.: 40) that, in each case, "the process of interpretation must stop—at least for some time—outside language—at least in the sense in which not every practical effect is a semiosic one".[11] Similarly (ibid.: 38), "it is irrefutable that in the act of indication (when one says *this* and points his fingers toward a given object of the world), indices are in some way linked to an item of the extralinguistic or extrasemiotic world." Semiosis is not a self-contained process. On the contrary, it is a process wherein and whereby nature and culture compenetrate within experience, and understanding progresses, not simply grows. Semiosis can involve cancerous mental processes and can degenerate into cancerous forms, but it is not itself a cancer but pro-

---

10 "In structuralistic terms," says Eco (1990: 28), "one could say that for Peirce semiosis is potentially unlimited from the point of view of the system but is not unlimited from the point of view of the process. In the course of a semiosic process we want to know only what is relevant according to a given *universe of discourse*."

Eco is speaking of a robust semiosis, to be sure, but I am not sure that associative drifts or even leaps do not have a subsidiary role in the process. To reduce semiosis to such associations, however, is quite another thing, as Eco has well shown with his distinction of semiosis as such from the various forms of cancerous drift that have tried to claim the name for their own vagary.

11 Eco continues (1990: 40): "It is true that even the practical effect must then be spelled out by and through language, and that the very agreement among the members of the community cannot but take the form of a new chain of signs. Nevertheless, the agreement concerns something—be it a practical effect or the possibility of a practical effect—that is produced outside semiosis."

gress in time. In semiosis,[12] a sign brings something not semiotic into the semiotic realm: it makes of a thing an object signified, a significate, an element reticulated in the net of experience, leading in turn to further signifieds, many of which are often new.

Eco (1990: 28) considers it a fundamental principle in Peirce's semiotics that "A sign is something by knowing which we know something more" (Peirce 1904: 8.332). According to Poinsot (1632a: 117/12–17), this is a fundamental principle of semiosis itself:

Indeed the manifestative element *of a sign* is found both with an order to another [as in the case of associationism or "drift"] ... and with a dependence on that other to which it is ordered, because a sign is always less than what it signifies and is dependent thereon as on a measure.

Thus Eco points to a fundamental difference between a process in which, by the knowing of one thing, we merely know something *else*, and a process in which, by the knowing of one thing, we are led thereby to know

---

12 "If perception is—as it is for Peirce—semiosis, then even at the original moment of our perceptive acquaintance with the external world the external world becomes understandable to us only under the form of an Immediate Object. For Peirce, when the sign is produced the Dynamic Object is no more *there* (and before the sign was produced it was not an object at all [it was, I should say, a bare physical entity or element in the environment, *regardless* of whether it is objectified, and, therefore, *even if* it is objectified; therefore too it cannot be said to be *not an object at all*—unless, of course, as such interpreters as Marmo might hold, it involved no thirdness, no cognizability, no relation, even prospectively, to mind and being apprehended]). What is present to our mind and to the semiosic discourse is only the Immediate Object to be interpreted by other signs. But the presence of the representamen as well as the presence (in the mind or elsewhere) of the Immediate Object means that in some way the Dynamic Object, which is not there, *was* somewhere. Being not present, or not-being-there, the object of an act of interpretation *has been*" (Eco 1990: 39)—and, I would add, might still be (there is not only the case of light from long vanished stars, dynamic objects which *once were*; there is also the case of light from stars still burning, dynamic objects which *now are*). I would also add that Eco's analysis of perception needs to be refined by the analysis of the sensory element within perception as such (cf. Deely 1994: Gloss 19). Such a refinement would reveal that the dynamic object not only was somewhere but, in fragmented and partial modes, *is* present within the immediate object as providing a common measure for disagreements about what is perceived.

something *more*. In other words, semiosis exhibits the central notion of the more classical and comprehensive analyses of causality, that of a *dependency in being* of sign upon signified, rather than a mere reversibility of association between the two. The process of being led to something more is irreducibly triadic; the process of being led to something other may or may not be. Insofar as it happens to be triadic, association provides at best an anemic form of semiosis. In itself, semiosis is something more than association of ideas, and indeed is a process whereby the mind, through and in its own products, is involved with something more than itself and its products. Understanding is that form of semiosis whereby the world in its totality gets to know something of itself, not only as, but as including, mind. Thus Peirce remarks (c.1909: 6.324) that thought "needs the existential facts, but regulates them. It is only imitation-thought"—i.e., a mental process, such as drift, which does not imply and does not regulate brute fact—"to which the adjective 'mere' is appropriate."

We are left then with two further possibilities for conceiving the causality proper to the sign, final causality or some variety of extrinsic formal causality.

b. Final Causality

The fact that the action of signs reveals laws in nature and works indirectly in the realm of physical change (efficient causality or "brute force") led Peirce at various points to identify the causality proper to signs with what we have identified above as intrinsic final causality (see Ransdell 1977). We can say at once that, if this be the case, then biology (the life-science) and semiotics (the sign-science) are indeed coextensive. On such an assumption, as Peirce put it (c.1909: 6.322), "the problem of how genuine triadic relationships first arose in the world" is an improved formulation of "the problem of how life first came about". A similar view is echoed today in the work of Thomas A. Sebeok. Regarding the genetic code as "the most fundamental of all semiotic networks", Sebeok (1968: 69) is prompted to suggest that "a full understanding of the dynamics of semiosis" may, "in the last analysis, turn out to be no less than the definition of life."

I have already given elsewhere detailed criticisms of this view (1978,

1982, 1990: esp. 86n32), and have not space to repeat them here. Suffice it to say that the view that biology and semiotics are co-extensive has the unfortunate result of omitting the object of physics from the semiosic process—omitting, that is to say, the realm of inanimate or inorganic matter.

Of course, one may remedy the situation by appealing to the hypothesis of panpsychism, as Peirce was sometimes inclined to do. And indeed, the daring of such a speculation would not daunt Sebeok, we may be sure. Nonetheless, even Peirce found the hypothesis a stretch, suggesting (c.1909: 6.322) a distinction between "metaphysical life" and "physiological life" to cover it. Yet, where it is a question of material bodies—as it always is with the universe of what appears in our experience to be "inorganic"—it is not easy to see what life other than "physiological life" would be. Nor does such a hypothesis appear convincing to the majority of observers, a statistical fact which does not prove it wrong, to be sure, but which justifies our assigning to the panpsychist hypothesis a degree of dubitability higher than would warrant its adoption.

The desire to include inanimate nature in the semiotic web, in short, is hardly sufficient motive to adopt the hypothesis of panpsychism. Yet it is clear that, within our experience, the world of stones and stars exists precisely as a constitutive part of the semiotic web which our experience is; however, that world may further or previously exist as well. Hence no notion of the action proper to signs which leaves the inorganic realm out of the process can be acceptable. In this sense, if we had no choice but to identify the action proper to signs with intrinsic final causality,[13] we would *eo ipso* be warranted in holding for panpsychism as well. But we do have a choice.

---

[13] Although there is also the question of extrinsic final causality, it seems to me so clear that extrinsic final causality cannot explain semiosis that the point is worth no more discussion than a passing note. For extrinsic final causality is, in every case, a matter of deliberate intention on the artificer's part, and no one can seriously maintain that the action of signs is restricted to the realm of deliberately uttered expressions. Of course, in a glottocentric semiotics, something approaching this absurdity is maintained; but that is another question.

c. Specificative Causality

In fact, the type of causality which best explains the action of signs is not final causality, but extrinsic formal causality of the specificative or "objective" type.[14] The terminology here, as far as I know, does not appear as such in the Peircean lexicon, though it has an approximating counterpart in the Peircean notion of "ideal" causality.[15] Formal causality in the specificative sense best explains the action of signs from every point of view. This causality can be exercised through the intrinsic constitution of the sign-vehicle (in the case of a natural sign) or not (in the case of an arbitrary sign), as the situation calls for. It is more general than the final causality typical of vital powers, inasmuch as it specifies equally both vital activity and the chance interactions of brute secondness at the level of inorganic nature. This is the causality that enables the sign to achieve its distinctive function of making present what the sign-vehicle itself is not, regardless of whether the object signified enjoys a physical existence apart from the signification. Only extrinsic specificative formal causality is equally suited to the grounding of sign-behavior in chance occurrences (as when the implosion of a star leads to the discovery of a new law of physics, or when accidental scratches become the clue leading to the apprehension of the criminal) and planned happenings.

14 Extrinsic formal causality of the exemplary type will not do to explain the action of signs, for semiosis is clearly not a *model* according to which interpretation occurs, but rather the very *process itself of interpretation* is a semiosic act.

At the same time, when speaking of specificative extrinsic formal causality as "objective", even though the term "objective" was applied to this variety of formal causality by the Latins themselves, I place it here in quotation marks to flag the fact that the sense of objective in this context is, more-or-less, the opposite of the sense the term has come to exercise in common speech today. See the analysis of objectivity in Deely 1990: 54ff. and *passim*; and especially in Deely 1994.

15 The choice of terminology here is unfortunate, for, as we have seen, unbeknownst to Peirce, the term "ideal causality" had already been applied by the Latins to the other great branch of extrinsic formal causality, exemplary causation, whereas "ideal causality" in Peirce's sense pertains rather to specificatory, or "objective", extrinsic formal causation, as distinguished from intrinsic final causality: see Deely 1985: 493–498. More detailed comparison on these points, along with a discussion of the ethical issues Peirce envisaged to be involved in such terminological questions, can be found in Deely 1994.

Once it is understood that the action proper to signs is explained by specificative causality, the central question for understanding the scope of semiosis becomes: "What is the essential difference between a sign that is communicated to a mind, and one that is not so communicated?" (Peirce 1904: 8.332)[16] On the one side of this line is the thirdness of experience, on the other side the thirdness of the laws of nature. How does semiosis link the two? The answer to this question is through the interpretant, which need not be anything mental, but must in every case provide the ground for objectivity. Hence Peirce elaborates on the central question thus (1904: 8.332):

If the question were simply what we *do* mean by a sign, it might soon be resolved. But that is not the point. We are in the situation of a zoölogist who wants to know what ought to be the meaning of "fish" in order to make fishes one of the great classes of vertebrates. It appears to me that the essential function of a sign is to render inefficient relations efficient,—not to set them into action, but to establish a habit or general rule whereby they will act on occasion ... A sign therefore is an object which is in relation to its object on the one hand and to an interpretant on the other, in such a way as to bring the interpretant into a relation to the object, corresponding to its own relation to the object.

To see how this is so, we need only consider the triadicity of semiosis as schematized in the semiotic triangle, first in abstract form, and then twice concretized, once where the interpretant is a concept or idea, i.e., "something mental", and once where the interpretant is itself a physical condition or state. We begin with the abstract schema (Figure 5, page 172). In this triangle, the sign will be understood to be any element or factor of experience ("A") so *determined by* an experienced object ("B") that, in *determining another* factor experienced ("C"), that other factor is mediately determined by the first object. Therefore C, in being immediately determined by A, is at the same time mediately determined by B. To use Peirce's own description of the abstract situation (1901: 2.303): A sign is "anything which determines something else (its

---

16 Several interesting versions of this question occur in Poinsot, such as: is the statue of a dead emperor still a sign of the emperor?; are the letters in a closed book still signs?; etc. See Poinsot 1632a, *passim*.

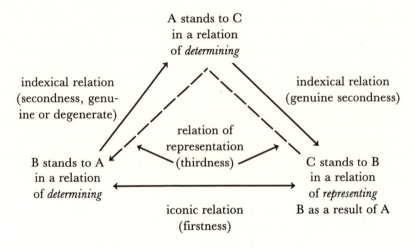

Figure 5. *Abstract form of the semiotic triangle*

interpretant) to refer to an object to which itself refers (its *object*) in the same way, the interpretant becoming in turn a sign, and so on *ad infinitum*.'' In the terms of our schema, the interpretant C is passive to the sign A in just the way that A is passive to the object B; but, precisely by reason of being passive in this way, C is virtually active respecting both A and B as a representation or representative element.

Now let A be the bone of a dinosaur uncovered in what has become a garden, and let B be the dinosaur long dead. C in this case would not be the effect of the bone on a gardener who knew nothing of paleontology, for that would not actualize the representative dimension of the bone to stand for the dinosaur it once helped structure. The effect of the bone on the ignorant gardener, in other words, would not make of this past relation a sign. Nonetheless, the element representative in this respect is there, identical with the bone as prospective representamen,[17] but needing in the present to be actualized. It is there, of a piece with the bone in physical being, but virtually distinct therefrom.

Suppose that a paleontologist happens just now to visit the gardener, and spies the recently dug up bone lying with some rubbish (which

---

17 Peirce's term for the element or factor of transcendental relativity in the sign, the sign-vehicle as founding or able to found a sign-relation as such.

rubbish, of course, has its own stories to tell to some other eyes). Recognizing the bone for what it is, the bone has a remarkable perceptual effect on the paleontologist. The virtual element whereby the bone is of a dinosaur now comes actually to represent the dinosaur. Hence Poinsot's formula (1632a: 126/3–5), mentioned above: "It suffices to be a sign virtually in order to signify in act".

Our schema is now concretized in a form where the interpretant is a mental condition or state (Figure 6):

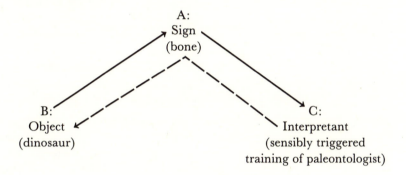

Figure 6. *First concretion of the semiotic triangle*

The relation of the bone to the dinosaur which once obtained in nature and was exercised through the bone can now be exercised in thought through the bone as understood and seen for what it is, to wit, a bone that once *belonged to* and *made part of* a living dinosaur. The same relation once existing only in nature now comes to exist (or re-exist) only in thought.

Finally, let us consider the semiotic triangle concretized a second way, where B is the dinosaur, A the bone, and C a geological formation in which the bone has been fossilized, thus (Figure 7, page 174).

In this case the interpretant is a physical rather than a psychical structure but one that has been so determined by A as to represent through A also B. In this way the interaction is a virtual semiosis, that is, a series of interactions at the level of secondness that, at the same time, provides an actual pathway through time whereby it is possible that what happened long ago might be partially understood. The present, indeed, from such a standpoint, might be regarded as a mosaic of traces from the past,

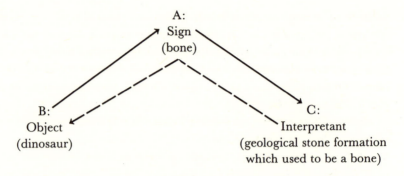

Figure 7. *Second concretion of the semiotic triangle.*

each providing, for a sufficiently knowledgeable present observer, the starting point of a journey into what used to be. Notice that the possibility in question need not be actualized in order for it to be virtually present. Nor is it merely "possible" in some abstract, conceptual sense. Our example of an interpretant for what was once purely and simply a bone, for example, exists in a geological formation. No longer a bone pure and simple, it is there still a bone virtually, that is, as a representamen of something that once was. And this something that once was, in turn, having been the bone of a dinosaur, can in its turn represent something else that once was, the dinosaur itself, and so on, in a chain of signs and interpretants becoming signs *ad infinitum*. The bone (A), or the rock formation that used to be a bone (C), is "not a sign formally but virtually and fundamentally", as Poinsot puts it (1632a: 126/12–18):

For since the rationale of moving or stimulating the mind remains, which comes about through the sign insofar as it is something representative even if the relation of substitution for the signified does not remain, the sign is able to exercise the functions of substituting without the relation.

The relation of the bone to the dinosaur was exercised through the structure of the bone as part of the dinosaur. That basis of the relation remains in the physical structure of the bone, and provides a ground capable of guiding some present or future observer, such as our paleontologist, in the direction of rightly understanding the function and place the bone once actually occupied. Inasmuch as that guiding basis is inscribed in the bone's very structure as a physical entity, the capacity of representing and standing-for the dinosaur that once was transfers to any physical structure that receives from the bone an impression of the bone's own structure, be that receiving structure the retina of the paleontologist connected with her appropriately trained nervous system or the fossilizing geological formation.

We see, thus, at once, three decisive points: (1) how the interpretant is fundamental to the semiosis; (2) that the interpretant need not be a psychological state or idea; and (3) why the interpretant is itself a sign or link in the chain of "semiosis toward the infinite" or "unlimited semiosis".

Since it is through the sign-vehicle as fundament (or intermediate term) of the sign-relation that the sign is a representamen, and it is through this being as representamen that the sign is involved in the brute force interactions of secondness and physical existence, it follows that the virtuality of signs is present and operative throughout the realm of nature, and not just among cognitive organisms where signs exist and function in their proper being actually as well.[18]

---

18 Poinsot extends extrinsic formal causality, that is, the objective causality of semiosis, from specification of vital powers to categorial or physical relations as such, in the following manner (*Artis Logicae Secunda Pars*, Q. 17, "De Praedicamento Relationis", Art. 6, "Unde Sumatur Distinctio Specifica et Numerica Relationis", 602b33–603a14; = *Treatise on Signs*, Appendix C, "On the Source of Specific and Individual Identity of Relations", 382/4–46): "Distinction has to be made between the terminus understood most formally in the rationale of an opposed terminus, and the terminus understood fundamentally on the side of the subjective being founding this rationale of terminating. In the former way a terminus concurs in a specification purely terminatively, but not by causing that specification, because so considered it is a pure terminus and simultaneous by nature and in cognition with the relation; therefore as such it is not a specifying cause, because a cause is not naturally simultaneous with but prior to its effect. If it is considered in the latter way, the terminus stands as an extrinsic formal cause and specifies in the manner of an object, and in this way a single specifying rationale of the relation arises from the foundation and terminus together, inasmuch as the foundation contains the terminus within itself by a proportion and power; for it is not relative to a given terminus unless it is a specific fundament, and conversely. In this way, to the extent that they are mutually proportioned, terminus and foundation together bring about a single ra-

Moreover, this virtual semiosis prior to any cognitive life is not restricted to passive reflections in present being of past interactions, such as those we have considered so far. Virtual semiosis is also at work in the ways that present interactions anticipate future conditions radically different from what presently obtains. In other words, present effects are virtual signs prospectively as well as retrospectively. They portend, and do so in two ways. First of all, in any given interaction of bodies, over and above the resultant relations of cause and effect (acting and being acted upon), there is the fact that each of the bodies involved interprets and twists the action according to its own intrinsic nature. In this way, as Powell puts it (1986: 300), "the extrinsic specification of causal relations always reveals indirectly the intrinsic species of the bodies which are their extrinsic specifying causes". For example, if I strike an armored vehicle, a porcelain bowl, or the trunk of a tree with a hammer, the relation of agent to patient is in all three cases the same, in that, as Powell well notes (ibid.), "spatio-temporal/real causal relational systems do not have determinate intrinsic species as bodies do". However, owing to the intrinsically diverse properties of steel, porcelain, and wood pulp, the effect will be likewise diversified in each case.

Thus, dyadic interactions, as extrinsically specified by the bodies involved at the level of secondness, also project a virtual level of thirdness that anticipates changes in future states respecting the interactions oc-

tionale specifying a relation which postulates both a specific foundation and a specific terminus corresponding thereto.

"From these remarks one can further gather what a formal terminus is in the rationale of something specifying. For although specifically different relations can be anchored to the materially same terminus, yet they cannot be anchored to the *formally* same terminus. But the formal specifying rationale in a terminus is understood in accordance with a correspondence and adequate proportion to its fundament ... Wherefore, as regards the specifying of any relation, in just the way that the fundament is understood under the final rationale of the grounding of the relation, so the terminus of the relation is understood under the proportion and correspondence of the terminating." (The original Latin text can be found in the Appendix of Longer Citations, pp. 258–259 below.)

See further in Index 4 to the *Treatise* (the Index Rerum/Index of Terms and Propositions) the entries under "Object", pp. 552–554, beginning with no. 4, referring the whole text to extrinsic formal causality of the specificative type. Also see the entries for "Foundation", p. 539.

curring here and now. And the measure of these interactions occurs through precisely the same type of causality operative in the sign, whereby semiosis achieves indifference to the being and non-being, presently considered, of what is signified.

Here, however, in the direction of future states, the virtuality of the semiosis is more complicated. The reason is that the direct deflection of the results of the interactions itself can lead to changes in the immediate constitution of what does the interacting—as, for example, when one of the interactants is destroyed by the interaction, or when the interaction triggers a new phase in the development of one of the interactants, or when a specifically new type of being (such as the formation of a new atomic element) results from the interaction. Here, Peirce's idea of scientific laws existing as habits in nature as a whole would seem to find, as it were, a semiotic grounding. For, over and above the individual interactions of bodies, there is a macroformation of the universe that takes place, over-all, directionally, toward the establishment of conditions under which virtual semioses can give place to actual ones. Physiosemiosis, let us say, moves in the direction of biosemiosis.

Out of cosmic dust, stellar systems form through subatomic, atomic, and molecular interactions. At various stages of the process, even as now on earth we can in laboratories bring into being a few elements not existent in nature itself, new elements not previously given in nature precipitate from the natural interactions. These new elements, in turn, prove essential to the formation in planetary systems of the conditions under which living beings become possible, and these beings, in turn, further modify the planetary conditions so that successive generations of living beings are incompatible with the original conditions of life. Oxygen, essential for life on this planet now, for example, was originally introduced as a waste product of living beings who neither needed nor could survive within a heavily oxygenated atmosphere.

Through this entire series of intersecting and often conflicting processes resulting in cosmic evolution over-all, the specificity and identity of any given process at each step is guaranteed not by individual bodies but by systems of commonly specified real relations between bodies, that is, by specifically identifiable existentially determined systems of ontological relations. Within these systems, individual bodies *further* determine their immediate interactions according to their own intrinsic natures. In the case of organisms, this determination in turn depends on a whole sub-system of interactions indisputably semiotic in nature, as Sebeok has pointed out (1977, 1988, 1989). The relational systems as a whole and the interactions within them form throughout a single web of at least virtual semiosis, governed at each point by the objective causality of the sign virtually at work throughout. This causality corresponds to the plan in von Uexküll's distinction (1934: 42–46) between goal and plan in nature, and removes the mist in Peirce's broadest conception of semiosis, as expressed in the following passage (c.1907: 205–206):

The action of a sign generally takes place between two parties, the *utterer* and the *interpreter*. They need not be persons; for a chameleon and many kinds of insects and even plants make their living by uttering signs, and lying signs, at that. Who is the utterer of signs of the weather ... ? However, every sign certainly conveys something of the general nature of thought, if not from a mind, yet from some repository of ideas, or significant forms, and if not to a person, yet to something capable of somehow "catching on" ... that is, of receiving not merely a physical, nor even merely a psychical dose of energy, but a significant meaning. In that modified, and as yet very misty, sense, then, we may continue to use the italicized words.

The modified sense ceases to be misty once it is understood that the specification of existential relations in the universe at large already puts into play the causality upon which the action of signs depends. Already at the level of their fundaments, signs are virtually present and operative in the dyadic interactions of brute force, weaving together in a single fabric of virtual relations the future and the past of such interactions.

This is semiosis, but semiosis of a specific kind. I have called it *physiosemiosis*, so as to bring out by the very name the fact that there is a question here of a process as broad as physical nature itself. For this process is at work in all parts of the physical universe as the foundation of those higher, more distinctive levels of the same process that come into existence as the conditions of physical being themselves make possible the successively higher levels, first of life, and then of cognitive life.

C. Conclusions

Illusion, deception, and the possibilities for alternative interpretation of texts and even perceptions (which are a kind of text: see Deely 1990,

1994) are among the phenomena which become foreground in a dramatic way once the notion of reality is given its primary sense as experience and this primary sense is allowed to displace as central the derivative notion of reality (which ruled the early moderns no less than the ancients) as what exists independently of human thought and feeling. Hence it is not surprising that the most notorious advocates of postmodernism tend to be thinkers stressing the irrational and modes of deconstructing objects. But this emphasis should not blind us to the fact that experience provides us as well with ample justification and room for a notion of mind-independent being reached and analyzed precisely from within experience itself: some objects, after all, we experience as also things. Postmodern philosophy is bound to have its fads, and it is to be expected that attention should focus for awhile, in a free play of objective causality (cf. Powell 1983–1991), especially on what previous paradigms neglected, explained away, and generally marginalized. But, in the end, philosophy's new age has as much room for science as for deconstruction (the witness of Peirce alone shows this), and for both because of the action and nature of signs. Postmodern philosophy will have to learn how to be anthropocentric inasmuch as it is grounded throughout in experience without being anthropomorphic and falling into the ancient sophism of making itself the measure of all things.

The place of language in all this is necessarily central, for it is language that structures consciousness insofar as it is species-specifically human and publicly communicable in adjudicable terms. But postmodern thought will have to overcome the vestiges of modern idealism so clearly manifested in much of structuralism and in all those many versions characterized scathingly and unforgettably by Paul Bouissac as "glottocentric". Nothing prevents avatars of late modern idealism from appearing in a postmodern disguise.

But language of its very nature has always been central to philosophy. What semiotics makes unmistakable in its foundational scheme is that linguistic semiosis is not a free-standing or isolated action of signs but one that draws upon and relies throughout on innumerable other forms of semiosis which are not species-specifically human to such an extent that language itself as species-specifically human would not be possible apart from those other forms including, ultimately, physiosemiosis. The age of philosophy as "linguistic analysis", i.e., the period during which it was credible to claim that language itself is the whole of the proper subject matter of philosophy, is as definitively past as is methodic doubt as a credible method for establishing the foundations of human knowledge and the external reality of nature. The age of idealism, which coincided with the period of classical modern philosophy in all its direct issuances, is behind us, save only for the avatars.

Mayhap the plainest sign of the centrality of language to philosophy throughout its development so far is the fact, insufficiently noted and analyzed, that previous philosophical epochs in Western thought corresponded with major linguistic shifts in the natural languages—first from Greek to Latin, then from Latin to the modern national languages. Postmodern thought, by contrast, corresponds rather with the establishment of an intellectual paradigm based not on the national languages but on an awareness of the semiotic mechanisms and nature of language itself as the principal vehicle of human understanding. Postmodern thought, by consequence, is centered more on the transcendence of the divisions of natural language which define and divide East from West than it is on Western culture as Western. By moving thought to such a vantage, postmodernism, contrary to the appearances created by some of its earliest proponents concentrating on its deconstructive opportunities exclusively, opens the possibility, at least in principle, of an era of a global perspective within the arts and sciences, explicitly achievable as such within philosophy. New parochialisms are but a temporary phase, and, at bottom, an aberration of the postmodern impulse to achieve a *prise de conscience* capable of beginning a new epoch of development in the history of ideas.

This new era does not find its limits in the physical universe itself taken as the measure of reality insofar as it can be assigned an existence independent of our thought, nor does it find its limits in the realm of thought considered as arising from the subjectivity of the knower and as intervening between the knower and things through the creation of an impenetrable veil of phenomena. The new era finds its limits only in semiosis itself which is coextensive both with thought and with the material universe not as two realms but as the one reality of experience wherein the threads of what is mind-dependent and mind-independent are made to weave a common fabric of objectivity.

It is true, of course, that, so far as we can judge, once all of physiosemiosis and even biosemiosis transpired without signs communicated to a finite mind. But our basis for thinking this has been established within present experience as providing signs of the past, and those signs also tell us that orientation to the future is part of the nature of semiosis as a process at any level. This orientation to the future does not necessitate the postulation of panpsychism, for, as we have seen, a distinction between a virtual semiosis, which depends on chance events for achieving its future orientation, and the semiosis of living matter, which essentially turns chance events toward the future, is sufficient to maintain this orientation, and, at the same time, suggests the boundary line between physiosemiosis (to the understanding of which physics and chemistry contribute) and biosemiosis (study of which produces the semiotics of living matter in general). Within biosemiosis, the emergence of cognitive beings dramatically quickened the pace of evolutionary development, foregrounding its semiotic character, and assimilating to itself even those antecedent levels which did not require cognition (but which of course can become objectified in cognition). Not only can anything fully signify through cognition, but also phenomena not in themselves actually semiotic are nonetheless entangled in semiosic virtualities.

Such is the situation that has to be accounted for. It plainly exhausts the possibilities for understanding possible within the confines of the modern paradigm. Hence a postmodern era becomes inevitable, forced upon us by the very growth of experience in modern times, and the requirements in philosophy for postmodernism are clear: we have to take account not only of the fact that all things become semiotic once an awareness of them dawns, but also of the fact that all things in the process of becoming objectified work as if *to have a say* in the semioticity of their objectification. Things of physical nature not only respond to the web they are caught in, they also make the web respond to what it has caught (this is the ultimate meaning of the transcendental relative).

Semiosis is above all an *assimilative* interactive process, especially as manifested biosemiotically, but not only there. Semiosis is the process whereby phenomena originating anywhere in the universe signify virtually in their present being also their past and their future and begin the further process of *realizing* these virtualities—especially when life intervenes and, within life, when cognition supervenes. The process does not begin with the advent of cognitive organisms, but merely enters a further phase, a new magnitude of thirdness. At this level, the level of anthroposemiosis, semiosis finally reveals itself for what it has been all along, a task that can be accomplished only in community, and over the indefinitely long run. Furthermore, in the case of anthroposemiosis, the preservation and generation of culture is future-oriented *beyond* mere biological propagation, a point that completes the grand view of a progression through past-future relations from physiosemiosis to anthroposemiosis.

Life is more than semiosis, and, conversely, semiosis is more than life. But of the two, semiosis is the more general process, and broader overall. Moreover, when it comes to living beings, the causality proper to signs is so completely interwoven with the fabric of interactions whereby life develops, so delicately maintained in the specification of the other channels of causality that structure that interaction, that to separate it in analysis from vital activity is already an achievement of intellectual abstraction in the scientific sense.

Looking to the modern era in its mainstream development, postmodern philosophy represents a break and a rejection. But if we look rather to early modern philosophy as regards its late Latin matrix, we see that the classical modern development was in many respects an impoverishment of speculative possibilities historically achieved, and that postmodernism represents the possibility of a retrieval of philosophy's historical continuity brought to a new level, and better suited for the long run.

7

The Grand Vision

A. The Originality of Peirce regarding Semiotic

As Descartes has come to be regarded as the father of modern philosophy in general and rationalism in particular, and as Locke is regarded as the father of empiricism in modern philosophy, so Peirce has justly come to be regarded as the father of contemporary semiotics. There is, however, this difference, and an important one it is: in the case of semiotics, Peirce's position was made possible by the accident of history whereby the highest developments of Latin thought after Ockham (partly owing to their having taken place in Iberia, partly owing to the very temper of modern thought as anti-historical, a temper to which Descartes mightily contributed) fell into oblivion, and the Iberian influence on the university life of Europe and the English-speaking parts of the New World, except as filtered through Suárez, became lost to modern times (see Beuchot 1980, Deely 1994).

As interest in semiotic has grown, motivating research into the ideas and figures prominently associated with its inception and development, the early notion, popularized by Morris and promulgated by Sebeok as late as 1974 (p. 220) that Peirce "was heir to the entire tradition of philosophical analysis of signs", has proven to be false in crucial particulars. For we now see enough to be able to say that, had the trajectory of semiotic development in Iberia defined by the work of Soto, Araújo, and Poinsot influenced the work of the French, English, and German founders of classical modern philosophy, Peirce would not have had to play the role of a backwoodsman clearing the way for the doctrine of signs; on the contemporary scene he would be not the father of semiotic tradition but one of its late systematizers.

In a way, the historical accidents which have created this anomalous situation respecting Peirce's place in the development of the consciousness of the requirements of a doctrine of signs are a testimony to the difficulty and exceptionally demanding circumstances attendant on the *prise de conscience* which places the sign at the center of the notion of experience and (hence) at the foundation of philosophy itself insofar as it is to be based on experience (which is to say, throughout). For if we look to the Iberian context within which the systematic requirements for a comprehensive *doctrina signorum* were first gestated, we find that the central figure, John Poinsot, had very much the omnivorous attitude to the work of his predecessors that Peirce himself exhibited in breaking with the typical modern attitude that the achievements of the past can be eschewed in the doing of philosophy today.

We perhaps need not go so far as went that devoted student of Peirce's thought, Walker Percy, when he wrote to me, in a letter of 27 October 1986, speaking about John Poinsot, whose *Tractatus de Signis* of 1632 had been published in a modern critical bilingual edition by the University of California Press in 1985, that "I have no doubt that a few years from now John will be recognized as one of the major founders, if not the founder, of modern semiotic." Yet even without going that far, as we saw above (p. 106), it is of considerable interest that Max H. Fisch, the Dean of Peirce scholarship, in his review (1986: 180), characterized Poinsot's *Tractatus* as, "within its limits"—the limits of a foundational inquiry (as distinct from an inquiry exploring also the superstructures of semiosis across the disciplines, such as Peirce undertook)—"the most *systematic* treatise on signs that has ever been written". For Poinsot had the advantage of maturing in an atmosphere which reverenced rather than contemned philosophical tradition. He was, as a consequence, truly "heir to the entire tradition of philosophical analysis of signs" as of the time of his writing. What he published in 1632, then, may well have been, as he himself seems to have thought (Deely 1985, 1988), the first systematic treatise establishing a unified object of semiotic inquiry by the identification of the sign as consisting essentially in ontological relation beyond all the further differences in types and variety of signs, such as natural, conventional, etc.

Hence it is doubly interesting to note that the contemporary founding of semiotic, which does trace principally to Peirce, traces to a man who, as a philosopher, stood out sharply from the crowd of moderns and contemporaries by his great respect for, and the depth of his involvement in, the writings of earlier philosophers from both ancient Greek and Medieval, Baroque, and Renaissance Latin times. For example, though he was ignorant of Poinsot's writing, Peirce at least knew the work of Poinsot's principal teachers in semiotic matters, the Conimbricenses, a group which had failed precisely where Poinsot subsequently succeeded, namely, in determining a *formalis ratio signi* which could be verified in all signs, natural and conventional alike (see Doyle 1984).

In both cases, then, in the historically first laying of semiotic's systematic foundations in Poinsot's work, and in the contemporary revival and full-scale development of semiotic after Peirce, we find a man who combined unparalleled historical learning with the highest philosophical capacity. From their different backgrounds and paths, moreover, the two arrive at remarkably convergent conclusions, as can be seen in the "Excursus on Peirce and Poinsot" in my edition of Poinsot's *Tractatus* (Deely 1985: 492–498,).

This unusual combination of philosophical ability and historical learning, I would suggest, is not just coincidental. There is, without a doubt, something exceptionally difficult about semiotics, something that places historicity at the very center of human thought rather than, as the modern philosophers all but unanimously supposed, at the margins of what is understood. That the doctrine of signs has begun to mature so lately in philosophical tradition, after its somewhat abortive earlier florescence in the university world of sixteenth and seventeenth century Iberia, is, I would suggest, a fact inherently related to the subtlety and complexity of its foundational issues with the demands they make on both learning and ingenuity, for reasons intrinsic to the nature of semiotic consciousness (see Deely 1990; Williams and Pencak 1991; Pencak 1993).

1. Shifting the focus from being to action

While the historical situation of semiotics is thus considerably more complicated and interesting than the early enthusiasms of Peirce scholarship allowed, at the same time, Peirce's originality in the field has been established at a deeper and more fundamental level than mere breadth of learning could provide. For while research into the historical development of semiotic consciousness reveals that Peirce was anything but the first pioneer to clear and open up "the doctrine of the essential nature and fundamental varieties of possible semiosis", he was indeed the first clearly to perceive that the proper subject matter for such inquiry is not so much the being of signs as it is the action such being gives rise to and depends upon for its sustenance throughout (see Deely 1990: 22–32), to which he gave the name *semiosis*.[1]

This peculiar type of causality or action, corresponding to the distinctive type of knowledge that the name semiotic properly characterizes, has long had some minimal recognition in philosophy in connection with investigations of the various types of physical causality. But in that connection, the "ideal" or objective factor, the pattern according to which the investigations themselves were able to establish the material, formal, and determinative dimensions of causality as constellated around the productive or "efficient" action of things in the order of "brute secondness" (as we might say), appeared as something marginal. This objective factor pertains more to the observation than to the observed in its independent existence. Hence this factor was not clearly pertinent to the results of investigations which did not have as their aim the establishment of any essential connection as such between observer and observed, such as would make "observation"—an extrinsic formal connection between subject knowing and object known—even possible in the first place. Here, as in so many areas of traditional philosophy, what was "marginal" in other problematics proves to be central for semiotic (see Deely 1991).

The minimal recognition of previous philosophers never reached the level of singling out the action in question as peculiar to signs and as constituting in this sense a distinct field of possible inquiry in its own right, as distinguished from its adjacency with other lines of immediate

1 Coming as he did at the end of the modern development of idealism, moreover, Peirce perforce struggled with a whole range of issues that had not even taken shape in Poinsot's day. Hence, while the two pioneers tend to converge on the foundational issues of semiotic, it is the writings of Peirce that best illustrate the range and complexity in detail of issues both scientific and philosophical that need to be clarified or rethought entirely in the perspective of semiotic.

investigation. The insight of the singling out, along with the naming of what was singled out as "semiosis", belongs decidedly to Charles Sanders Peirce. Hence we may fairly say that the true originality of Peirce in relation to semiotics today lies in the fact that it was he who first saw that the full development of semiotic as a distinct body of knowledge required a dynamic view of signification as a process. I think that this is also the main reason why the third element in the action of signs, the *Interpretant*, did not receive a proper name before Peirce assigned it one, despite the fact that the triadic nature of the sign relation had been definitively established in the original Iberian establishment of semiotic foundations (see the summary in Poinsot 1632a: Book I, Question 3).

To achieve its full scope, semiotics could not be envisioned, as it mainly was for Peirce's semiotic forebears, as merely a response to the question of the being proper to signs ontologically considered. Semiotics must also be a response to the further question of the *becoming* which this peculiar type of being enables and by which it sustains itself. Symbols do not just exist, they also grow; and, uniquely, they grow by a process which need not consist exclusively of actually existing nutrients.

Peirce's way of characterizing this odd state of affairs was by pointing out that semiosis is a uniquely irreducible form or type of activity in nature. In all other types of action, the actors are correlative, and, hence, the action between them, however many there may be, is essentially dyadic and dynamical. For it to occur, both terms must exist. But a sign can signify what is no longer or never was or never will be there in nature.

This irreducible factor or element in semiosis Peirce has made familiar to us under the name of "thirdness", something which, as he put it, when "*thoroughly* genuine" is entirely separated from the worlds of law and fact by existence "in the world of *representations*" (c.1896: 1.480). And the question becomes: How far is this notion to be extended vis-à-vis the world of experience and the world of nature generally?

2. Extending the action to the universe as a whole

What I mean by the "Grand Vision" in my chapter title is simply the Peircean idea that the whole of nature, not just our experience of it, but the whole of nature considered in itself and on the side of its own and proper being is the subject of semiosis—the process and product, that is, of an action of signs coextensive with and constructive of the actual world as well as of the world of experience and imagination. Such a vision is unmistakable, for example, in the claim that thought—that is to say, thirdness—"is not necessarily connected with a brain" but "appears in the work of bees, of crystals, and throughout the purely physical world"; and, "as there cannot be a General without instances embodying it, so there cannot be thought without Signs" (Peirce 1905: 4.551). But the requirements of the vision are suggested no less clearly at many points throughout the Peircean writings.

The anticipation of such a vision I found in Poinsot's formula (1632a: 126/3-4): "it suffices to be a sign virtually in order to signify in act", inasmuch as there is every reason to think that sign activity has also been at work in an anticipatory way even at inorganic levels before the advent of life in nature.[2]

Nonetheless, the actual attempt to articulate such a Grand Vision was original with Peirce, and something he struggled to establish from the famous date of the publication of his categories throughout the entire rest of his life, and against all the odds created by the state of philosophy and science in his day, as he himself has testified (c.1909: 6.322):

For forty years, that is, since the beginning of the year 1867, I have been constantly on the alert to find a *genuine* triadic relation—that is, one that does not consist in a mere collocation of dyadic relations, or the negative of such ... — which is not either an intellectual relation or a relation concerned with the less comprehensible phenomena of life. I have not met with one which could not reasonably be supposed to belong to one or other of these two classes ... Of course, the fact that a given individual has been persuaded of the truth of a proposition is the very slenderest possible argument for its truth; nevertheless, the fact that I, a person of the strongest possible physicistic prejudices, should, as the result of forty years of questionings, have been brought to the deep con-

---

2 This formula in Poinsot's writing derives from carefully considering the fact that all that pertains to secondness and dyadic interaction in semiosis belongs to signs strictly through what in them provides the foundations or fundaments whence result, or might result, relations of representation of another in which signifying consists formally as thirdness.

viction that there is some essentially and irreducibly other element in the universe than pure dynamism may have sufficient interest to excuse my devoting a single sentence to its expression.

The volume in which Peirce conditionally intended to embody the reasons for his deep conviction of the coextensiveness of semiosis with nature (c.1909: 6.322), unfortunately, he did not live to write. But this tantalizing testimony as to the firmness with which he held to his Grand Vision bears eloquent witness also to what was truly original and vital in his conception of the doctrine of signs—or perhaps I should better say his conception for the possibilities open before the doctrine of signs.

On this view of things, there is not only the macroscopic realm of *biosemiosis*, in contemporary parlance, there is also the more inclusive macroscopic realm of evolution in general affecting even the stars. This realm in its material substructure now must be conceived rather under the form of a *physiosemiosis*, an activity virtual by comparison with biosemiosis but no less replete with the objective causality whereby the physical interaction of existing things is channeled toward a future different from what obtains at the time of the affected interaction. This is a process whereby first stars and then planetary systems develop out of a more primitive atomic and molecular "dust"; but these systems in turn give rise to conditions under which further complexifications of atomic structure become possible. Some of these, inevitably, become actual as well, continuing the process, as I have shown elsewhere (1969: shown, that is, as definitively as anything can be shown in the absence of directly observed data), along an overall trajectory inevitably pointing to the establishment of biosemiosic and even anthroposemiosic phenomena.

In this view and hypothesis, semiosis, as providing the subject matter of semiotic investigation, would establish nothing less than a new framework and foundation for the whole of human knowledge, a framework embracing not only the so-called human and social sciences, as we have already seen from the partial tradition of semiology after Saussure, but also the so-called "hard" or natural sciences, precisely as they, too, arise from within and depend in their development upon experience and the processes of anthroposemiosis generally.

A hypothesis of such sweep and daring is indeed a grand vision, an abduction of the most improbable scope. But can it be verified inductively? For how are we to understand the actions of signs outside the context of organisms and cognitive life? If such an understanding could be achieved, the scope for semiotic as a possible science would become as wide as could be, for it would be commensurate with an activity and type of causality coextensive with the physical universe. And it was nothing less than such a ''broader conception'' of the sign, as Peirce put it, that his Grand Vision called for, as appears in the passage we had occasion to cite in the last chapter (p. 178 above) as indicative of some obscurity in Peirce's conception::

The action of a sign generally takes place between two parties, the *utterer* and the *interpreter*. They need not be persons; for a chameleon and many kinds of insects and even plants make their living by uttering signs, and lying signs, at that. Who is the utterer of signs of the weather ... ? However, every sign certainly conveys something of the general nature of thought, if not from a mind, yet from some repository of ideas, or significant forms, and if not to a person, yet to something capable of somehow 'catching on' ... that is, of receiving not merely a physical, nor even merely a psychical dose of energy, but a significant meaning. In that modified, and as yet very misty, sense, then, we may continue to use the italicized words [*utterer* and *interpreter*].

Peirce's oft-cited remark (1905–1906: 5.448n) that ''this universe is perfused with signs, if it is not composed exclusively of signs'', may be regarded as a kind of capsule summary of this broader conception. And his earlier, otherwise enigmatic, assertion (1868a: 5.314) that ''man is a sign'' would be a kind of corollary to this conception.

B. The Problem

But can this broader conception be justified? Is it warranted by the nature of semiosis? Clearly, the very attempt at such justification would require going beyond the bounds conventionally established for scientific thought, which we may say had already by Peirce's day more or less dogmatically embraced the view of nature as engaged exclusively in chance interactions of a brute force character. Conventional boundaries as such, of course, had no interest for Peirce when the inquiry demanded their violation, and such seemed the case with the problem at hand.

1. First attempt at resolution: teleology

To Peirce, the fact that a sign always signifies something to or for another suggested the need to reconsider the taboo notion of final causality, or so-called teleology.[3]

At least in the context of the biological sciences, such a move was to some degree inevitable. Later biologists (for example, Simpson, Pittendrigh, and Tiffany 1957; Pittendrigh 1958; Mayr 1974, 1983) would prefer to speak of "teleonomy", to make the point that actual purpose in the individual sense is not necessary to account for the behavior (such as the seasonal climbing of the female turtle onto the sand and laying its eggs) that the observer must ascribe to plan in nature in order to make scientific sense of the observations (a point also made by von Uexküll).

But, in the larger physical universe of atoms, stars, and intergalactic dust, even such a moderate version of teleology is extremely difficult

---

[3] Ransdell (1977: 163) points out that Peirce expressly "thought of semiotic as precisely the development of a concept of final cause process and as a study of such processes", a fact that his would-be commentators so far have treated as "an embarrassment, a sort of intellectual club foot that one shouldn't be caught looking at, much less blatantly pointing out to others"—which explains "why the topic of final causation is so strangely absent in criticisms and explanations of Peirce's conception of semiotic and semiosis", despite its centrality in Peirce's own reflections and explanations.

This situation is beginning to change, as can be seen in Short (1983) and in Pape (1993). The trouble with these commentators is that, functioning primarily as exegetes, they do not see beyond the Peircean corpus itself enough to realize that the main "originality" in Peirce's idea of final causality, as the work of Santaella-Braga especially makes clear (1994), results from his conflating final with extrinsic formal or objective causality in the senses discussed in our last chapter. Philosophers at least, if not exegetes, are bound in Peirce's mind by an Ethics of Terminology (Peirce 1903: CP 2.219–2.226, reproduced with comments in Deely 1994: 173–174, and applied to the case at hand throughout, esp. ¶s 93–115) that demands in this area of investigation something more than faithful exegesis.

It remains to be noted, accordingly, that for Poinsot, too, the question of final causality arises in the context of semiotic (1632a: Book I, Question 4, and editorial notes 10–12 thereon, pp. 174–178), but as expressly distinguished from the causality specific to the sign (see esp. 174/18–178/7), which is restricted neither to the order of actual existence nor to the order of intention (to signs as bearing an intention) and is virtually operative even in chance events (inasmuch as they signify as well as occur "unplanned") independently of any processes involving intention or cognition.

to sustain as pertaining to the particles and interactions themselves, especially those of a more random sort such as meteor showers, the bombardment of cosmic rays, the dispersion of light, etc. True, there is the fact of stellar evolution and planetary formation, in relation to which the formation of the elements out of more primitive atomic materials and the distribution of matter seems to be law-governed in statistically determinable ways rather than random. This non-randomness led thinkers such as Henderson (1913: 305) to argue with considerable persuasiveness and empirical support that "physical science... no less than biological science appears to manifest teleology". But the "teleology" here, if such it can be called, appears to be entirely external to the interactions themselves.

The problem is that, before the advent of living matter, and afterwards in the inorganic environmental factors taken in their own right, the inorganic components themselves (no matter how much they may be modified and dominated by vital processes and organic symbioses in a Gaia situation, the situation of a living planet), seem overwhelmingly to enter the process of cosmic evolution only indirectly, through the direct process of random or chance interactions. Once these have occurred, the inorganic components are inevitably redirected by the nature of the particles or bodies interacting, and this results in processes of complexification and overall cosmic development. The consequent overall development, however, does not disguise the fact of the random foundation. This undeniable substructure of chance encounters in a realm of brute secondness seems to pose a barrier to any possible extension of semiosis beyond the boundaries of the living world.

2. Contemporary application by Sebeok

Nonetheless, by linking the action of signs to future-oriented changes in the world of nature, Peirce had clearly pointed the way to what Sebeok called attention to in the early 1960s as "a vision of new and startling dimensions: the convergence of the science of genetics with the science of linguistics ... in the larger field of communication studies". In this view (Sebeok 1968: 69):

the genetic code must be regarded as the most fundamental of all semiotic networks and therefore as the prototype for all other signaling systems used by animals, including man. From this point of view, molecules that are quantum systems, acting as stable physical information carriers, zoösemiotic systems, and, finally, cultural systems, comprehending language, constitute a natural sequel of stages of ever more complex energy levels in a single universal evolution. It is possible, therefore, to describe language as well as living systems from a unified cybernetic standpoint ... A mutual appreciation of genetics, animal communication studies, and linguistics may lead to a full understanding of the dynamics of semiosis, and this may, in the last analysis, turn out to be no less than the definition of life.

Sebeok's, too, is a kind of grand vision for contemporary semiotics, diminished by comparison with Peirce's own, it is true, but of decidedly Peircean inspiration nonetheless. Sebeok's version falls considerably short of the broader conception Peirce had in mind in linking the sign to final causality.

At the same time, Sebeok's lesser version of Peirce's Grand Vision is probably as far as a conception of semiosis can effectively be made to reach on the basis of linking the causality proper to signs with any defensible notion of final causality.[4] The linkage, quite apart from the question of its correctness, is insufficient to establish the range of the connection required for semiosis to pervade nature all the way to its cosmic foundations.

Thus, while the "vision of new and startling dimensions" as proclaimed by Sebeok (1968: 69) considerably propelled contemporary semiotics beyond the boundaries of a glottocentrically conceived anthroposemiosis and in the direction of considering sign processes as at work throughout the biological world, it still provided no ground for a notion of physiosemiosis, for seeing the action proper to signs as already at work in physical nature itself beyond the bounds of organic matter or prior to its advent. I also think that the conclusion is inescapable that Peirce's attempt to justify his Grand Vision on the grounds of teleology falls short. At best, Peirce's attempt provides the ground for Sebeok's

---

4 The qualification is a crucial one, for only a very limited range of the notions associated historically with the notion of "final causality" retains any claim to critical consideration today. See the discussion of this point in the editorial notes to Book I, Question 4 of the *Tractatus de Signis* (Poinsot 1632a).

lesser vision of the sign-science as coextensive with life-science. For the Grand Vision, further ground is needed. To provide this further ground and to establish the Peircean broader conception of semiotic, therefore, would be the same thing.

C. The Decisive Step

To say that Peirce's first attempt to vindicate the Grand Vision failed, of course, is not to assert that the vision should be abandoned as false. As we shall see, Peirce was sometimes discouraged in his pursuit of the Grand Vision, but he never abandoned it. Happily, the justification that eluded him is there to be found. The justifiability of the Grand Vision vindicates Peirce's tenacity in holding to it, demonstrates in a decisive way his originality and foremost place in the final establishment of contemporary semiotics, and assures his role, in Guy Debrock's fine expression (1989), as a "philosopher for the 21st century". The new era of postmodern philosophy may be expected to achieve the *prise de conscience* of realizing its finality as the era of semiotics and of semiotic consciousness.

One further step, following upon the Peircean step of bringing into thematic focus the action along with the being of signs, is all that is required to establish the full possibilities for a doctrine of signs. The one further step, therefore, is also the decisive step. The taking of this step depends on the further discovery that there is a more general causality at work in the sign than the final causality typical of the vital powers (Deely 1991; 1993, esp. pars. 88–115; 1994, Appendix). This more general causality specifies vital activity but specifies also the causality at work in chance interactions of brute secondness. As we saw in the last chapter, it is this causality, not final causality, that is the causality proper to the sign in its distinctive function of making present what it itself is not, for it is this causality, not final causality, that transforms, for example, accidental scratches into a clue leading the detective to the apprehension of the murderer.

The causality distinctive of semiosis, in its contrast with physical modes of causality, need not be goal-oriented in any intrinsic sense. On the contrary, it needs to be a causality equally able to ground sign-behavior in chance occurrences and planned happenings. On any construction, final causality cannot do this.

The decisive step in this regard seems never to have been taken fully by any single thinker. I owe to Ralph Powell (e.g., 1986) the realization that it can be taken from what is set forth in Poinsot's *Treatise on Signs* (1632a: Book I, Question 4, and Appendix C),[5] but only once the problematic of the sign as a whole has been redefined so as to make the action of signs equiprimordial with their being—that is to say, only after Peirce, and by looking over, as it were, as well as standing upon, his shoulder. Thus, taking the decisive step requires first that we straddle the work of two thinkers, even though the step to be taken is more immanent to what Peirce had in mind for semiotic than it is to anything Poinsot explicitly envisioned for the doctrine of signs. When one takes a view of the paths of both men together, one sees that they converge toward a doctrinal point which provides the basis for the decisive final step, the step needed to warrant extension of semiotic understanding beyond the sphere of cognitive phenomena to the whole of nature itself— to warrant, in sum, the Grand Vision.

---

5   As Powell wrote to me in a letter of 16 December 1988 (which became the plan for Chapter 6 in *Basics of Semiotics*): "the extension of extrinsic formal causality from specifier of vital powers, active and passive (Poinsot 1632a: Book I, Question 4), *to specifier of categorial relations (ibid.: Appendix C: 382/14ff.) concerns precisely physiosemiosis*. For the specification of categorial relations extends to the universe at large ...".

Concerning this Appendix C, we had already explained in 1985 (p. 450) that we had added it to the Books of Poinsot's *Treatise* with a view to the questions of research strategies, "but in a very specific way. It is provided to ground in Poinsot's text the Peircean idea of extending semiotic understanding beyond the sphere of cognitive phenomena to the whole of nature itself as a network virtually semiosic in character ... The discussion in this Third Appendix ... extends and completes the discussion of objective causality in Book I, Question 4, of the *Treatise on Signs*."

Moreover, in Peirce's work a tendency toward what is set forth in Book I, Question 4, specifically as completed by the ideas of the editorially added Appendix C, is definitely marked, inasmuch as Peirce groped in the direction of a distinction between "ideal" and "final" causality along the lines Poinsot had earlier established for semiotics under the rubric of "objective" or "extrinsic formal" causality.

I would again call to the reader's attention that the texts from Poinsot's *Cursus Philosophicus* completing his discussion of relation in nature have been added to the expanded Appendix C of the electronic edition of Poinsot's *Tractatus de Signis*, as a PC database released by Intelex Corporation in 1992.

With this step, the broader conception Peirce dreamed of becomes realized.

1. Poinsot's formula applied to Peirce's idea of Interpretant

To see how the dream becomes real, let us begin at the point where Peirce was tempted to despair of establishing his broader conception. Then, by expanding outward from this point, removing step by step each of the reasons for a temptation to settle for a more restricted notion of the sign, we will be able to end up with a warranted version of the broader conception.

Before there are actually signs, there are signs virtually, that is, there are beings and events so determined by other beings and events that, in their own activity as so determined, they determine yet further series of beings and events in such a way that the last terms in the series represent the first terms by the mediation of the middle terms. To this situation can be applied Craik's observation (1967: 59): "It is only the sensitive 'receptors' on matter, and means of intercommunication ... which are lacking".

The actions and relations in such a series are actually at the level of secondness. But, even at that level, they anticipate the intervention of cognition and experience: they so stand to one another in relations of determining and being determined that they constitute a *pattern of knowability*, a *virtual* thirdness, which, should it come to be actually known in some context of experience, will exhibit precisely that element of thirdness, that irreducible elemental type of representation, constitutive of the sign relation.

The years 1908 and 1909, in this respect, seem to have been a period of crisis and some despondency for Peirce in his project of thus broadly establishing semiotic. In 1908, in a letter to Lady Welby, he tossed in despair his famous "sop to Cerberus", introducing the notion of "person" into his definition of sign (1908: 80–81):

I define a sign as anything which is so determined by something else, called its object, and so determines an effect upon a person, which effect I call its interpretant, that the latter is thereby mediated by the former. My insertion of the term 'upon a person' is a sop to Cerberus, because I despair of making my own broader conception understood.

If, as is to be expected, the term "person" here is equivalent to "human being", then the term "sign" so qualified would be restricted to the region of anthroposemiosis. In order to reach Peirce's "broader conception", therefore, it is necessary to remove this qualification and consequent restriction, which is in fact how we arrived at the abstract formula of our last chapter: a sign will be any A so *determined by* a B that in *determining* C that C is mediately determined by B. Thus, B determines A, and, precisely in the respect in which B has determined it, A determines C. Therefore C, in being immediately determined by A, is at the same time mediately determined by B. We see here again the most primitive and abstract form of the semiotic triangle described above (see Figure 4 in Chapter 6).

In this triad of factors, as we saw, C is passive to A in just the way that A is passive to B; but, precisely by reason of being passive in this way, C is virtually active respecting both A and B as a representation or representative element. Let B be rain and A the clouds whence the rain precipitates, and C be the experience of an organism caught in the rain. The effect of being caught in the rain will establish for the organism a new relation to B whereby A will henceforward exist for C as a sign of B, thus (Figure 8):

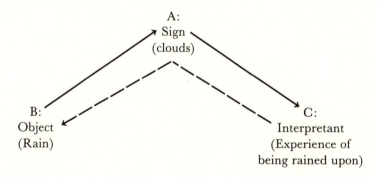

Figure 8. *The Semiotic Triangle with a Generically Zoösemiotic Interpretant*

For the case of conceiving the triad of semiosic factors in terms of a specifically anthroposemiotic interpretant, simply recall our example from the last chapter: let A be the buried bone of a dinosaur, and let B be the dinosaur long dead. In this case, C would not be the effect of the bone on any gardener who, while chancing to dig it up, was wholly ignorant of dinosaurs. Nonetheless, the element representative in this respect is there, identical with the bone, but needing to be actualized. The element of representation is there, of a piece with the bone in physical being, but virtually distinct therefrom. When a paleontologist comes along, however, this virtuality is actualized.

The "chance of the actualization", thus, in our example, depends upon two factors in a fourfold combination: one factor is the structure of the bone, which is [1] intrinsic to the bone but [2] extrinsic to the paleontologist; the other factor is the training of the paleontologist which is [3] intrinsic to the paleontologist but [4] extrinsic to the bone. The web of relations resulting from the meshing of these factors constitutes an actual experience in which the chance of the actualization comes about as a realized fact. The perceptual effect of the bone on the paleontologist, but not on the gardener, triggered the virtual element whereby the bone actually represents the dinosaur. Hence Poinsot's formula (1632a: 126/3-5): "It suffices to be a sign virtually in order to signify in act".

This formula applies just as well, as we saw above (pp. 173-175), where the interpretant so determined by A as to represent also B through that determination is a physical rather than a psychical structure—as when C is a geological formation of stone formed around a bone, or one which the bone itself has become through fossilization. It is this formula which explains generally how the present is always linked to the past semiotically in more than conscious ways, and guides the present toward a future whose possibilities reflect not only what has been but what might have been and what might or might not still be as well.

This virtual semiosis constitutes a network in its own right, in which the actual semioses of cognitive and affective experience are constantly caught up, even when they—as frequently happens—they introduce breaks and new strands wrought by action proper to themselves into the larger network.

We saw in the last chapter that the objective or extrinsic formal causality at work in relational systems as a whole and the interactions within them removes the mist in Peirce's broadest conception of semiosis, and we need also to note at the same time that this causality is, as Powell pointed out (1988b: 180, 186), "prior to the well-known Aristotelian four causes, the agent, the final, the formal, and the material cause":

It is precisely the function of extrinsic formal causality to displace the agent and final causes by a more elementary cause which is not committed to explaining how interaction could be understood. Thus the solar system is explained as a mechanism specified by extrinsic formal causes without needing any explanation by agent causes (let alone by final causes which have not been recognized by science since the seventeenth century). For Einstein's general theory of relativity precisely eliminated gravitational forces from explanation of the solar system, by substituting the curvature of space time for gravitational forces (Hawking 1988: 29–30). Now gravitational forces are agent causes, whereas the curved space-time that governs the path of the earth around the sun is an excellent example of extrinsic formal causality ... because that path consists of specified temporal relations between the earth and the other bodies of the solar system ... plain cases of extrinsic formal causality.

Thus, once it be understood that the specification of categorial relations in the universe at large already puts into play the causality upon which the action of signs depends, Peirce's discouragement at establishing his broadest conception of semiosis proves unnecessary, along with his earlier desperate resort to panpsychism as a ploy for introducing thirdness into the realm of inorganic matter (1892: 6.158, 1892a: 6.268). This ploy, by his own accounting, failed to solve the problem of *experienced* thirdness (c.1909: 6.322) as required by the sign for its proper and formal being. But this problem is circumvented once we are able to say that, already at the level of their fundaments, signs are virtually present and operative in the dyadic interactions of brute force, and weave together in a single fabric of virtual relations the future and the past of such interactions.

In other words, physiosemiosis subtends all the forms of embodiment, and links them in an action of signs as broad as the physical universe itself, the realm of nature itself. There is no part of nature untouched by the action of signs. At its broadest level, physiosemiosis depends largely on tychistic factors—chance events—for achieving its future orientation. Yet this dependence on tychism decreases as thirdness grows in the world, as law-governed structures take form. Once the organization of matter crosses the threshold of living networks, of course, the action of signs is not only less dependent on tychistic factors but also often essentially oriented from within to the future, specifically through the actions aimed at the preservation, propagation, and fluorishing of the relational networks of units interacting.

The semiotic point of view lends, in this way, an unexpected credence to the early environmentalist view of Henderson, so unorthodox in its own day (1913: 305), that "physical science ... no less than biological science appears to manifest teleology".[6] Nonetheless, the above distinction between physiosemiosis, which depends principally on tychistic factors for achieving its future orientation, and the semiosis of living matter, which essentially turns chance interactions toward the future, suggests the boundary line between physiosemiosis and the semiosis of living matter—biosemiosis in general.

2. The Grand Vision vindicated

By suggesting the boundary between matter and life in this way, to wit, in such a manner as to show that it is semiosic on both sides, we have suggested also that the Grand Vision is not merely grand, but also fundamentally true. Along with his "New List of Categories", it is perhaps Peirce's finest bequeathment to the development of semiotics today. His vision is a seed sprung of many centuries, the prospect of a tradition, to cite again Winance's expression (1983: 515), wherein "Logic becomes Semiotic, able to assimilate the whole of epistemology and natural philosophy as well", where the term "epistemology" is to be taken as a synecdoche for the human sciences, and "natural philosophy" as a synecdoche for the natural sciences including, as Aquinas noted (c.1269: Book I, lectio 1, n. 2), "even metaphysics".

In this Grand Vision, originally and integrally Peircean, semiotics becomes the name for a distinctive series of investigations, distinctive for the same reason that any investigation is distinctive, namely, by reason of what it studies. In the present case, the study is of semiosis as subtending the whole of nature, including, in Sebeok's fine way of skewing the matter (1984: 3), "that miniscule segment of nature some anthropologists grandly compartmentalize as culture".

---

6 If the power of Henderson's arguments was outweighed by their unorthodoxy in the scientific community of his day, that is rapidly ceasing to be the case in the age of Gaia (Lovelock 1979), where the recognition at last of delicate interdependencies, both within our own planetary ecology and between that ecology and the solar and cosmic radiation through which our planet moves, have begun at long last to become themselves objectified as well as physical.

8

Renvoi

In Chapter 6 we had occasion to identify the specific effect of the action of signs as the creation of a specific type of relation with an intermediate term that sends the discourse of an observer beyond itself to an object signified, and we called this effect, the relation among all relations which is specifically a relation of signification, ''renvoi'', after the suggestion of Roman Jakobson. There we mentioned renvoi only in passing, since the interest of the chapter was not renvoi itself but the underlying causality through the exercise of which renvoi is brought about.

Now, in bringing this study to a close, I want to look rather directly at renvoi itself, its own structure and requirements, in order to achieve a technically correct and exact understanding of the classic formula according to which a sign always represents something other than itself.

A. Renvoi

Renvoi, as has been said, is the term by which Roman Jakobson ''deftly captured and transfixed each and every sign process conforming to the classic formula, *aliquid stat pro aliquo*'' (Sebeok 1984: 66). I myself first encountered the term in reading Jakobson's ''Coup d'Oeil sur le Developpement de la Sémiotique''[1], opening the June 1974 Proceed-

---

1 ''Malgré toutes les différences dan les détail de la présentation, la bipartition du signe en deux faces conjointes, et en particulier la tradition stoïcien qui conçoit le signe (σημεῖον) comme un renvoi de la part du signifiant (σημαῖνον) au signifié (σημαινόμενοω), reste en vigeur dans la doctrine de Peirce'' (Jakobson 1974: 9)—''Notwith-

ings of the First Congress of the International Association for Semiotic Studies (Jakobson 1974), where, despite using the term in connection with the semiotic doctrine of Peirce, Jakobson gives it a quasi-Saussurean interpretation. The word itself is French, rich in meanings, including reflection (of light), reverberation, a sending-back, a reference, etc. Although Jakobson himself (1980: 22) approved an English rendering of *renvoi* as "referral", here I propose rather to retain the French spelling and use it simply to create in English a technical term expressing the irreducibly triadic character which distinguishes the sign relation within the order of relations from all other relations, in particular dyadic relations of brute force (or "efficient causality").

Every relation is a referral of one thing to another. Smoke refers to fire as an effect, clouds refer to rain as a source. But not every relation is a sign relation. Even the examples of physical relations we have just mentioned, and which are commonly cited as examples of natural signification, are in fact not of themselves sign relations. For smoke to become a *sign* of fire the connection between the two must not simply be but be experienced. And the initial experience will not be of the one as *sign* of the other, but simply of the two objects as occurring in relation to one another, whence the one comes subsequently to signify the other even in the other's absence.

Smoke cannot be the effect of fire in the absence of fire, nor can clouds be the cause of rain in the absence of rain. The causal relation requires the co-presence of both its terms, and refers the one to the other. But once the causal connection between clouds and rain or fire and smoke has become a matter of experience, clouds can portend rain and smoke can portend fire even before the rain falls or the fire is seen as a co-occurrent object.

B. Referral in the Order of Things

We consider ourselves to be experiencing "something real", a "real thing", when we encounter within our experience objects which seem to

standing all the differences in the detail of the presentation, the bipartition of the sign into two conjoined faces, and in particular the Stoic tradition which conceives the sign (σημεῖον) as a referral from the part signifying (σημαῖνον) to the part signified (σημαινόμενοω), remains central in the doctrine of Peirce".

exceed our ability to control and which, moreover, appear to come and go not simply as part of, or from within, our psyche but according to causes of motion which have to do more with the object's internal constitution as a material reality and other influences independent of us than on anything we desire or consider intrinsic to our identity and bodily existence.

This seemingly simple concept of reality is anything but simple. Nor, on analysis, is it by any means restricted to that which appears to be independent of us—for otherwise we ourselves, or at least aspects and parts of ourselves, would have to be considered unreal. Yet reality, like being pregnant, does not admit of degrees insofar as it is a question of actual existence.

Not only is the notion of reality complex, but its analysis reveals elements very close to antinomic. For even though some object supposed to be a thing is thought through the concept of what exists independently of me, our arrival at this concept is far from a matter independent of experience. As experience is precisely a matter of what we are, have been, and are becoming aware of and the consequent influences upon us through memory, imagination, and calculations of interest as well through the immediate aspect of what is "here and now" filling our channels of exteroception, "real things" only appear within experience by way of contrast with other objects and aspects of objects which we take, perhaps mistakenly, to be "unreal" or "mere objects", etc. Since the record of human mistakes in the classification of objects as "real" and "unreal" is amply long, both collectively and individually, on both sides of the accounting (that is, not only are we often mistaken in what we think to be real, but we are also often mistaken in what we think to be unreal), this record needs to be accorded a theoretical footing and not brushed aside as an inconvenience or embarassment. Such a footing can be gained only if we make of "reality" and "things" subordinate rather than primary categories for an understanding of experience in the whole of its texture and proper consistency. The indifference of the sign relation as such to its physical status, in short, turns out to be the *raison d'être* of fallibilism, and the reason for the dependence of present thought on future thought and, in general, on "what will be" as well as on what presently is.

Granting all this, it must also be granted that experience entitles us to think in the abstract of a universe existing without us, both in the sense that there is an order of existence to which our presence is not essential even though we are a part of it, and in the sense that we have every reason to believe that this order of existence perdured prior to our appearance and was involved in its own evolution and development over billions of humanless years thanks to which, indeed, our emergence as individuals and as a species became possible in the first place.

In other words, in raising the question of referral in the order of things, I am thinking of that impoverished, indeed, but fundamental notion of reality which inspired the beginnings of modern science. This is the notion of a world of bodies in motion, subject to mathematical analysis by virtue of being bodies (quantities) in space (another quantity), and acted upon by forces of brute secondness sending them hurtling down trajectories and constrained within orbits by a network of relations capable of direct mathematical expressions predictive of the bodies' future courses.

Peirce called this realm of brute force the domain of Secondness. Whether we consider the celestial mechanics of Newton or the homely case of a temperature regulating device, we find at this level of reality nothing of the sign. If a thermometer is dynamically connected with a heating and cooling apparatus ''so as to check either effect'', Peirce notices (c.1906: 5.473), ''we do not, in ordinary parlance, speak of there being any semeiosy, or action of a sign, but, on the contrary, say that there is an 'automatic regulation', an idea opposed, in our minds, to that of semeiosy''.

Nonetheless, we should not be too hasty in our assessment, for this order of things cannot be the whole of reality, nor are the bodies occupying it mere quantities undifferentiated within themselves. On the contrary, they are stars and planets and all manner of interstitial debris, differentiated from one another not only by space and size but by internal composition as well. They are linked, moreover, through the forces that move them into systems and subsystems of various sorts, some relatively independent of one another, like the Milky Way and the Andromeda nebula, say, but quite tightly woven within themselves, as is our own solar system.

There are not only bodies in the world of things but systems of bodies, and the order of things is made up of systems both between and within the bodies that occupy it with their masses and interactions. Referral in this order of things seems to be nothing more than the fact that the action of any given body, the earth, say, requires for its explanation reference to the surrounding bodies with which it interacts, such as the sun and moon, inasmuch as it exhibits a pattern of behavior which is not the same pattern as would obtain were the relevant other bodies to be removed.

Now this notion of system is problematic. How does the system as such exist? Not apart from the bodies, to be sure; but not as the bodies either. The bodies exist, each of them, in themselves, that is, as internally constituted in this or that way, while the system as such exists rather in between them, as the pattern of their interaction.

This contrast between the intrinsic constitution of a thing and its relations to other things provides us with the fundamental contrast between the *subjective* and the *intersubjective*, between what things are in themselves and what they are as elements or parts of a system, that is, relative to other things. Of course, what things are "in themselves" is also a kind of system (see, for example, Sebeok 1977a, 1988).[2] The brain is distinct from the lungs, liver, and heart, and all of them together, along with many other organs and tissues, constitute an organic system which is the whole of our body. So perhaps, fully to establish our contrast, we need to distinguish between systems whose parts are contiguous (*subjective* entities) and systems whose parts are spatially removed but which nonetheless belong to an organized whole. The relation between the parts of the latter sort of system precisely as spatially separated would then illustrate what we mean by *intersubjective*, or *between* rather than *within* the noncontiguous parts. Of course, even within a system of contiguous parts, such as our bodies, there is an internal differentiation in the constitution of the various organs which separates them from one another.

---

[2] As a student in graduate school, I was introduced to the complexities of this problem through a paper essayed, but never published, by one of my best professors under the title "The Problem of Identifying More or Less Unitary Beings in Our World". Of course, this is the classical problem of substance, but now stated and posed in a way that makes the neglected problematic of relation itself relevant in the very context where it has usually been neglected. Years later, this same professor did manage to bring to publication a very strange book (Powell 1983a) rich in source materials regarding the history of relation; and I myself tried my hand with the problematic of substance as such (Deely 1969). The gist of Powell's "problem" can be seen in the "The Metaphysical Issues: Rationale" section of Deely and Nogar 1973: 251–254. But this earlier essay of Powell's, c.1967, I would like to exhume from an archive one day and bring to publication.

But this internal differentiation still belongs to the notion of *subjectivity* as whatever goes to make up an individual entity in its proper being as a whole relatively enclosed and unified.

As parts of a system (in the noncontiguous sense), each part refers to each other part in various ways: the sun influences the behavior of all its planets, but within this general influence each planet contributes a specific influence of its own on the other planets. The importance of subjective being to the understanding of reality as that which obtains independently of us is so evident that, in the middle ages and throughout most of modern times, the notion of intersubjective being was regarded primarily as a fiction contributed by the mind to our experience of bodies. Such was not only the opinion of the great Kant, master of the moderns, but also of William of Ockham, the hero of nominalism, and Francisco Suárez, who was the principal channel through which Latin philosophizing influenced the development of modern philosophy.

In short, the notion of referral in the order of things was generally reduced to a comparison some observer makes between two or more bodies, rather than seen as an actual part of the mind-independent reality observed. A shoulder bone fits into a shoulder socket and not into a knee socket: the "relation" between shoulder bone and a shoulder socket consists in nothing more than the way the bone is contoured, on the one hand, and the way the shoulder itself is contoured, on the other hand, not in anything "intersubjective" as over and above either or both of them. Over and above the shape of the bone and the contour of the socket there is room for the mind to compare the two and see the "fit" that an actual joining of the two realizes; but there is no "relation" between them over and above this fit. Similarly for all so-called relations: there is nothing in reality but the related things, the relation "between" them being nothing more than the comparison of them made by some observer. The shape of the bone is a referral to the contour of the socket, and conversely. The contour of the socket is a representation of the shape of the bone, and conversely. Each is relative to the other in this sense: the shape of the bone fits the contour of a shoulder socket rather than some other, and the contour of the socket fits the shape of the shoulder bone rather than some other bone.

In this way, the intrinsic constitution of a thing, its subjective or own being, has inscribed within itself a story, the story of where it fits and "belongs" in the universe of things, regardless of whether anyone observing it has the requisite knowledge to grasp what that intrinsic constitution is saying about its place in the nature of things.

Relative being in this sense, the referral of one thing to another through the intrinsic constitution of each of the entities "referred" as a being in its own right is of the essence of indexical representation, and was called "transcendental relation" in the Latin Age, a term we encountered several times in Chapter 4 above.[3] Many medievals, as I have mentioned, considered this to be the only real form of relation, that is to

---

3 The Latins called these elements of physical being as internally codetermined "transcendental relatives", a difficult term discussed in detail in Poinsot 1632a: esp. Second Preamble, Arts. 1 and 2, and in Deely 1990: esp. 35–46. Eugen Baer (1992: 353), discussing the contrast between transcendental and ontological relations (which latter relations alone are truly and fully relations, and of which the relations of renvoi form an irreducible subclass), has best summarized the medieval notion of transcendental relation as an aid to understanding "how objects become signs in experience": "Transcendental relations constitute a given thing, say, a rock, and provide thus the possibility of understanding it, once it becomes an object in experience. Ontological relations characterize the interactions a thing may assume in addition to being a thing. Here thing becomes a little tricky," Baer notes, "because it is often difficult to say what exactly a thing is, since [see particularly ¶s 38–60 in *The Human Use of Signs* (Deely 1994)] things are accessible only by becoming objects in our experience, and the 'thingness' in objects might precisely be the element which resists our understanding. It is perhaps best to say that transcendental relations," as I would put it, in the sense relevant to semiosis, "constitute things in the first place which then may or may not engage in additional relations with other things already established in their own right. These additional relations would then be ontological relations. They exist not as things but 'between things'." Baer concludes (ibid.): "While transcendental relations provide the possibility for our understanding a thing as thing (say, a rock as a rock), ontological relations provide the possibility of experiencing that thing as an object in various contexts, not all of which need be physically real. A rock can become a weapon; I would say, it then assumes for the time being an ontological relation with perhaps tangible physical results. But what happens if it becomes a tombstone, one of the oldest signs of humankind, distinguishing the human species clearly from all others? Here the ontological relation reveals its true essence as an imperceptible relation which nevertheless makes a huge difference in relating a rock to the memory of the dead. A rock can be weapon, tombstone, furniture or, as in the case of our paleontology student, a piece of scientific information. Semiosic relations are ontological relations which provide the possibility for experiencing objects as bringing other objects into view. A rock recognized

say, the only sort of relativity to be found as such in the order of mind-independent being. And I think that the importance of this sort of "referral" for science and detective work of any kind is abundantly clear. However, this sort of referral is not sufficient to constitute referral in the sense of renvoi.

Nor is such referral sufficient to account for the order we find in, rather than impose upon, such systems as we encounter among army ants on the march or planets subordinate to a particular star. The relations between the parts of noncontiguous systems do not reduce to the shape and contours of the parts, for the system can be cast into disarray without the shape and contours of its parts being affected. There is clearly a difference not reducible to the observer between, say, an army on the march and an army in rout. The relations in such cases, while doubtless involving and not independent of the parts, are nonetheless something over and above the parts, something "intersubjective" respecting those parts and something which does not reduce to a comparison made by an observer, inasmuch as the intersubjectivity in question obtains on the side of the things observed. Such was the argument of Thomas Aquinas in insisting, with Aristotle, that there is a pure sort of relative being in nature demanding to be recognized as such. Poinsot summarized the argument for this position as follows:

We know there are forms of quantity and quality from seeing their effects. In the same way, from seeing in the world of nature the effect of some things ordered and having a condition relative to other things, such as similitude, paternity, order, etc.; and from seeing that in these things this effect of respecting is without admixture of any absolute rationale, that their whole being consists in a respect; it is from seeing this, I say, that we best gather that there is this pure sort of relative being, just as we gather from absolute effects that there are absolute entities.[4]

This is still not the referral of renvoi, for we are not talking here at all of semiosis. What we are talking about is nonetheless important—I

by the appropriate interpretant as a fossil bone begins to tell a story." See further Baer 1977; and note 11 in this Chapter, p. 226 below.

4 *Tractatus de Signis* (1632a), Second Preamble "On Relation", Article 1, "Whether There Exist on the Side of Mind-Independent Being Intrinsic Forms Which Are

would say crucial—for understanding eventually the renvoi effected by semiosis, if semiosis stands indeed, as Sebeok has always insisted (and I think rightly insisted), "at the intersection of nature and culture". For what the renvoi of semiosis establishes is precisely communication, and communication requires in the nature of the case a transcendence of subjectivity if it is to be more than apparent, more, we might say, than a transcendental illusion.

Intersubjective being in the physical world, it has been said (Aquinas c.1254–1256: 1 Sent. d. 26, q. 2 ad 2), is the thinnest of all the modes of real existence, the "*ens minimum*" of the material world. Among material objects, relations exist not only dependently on the objects related, but they do not appear to the eye—that is, they are not directly accessible by any channel of sensation. Only the related things can be seen and touched. To be sure, patterns of things as related can be perceived; but to consider the relations themselves forming the pattern apart from the patterned things is an act of intellectual abstraction beyond the reach of a purely perceptual intelligence. When it is a question of understanding the constitution of bodies and secondness of material interactions, moreover, the abstraction in question is not evidently useful to make.

Still, so far as it is a question of a scientific intelligence aiming to know reality, what we have achieved at this point is not a little. It is interesting to know that intersubjectivity is a mode of being verified independently of our seeming experience of it in communication. This fact already suggests to us that the experience of communication is not a purely cognitive phenomenon but a participation of cognition in a more gene-

Relations'', 86/9–19 (= *Artis Logicae Secunda Pars*, Quaestio 17, Articulus Primus, "Utrum a Parte Rei Dentur Relationes, Quae Sint Formae Intrinsecae", Reiser ed. 577a7–28: "Ad tertium dicitur, quod non est minor necessitas ponendi hoc genus entitatis relativae quam genus quantitatis vel qualitatis. Quia enim videmus effectus quantitatis et qualitatis, inde tales formas dari colligimus. Sic etiam quia videmus dari hunc effectum in rerum natura, scilicet ordinari aliqua et habitudinem habere ad alia, sicut similitudo, paternitas, ordo etc., et in istis non est iste effectus respiciendi mixtus cum ratione absoluta, sed totum esse eorum consistit in respectu, inde optime colligimus dari hoc genus entitatis relativae, sicut ex effectibus absolutis entitates absolutas. Nec est necessaria ad hoc maior experientia quam in aliis formis accidentalibus, in quibus experimur quidem effectus, sed non earum distinctionem a substantia.") See Chapter 4, p. 100 above, text and footnote 69.

ral feature of reality. This realization is highly pertinent to our impression that semiosis, wherein our *experience* of communication perforce resides, is permeable to nature as well as to culture. In other words, by obtaining as an intersubjective possibility at the level of the physical environment itself, relation opens the way to an intersubjectivity cognitively realizable within experience itself, insofar as experience includes assimilation through cognition of parts and aspects of the physical environment itself in its otherwise mind-independent being. This vindicates, against the Kantian notion of *noumenon*, the medieval formula, *ens et verum convertuntur.*

C. Objective Referral

Experience is not directly of things, but of objects. Things, we have already noted, are represented through a derivative notion, a notion derived from our experience of objects as including in *their* constitution—that is, their constitution as known—aspects and elements that do not reduce to our experience of them. An easy example of this irreducibility is found in the contrast between smoke as a sign of something burning and a flag as a sign of a country. The referral of smoke to fire, we have seen, is something physical, indeed, inscribed in the very subjective constitution of smoke as an environmental phenomenon. But this is not the referral of smoke to fire as *sign* of fire. The smoke as an effect of fire requires something more in order to become also a sign of fire. Smoke requires, in addition to its relation of effect to cause based on secondness, an *interpretant* through which it acquires the thirdness according to which it becomes, now, a sign of burning. The *causal relation* between burning and smoke is not what constitutes the smoke as sign. The *experience* of smoke and fire, on the other hand, *does* constitute the smoke as a sign. The fact that our experience of the connection of smoke with fire leads us to believe, indeed, that the two phenomena have a causal connection such that, regardless of our experience or whether anyone observes a given plume of smoke, wherever a plume of smoke appears there is something burning. This belief, in turn, leads us to call smoke traditionally a *natural* sign. But this fact and the belief it grounds has no bearing on the fact that the sign relation itself is something more than the cause-effect relation, since the latter can occur without the former.

The case is quite different in the relation between flag and country.

Here experience gives us every reason to believe that in the absence of human beings there would neither have been a physical construct of the sort this flag is nor even less any relation between it and any country. The flag-country relation has no being at all apart from the context of human experience, whereas the smoke-fire relation has a dimension which goes beyond our experience of it and obtains independently of that experience. But that is because smoke and fire as environmental phenomena are related *things* as well as related *objects*, whereas flag and country as cultural phenomena are related *objects* but are quite unrelated as things at the level of physical environment as such. Indeed, environmentally, the flag is no more than a grouping of threads, and the country no more than a land mass. The fact that our experience of the connection of flag with country leads us to believe that the two are connected with one another only in the context of human experience, indeed, is what traditionally leads us to call flags *conventional* signs.

While our analysis so far is sufficient to exclude a naive idea of natural signs as causally connected to their significates, inasmuch as we now realize that the connection of sign to signified in such cases cannot simply be identified with the dyadic cause-effect relation, our analysis is anything but sufficient to preserve an idea of natural *sign*. For this it is not enough to demonstrate that whatever cause and effect relations there may be in the environment, sign relations are something that must be further added. For if sign relations are in every case *added* to environmental phenomena as physical, how is the relation of natural signs *as signs* any different from the relation of conventional signs *as signs*?

The answer to this question is that the *sign*-relation as such in the two cases is not different, even though there is a great difference in the way the *sign-vehicle functions* in the two cases vis-à-vis the physical environment. In both cases, the sign-relation *as such* is an intersubjective mode of being resting or dependent upon some aspect of subjectivity. But the *manner of this dependence* is different in the two cases, something possible as a consequence of the difference between subjective and intersubjective being as modes of reality, which we must now examine more closely.

For a being to be subjective, it must be conceived as existing or able to exist independently of the conception of it. The conception specifically applied in any given case may be mistaken: many are the objects once thought to have subjective existence which proved on further investigation to be veritable chimeras. But that is beside the point. Capacity for an existence in the environment independent of being cognized is an essential constituent of the notion of subjective being, not of objects to which that notion may be mistakenly applied. By contrast, the conception of intersubjectivity is the conception of a relation between two objects, regardless of whether the objects are existent things or not. True, for the intersubjectivity to be conceived as obtaining in the environment independently of our conception of it, it must be conceived as obtaining between two or more things existing in the environment and related in the manner we conceive of them to be related. And for the intersubjectivity to exist in the environment there must be two or more related things. But the present point is quite different. Here the point is that the intersubjective relation in its possible being as physical involves not existence in itself but existence between existents in themselves. And this possibility of physical being, unlike any subjective possibility of physical being, does not exclude realization indifferently in nature or in cognition.[5] Whence it is that, in nature, relations always involve an

---

5 Poinsot, *Tractatus de Signis*, Second Preamble "On Relation", Article 2, from the "Resolution of Counter-Arguments", 94/37–95/45 (= *Artis Logicae Secunda Pars*, Q. 17, Art. 2, "Solvuntur Argumenta", Reiser ed. 581a11–581b23): "From that content by which the relation is considered toward a terminus, it both exists positively, and is not determinately a mind-independent form, but is indifferent to the exercise of a mind-independent or a mind-dependent act of existence, even though a physical exercise of being-toward would also be mind-independently founded. [It is thus not a question of] which relation would be mind-independent or which mind-dependent, but [a question rather of] the rationale or content owing to which relation is [peculiarly] able to be mind-independent or mind-dependent, namely, the rationale or content whereby it is toward a terminus; for even though it can have a mind-independent existence there, yet it does not have a mind-independent existence *from* there. [This point has been expressly made by an unknown Latin author in a work long attributed mistakenly to Aquinas, the so-called] *Commentary on the Sentences Written for Annibald*, Book I, dist. 26, q. 2, art. 1, where he says that 'relation can be considered in two ways. In one way, as regards that toward which it is said to be [i.e., its terminus], from which it has the rationale of a relation, and in this regard it need not posit anything, although too it need not for this reason be nothing; for there are certain respects which are something in the order of being as it exists independently of mind, but certain others which are nothing in the order of mind-independent being. In another way, relation can be considered as regards

element of reciprocity,[6] whereas in experience there can be one-sided relations, as any spurned lover can testify.

There is more to this situation than the possibility of unrequited love. A relation formed in cognition may be the same in its referral as a relation formed in nature, but its conditions of realization are anything but the same. In nature, for the relation to exist, both the subject of the relation and the terminus of the relation must exist. In cognition, for the relation to exist, it is sufficient that the relation be thought, for in this case it is from the idea of the knower that the relation springs as between two objects experienced or known, and the question of whether that relation also obtains independently of being thought is purely in-

that in which it is, and so when it has existence in a subject, it is in the subject independently of mind'...

"But how this is peculiar to the case of relation and is not found in the other categories ... is owing to the fact that in the other categories their proper and most formal rationale cannot be understood positively unless it is also understood entitatively, because their positive rationale is toward themselves only and subjective, and for this reason is not understood positively unless also entitatively; for that which is toward itself is an entity [just as that which is toward a knower is an object, and that which is toward another than itself a sign]. Only relation has [both] to be being and toward being, and from that content by which it is toward being, it exists positively, yet it does not have thence the rationale of being mind-independent. But a mind-independent existence comes to relation from one source, namely, from a fundament, the positive rationale of toward from elsewhere, namely, from the terminus, from which the relation does not have to be being, but toward being, although that toward is truly mind-independent when it is founded [and the terminus exists]. That therefore something can be considered positively, even if it does not exist entitatively independently of mind, is proper to relation. And this is [what Cajetan meant when he said, 1507: *In I* q. 28. art. 1] that a mind-dependent relation is a true relation, not by the truth of an entity and of an informing form, but by the truth of an objective and positive tendency toward a term. ... in the case of a physical relation, the very toward is not something constructed [but] is truly instantiated mind-independently." (Latin text in Appendix of Longer Citations, p. 254 below.)

6 The point here is not that there are not to be found in nature relations of measured to measure, such as Peirce's example of the diamond which scratches glass without being scratched in return (and similar examples found in Poinsot 1634—cf. Deely 1985: 495–496), which provide for the scientist what clues are for the detective. The point is that the *pure relational* aspect of these situations, insofar as they are rooted in action and passion, always involves the mutual existence of both actor and acted upon.

cidental, although it can well be the case. We see that this uniqueness of relation as indifferent to its subjective ground opens the way to error: a relation I conceive to be fictional may in fact be real, just as a being I conceive to exist subjectively may in fact be a tissue of fictive relations. But the uniqueness of relations as indifferent to their subjective ground also opens the way to knowledge of the past. When, for example, the paleontologist correctly sees the bone as *of a dinosaur*, a relation which once existed in fact but now exists only representatively in the bone as a foundation is made to re-exist in cognition just as it once existed in nature itself. And the uniqueness of relations as indifferent to their subjective ground opens the way to a community among organisms based in part on relations that have no existence except through the psychological constitution of its members bringing into existence among themselves a *network* of intersubjective bonds which are physical, indeed, but only as among conspecifics sharing common ways of cognizing and cathecting. Networks of this sort obtain not only within human societies with their differing civil and constitutional structures. They obtain also zoösemiotically for each species of animal. But I think that the species-specific networks of phytosemiotic relations do not share in the possibility for one-sidedness of relations that cognition introduces into nature and that makes possible a second level, as it were, of mutual relations that are not mutual perforce but only through the forging of common perceptions and understandings surrounded by misunderstandings (and open always to the possibility of misunderstanding precisely because, in cognition, any given relation, even one which *was* mutual in the physical environment, need not be mutual). We will see more of this shortly.

For the moment, suffice it to say that, as we glimpsed in Chapter 4, this peculiarity of relation was grasped quite late in the history of philosophy. Yet, except for the theory of the Trinity developed in theology by Thomas Aquinas, no one seems to have known what to make of it. "A rose existing only in thought is not a rose", Cajetan wrote cryptically (1507: *In 1*. 28. art. 1. par. 9), "but a relation existing in thought is truly a relation." Not until sixteenth and seventeenth century developments in logic and epistemology carried out systematically in the work of Iberian thinkers, soon to be forgotten in the mainstream development of classical modern philosophy, did anyone realize that what is at stake in this peculiarity of relation as an intersubjective mode of being is the very possibility of semiosis—or, perhaps I should better say, the opening in physical nature itself to an action of signs not reducible to the more typical, or at least more widespread, brute force interactions of secondness constitutive of subjective being and the physical environment of material objects.[7]

Let us consider further our case of smoke as a "natural sign" of fire. The effect-to-cause relation of smoke to fire is not in and of itself a sign relation, for it lacks an interpretant. Yet when the interpretant is added, nothing prevents this very relation given in nature from being assimilated according to its intersubjective character within experience and becoming in just this way a *part* of the sign relation. In other words, the fact that the cause-effect relation can obtain prior to and independently of the sign-relation does not preclude its inclusion *also* within the sign-relation. The very effect-to-cause relation which is dyadic in the physical environment becomes triadic through the experience of an organism, i.e., as assimilated thereto, and as such constitutive of a relation of sign. Thus the relation of a natural sign is, like that of a conventional sign, always as such objective; but *in that very objectivity the relation is not preclusive of the physical dimension of environmental phenomena but only indifferent to it.* Whence fake smoke can also signify fire no less effectively than real smoke, a fact, for example, useful in certain guerilla situations where a deception is helpful or even essential to the successful outcome of a given operation.

The reason the referral constitutive of the intrinsic being of the ground of some relation—say, the constitution of a bone which makes it the bone *of a mastodon* and not the bone *of a bison*—does not constitute the referral constitutive of the sign, in short, is the same as the reason a representation as such is not a sign but an object. The constitution of the bone represents first of all itself. Practically anyone, even a dog, can see that it is a bone. But only a more elite few can see that it was the bone *of a mastodon*. Adding "of a mastodon" to a fossil bone, for example, is a cognitive act over and above the experience of the bone as a material

---

[7] For a detailed discussion of the case of sign-relations that have no physical reference see "Reference to the Non-Existent" (Deely 1975).

object. After all, the bone is present here and now, the mastodon is not. Yet the relation added in such a case as suprasubjective to the bone is achieved in an awareness which recognizes and cognitively duplicates the fit between bone and mastodon no differently than that fit once obtained in the physical environment. In the past, the mastodon in question existed only subjectively; in the present, he (for this mastodon happened to be male) exists only objectively as signified. *As signified* he exists fundamentally in the bone and terminatively as the object *through* the "relation between" the bone and what was, now duplicated, or recreated, purely objectively through the bone's objectification within the context of the cognitive experience and training of the paleontologist.

That the sign must be identified with the suprasubjective and prospectively intersubjective referral over and above the referral constitutive of the intrinsic being of the (perhaps former) ground of some relation is plainest, of course, in the case of symbols (linguistic signs, for example, which are neither iconic nor indexical as such) which give no clue at all to their referral except through the habit structure of a population quite extrinsic to their own physical constitution as sounds or marks. This identification of the sign with a referral in a suprasubjective sense is precisely what situates the sign at the intersection of nature and culture, rather than determinately in one or the other of the two domains. Therein lies the reason both for the possibility of natural signs in the first place and for the possibility of the naturalization of conventional signs (Deely 1978a). For the opposition of natural to conventional signs does not preclude the relation constituting *either* type of sign from being sometimes physical as well as objective and sometimes only objective.

D. Objective Constitution

"Things are stories" is Eugen Baer's way of making the point that all experience is of objects, from which experience the notion of things is derived. Things are those objects which have a subjective constitution, which is far from the case with all objects. Even in the case of those objects which do indeed have a subjective constitution in their own right, it is far from the case that this subjective constitution is always what is of primary interest to us about their objectivity, although it often is. For example, the subjective constitution of wood is precisely what makes it a more suitable material for construction of a house than is cardboard. The subjective constitution of a given virus is what makes it deadly for humans but not for some other animals. And so forth.

But objective constitution in its own right is something entirely different from whatever subjective being objects may happen to have through their incidental participation in the physical environment in its own being. Objective constitution as such is a matter of intersecting relationships which may or may not in any particular regard coincide with relationships in the physical environment as such, although in the modalities of sensation as such analytically prescissed within perception and intellection it is possible to identify certain minimal coincidences of objective and physical relationships which are necessary and not contingent (Deely 1992), thus constituting the semiosis engendering experience of objects precisely, as Sebeok has said, "at the intersection" (or *as an interface*) of nature and culture.

The priority of relations over the intrinsic constitution of subjective being in the case of objects in their difference from things has best been stated in semiotics by Louis Hjelmslev. When it comes to objects as such, Hjelmslev notes,[8] "it soon becomes apparent that the important thing

---

[8] A fuller context of my brief citation in the text is helpful (from Hjelmslev 1961: 22-23): "Naive realism would probably suppose that analysis consisted merely in dividing a given object into parts, i.e., into other objects, then those again into parts, i.e., into still other objects, and so on. But even naive realism would be faced with the choice between several possible ways of dividing. It soon becomes apparent that the important thing is not the division of an object into parts, but the conduct of the analysis so that it conforms to the mutual dependences between these parts, and permits us to give an adequate account of them. In this way alone the analysis becomes adequate and, from the point of view of a metaphysical theory of knowledge, can be said to reflect the 'nature' of the object and its parts.

"When we draw the full consequences from this, we reach a conclusion which is most important for an understanding of the principle of analysis: both the object under examination and its parts have existence only by virtue of these dependences; the whole of the object under examination can be defined only by their sum total; and each of its parts can be defined only by the dependences joining it to the other coordinated parts, to the whole, and to its parts of the next degree, and by the sum of the dependences that these parts of the next degree contract with each other. After we have recognized this, the 'objects' of naive realism are, from our point of view, nothing but intersections of bundles of such dependences. That is to say, objects

is not the division of an object into parts, but the conduct of the analysis so that it conforms to the mutual dependences between these parts, and permits us to give an adequate account of them." Once we have recognized this, the 'objects' of naive realism, i.e., the supposed things of direct experience, are seen to be rather "nothing but intersections of bundles of such dependences"—which may of course include, as we have seen, objectifications of natural dependences among things which may be subsequently analysed out of the whole by standard techniques of experimentation and critical control of objectification. "The dependences," Hjelmslev concludes, "which naive realism regards as secondary, presupposing the objects, become from this point of view primary, presupposed by their intersections."

The point may be illustrated with a simple example. If I were to appear before most readers of this book wearing a high-necked black cape, with my hair dyed black and slicked back, perhaps adding for good measure two long incisors, each would think at once of Dracula, a creature who, some think, does not exist. A perceived pattern is what constitutes an object of experience, not an existing thing. Our experience consists in the building up of a structure or network of cognitive and cathectic relations which constitute an objective world. This world partially includes aspects of the physical environment, to be sure, but it includes such elements according to its own plan and without being reducible to them. If we consider the environment to be the world of things, then the objective world is constructed according to a quite different plan, and divisions in the one world vary relatively independently of divisions in the other world. Moreover, each world extends beyond the other's boundaries: not all things are known to us, and not all objects known to us are things.

In semiotics, it has become customary to speak of this difference between environment and objective world in terms of the notion of *Umwelt*, a term first established in the sense appropriate for semiotics by the German biologist Jakob von Uexküll. Each individual, von Uexküll ex-

can be described only with their help and can be defined and grasped scientifically only in this way. The dependences, which naive realism regards as secondary, presupposing the objects, become from this point of view primary, presupposed by their intersections."

plained, is surrounded by an invisible bubble within which alone the environment is rendered meaningful. Von Uexkull also compared the world of experience to a web: "As the spider spins its threads, every subject spins his relations to certain characters of the things around him, and weaves them into a firm web which carries his existence" (J. von Uexküll 1934: 14).

To understand the constitution of objects, I think it is helpful to combine these two notions of bubble and web into the single model of a kind of geodesic sphere whose interior as well as its surface consists of a series of intersecting lines. (The spherical image, however, is only analogous, for in fact the surface of the "sphere" will be perforce highly irregular, according to the distance and type of the radii relations linking the individual to stimuli from the physical surroundings, some as near as the ground at our feet, others as remote as alien galaxies.) Each intersection is an object, each line a relationship. Lines radiate outward from the center where each of us stands to the surface of the sphere, and lines extend also crosswise, intersecting the radii. The radii lines represent relations between ideas and objects, the intersecting lines represent relations between objects, and the intersections themselves represent the objects. Thus, the objective world is the sphere of an individual's experiences built up out of relationships, and the internal constitution of this sphere is precisely that of a web the various intersections of whose strands present to us the objects according to the meaning of which we lead our lives. At the center of such a three-dimensional spider's web, by maintaining and elaborating it, we live our lives.

The physical environment impinges upon our bodies, and according to their intrinsic constitution we respond to those impingements. Of most of the impingements we are sublimely oblivious; of a small subset we become aware. All the impingements establish relationships between us and the physical surroundings, but only the impingements of which we have an awareness partially transform the physical surroundings into objective surroundings.

Take the simple case of the classical "external senses": the eye objectifies only colors, the ear only sounds, the tongue only flavors, the nose only odors, the touch only textures and temperatures. All five have in common that they reveal the surrounding environment only insofar as it here and now acts upon our organs of sense. That is to say, all five have in common that they reveal things of the environment not according to the subjective constitution of those things as such, but according as that subjective constitution is here and now affecting our own subjective constitution as organisms. In other words, all five senses have in common that they reveal things not as they are independently but partially as they are bodies here and now in interaction with our bodies, an "interested intersubjectivity", as we might say. We may regard the cognitive relation whereby each sense aspectually objectifies the body or bodies immediately acting upon it as basic radii in the construction of the geodesic sphere of experience, which guarantee that the sphere will always include objectively elements of the physical surroundings as such. So at its surface will remain always a virtual intersection or interface between nature and culture, no matter how elaborate the sphere subsequently becomes on the ideal side of its construction.

However, radii connecting eye with colors, ear with sounds, taste buds with flavors, nose with odors, and touch with textures and temperatures are far from the whole story of sensation. Along with colors are conveyed shapes, movements and positions, as also along with touch. Hearing, too, directionalizes and localizes its stimuli, as does smell and, to a much lesser degree, taste. Thus, between the direct objects of the external sense, right from the start, a series of lateral relations are also given, relations which depend on the direct or proper objects, to be sure, but which are given simultaneously with those objects and as giving to those objects an incipient or nascent objective contour and structure: the color is not only a color, but a color with certain contours and a relative position, whether moving or at rest. In other words, the radii relations at this primitive level already present to the sense organs something that the sense organ itself is not, namely, its object, and so these relations are sign relations. The proper objects are, moreover, involved in relations which further convey what they themselves are not, such as shapes, movements, positions, and the like, and so are themselves sign-vehicles right from the start. Already you see the beginning structure of the interior of the sphere taking form: radii relations form objects at the surface of the sphere, and between these objects are other relations which further structure the objects themselves and interrelate them. The relations between the objective elements give rise to further objectification: the sound is not only heard, it is heard from behind me and as moving away, etc. Both the radii relations and the relations interconnecting them are, thus, sign relations.

Memory, imagination, and estimation of interest build upon these sensory elements, both by adding new radii and further intersections. The sensory strands of the sphere are further woven into a *perceptual* network of ever more complex objects and objectifications. In this network not only here and now physical environmental influences are at work, but objective influences from the past as well, and subjective influences from the needs and interests of the organism. The objective and subjective influences alike, as arising here and now, enter into the objective world through the same cognitive and affective relational network by which the objective world exists in the first place and filters what from the past is brought to bear on the here and now structure of objectivity.

Thus far the three-dimensional web of experience exists as tied to the biological type of the organism experiencing. Hence von Uexküll says that each species lives in its own *Umwelt*, that is to say, in our terms, each species lives in a species-specific objective world. This is also true of the human animal: its objective world is a biological *Umwelt* first of all, populated by objects that do not exist in the physical environment as such and objects that exist otherwise in the Umwelt than they do in the physical environment as such. But the human animal becomes aware of what the other animals do not, namely, the relational strands which constitute the web and structure the objects, and can now begin to play with those strands in their own right. At that moment, language in the species-specifically human sense is born, only later to be exapted into the communication system we call speech (cf. Sebeok 1993, 1987). At that moment also the strict proportion between biological heritage and objective world is transcended, and the possibility of reconstruction of the Umwelt along radically alternative lines of objectification opens up— such as an inquiry to satisfy some human curiosity about ''the environment as it appears through the eye of a fly''. It is in this way, for example, that legal systems are devised, distributing, say, property, not along biological lines of species territoriality, but according to an abstract plan of objective boundaries imposed upon the physical environment as identified with this or that of its features, for example, the Mississippi River as separating Iowa from Illinois for a certain stretch. The way is also opened to science, in the sense of an investigation into the subjective dimension of physical objects, that is to say, an investigation seeking to determine their intrinsic constitution.

Thus, the sphere of human experience, unlike a purely zoösemiotic Umwelt, does not remain completely closed unto itself but is able both to be restructured from within and to draw within itself, through the radii of sensations-intellectually-elaborated, increasingly remote and alien parts of the physical universe itself made objects of understanding and indirect experience. This facility is precisely what Peirce envisioned as the point of what he called Pragmaticism (in contrast to "pragmatism"), in recognizing the specifically intellectual component of anthroposemiosis.

E. The Interpretant

Now we come to the theoretical point which poses one of the greatest, if not the greatest, of difficulties for contemporary semiotics: how to explain the notion of interpretant? This notion is the fulcrum of semiosis in the writings of Peirce, and, in my mind, of semiotics as the doctrine of signs. Doctrine, after all, is measured by its object, in this case semiosis, the action of signs. And the action of signs is precisely the production of an interpretant as its proper effect.

The "intended" or proper[9] effect of a sign, of course, is to signify, i.e., to make present an object other than itself. This object may or may not, as we have seen, be a thing. An interpretant, accordingly, is the reason for the sign's being seen as related to something else as signified. An interpretant may or may not be itself mental, and may in turn become an object signified with *its* own interpretant, and, as an object signified, of course, it may also become a sign with its own object and further interpretant, and so on, in a cycling spiral of unending semiosis coextensive with our life, even though any particular aspect of the total process has definite resolutions and outcomes. The process as a whole is unlimited, not the stages and steps in the process. Otherwise, of course, there would be no *process* at all but only a vortex of signs failing on every side to signify, a kind of black hole illuminating nothing and obliterating everything.

---

9 For, even within anthroposemiosis, not all signs by any means convey an intention.

What is essential to the interpretant is that it mediate the difference between physical and objective being, a difference that knows no fixed line. This is why the triadic production of the interpretant is essential to the sign, while, at the same time, the interpretant need not be a mental mode of being, although, considered as founding a determinate relation of signification for some animal, it will indeed involve the mental.

We need to clarify at this juncture two points. First, how, as a result of the action of signs, a mediation of the objective is effected vis-à-vis our situation in the environment as physical entities which happen to know; and, second, what is unique about the interpretant when the spiral of semiosis happens to turn upon a mental event whether emotional or ideal (although especially the interpretant in its intellectual character distinguishes anthroposemiosis).

1. Mediation of the Objective

I would like to clarify the first point by expanding on an analysis presented in Chapter 3 of *Basics of Semiotics* (Deely 1990: 23–27). The idea of surrounding temperature produced by the physical apparatus we call a thermometer when that apparatus functions as sign represents to the interpreter of the thermometer something that itself is neither the idea nor the thermometer, namely, the condition of the environment presumed indexically represented by the thermometer. The idea as a mental representation, that is to say, a psychological reality, belongs to the order of subjective existence as the immediate object of the thermometer as sign.[10] But, within that subjective and physical order, the idea also functions to engender or found a relation to something other than itself, namely, a condition of the environment surrounding the thermometer. This condition admits, now, of two possibilities: 1. it is both objective (known) and physical (something existent besides being known), presuming the thermometer accurate; or 2. it is objective but deviant from the physical situation rather than coincident with it—it is

---

[10] Peirce c.1906: 5.473: "In these cases"—the rise of mercury in a glass tube thermometer or the bending of the double metallic strip in a metallic thermometer as indexical of an increase of atmospheric pressure—"a mental representation of the index is produced, which mental representation is called the immediate object of the sign".

merely objective—presuming the thermometer defective. As founding this objective relation through which the interpreter is put in a position to form an opinion or judgment, whether correct or mistaken (because the relation is in every case objective, but only in some cases coincidentally physical as well), about the represented state of affairs, the idea itself produced by the thermometer has in turn produced "the proper significate outcome" of the thermometer as sign, i.e., it has produced what Peirce calls the *interpretant*.

From the situation thus far described Peirce (c.1906: 5.473) considers that "it is very easy to see what the interpretant of a sign is: it is all that is explicit in the sign itself apart from its context and circumstances of utterance". The *sign* is the thermometer. The *context and circumstances of its utterance* are the ambient warmth or atmospheric pressure producing a certain level of the mercury correlated—accurately or inaccurately—with a scale, the whole of which apparatus is seen and recognized as a temperature-measuring device. And *what is explicit in the sign itself apart from this context and these circumstances* is representation of something other than the thermometer, namely, the ambient temperature objectively taken, as being presumably what the thermometer indicates it to be (although this may be wrong due to defect in the mechanism). In other words, all that is explicit in the sign itself apart from its context and circumstances of utterance, what is in Peirce's description the "proper significate outcome" of the sign acting as sign, is *the objective element of the situation as involving representation of one by another, irreducible to the dynamical interactions involved, and establishing channels and expectations along which some of the interactions will be diverted in ongoing exchanges* (if the temperature is high, you are not going to wear a heavy coat, etc.).

Notice especially that, although the idea of the thermometer enabling the thermometer to function as a sign was in the first instance a mental representation, it is not as a mental mode of subjective being that the perception produced by the thermometer functions in bringing about the interpretant. On the contrary, the idea of the thermometer enables the physical apparatus as perceived to educe yet another idea having as *its* object, rightly or wrongly, a certain ambient environmental temperature. And, as Peirce rightly says (*ibid.*), "this object does triadically produce the proper effect of the sign strictly by means of another mental sign". The irreducibility of the triadicity in the case appears when we schematize the factors involved. The situation requires a diagram of at least two triangles (Figure 9):

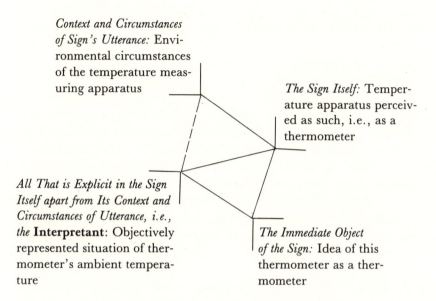

Context and Circumstances of Sign's Utterance: Environmental circumstances of the temperature measuring apparatus

The Sign Itself: Temperature apparatus perceived as such, i.e., as a thermometer

All That is Explicit in the Sign Itself apart from Its Context and Circumstances of Utterance, i.e., the **Interpretant**: Objectively represented situation of thermometer's ambient temperature

The Immediate Object of the Sign: Idea of this thermometer as a thermometer

Figure 9. *The Irreducibility of the Action of Signs*

These two triangles collapse into one when the thermometer reading is in fact accurate, i.e., when the thermometer is both correctly read and properly functioning (for then the objective context and circumstances and the physical context and circumstances in this particular coincide). But the triangles stand as two indeed when the thermometer reading is false, whether through an incorrect reading or a faulty mechanism or both (a consideration which would enable us to multiply the semiosic triads at play to three or four, without changing the principle that the sign always brings about its result triadically, as a mediation between physical and objective being). What is decisive is that, on either assumption, whether the thermometer reading be taken as true or whether it be taken as false, the intervening variable of signification prevents its reduction to the forces acting upon the physical apparatus of the thermometer "in a purely brute and dyadic way". Semiosis, not error, introduces a third factor. Error may help to make the third factor evident, but removal of error does not at all take the third factor away.[11]

2. The Interpretant as Mental Event

The ideas of our minds as psychological conditions and states are signs, inasmuch as all thought is through signs. But, as we have seen, every sign can also be an object or an interpretant, depending on its momentary place in a given spiral of semiosis. In addition, we need to note that ideas are not like atoms or material particles of any type. Peirce's synechism (his doctrine of continuity), whatever is to be said of it vis-à-vis the realm of material structures and objects as part of the physical environment, holds absolutely in the psychological realm of ideas and emotional interpretants, both as regards its conscious and unconscious dimensions which, as we now know, shade at times imperceptibly into one another. The "idea of thermometer" is not a discrete event, but a disposition in us toward recognizing certain physical structures encountered in perception and, by recognizing them, to enable them to be also signs in their own right, that is to say, objects which are also signs, or, more exactly, sign vehicles.

What is unique about ideas as signs is simply that, of all the things in our universe of experience, they are the only items that are signs before being objects, interpretants, or anything else at all. Every object, though not every aspect of every object (if what we have observed above about the unique status of sensations analytically prescissed within perception and intellection is accurate), presupposes a sign, and every sign an interpretant. The prime interpretant in the case of cognitive organisms, of course, is the biological nature of the organism itself, which determines indeed not what sensations will be actual, but what will be possible in the first place for perception to elaborate and, in our case, intellection to assimilate as best it can. Thus "man" or "woman", no less than

---

11 This is why I said in *Basics* (Deely 1990: 23) that "the distinctiveness of semiosis is unavoidable when we consider the case of two existing things affected in the course of their existence by what does not exist, but, if we understand what is distinctive about semiosis, that distinctiveness remains unmistakable even when the three terms involved in a semeiosy happen also to be all three existent."

"male bat" or "female bat", provides the initial interpretant for the signs we call ideas, and, in this regard, all that is unique about ideas as specifically anthroposemiosic is that they eventually open unto the universe in its totality as their Object. This openness in principle to totality is not at work for animals unable to thematize the difference between Umwelt and physical environment as such.

Common to all ideas, thus, is their initial formation and status as signs *before* they can *subsequently* function as either objects in reflective awareness or interpretants in awareness of environmental objects as signs in their own right, whether "natural" or "conventional". What is unique about ideas thus is that they *begin* as signs, whereas all other signs *begin* as objects. Thus, what is unique about the interpretant as a mental event is that it was, in its initial being, always a sign, not an object nor an interpretant, as it will subsequently become as the semiosis advances. This is not true of any other interpretants; neither is it true of objects which are such (logically speaking) before becoming signs. The first interpretant is the nature of the organism, its biological heritage; the first object is the environment aspectually influencing the organism through its cognitive channels; but the first sign is the idea objectifying the environmental influences as desirable or undesirable, i.e., constituting experience in the first place. Subsequent ideas will greatly elaborate the objective structure of experience and progressively differentiate it from the being of the physical environment. But every idea will stand in the first place as sign to an object signified, in the absence of which that object would dissolve into bare sensations and, beyond that, disappear entirely.

The interpretant as mental event is thus like the world of objects in one particular: both alike depend entirely on the being of ideas as signs. At the origin of the objective world of experience, at the base and at every subsequent turn of the spiral of semiosis through which experience is constructed, lies the idea as sign, the sign which is a sign before it can be either object or interpretant, the sign every perceptual or intellectual object as such presupposes in order to be as object. Thus we need to examine the "idea of idea" in order to understand the foundation of semiosis, not in nature (which is another question entirely,[12]

---

[12] See *Basics of Semiotics* (Deely 1990), Chapter 6. Using the term "thought" for what I would call objective being in the sense of "knowable as such", regardless of what

though still involving objective being in its contrast with the physical) but insofar as it involves experience in any cognitive sense.

F. The Idea as Sign

We saw above that such physical structures as smoke and bones are sometimes called "natural signs" fundamentally owing to the fact that their very physical constitution serves to guide the formation in experience and cognition of objective relations. These relations duplicate the essential structure of intersubjectivity which at least at one time obtained independently of and prior to the experience in which such objective relations are here and now formed. In fact, the relation itself so formed constitutes the sign in its actual being as sign, so that, technically speaking, the smoke and bones are not signs but rather sign-vehicles, or are signs *fundamentally* but not *formally*.

The sign-vehicle, thus, in contrast to the sign-relation, is the representative element in the sign, while the relation arising *from* this foundation, obtaining (or obtainable) *over and above* the foundation, and *terminating* at a signified object, alone makes this representative element a representation of *something other than itself*. In the absence of this relation, hence, the foundation becomes merely virtual or material *as* a foundation and is then experienced instead simply as a *self*-representation or object.

is actually known, Max Fisch (1978: 360) has described the situation of what I have proposed we call "physiosemiosis" thus: "Marine fossils found on a mountain are interpreted by the paleontologist as signs of the sea level having been higher than the level of deposit of those fossils, at far distant dates the paleontologist proceeds to estimate. But the number of such fossils that ever has been, and perhaps that ever will be, accessible to paleontologists or to other interpreters is an extremely small fraction of their total number. Those that never have been and that never will be interpreted are nonetheless signs. Again, how extremely rare is it for an ill human being or other animal to be observed at all by a trained and skilled diagnostician, and how much escapes even the most skilled! But the symptoms and other signs are there, and so are the interpretants to which they *would* lead an equally qualified observer and interpreter. The thought is 'there', though there be no thinker of it." This situation is roughly what the Latins meant by "transcendental relation", discussed in note 3 of this Chapter, p. 207 above, and below in Appendix 1, p. 249 ff.

The concept or idea, indeed, the percept of a pure zoösemiosis no less, is a sign-vehicle in just this sense, i.e., it is a subjective structure or modification which according to its intrinsic being guides the formation of a relation to an object signified, and as such the idea is a sign fundamentally rather than formally. But, unlike the fossil bone or plume of smoke which can exist without being apprehended or known, the idea exists only insofar as it guides an apprehension to the awareness of this rather than that object: it is the knowing that forms the idea, so that the idea cannot be *except* as an idea *of* its object. The bone, of course, is the bone *of* some animal and the smoke *of* some fire; but here the *of* refers to the *productive source* of the bone or the fire, whereas the *of* in the idea refers not to the mind as producing the idea but to *that of which the idea makes the mind aware in producing it.* In other words, the *of* distinctive of the idea as such refers not backward to the idea's productive source as *my* idea or *your* idea, but outward to the objective term of an experience in principle suprasubjective and, insofar, accessible to others besides the one here and now forming the idea making that object present.

It is necessary to be quite precise in symbolising this situation.[13] Up to now we have spoken of relation as an intersubjective mode of being, because up to now we have been considering relations as able to obtain in the physical as well as the objective order, and in the physical order a relation always requires a physically existent source as well as a physic-

---

13 For example, the considerations of the preceding paragraph suggest that the late Latin designation of the concept as a *signum formale*, while justified by the fact that the idea cannot exist *without* founding a relation to an object, is also problematic inasmuch as the idea (or concept) in itself is not the *suprasubjective* referral or relation as such required for renvoi but only the *subjective* referral or fundament on which that relation—in which alone the sign *formally* consists—is based. The existential inseparability of the two in the case of the idea (which is why an idea, in contrast to, say, our fossil bone, has no existence apart from its semiosic one) does not gainsay the modal real distinction of relation from its foundation, or the fact that the foundation as such is neither suprasubjective nor (still less) intersubjective but subjective. By speaking of *the concept* as a "formal sign", the scholastic analysis did not foreclose the very confusion I am about to criticize in Jakobson's version of the classical Latin formula for *signum*. Indeed we find, in Pedro da Fonseca, for example (1564: lib. I, cap. VIII), the very reduction of sign to sign-vehicle that would become in Descartes and Locke the irredeemably solipsistic equation of objects with ideas.

ally existent terminus in order to obtain. Whence, even though there can be relations of measured to measure in the order of physical existence, as when a meteor crater reveals (to the sufficiently cognizant observer) the weight, size, speed, and perhaps even composition of the meteor, or a gunshot wound reveals the calibre of the weapon and angle and distance of its firing, these relations as dyadic are necessarily intersubjective, grounded in action and reaction. They are never strictly one-sided in the sense that cognitive relations can be. For the cognitive relation is not dyadic but irreducibly triadic, and the dyad of mind as forming the idea and ideas as formed by the mind cannot but engender an irreducible triad, because the very formation of an idea necessarily guides the mind to an awareness of the formal correlate of the idea as sign, namely, the object represented—the object to which the idea as sign points as to what is signified. The content of the idea is a representative content, to be sure, but a content representative of *something the idea is not*.

We see here an essential flaw in Jakobson's accepted formula for the sign as *aliquid stat pro aliquo*. In phrasing his formula thus, Jakobson has left open a Cartesian interpretation of the sign, and of the idea as sign. For an object stands within experience for something, namely, itself, regardless of whether it is a thing or not, and even when it misleads us in this particular. By contrast, a sign stands within experience only for something *other* than itself, something which it itself is not, and insofar as it fails to do this it fails or ceases to be a sign. A formula more exact than *aliquid stat pro aliquo*, therefore, is *aliquid stat pro alio*: a sign is anything that stands for something other than itself. In order to consider any object, the mind must first form an idea of that object, *first* as a logical priority, but simultaneously as a temporal experience, for *as soon as* and *while* the mind forms a concept the object too is formed and made present as the term of the sign relation. Knowing from past experience what bluejays are, we retain a disposition to see a bluejay when one flies into our perceptual field. The bluejay objectified becomes, as physical organism, an instance of what we know: a particular object terminating dyadically a more general objective structure that exists apart from the particular instance not dyadically but triadically and through a semiosis.

This triadic structure thus enables us to think of objects in the absence of their physical presence within our perceptual field, as in memories, because, "a relation has specification from its foundation as from its cause and specifying principle,'' as Poinsot put it (1632a: 380/13–17[14]), ''while it has specification from its term not as from the cause of the specification but as from a factor completing and terminating the rationale of the specifying''.[15]

[14] ''A fundamento habet relatio specificationem tamquam a causa et principio specificante, a termino autem non ut a causa specificationis, sed ut a complente et terminante rationem specificandi.''

[15] ''The reason for these remarks is taken from what has been said, because the whole reality of a relation is from its foundation according to the order to a terminus, since indeed the entire being of a relation is toward another, as the definition of relation says. Whence since a relation essentially requires both foundation and terminus, it ought not to be understood to be from one in any way that precludes its being understood to be from the other also.

''But the second part of the conclusion [i.e., the statement cited in the text above], about the way in which these two work together in effecting the specification, must not be thought to assert that each partially concurs in such a way that the fundament provides a part of the specification and the terminus a part, but must be understood to assert that each provides the entire specification in different orders of causality. Some explain this situation by saying that the fundament concurs by initiating and the terminus by completing, others by saying that the fundament works in the order of an efficient cause and the terminus in the order of an extrinsic formal cause, and others again by saying that the fundament specifies as virtually precontaining within itself the terminus to which it is proportioned, in this way dissolving the diversity of foundations into the diverse formalities of the termini.

''Yet the distinction has to be made between the terminus understood most formally in the rationale of an opposed terminus, and the terminus understood fundamentally on the side of the subjective being founding this rationale of terminating. In the former way a terminus concurs in a specification purely terminatively, but not by causing that specification, because so considered it is a pure terminus and simultaneous by nature and in cognition with the relation; therefore as such it is not a specifying cause, because a cause is not naturally simultaneous with but prior to its effect. If it is considered in the latter way, the terminus stands as an extrinsic formal cause and specifies in the manner of an object, and in this way a single specifying rationale of the relation arises from the foundation and terminus together, inasmuch as the foundation contains the terminus within itself by a proportion and power; for it is not relative to a given terminus unless it is a specific fundament, and conversely. In this way, to the extent that they are mutually proportioned, terminus and foundation together bring about a single rationale specifying a relation which postulates both a specific foundation and a specific terminus corresponding thereto.

''From these remarks one can further gather what a formal terminus is in the rationale of something specifying. For although specifically different relations can be

The mind of the knower, the cognitive capacity of the cognitive organism as being of a definite biological type, thus serves as interpretant to the idea as sign. The power actuated in the formation of *this* idea is aware of *that* object rather than some other. The object itself, if it has a physical structure and is here and now acting through that structure upon the physical subjectivity of the organism as cognitive, indeed participates in the specification of the mind to form this idea rather than some other one. But it is not the dyadic aspect of such interaction that constitutes the objective relation of idea to object signified. And the objective relation of idea to object signified is indeed rendered in such a circumstance physical as well as objective.[16] But when the circumstances change and the objective relation ceases to be physical it remains unchanged in its essential being as trirelatively objective. It remains a suprasubjective mode englobing the knower at the center of a relative sphere open in principle to communication with another cognitive organism properly disposed in its psychological subjectivity, that is, one which has formed a similar idea and hence engendered an

anchored to the materially same terminus, yet they cannot be anchored to the formally same terminus. But the formal specifying rationale in a terminus is understood in accordance with a correspondence and adequate proportion to its fundament ... Wherefore, as regards the specifying of any relation, in just the way that the fundament is understood under the final rationale of the grounding of the relation, so the terminus of the relation is understood under the proportion and correspondence of the terminating." Poinsot, *Tractatus de Signis*, Appendix C, "On the Source of Specific and Individual Identity of Relations", 381/25–386/46 (Latin text in Appendix of Longer Citations, pp. 255 below).

16 "I answer the question before us therefore by saying: The relation of a natural sign to its significate by which the sign is constituted in being as a sign, is mind-independent and not mind-dependent, considered in itself and by virtue of its fundament and presupposing the existence of the terminus and the other conditions for a mind-independent or physical relation."—"Respondeo ergo et dico: Relatio signi naturalis ad suum signatum, qua constituitur in esse signi, realis est, et non rationis, quantum est ex se et vi sui fundamenti et supponendo existentiam termini ceterasque conditiones relationis realis." Poinsot, *Tractatus de Signis*, Book I, Question 2, "Whether the Sign-Relation in the Case of Natural Signs is Mind-Independent or Mind-Dependent", 137/8–14 (= *Artis Logicae Secunda Pars*, Quaest. XXI, "De Signo Secundum Se", Art. 2, "Utrum in Signo Naturali Relatio Sit Realis vel Rationis", Reiser ed. 656b20–26).

overlapping sphere similarly suprasubjective and at that moment constituting, insofar as overlapping, an *intersubjective moment* or *commens*, in Peirce's terminology, a *cominterpretant* or shared object transcendent to the physical circumstances as such (see Johansen 1993, 1993a).

When we are speaking of relations as physically realized, whether the relations in question be products of brute force or products of semiosis—whether the relations be dyadic in their causal provenance or triadic—they constitute an intersubjective zone. But when we are speaking of relations precisely as objective, that is, precisely as semiosic and so far indifferent to the actual existence of their objective termini as specified through their ideal fundament in the psychological subjectivity of the knower, it is not necessarily an *actual* intersubjectivity that prevails. What prevails necessarily is only a suprasubjectivity *in principle able to be further realized intersubjectively* through an adequate social interaction, regardless of whether the environmental conditions are otherwise such as to allow this intersubjectivity realized objectively to also be physical.

We see then what becomes of the "idea of idea" in the context of a thematically developed doctrine of signs. When we realize that ideas as representations of objects are so only insofar as they formally guide the mind to an apprehension of this rather than that object through a relation of sign to signified, we understand also that ideas psychologically considered, like bones and puffs of smoke physically considered, are *sign-vehicles* which, by their very constitution, are proportioned to one object rather than to another, and under this consideration are called "natural signs" in the same sense that bones and puffs of smoke are so-called within the context of cognitive experience. But we also understand that these concepts or ideas are unlike bones and puffs of smoke in that they cannot exist *except* in the context of actual experience. Hence, unlike bones and puffs of smoke, concepts or ideas cannot be objects before (or without) being signs, because the relation to their significate which defines them—or, rather, *constitutes* them—as signs cannot be prescinded from. The reason for this was well noted by Poinsot (1632a: 382/4–12): the terminus of a relation understood most formally in the rationale of an opposed terminus concurs in a specification purely terminatively, but not by causing that specification, because so considered it is a pure terminus and simultaneous by nature and in cognition with the relation.

At the same time, inasmuch as the cognitive relation as existing within experience is precisely triadic and not dyadic, its terminus, i.e., its significate, "understood fundamentally on the side of the subjective being founding this rationale of terminating, stands as an extrinsic formal cause and specifies in the manner of an object, and in this way a single specifying rationale of the relation arises from the foundation and terminus together, inasmuch as the foundation contains the terminus within itself by a proportion and power; for it is not relative to a given terminus unless it is a specific fundament, and conversely."[17] Whence the object need not exist apart from the semiosis, even though it *may* so exist in the right circumstances. Not only is the universe perfused with signs but, insofar as it is an objective universe, it does not exist at all except through signs, even though, after all, it is not composed exclusively of them—at least, not in every respect.[18]

We can summarize our results so far as follows.

Idea and object in every case differ as that which is known from that on the basis of which it is known. In representational terms, idea and

---

17   The citation in the text above corresponds to Poinsot 1632a: Appendix C, 382/14–21, with the liberty taken of explicitating the antecedents of the indefinite articles. The justification and accuracy of the expansion is clear from the larger Latin context of 382/4–27 (= *Artis Logicae Secunda Pars*, Q. 17, "De Praedicamento Relationis", Art. 6, "Unde Sumatur Distinctio Specifica et Numerica Relationis", 602b33–603a14), which I cite: "distinguendum est, quod terminus vel sumitur formalissime in ratione termini oppositi, vel fundamentaliter ex parte absoluti fundantis istam rationem terminandi. Primo modo terminus concurrit pure terminative ad specificationem, non autem causando illam, quia sic est purus terminus et est simul natura et cognitione cum relatione; ergo ut sic non est causa specificans, quia causa non est simul natura, sed prior effectu. Si secundo modo consideratur, habet se ut causa formalis extrinseca et specificat ad modum obiecti, et sic ex fundamento et termino consurgit unica ratio specificandi relationem, quatenus fundamentum continet in se terminum in proportione et virtute; non enim est ad talem terminum, nisi sit tale fundamentum, et e converso. Et sic quatenus inter se proportionantur, conficiunt unam rationem specificandi relationem, quae et tale fundamentum postulat et talem terminum ei correspondentem."

18   I am thinking here of one of the finest upshots of the Urbino conference at which Watt and Sebeok overstated the case for semiotics to the point of provoking Dines Johansen's exhortation to "Let sleeping signs lie". See Watt 1993 and Johansen 1993 for particulars. See also Deely 1992a.

object differ as that which is represented from another which represents it, regardless of whether that which is represented has or ever had a mind-independent physical existence. Ideas in our minds are representamens, but representamens *of something besides themselves*, something irreducibly other. This "something besides" the idea is the object of the representation. The connection between the two, idea and object, is a pure relation. In some cases, namely, when the object thought of is also a physical being and existing at the time that we think of it, the relation between idea signifying and object signified is also a physical relation. But it is not the fact of being physical that makes the relation in question be an objective relation. On the contrary, the relation need not be physical in order to be objective, and it remains as a relation even when the conditions for physical existence do not obtain, as is notably the case when the terminus of the relation does not, or does no longer, exist. The relation is objective because, in every case, it terminates at an object. It obtains between that which as such, by its intrinsic constitution, represents something other than itself, and that which, as such, represents itself (and may not even have an intrinsic, a subjective, constitution) and exists as a pure terminus, a creature of the very relation through which it is presented, though it *may* also be more than this.

In the case of a physical relation, the foundation or fundament of the relation—the characteristic of an individual on the basis of which it is related to another individual—is distinct from the other individual which is the terminus of the relation and from the relation itself (the fundament exists within or as part of the individual related, whereas the relation itself is always something over and above the individual related and intersubjective between the individuals related). Just so, in the case of an objective relation, the idea as a representation provides but the fundament or foundation for the idea as a relation to its object. And, just as in the case of a physical relation it is the relation itself that makes the terminus be a terminus even though that terminus may also have an existence in its own right as a material object, so in the case of an objective relation the relation itself makes the terminus be as terminus even though in this case the terminus need have no further existence in its own right and may be nothing material. (Similarly, in the case of a photograph or a statue of a dead person, the photograph or statue in its own being is fundamentally a representation; but this representation, on being perceived, becomes the ground for a cognitive relation which goes beyond the physical photograph to the very nonexistent person of whom the photograph was taken. The sign formally consists in this relation, not in the representation that constitutes it only fundamentally.)

The idea as a sign is thus conceived as always and necessarily, by virtue of its proper being, creating as it were a suprasubjective zone or objective sphere around the individual thinking, a four-dimensional web which is always at the same time in some parts actually and in all parts at least virtually intersubjective. This realm is actually intersubjective whenever some object of thought is also being actually considered by another thinker, as also in its sensory channels as such. It is virtually intersubjective when the thought concerns a nonexistent object which, as object, could also be constituted as terminus of thought for another should the requisite representation be formed fundamentally in that other's mind. The objects of thought, regardless of their status vis-à-vis the physical environment, always exist as objects at the intersecting termini of idea-based relations, and communication is possible in exactly the same way that any two things can be related to a common third.

G. Renvoi Again

Ken Ketner has recently argued (1993) that the irreducibility of triadic relations to any combination of dyads requires that we think of intersubjective communication events as noncausal phenomena, and hence that causal thinking must be transcended in order to gain any understanding of Thirdness as irreducible to brute interactions, the realm of ''Dyadic Science'', where alone causal statements apply. I think enough has been said about the nature of semeiosy at this point for anyone to realize that the problem of understanding the action of signs is not rooted in the fact that causality is not operative in such action, but rather in the fact that the causality at work in the production of renvoi requires a more sophisticated analysis of causality than is possible within a conceptual scheme which sees in relation nothing more than a contribution constructed and imposed by the mind on a world of interacting physical objects. The problem with understanding the effect proper to signs is bound up with understanding the nature of relation as an intersubjective reality of the physical universe whereby the way is opened to suprasubjective objective relations. These relations remain virtually intersubjective even under those circumstances where an actual intersubjectivity cannot obtain, either because the objective terminus sustained by the web of renvoi no longer exists apart from that web, or because there is at the moment no overlap between two or more networks of experience that includes the objective terminus sustained from the center of one such web, such as happens when a new proposal or invention has been made within an Innenwelt (the inner correlative of Umwelt) but not yet coded—not yet exapted—so as to become accessible through language at the level of Umwelt.

Indeed, the peculiarly indirect character of the objective causal action proper to signs is already found adumbrated in the physical order itself, by the fact that relations cannot be produced directly by dyadic interactions but only *result from* something that has been so produced, as circumstances allow.[19] "And the reason for this is that relation, on

---

19 "A relation accrues to a subject without any change that is directly and immediately terminated at the relation, but not without a change that is terminated mediately and indirectly at that relation. Just as risibility results from the same action by which a man is produced, so from the production of a white thing is produced similitude to another existing white thing. But if another white thing did not exist, by virtue of the generation of the first white thing, that similitude and any other relation that would result from the positing of its terminus would remain in a virtual state. Whence distance neither conduces to nor obstructs the resultance of a pure relation, because these relations do not depend upon a local situation; for far or near, a son is in the same way the son of his father. Nor is the relation in the other extreme produced by the terminus itself through some emission of power when it is brought into existence. Rather is the existence of the terminus the condition for a relation's resulting from an already existing fundament by virtue of the original generation whereby that fundament was brought into being as inclining toward any terminus of such a fundament. Whence even though the generating has now ceased, it yet remains in its effect or power, inasmuch as it leaves a fundament sufficient for a relation to result."—"Relatio advenit subiecto sine aliqua mutatione, quae directe et immediate terminetur ad relationem, non tamen sine mutatione, quae mediate et indirecte terminetur ad illam. Sicut eadem actione, qua producitur homo, dimanat risibilitas, sic ad productionem albi producitur similitudo ad aliud album, quod existit. Si autem non existit, manet ex vi generationis albi quasi in virtute illa similitudo et quaecumque alia relatio, ut resultet posito suo termino. Unde ad hoc nihil conducit vel obstat distantia, quia relationes istae non dependent a locali situatione; eodem enim modo

account of its minimal entitative character, does not depend on a subject in precisely the same way that direct determinations of subjectivity do, but stands rather as a third kind of being consisting in and resulting from the coordination [in time] of two extremes; and therefore, in order to exist in the nature of things, a relation continuously depends on the fundament coordinating it with a term, and not only on a subject and productive cause.''[20] From this becomes possible the difference between the vehicles for traditionally so-called ''natural'' and ''conventional'' signs which we considered above, as described by an unknown author of the Latin Age whose work has so far come down to us pseudonymous-

est filius sui patris filius distans et indistans. Neque enim ab ipso termino, quando ponitur per aliquam emissionem virtutis, producitur relatio in alio extremo, sed positio termini est conditio, ut ex fundamento antea posito resultet relatio ex vi primae generationis, qua positum est in rerum natura ut petens respicere quemcumque terminum talis fundamenti. Unde licet generans iam desierit, remanet tamen in sua virtute, quatenus relinquit sufficiens fundamentum, ut resultet relatio.'' Poinsot , *Tractatus de Signis,* First Preamble ''On Relation'', Article 1, ''Whether There Exist on the Side of Mind-Independent Being Intrinsic Forms Which Are Relations'', 84/45-85/22 (= *Artis Logicae Prima Pars*, Q. 17 ''De Relatione'', Art. 1, ''Utrum a Parte Rei Dentur Relationes, Quae Sint Formae Intrinsecae'', 576a36-576b19).

20 Poinsot, *Tractatus de Signis*, Second Preamble, ''On Relation'', Article 2, ''What Is Required for a 'Categorial' Relation'', 89/13-20 (= *Artis Logicae Secunda Pars*, Quaest. 17 ''De Relatione'', Art. 2, ''Quid Requiratur, ut Aliqua Relatio Sit Praedicamentalis'', Reiser ed. 578a13-23): ''Et hoc ideo est, quia relatio propter suam minimam entitatem non praecise dependet a subiecto sicut aliae formae absolutae, sed se habet ut entitas tertia ex coordinatione duorum extremorum consistens et resultans, ideoque ut sit in rerum natura debet dependere a fundamento coordinante illam ad terminum, et non solum a subiecto et causa productiva.''

See also *ibid.:* 88/18-27 (= 577b31-42): ''though a cause is required for every entity and form, yet in a special sense a fundament is said to be required for a relation, because other forms require a cause only in order to be produced in being and exist, whereas relation—owing to its minimal entitative character and because in terms of its proper concept it is toward another—requires a fundament not only in order to exist but also in order to be able to remain in existence, that is, in order to be a mind-independent rationale of physical being.''—''Et licet ad omnem entitatem et formam requiratur causa, specialiter tamen ad relationem dicitur requiri fundamentum, quia aliae formae solum requirunt causam, ut producantur in esse et existant, relatio autem propter suam minimam entitatem et quia ex proprio conceptu est ad aliud, requirit fundamentum non solum ut existat, sed etiam ut sit capax existendi, id est ut sit entitas realis.''

ly:[21] "according to its proper rationale relation need not be anything in that of which it is predicated," as when a flag is taken to signify a country, "although it sometimes is this owing to the cause of the relative condition", as when a Brontosaurus bone is correctly identified by a paleontologist. But whence becomes possible also mistaken identifications and lies generally, wherein the fact that relation need not be verified in that of which it is predicated becomes the occasion for someone being misled, a possibility which traces directly to the indirect character of the causality whence relations result and open the way to semiosis. Hence the accuracy in Umberto Eco's famous assertion of "the possibility of lying" as "the proprium of semiosis" (Eco 1976: 58–59). Semiotics indeed studies everything which can be used in order to lie, inasmuch as there is signification wherever there is a lie. But this is only because semiotics studies more generally everything which, on being known, reveals something more.

Of course, as we have seen, the special sense in which a fundament is required as cause of a relation makes possible the singularly semiosic character of ideas as founding relations to objects in their difference from things. This difference consists precisely in the requirement that an object represent itself to a knower, whereas a thing in its proper being is indifferent to being represented or known, though without precluding it. Every object presupposes a knower through relation to which the object as such is constituted as a terminus of knowledge, while at the same time standing over against the knower through the specification it has as terminus exercised through the fundament of its proper idea. But every thing presupposes a knower only if and to the extent that it becomes assimilated to experience through the net of renvoi, which need not happen except according to circumstance.

So it is not that semiosic phenomena are noncausal, as Ketner proposes, but rather that causality in semiosis depends upon renvoi, the actualization through experience of the difference between objective and physical being, between Umwelt and physical environment. In this estab-

---

21 Cited in Poinsot 1632a: 89/1–5: "Relatio non est aliud quam habitudo unius ad alterum; unde secundum propriam rationem non habet, quod sit aliquid in eo, de quo dicitur, sed hoc aliquando habet ex habitudinis causa."

lishment the role of relation is central, because only through the indifference of relation to its subjective ground—that is to say, only through the proper nature of relation as suprasubjective in every case, regardless of the difference between objective and physical existence—is semiosis able to constitute an interface between nature and culture, and to transpire at their intersection.

The action of signs is exercised through relations. And as such it participates in the very same causality by which relations are specified, which is to say the constitution of their fundaments as *ordered to* a terminus—with the difference that, for the relation to be physical and not just objective, that terminus must also have a physical existence. This constitution of a fundament indeed comes about through productive and material causality. But insofar as the fundament materially constituted is correlated with a terminus it is a question of formal causality, of an iconic or indexical character intrinsic to the fundament (especially in the case of natural signs), indeed, but a formal causality which is at the same time *extrinsic* to the fundament insofar as the fundament has for its correlate a terminus other than itself (for otherwise it would not be a fundament), which terminus, when it is an object, is already in principle distinct from physical being and superordinate to it.

The analysis of causality refined to this level of explanation was one of the last achievements of Latin thought, from an era and an area consigned to oblivion by mainstream modern thought for centuries now. This thought is destined to live again as the pressures of postmodern developments in philosophy, science, and culture make the study of signs and the action proper to themselves a central problematic. Among the moderns, only in the last of them do we find a lexicon which approaches the requirements for laying bare the intelligibility of semiosis. In this regard, Peirce is not only the last of the moderns but the first of the postmoderns, occupying a position analogous to that of Augustine as last of the Fathers and first of the medievals. Peirce saw clearly that the causality whereby semiosis effects renvoi must be one which both constitutes and transcends the given material structure with which it is involved. This double criterion of at once constituting and transcending a given sign vehicle is precisely what suggested to him final causality as the causality proper to semiosis, a hypothesis which in turn led him to consider panpsychism in order to understand semiosis.

But, as we saw in Chapter 6, it is not necessary to go this far in order to discover the causality adequating semiosis. The dependency in being that knowledge as such has upon the object known is specificative more fundamentally than it is intentional. It is not a question of teleology, but of specification. Whence the type of causality required to explain the action of signs is not final causality, but extrinsic formal causality of the specificative or 'objective' type. This terminology does not appear as such in the Peircean lexicon, though it has an approximating counterpart in the Peircean notion of 'ideal' causality (a terminology we are required to abandon by fully three of Peirce's eight rules for an Ethics of Terminology[22]). Formal causality in the specificative sense, as we saw in Chapter 6, is the causality that enables the sign to achieve its distinctive function of making present what the sign-vehicle itself is not, regardless of whether it is itself an object or a psychological condition—an idea—enabling a knower to be aware of an object, and regardless of whether the object signified further enjoys a physical existence apart from the signification.

There is no need to repeat in these concluding remarks the details of the analysis of the question of causality laid out in Chapter 6. But I would like to supplement those remarks here with an example which demonstrates that the abstract discussion of causality according to the various modes of dependency in being (which is the underlying notion of causality as such), particularly as it applies to semiosis, has a very concrete bearing. The following example is taken from ¶109 of *The Human Use of Signs*.

Think simply of an actual conversation. The words spoken provide a physical sign-vehicle in the sound-waves which strike the ear as the efficient cause of the nerve reactions in the speaker. The relation of these spoken words to an objective content, conveyed along with the sound-waves but superordinate to them and differentiating them from ''mere noises'', makes of them linguistic signs rather than ''sounds signifying nothing but themselves''. This objective content gives the discourse its

---

22 Peirce's mature formulation of these rules is reproduced as an Appendix to *The Human Use of Signs* (Deely 1994), pp. 173–174, and the rules are applied to the case at hand in ¶s92–108, esp. ¶107.

specific form as about *this* rather than that, and this form of the discourse in turn focusses the attention of the hearer. Here the objective content of the discourse functions as the extrinsic formal cause specifying the listener to attend to *this*. If the information thus conveyed was "a word of advice" and the hearer heeds the advice in some subsequent action, the objective content of the advice is now functioning for the actor rather as an exemplary cause, an ideal type or model against which the action is being measured. We see in this way both that extrinsic formal causalities of both the specifying type and the ideal or exemplificatory type are at work all the time in animal life and that objective causality as underlying all understanding (and indeed cognition generally) is actually far more fundamental to human culture than the efficient causality which is otherwise a blind force of nature. This is the point Ketner was trying to make with his otherwise too-hasty proposal—reminiscent, ironically (inasmuch as Democritus was a reductionist), of the "swerve" Democritus assigned to movements of atoms—of "noncausal phenomena".[23]

---

[23] Ketner 1993: 55: "I had often thought that the social sciences might be secure if only one could arrive at a dramatic breakthrough, a convincing new crucial experiment or observation based upon some technique derived from a lightning-flash of insight. Mired in that rut, I would often mutter to myself, 'Be patient, a Newton of the social sciences will arrive some day'. I now think this way of thinking is a mirage. For if such a new technique were based upon dyadic considerations, as this thought seems to presuppose, it would fail for the reasons already noted.

"Then what is to be done? In fact, that which is to be done is in kind already being done. Every day each of us accomplishes multiple acts of understanding. The requisite breakthrough occurred many thousands of years ago when one of our ancestors, instead of merely reacting to the course of events, somehow first understood something. The Newton of the social sciences is that unknown ancestor who first understood and conveyed that ability to descendants.

"This seems to imply that what has been called 'commonsense psychology' or routine experience is a likely starting point in social science. ... Although it cannot be argued here, I suspect that unanalyzed common-sense abilities, which are rich in triadic relations, lurk in the background everywhere in contemporary science of all kinds, and that these factors constitute irreplaceable contributions and indeed make the otherwise unintelligible Dyadic Science approach (which doesn't recognize these factors) semi-palatable and serviceable in a jury-rigged sense.

"If we do that ... we might understand understanding better. At the very least we could avoid destructive reductionism."

Because formal causality ties intelligibility to the intrinsic constitution of an entity, whether the entity be natural or artifactual, the objective exercise of this causality in semiosis through the action specifically proper to signs: renvoi, the reference whereby objects exist in experience, and of any object beyond itself—ensures that semiotics cannot be confined to the order of culture alone, but, like semiosis itself, constitutes an interface between the two orders. At this interface, the sign manifests itself not at all as a physical thing, nor even as a peculiar type and variety of object. The sign appears, rather, as the linkage whereby objects, be they bodily entities or purely objective, come to stand one for another within some particular context or web of experience. And semiosis appears as the process whereby phenomena originating anywhere in the universe signify virtually in their present being also their past and their future and begin the further process of *realizing* these virtualities—especially when life intervenes and, within life, when cognition supervenes. The process does not begin with the advent of cognitive organisms, but merely enters a further phase—a new magnitude of thirdness. At the level of anthroposemiosis, semiosis finally reveals itself for what it has been all along, a task that can be accomplished only in community, and over the indefinitely long run. Furthermore, in the case of anthroposemiosis, the preservation and generation of culture is future-oriented *beyond* mere biological propagation, a point that completes the grand view of a progression through past-future relations from physiosemiosis to anthroposemiosis, and vindicates Peirce's intuition that, at some point and in some fundamental way, teleology is a part of semiosis overall. "In other words," to borrow a summation of Santaella-Braga (1992: 313), "where there is a sign, there is a temporal process, seeing that the action of the sign is to develop itself in time", as link builds upon link in the objective constitution and elaboration of human experience as being, finally, a growth of understanding in time.

H. Conclusion

Not only according to Peirce (c.1897: 2.228) but for all the major investigators of signs before him, "a sign is something which stands to somebody for something in some respect or capacity". The classic formula for the sign, as a concept first born among the Latins in the usage that has become contemporary (that is, as transcending whatever divisions there are between nature and culture[24]), needs to be reformulated thus: *Aliquid stat pro alio ad aliquem*. If we are to shorten it for convenience, then it should be, for the reasons we have considered in some detail, *aliquid stat pro alio*, in preference to *aliquid stat pro aliquo*, a formulation which lends itself to a confusion of signs with objects in the very manner that Descartes took as his basis for launching classical modern philosophy.

With this qualification in place, my final suggestion in this work is that Jakobson's French *renvoi* indeed stands, as Sebeok said (1986: 66), as a word by which Jakobson "deftly captured and transfixed each and every sign process conforming to the classic formula". Thus qualified and understood, it is time that we make of this term a common part of the technical vocabulary of contemporary semiotics.

---

[24] Eco *et al.* 1986: 65: "one must realize that Greek semiotics, from the corpus Hippocratum up to the Stoics, made a clearcut distinction between a theory of verbal language (ὀνόματα) and a theory of signs (σημεῖα). Signs are natural events acting as symptoms or indices, and they entertain with that which they point to a relation based upon the mechanisms of inference ('if such a symptom, then such a sickness'; 'if smoke then burning'). Words stand in quite a different relation with what they signify. This relation is based upon the mere equivalence or biconditionality which appears also in the influential Aristotelian theory of definition and tree of Porphyry which springs from it.

"It was Augustine who first proposed a 'general semiotics'—that is, a general 'science' or 'doctrine' of signs, where sign becomes the genus of which words (ὀνόματα) and a theory of signs (σημεῖα) are alike equally species.

"With Augustine, there begins to take shape this '*doctrina*' or 'science' of *signum*, wherein both symptoms and the words of language, mimetic gestures of actors along with the sounds of military trumpets and the chirrups of cicadas, all become species. In essaying such a doctrine, Augustine foresees lines of development of enormous theoretical interest; but he suggests the possibility of resolving, rather than effects a definitive resolution of, the ancient dichotomy between the inferential relations linking natural signs to the things of which they are signs and the relations of equivalence linking linguistic terms to the concept(s) on the basis of which some thing 'is'—singly or plurally—designated."

Precisely the resolution of the dichotomy between inferential relations and equivalence relations through the identification of the indifference of relation to its subjective ground and univocal realization as objective in sign natural or conventional alike, then, was, as we said in Chapter 4 above, pp. 69-70, the achievement of Poinsot's *Tractatus* at the close of the Latin Age.

Transition to the Future

The Way of Signs

Ancient philosophy, both Greek and Latin, set out upon the way of things. Modern philosophy took what its classical mainstream founders saw as "the way of ideas".[1] But modern philosophy from its beginning failed to understand the difference between either the things of nature or the objects of experience from which such things are prescissed, on the one hand, and the pure signs that both objects and things alike presuppose in order to be presented within experience and set off critically against one another.

The result, to borrow one of Whitehead's felicitous titles (1933), was a series of "Adventures of Ideas" which gave us realism as well as idealism. Idealism was the result of the development of the epistemological paradigm proper to modernity, whereas realism developed by way of reaction and opposition to the loss of the world of nature and things now deemed forever and irretrievably veiled behind phenomena spun of the mind's own workings. The struggle to the death of these philosophical adversaries provided us with the spectacle of the death throes of modernity itself, consequent upon the exhaustion of its epistemological paradigm in the refined development of its utmost consequences as solipsism. Just as the Latin Age finally "exhausted itself in the plenitude of its refinements",[2] so the Modern Age finally wore itself out with the consequences of the way of ideas construed as objects thrown up by the

---

[1] The actual expression is from Leibniz's Preface to his *New Essays concerning Human Understanding* of c.1704.

[2] In Simonin's description (1930: 145-146).

mind under the provocation of things both psychic and physic forever hidden from the grasp of human understanding.

The discovery of renvoi in the Iberian currents of late Latin development was too feeble and, ultimately, too isolated by the political and religious currents of classical early modernity to turn the way of ideas into what it no doubt should have been (given the true nature of ideas and their role in semiosis), namely, the way of signs. As it happened, philosophy took a four-hundred-year time-out from its normal development, to explore the consequences of conflating representation and signification in the idea of ideas.

The time-out was far from a stagnation. It appears to have been an almost necessary *prise de conscience* in which thought struggled within anthroposemiosis to come to terms with itself. To the admonition of the late Latin scholastics who had begun the decisive move toward a semiotic consciousness—"et disces elevare ingenium, aliumque rerum ordinem ingredi"—the mainstream early moderns turned a deaf ear. Whence it fell to a late modern, Charles Peirce, to realize that the way out of the idealism-realism impasse lay not in a return to some earlier system of philosophy but in the development of an entirely new categorial scheme capable of accounting for the compenetration within experience of consequences arising both from the nature of things and from the workings of thought in the constitution of the Umwelt (technically, rather, the *Lebenswelt* or *objective world*, as I have explained in detail elsewhere[3]) within which science, philosophy, and morality alike unfold as postlinguistic consequences of an objective world species-specifically open to remodelling based on the grasp of being in its transcendental amplitude.

With this discovery, what was only adumbrated by the Iberian scholastics became an actual movement of thought vital today under the banner of semiotics. This movement has for its maxim not "To the things themselves" but the subtler realization that "There is nothing in the understanding nor in the perception of sense that is not possessed through a sign". Reality is not only what it is, but also what it will be; and in this becoming we are participants through semiosis. The classical ideal of the detached observer gives place to the semiotic reality of the participant in creation, for which thought itself turns out to be essential.

---

3 In *The Human Use of Signs*, passim.

What is decisive in the role of thought in semiosis turns out to be not the presentation of objects to be grasped as such but the factor of renvoi, whereby thought always represents and is measured by an object beyond itself that proves to be in turn a mélange of signifiers linked always in some unexpected ways to yet further ranges of signifieds.

This new beginning labels itself "postmodern" for want of a better name, since it knows in its nascence what it is *against* (modernity) more clearly than what it will itself become. Positive features of postmodernity will be acquired by advancing along the way of signs. "The identity of man", Peirce wrote with his decidedly prefeminist consciousness of 1868 (5.315-6), "consists in the *consistency* of what he does and thinks, and consistency is the intellectual character of a thing; that is, its expressing something ... so that reality depends on the ultimate decision of the community"—just as the divine reality, Poinsot tells us (in this following the trajectory of thought taken over from Aquinas), consists in a community of Persons.

The way of signs is thus different from the way of ideas which the moderns entered upon in search of certitudes. It is also different from the way of things which the ancients entered upon in search of what is what it is independently of human thinking and doing. The way of signs is the path of the infinite long run. In entering upon this path, we are not likely soon to reach a final resting place or dead-end, unless, of course we forget (or fail to learn in the first place) the lessons of modernity, and continue to stagnate in the presemiotic understanding of ideas which mistakes the objective world as created and sustained by signs for the world of unchanging Parmenidean being. This would be to prefer *mythos* to *logos* before the disquieting discovery of historicity that our overall view of reality in the nature of the case is not known to reduce to fact. There is no *fundamentum inconcussum veritatis* for the finite mind, only the fallibilism of "the existence of thought now" which "depends on what is to be hereafter."

Along the way of signs, it matters not a whit whether, as Heidegger grandly claimed,[4] "future thought is no longer philosophy, because it

---

4 Martin Heidegger, *Platons Lehre von der Wahrheit, mit einem Brief über den Humanismus* (Bern: Francke, 1947), p. 119: "Das künftige Denken ist nicht mehr Philosophie, weil es ursprünglicher denkt als die Metaphysik, welcher Name das Gleiche Sagt."

thinks more originally than metaphysics, which name says the same''. From the standpoint of experience, semiotics already occupies that more original ground.[5] On the path of signs, what matters is that, as Sebeok put it in his most balanced formulation, "we must in any case think of ourselves as *both* working within a tradition that changes over time *and* trying to grasp things as they 'really are'."[6] For both the being and the grasping of being the sign proves to be, if not *inconcussum*, at least *sine qua non*.

The purpose of human life is to bring to expression the stories things are. In the telling is the living of our lives as human. We are explorers and inquirers, and when society turns in from that, it dooms itself to suffocation. *In intelligentibus, intelligere est vivere.* For intelligent beings, to understand is to live. The Latin Age, long past, is rendered thus for postmodernity *aufgehoben*,[7] integral to its future in its new beginnings.

---

[5] This claim is not made lightly but in the wake of externsive analysis and argumentation throughout my work in semiotics, but especially in Deely 1987, 1992, and 1994.

[6] Sebeok 1991: 2, italics added.

[7] *Aufgehoben*: illustrative of the progress of the spirit; synthesized; contraries lifted beyond themselves and transcended.

Appendix 1

Contrasting Ontological and Transcendental Relatives

When I first undertook to understand Poinsot's account of the being proper to signs, I was soon brought up short by Poinsot's introduction of the distinction between *relatio secundum esse* and *relatio secundum dici* as the key to the work. Knowing of the huge study by Krempel of *La Doctrine de la Relation chez Saint Thomas* (1952), I turned to that work for assistance. I found in Krempel a wealth of historical detail combined, in the end, with a disappointing poverty of philosophical understanding. Krempel correctly traced the terms in Latin back to Boethius in the sixth century, and, through Boethius, to Aristotle's own discussion of the categories, as I discussed in first presenting Poinsot's *Tractatus* in English (see Deely 1985: 472ff.). But, when it came to the heart of the matter, Krempel throws up his hands, advising the reader that it is impossible to arrive at a satisfactory rendering of the two expressions (*op. cit.* 394). Either Krempel had to be wrong, or Poinsot's theory had to be inscrutable. I suspected the deficiency lay on Krempel's side.

Years of study followed before I was able to demonstrate to my own satisfaction that Krempel was indeed mistaken. The distinction in question was chosen by Poinsot to begin his treatment of signs for an excellent reason: properly understood, the *secundum esse* and *secundum dici* relatives both divide and exhaust the notion of relation in its total possible amplitude. Having grasped the point, I set out to explain it to others, for the purpose specifically of making Poinsot's revolutionary account available. I tried first in *Introducing Semiotic* (Deely 1982: esp. note 9, pp. 168-179), then in the Editorial AfterWord and notes to the *Treatise* itself (Deely 1985), and again in *Basics of Semiotics* (Deely 1990: esp. Ch. 4), as well as in numerous ancillary articles I placed in learned journals over these years.

The account which I felt was finally satisfactory was the account in *Basics*, worked out during my year of teaching in Brasil. Imagine my discouragement, then, after all that effort, to receive the following inquiry from my very best student over the years, now Professor Júlio Jéha of the Federal University of Minas Gerais. He had studied with me my whole time in Belo Horizonte, had come afterwards to the States where he completed his doctoral dissertation in semiotics in consultation with me, and had just himself completed a course he had taught using *Basics* as the text (letter of July 12, 1992):

One thing, however, wasn't very clear for me (and for the students). It's something I had trouble with when you first taught the course here: the difference between transcendental and ontological relations. Much as I tried to understand it from *Básica* [the Portuguese edition of *Basics*, which Júlio had helped to translate], it never became clear to me. Or for the students. When you are teaching, you need examples to make sure learners understand the concept concretely. I'd appreciate it very much if you could explicate that rather obscure point for me.

This letter had a very discouraging effect on me. I felt as if all my efforts to explain this point had come to nothing, that I had not succeeded at all in removing the major obstacle to Poinsot's semiotic becoming available to the community of contemporary linguists, philosophers, anthropologists, and students of the sciences generally. This was the period in which I had to face presenting a major paper for the October 14-17, 1993, conference on "Hispanic Philosophy in the Age of Discovery", which Dean Jude Dougherty had organized at the Catholic University of America to commemorate the quincentenary of Columbus' opening a way to the Americas.

Determined to make the paper succeed, I decided, in the despair brought on by Júlio's letter, to try to present the whole problematic Poinsot addressed without centering the discussion, as Poinsot himself had originally done, on the contrast between relation as *secundum esse* (or "ontological", as I came to say) and *secundum dici* (or "transcendental", as Poinsot and the Latins themselves came to say). That paper, "A New Beginning in Philosophy: Poinsot's Contribution to the 17th Century

Search'', establishing the approach I followed in Chapter 4 above of backgrounding the foundational distinction of Poinsot's Latin text, was a decisive influence on my original idea for this book.

Not until September, when I was well advanced in my plans for avoiding the point on which Júlio had oppressively pressed me, did I undertake to answer his letter. I wrote as follows concerning the main point of unclarity, somewhat tongue-in-cheek, as I was not optimistic of the outcome of the effort (letter of 29 September 1992):

... let me make a few remarks of such clarity that, despite their brevity, all will become self-evident (I hope).

The distinction between transcendental and ontological relation is the difference between a relation as such, which cannot be perceived, and the thing which is, on the basis of one or another of its characteristics, related to some other thing. The thing related and the thing to which it is related, together with all their characteristics, are transcendental relations: that is to say, neither of them is a relation, but they are involved in a relation. The relation they are actually involved in, that is an ontological relation. Voila!

Recently, in a lengthy essay I shall soon be sending you (I had to write it before answering your letter), I have undertaken to explain Poinsot's doctrine without speaking at all about the transcendental relative in its contrast to the ontological relative. I think the effort works; still, to understand the *Tractatus* itself, one has to grasp the distinction, the point of which is that, within human experience, *every* being is relative, i.e., involved with and dependent in various ways upon things other than itself. As such every being provides the basis for an indefinite number of sign-relations, and, besides, is involved in many physical relations of cause-effect, similarity, etc. But each of the things involved in relationships is not itself a relationship; in itself, it is some kind of individual existent with various characteristics, various subjective traits—traits belonging to it in its individuality and distinctness, even though others may have similar traits. The relations themselves in which the individual is involved, these alone, are ontological relations. The individuals, which are not themselves relations although they are involved in relations, cannot be fully understood in what they are unless the relations in which they are involved are also understood. Thus, on meeting a man, I may be surprised to later learn that that man was President of Brasil, or a homosexual, or a leader of a drug cartel, or the man who killed my mother. The man is transcendentally relative, in that he is not fully known unless his having murdered my mother is also known. His having murdered my mother is a cause-effect relation, an ontological relation, but it is not he. He is just an individual, who at one time had not murdered my mother. He is, of course, being prior to test-tube babies, some other mother's son. He is not his mother, but he is related to his mother. That relation is an ontological relation. He is transcendentally relative to his mother, that is to say, he, in order to be fully known for who he is, requires being known as the son of this mother, even though the relation to this mother, here and now, is something over and above his being in his own right.

Thus all being is relative, either transcendentally, or ontologically—that is, every being in the finite universe is an individual with its characteristics or a relation between individuals with their characteristics. The distinction is exhaustive and exclusive. (That is why the sign, a relative being, must be either the one or the other, though it may involve both: the point of departure of Poinsot's *Tractatus*.) A being transcendentally relative—just another way of saying a being finite, a being dependent in its existence on many factors outside itself, with emphasis on the dependency—is then *called* a "transcendental *relation*" by a kind of extension and, be it said, an abusive extension, of the meaning of terms. It is emphatically *not* a relation, it is a relative being existing in its own right or as a characteristic of a being existing in its own right, an individual or some or other characteristic of an individual. Usually, of course, at least in ordinary experience (leaving out atoms and the like), such individuals can be perceived, and their characteristics can also be perceived.

So I can see that my mother's murderer is tall and has a hooked nose, but, unless I witness the deed, I cannot see that he is the murderer of my mother. This, however, unfortunately for him, I can come to understand. What I understand, when I realize that, and assuming I am not mistaken, is something real: it is, in fact, an ontological relation. Now his peculiarly hooked nose, in fact, itself not a relation but a characteristic of an individual (a characteristic *relative* to an individual, indeed), may even become for me *a sign* of my mother, of her murder, and of her murderer. This hooked nose is a *transcendental "relation"* or, as I should prefer to say, a transcendental *relative*, in several respects: it is visibly relative to its owner, but it is also invisibly relative to the murdering of my mother (presuming the nose was present at the crime when performed by the man on whose face it resides).

I hope this helps. If it doesn't please let me know, and try to be as specific as possible, because if you and I can't get clear about this distinction, despair is in order.

I next heard from Júlio in December of the same year, when his letter dated November 15, 1992, arrived. Although I normally like to hear from him, in this case I felt a bit anxious, especially as the letter appeared to be lengthy. I was not in the mood, at the moment at least, for further discourse on the matter. Imagine how my spirits lightened when I reached the dreaded part of the letter to read only this:

As for explanations, thank you. Why didn't you say that when you wrote the book? Though the example is grim—to say the least—it's effective and likely to impress the reader.

My friend was actually satisfied. I could not believe it. Was it really the clarity and simplicity of my latest letter, or was it rather the accumulated weight of the letter on top of Júlio's own years of study and reading of most of my earlier attempts at exposition of the distinction, together with some direct wrestling of his own with Poinsot's Latin text? I preferred to believe that the letter alone explained his new-found understanding, and, since it succeeded in cutting through what Krempel considered a hopeless—even a Gordian?—knot, I place the correspondence here at the end of a study intended to motivate a new generation of students to return to the sources and join in the task of telling a new and more interesting story of the ferment of early modern philosophy as it bears on present and future concerns.

Appendix 2

Longer Latin Citations

Chapter 4, note 5, pp. 55-56 (Poinsot 1635: 77b26–78a46, cited in Deely edition of Poinsot 1632a: 190n35): "... non attendi formaliter in obiecto potentiae realitatem seu entitatem, prout habet esse in se, sed proportionem et coaptationem ad potentiam. Quae quidem proportio, ut subiective existat in re, debet esse realis, sed secundum comparationem ad potentiam non consideratur formaliter, quod sit subiective in ipsa re, sed quod se habet obiective ad talem potentiam, licet aliunde, si potentia ipsa solum respiciat ens reale, etiam in ratione obiecti realitatem petat non prout existentem, sed prout comparatam ad potentiam. Existentia enim semper est in ordine ad se et subiective, ad potentiam autem semper se habet obiective. Unde ens rationis, licet in se subiective non habeat realitatem, potest tamen esse obiectum actus intellectus et specificare illum ratione proportionis obiectivae, quam induit in ordine ad intellectum, quando habet fundamentum reale et ad instar realitatis concipitur. Tunc enim perficere et specificare potest intellectum perfectione reali, non innata sibi aut existente in se, sed emendicata et appropriata ab entitate reali, ad cuius instar obiective concipitur, ut diximus in Logica q. 1. art. 3. ad 1. Et ita, licet realitas et entitas subiective considerata conveniat enti reali et rationis analogice, et non eodem modo simpliciter, obiective tamen simpliciter et univoce inveniri potest in ente rationis, quia supposita emendicatione ab ente reali et fundamento ipsius, proportio ipsa et coaptatio ad potentiam, quae sola pertinet ad rationem obiectivam, per se invenitur, quia vere et proprie coaptatur, ita ut verum et proprium actum intelligendi terminet sicut alia obiecta.

"Nec obstat, quod ens rationis habet esse per ipsum actum intellectus; ergo non perficit nec specificat illum, sed perficitur ab illo. Respondetur enim, quod ens rationis habet esse ab intellectu per modum existentiae non realiter, sed denominative, scilicet quantum ad denominationem cogniti, quae consequitur actum intellectus. Et ideo talis denominatio consecuta non est ratio perficiens intellectum, sed ut effecta et consecuta, perficit autem ens rationis intellectum, in quantum antecedenter ad istam denominationem, ratione sui fundamenti induit coaptationem et proportionem obiectivam, qua vere et proprie terminat ut obiectum intellectus, eo quod licet sit ens fictum, non tamen ficte obicitur et intelligitur, sed verum actum terminat vera terminatione, etsi ficta entitate.''

Chapter 4, note 20, pp. 67-68 (Poinsot, *Artis Logicae Secunda Pars*, Q. 17 ''De Praedicamento Relationis'', Art. 2 ''Quid requiratur, ut aliqua relatio sit praedicamentalis'', 581b24–582a16; = *Tractatus de Signis*, Second Preamble, Article 2, ''What Is Required for a 'Categorial' Relation'', 96/1–36): ''Quando vero instatur, quod etiam alia genera possunt hoc modo dici aliquid rationis, sicut substantia rationis erit chimaera, quantitas rationis spatium imaginarium, et sic de aliis: Respondetur, quod, ut supra dictum est [in] Praeambulo Primo art. 1., non dicitur ens rationis illud, ad cuius instar formatur; formatur enim ens rationis ad instar entis realis, sed dicitur ens rationis illud non reale, quod ad instar realis entis concipitur. Non datur ergo substantia rationis nec quantitas rationis, quia licet aliquod non ens concipiatur ad instar substantiae, v. g. chimaera, et aliquid ad instar quantitatis, v. g. spatium imaginarium, non tamen ipsa substantia vel aliqua substantiae ratio concipitur per rationem et formatur in esse ad instar alterius entis realis. Et ideo illa negatio seu non ens chimaerae, et illud non ens spatii imaginarii dicetur ens rationis. Sed hoc est ens rationis, quod vocatur negatio, non autem erit substantia rationis, cum non ipsa substantia ut ens rationis ad instar alicuius realis concipiatur, sed negationes seu non entia ad instar substantiae et quantitatis. At vero in relativis non solum aliquod non ens concipitur ad instar relationis, sed etiam ipsa relatio ex parte respectus ad, cum non existit in re, concipitur seu formatur ad instar relationis realis, et sic est, quod formatur in esse, et non solum id, ad cuius instar formatur, et ratione huius datur relatio rationis, non substantia rationis.''

Chapter 4, note 48, pp. 92-93 (Poinsot 1632, *Artis Logicae Secunda Pars*, Q. 2, ''De Ente Rationis Logico, Quod Est Secunda Intentio'', 291b2-46; = *Treatise on Signs*, ''First Preamble: On Mind-Dependent Being'', Article 2, ''What Is the Second Intention and Logical Mind-Dependent Relation and How Many Kinds Are There'', 60/7–44): ''**non omnis relatio rationis est secunda intentio, omnis tamen secunda intentio formaliter sumpta, et non solum fundamentaliter, est relatio rationis, non forma realis, non denominatio extrinseca, ut male aliqui putant.**

''Prima pars constat manifeste, quia licet omnis relatio rationis resultet ex cognitione, non tamen omnis ista relatio denominat rem solum in statu cogniti, qui est status secundus, sed etiam in statu existentiae extra cognitionem, sicut relatio Creatoris et Domini non denominat Deum in se cognitum, sed Deum existentem, et similiter esse doctorem, esse iudicem. Neque enim homo ut cognitus est doctor aut iudex, sed homo existens, et ita denominant illae relationes pro statu existentiae.

"Ubi discerne, quod licet cognitio sit causa, ex qua resultat relatio rationis (quod omni enti rationis commune est), et ita ut conveniat et denominet relatio rationis aliquod subiectum, necessario exigat cognitionem, non tamen semper cognitio reddit ipsum obiectum aptum et congruum susceptivum talis denominationis, ita ut solum conveniat illi in esse cognito, sed solum hoc contingit in intentionibus secundis. Et ita relatio Creatoris et Domini, iudicis et doctoris, ut denominet subiectum, requirit cognitionem, quae talem relationem causet, sed non quae constituat subiectum in esse cognito capax, ut denominationem illam suscipiat. At vero esse genus vel speciem non solum supponit cognitionem causantem tales relationes, sed etiam supponit cognitionem, quae reddat subiectum abstractum ab inferioribus, et super rem sic abstractam cadit illa denominatio."

Chapter 4, note 53, p. 94 (Poinsot, *Artis Logicae Secunda Pars*, Q. II, *De Ente Rationis Logico, Quod Est Secunda Intentio*, Art. 2, *"Quid Sit Secunda Intentio et Relatio Rationis Logica et Quotuplex"*, 292a33–293b12, = *Tractatus de Signis*, First Preamble, "On Mind-Dependent Being", Article 2, "What Is the Second Intention and Logical Mind-Dependent Relation, and How Many Are There", 61/31–62/18): "Secundo sequitur, quod licet prima intentio absolute sumpta debeat esse aliquid reale vel conveniens alicui in statu realitatis, alias non esset simpliciter prima, quia semper id, quod est reale, praecedit et prius est eo, quod est rationis, nihilominus tamen non repugnat etiam in ipsa secunda intentione aliam secundam intentionem fundari, et tunc secunda intentio fundans induit quasi conditionem primae intentionis respectu alterius fundatae, non quia sit simpliciter prima, sed quia est prior illa, quam fundat.

"Nam cum intellectus sit reflexivus supra suos actus, potest ipsam secundam intentionem reflexe cognoscere et super ipsam cognitam fundare aliam secundam intentionem; sicut intentio generis, quae tribuitur animali, iterum ut cognita potest fundare secundam intentionem speciei, quatenus intentio generis est quaedam species praedicabilis. Et tunc secunda ista intentio fundata denominat priorem fundantem, ratione cuius dicitur, quod genus formaliter est genus et denominative species. Quod frequenter contingit in istis secundis intentionibus, quod secundum se una formaliter sit talis, et denominative ut cognita sit alia. Et nihilominus omnes istae dicuntur secundae intentiones, licet una fundetur super aliam, non tertia vel quarta intentio, quia omnes conveniunt obiecto ut cognito, esse autem cognitum est semper status secundus rei. Et quia una intentio ut fundat aliam, induit quasi conditionem primae respectu illius, et sic illa, quae fundatur, semper dicitur secunda.''

Chapter 6, note 18, pp. 175-176 (*Artis Logicae Secunda Pars*, Q. 17, *De Praedicamento Relationis*, Art. 6, *"Unde Sumatur Distinctio Specifica et Numerica Relationis"*, 602b33–603a14; = *Treatise on Signs*, Appendix C, "On the Source of Specific and Individual Identity of Relations", 382/4–46): "*Sed tamen distinguendum est*, quod terminus vel sumitur formalissime in ratione termini oppositi, vel fundamentaliter ex parte absoluti fundantis istam rationem terminandi. Primo modo terminus concurrit pure terminative ad specificationem, non autem causando illam, quia sic est purus terminus et est simul natura et cognitione cum relatione; ergo ut sic non est causa specificans, quia causa non est simul natura, sed prior effectu. Si secundo modo consideratur, habet se ut causa formalis extrinseca et specificat ad modum obiecti, et sic ex fundamento et termino consurgit unica ratio specificandi relationem, quatenus fundamentum continet in se terminum in proportione et virtute; non enim est ad talem terminum, nisi sit tale fundamentum, et e converso. Et sic quatenus inter se proportionantur, conficiunt unam rationem specificandi relationem, quae et tale fundamentum postulat et talem terminum ei correspondentem.

"*Ex quibus etiam colliges*, quid sit formalis terminus in ratione specificantis. Licet enim ad eundem materialem terminum diversae relationes specificae terminari possint, non tamen ad eundem formaliter. Sumitur autem formalis ratio specificans in termino secundum correspondentiam et proportionem adaequatam suo fundamento. V. g. album constituit formalem terminum relationis similitudinis, ut correspondet convenientiae et identitati, dissimilitudinis, ut correspondet disconvenientiae; paternitatis aut filiationis, ut correspondet generationi, et sic de aliis. Quare sicut fundamentum ad specificandum consideratur sub ratione ultima fundandi, sic terminus sub proportione et correspondentia terminandi.''

Chapter 8, note 5, pp. 212-213 (Poinsot, *Artis Logicae Secunda Pars*, Q. 17, *De Praedicamento Relationis*, Art. 2, *"Quid Requiratur, Ut Aliqua Relatio Sit Praedicamentalis"*, ex sectione "Solvuntur Argumenta", 581a11–b23; = *Tractatus de Signis*, Second Preamble "On Relation", Article 2, "What Is Required for a Categorial Relation", from the "Resolution of Counter-Arguments" section, 94/37–95/45): "... ex illa parte, qua consideratur ad terminum, et positive se habet et non est determinate realis forma, sed permittit, quod sit ens reale vel rationis; licet ad praedicamentale et fundatum reale sit. Et ita non voluit D. Thomas significare, quae relatio sit realis vel quae rationis, sed ex qua parte habet relatio, quod possit esse realis vel rationis, scilicet ex parte, qua est ad terminum; licet enim ibi realitatem habere possit, non tamen inde. Quod expressit S. Doctor in 1. ad Annibaldum dist. 26. q. 2. art. 1. *Pa* XXII. 76 a) dicens, "quod relatio potest dupliciter considerari, uno modo quantum ad id, ad quod dicitur, ex quo rationem relationis habet, et quantum ad hoc non habet, quod ponat aliquid, quamvis etiam ex hoc non habeat, quod nihil sit; sunt enim quidam respectus, qui sunt aliquid secundum rem, quidam vero, qui nihil. Alio modo quantum ad id, in quo est, et sic quando habet eam in subiecto, realiter inest" ...

"Quomodo autem hoc sit peculiare in relatione et in aliis generibus non inveniatur, dicimus ex eo esse, quia in aliis generibus ratio propria et formalissima eorum non potest positive intelligi, nisi entitative etiam intelligatur, quia positiva eorum ratio est ad se tantum et absoluta, et ideo non intelligitur positive nisi etiam entitative, quod enim est ad se, entitas est. Sola relatio habet esse ens et ad ens, et pro ea parte, qua se habet ad ens, positive se habet, nec tamen inde habet entitatem realem. Sed aliunde relationi provenit realitas, scilicet a fundamento, aliunde positiva ratio ad, scilicet ex termino, ex quo non habet esse ens, sed ad ens, licet illud ad vere reale sit, quando fundatum est. Quod ergo aliquid possit considerari positive, etiamsi non entitative realiter, proprium relationis est. Et hoc solum voluit dicere Caietanus cit. loco [*In I.* q. 28. art. 1. par. 9, cited in Deely ed. of Poinsot 1632a: 95n18], cum dixit relationem rationis esse veram relationem, non veritate entitatis et formae informantis, sed veritate obiectivae et positivae tendentiae ad terminum. Neque Caietanus dixit, quod in relatione praedicamentali ipsum ad est aliquid rationis; expresse enim dicit, quod vere realizatur."

Chapter 8, note 15, pp. 231-232 (Poinsot, *Artis Logicae Secunda Pars*, Q. 17, "De Praedicamento Relationis", Art. 6, "Unde Sumatur Distinctio Specifica et Numerica Relationis", 602b4-603a34; = *Tractatus de Signis*, Appendix C, "On the Source of Specific and Individual Identity of Relations", 381/25-386/46: "Ratio autem istorum ex dictis sumitur, quia tota realitas relationis est ex fundamento secundum ordinem ad terminum, siquidem totum esse relationis est ad aliud, ut dicit eius definitio. Unde cum essentialiter utrumque petat, scilicet fundamentum et terminum, non ita debet sumi praecise ab uno, quod non sumatur etiam ab alio.

"Secunda vero pars conclusionis de modo, quo ista duo concurrunt ad specificandum, non est existimandum, quod ita partialiter concurrant, quod partem specificationis det fundamentum, partem terminus, sed unumquodque dat totam specificationem in diverso genere causae. Quod *aliqui* explicant dicendo, quod fundamentum concurrit initiative et terminus completive. *Alii*, quod fundamentum in genere causae efficientis et terminus in genere causae formalis extrinsecae. *Alii*, quod fundamentum specificat ut virtualiter praehabens in se terminum, cui proportionatur, et sic diversitas fundamentorum refunditur in diversam formalitatem terminorum.

"Sed tamen distinguendum est, quod terminus vel sumitur formalissime in ratione termini oppositi, vel fundamentaliter ex parte absoluti fundantis istam rationem terminandi. Primo modo terminus concurrit pure terminative ad specificationem, non autem causando illam, quia sic est purus terminus et est simul natura et cognitione cum relatione; ergo ut sic non est causa specificans, quia causa non est simul natura, sed prior effectu. Si secundo modo consideratur, habet se ut causa formalis extrinseca et specificat ad modum obiecti, et sic ex fundamento et termino consurgit unica ratio specificandi relationem, quatenus fundamentum continet in se terminum in proportione et virtute; non enim est ad talem terminum, nisi sit tale fundamentum, et e converso. Et sic quatenus inter se proportionantur, conficiunt unam rationem specificandi relationem, quae et tale fundamentum postulat et talem terminum ei correspondentem.

"Ex quibus etiam colliges, quid sit formalis terminus in ratione specificantis. Licet enim ad eundem materialem terminum diversae relationes specificae terminari possint, non tamen ad eundem formaliter. Sumitur autem formalis ratio specificans in termino secundum correspondentiam et proportionem adaequatam suo fundamento. V. g. album constituit formalem terminum relationis similitudinis, ut correspondet convenientiae et identitati, dissimilitudinis, ut correspondet disconvenientiae; paternitatis aut filiationis, ut correspondet generationi, et sic de aliis. Quare sicut fundamentum ad specificandum consideratur sub ratione ultima fundandi, sic terminus sub proportione et correspondentia terminandi."

References

Note on Reference Style: This work has been prepared in accordance with the Style Sheet of the Semiotic Society of America (*The American Journal of Semiotics* 4.3–4 [1986], 193–215; "Brief Version", *Semiotic Scene* [Winter, 1990], n.s. Volume 2, Number 3, 11–12), as modified to include page-bottom footnotes.

This means basically three things.

First, barring some oversight, only those works are included in the final list of References which have actually been mentioned or cited or used for dating, as distinguished from works read, consulted, or relevant to the various topics such as are often included in scholarly bibliographies designed to display breadth of acquaintance independently of actual use.

Second, punctuation marks are placed outside quotation marks except in those cases where the punctuation itself is part of the quoted material, a procedure that follows as a logical consequence of the purpose for which quotation marks are to be used: "to indicate the beginning and the end of a quotation in which the exact phraseology of another or of a text is directly cited" (see Deely, Prewitt, and Haworth 1990).

Third, all the sources have been historically layered, i.e. (see Deely and Prewitt 1989), cited according to a primary reference date from within the lifetime of the author cited, with the relations to translations or later editions of the source work (the actual access volumes) set forth in the complete reference list.

The main merit of this style of reference is that it establishes an invariant reference base of sources across all the linguistic, chronological, and editorial lines of access volumes used—an outcome so useful to the scholarly community as to recommend the adoption of historical layering as the organizing principle for all style sheets.

A specific convention concerning the dating of the works of authors which can be assigned only an approximate date needs to be mentioned here. In such cases the following prefixes to the assigned dates are used: a. = *ante* or before; c. = *circa* or approximately; i. = *inter* or between; p. = *post* or after. The abbreviation q.v. means *quod vide* or "which see", referring to a source in this list of references.

ADAMS, Marilyn McCord.
> 1987.   *William Ockham*, 2 Volumes (Notre Dame, IN: Notre Dame University Press). Used for dating the Venerabilis Inceptor.

ALLEN, Barry.
> 1995.   "Is Locke's Semiotic Inconsistent?", *The American Journal of Semiotics*, 10.3/4, forthcoming.

ANDERSON, Myrdene, John DEELY, Martin KRAMPEN, Joseph RANSDELL, Thomas A. SEBEOK, and Thure von UEXKÜLL.
> 1984.   *A Semiotic Perspective on the Sciences: Steps Toward a New Paradigm* (Toronto Semiotic Circle Working Paper), since published under the same title as a "position paper" article in *Semiotica* 52.1/2 (1984), 7–47; and, with further refinements, as Chapter 3 of Sebeok 1986a: 17–44 (q.v.), to which final version page references are keyed in this book.

ANGELELLI, Ignacio.
> 1992.   "Logic in the Iberian Age of Discovery: Scholasticism, Humanism, Reformed Scholasticism", paper presented October 15 at the "Hispanic Philosophy in the Age of Discovery" conference held at the Catholic University of America, October 14–17.

AQUINAS, Thomas.
> i.1252–1273. *S. Thomae Aquinatis Opera Omnia ut sunt in indice thomistico*, ed. Roberto Busa (Stuttgart-Bad Cannstatt: Frommann-Holzboog, 1980), in septem volumina:
> 1. In quattuor libros Sententiarum;
> 2. Summa contra Gentiles, Autographi Deleta, Summa Theo-
> . logiae;
> 3. Quaestiones Disputatae, Quaestiones Quodlibetales, Opuscula;
> 4. Commentaria in Aristotelem et alios;
> 5. Commentaria in Scripturas;
> 6. Reportationes, Opuscula dubiae authenticitatis;
> 7. Aliorum Medii Aevi Auctorum Scripta 61.
> c.1254–1256. *In Quattuor Libros Sententiarum*, in Busa ed. vol. 1.
> c.1256–1259. *Quaestiones Disputatae de Veritate*, in Busa ed. vol. 3, 1–186.

c.1265-1267. *Quaestiones Disputatae de Potentia*, ed. Paul M. Pession, in *Quae-
tiones Disputatae*, vol. II, 9th ed. rev. by P. Bazzi, M. Calcaterra,
T. S. Centi, E. Odetto, and P. M. Pession (Turin: Marietti, 1953),
7-276; in Busa ed. vol. 3, 186-269.

c.1266-1273. *Summa theologiae*, in Busa ed. vol. 2, 184-926.

c.1268-1272. *In duodecim libros metaphysicorum Aristotelis expositio*, in Busa ed.
vol. 4, 390-507.

c.1269.   *Sententia libri ethicorum (In Decem Libros Ethicorum Aristotelis ad Nicoma-
chum Expositio)*, in Busa ed. vol. 4, 143-234.

c.1269-1272. *Quaestiones quodlibetales*, in Busa ed. vol. 3, 438-501.

c.1269-1274. *In Aristotelis libros perihermenias expositio* (completed by Aquinas
only as far as Book II, lect. 14), ed. R. M. Spiazzi (Turin: Marietti,
1955), in Busa ed. vol. 4, 327-341.

ARAÚJO, Francisco de.
    1617.   *Commentariorum in universam Aristotelis Metaphysicam tomus primus*
(Burgos and Salamanca: J. B. Varesius).

ARISTOTLE.
    Note: citations are from the 12-volume Oxford edition prepared
under W. D. Ross Ed. 1928-1952 (Oxford, England: Clarendon
Press); for the convenience of the reader, after the abbreviation
RM, we also give the pages where applicable to the more readily
available one-volume edition of *The Basic Works of Aristotle* prepared
by Richard McKeon (New York: Basic Books, 1941), using the
Oxford translations. Chronology for the works is based on
Gauthier 1970, as follows:

c.348-330BC. *Metaphysics*, Oxford Vol. VIII (trans. W. D. Ross; RM 681-
926 complete).

c.335-4BC. *Nicomachean Ethics*, Oxford Vol. IX 1094a1-1181b25 (trans. W.
D. Ross; RM 927-1112 complete).

ASHLEY, Benedict M.
    1952.   "Research into the Intrinsic Final Causes of Physical Things",
in *ACPA Proceedings* XXVI, 185-194.

ASHWORTH, E. J.
    1974.   *Language and Logic in the Post-Medieval Period* (Dordrecht, Holland:
D. Reidel Publishing Co.).
    1978.   "Multiple Quantification and the Use of Special Quantifiers in
Early Sixteenth Century Logic", *Notre Dame Journal of Formal Logic*
XIX, 599-613.

1988.   "The Historical Origins of John Poinsot's *Treatise on Signs*", *Semiotica* 69.1/2, 129–147.

1990a.   "Domingo de Soto (1494–1560) and the Doctrine of Signs", in *De Ortu Grammaticae. Studies in Medieval Grammar and Linguistic Theory in Memory of Jan Pinborg*, ed. G. L. Bursill-Hall, Sten Ebbesen, and Konrad Koerner (Amsterdam: John Benjamins), 35–48.

1990b.   "The Doctrine of Signs in Some Early Sixteenth-Century Spanish Logicians", in *Estudios de Historia la Logica. Actas del II Simposio de Historia de la Logica: Universidad de Navarra Pamplona 25–27 de Mayo 1987*, ed. Ignacio Angelelli and Angel d'Ors (Pamplona: Ediciones EUNATE), 13–38.

AUGUSTINE of Hippo.
   c.397–426. *De doctrina christiana libri quattuor* ("Of" or "Concerning Christian Doctrine"), in P.L. 34, cols. 15–122.

BAER, Eugen.
   1977.   "Things Are Stories: A Manifesto for a Reflexive Semiotics", *Semiotica* 25.3/4, 293–205.

   1992.   "Via Semiotica", review of Deely 1990, *Semiotica* 92.3/4, 351–357.

BALDWIN, James M., Editor.
   1901–1902. *Dictionary of Psychology and Philosophy*, "giving a terminology in English, French, German, and Italian. Written by many hands and edited by J. M. Baldwin", in 3 Volumes, Vol. 3 being a Bibliography of Philosophy, Psychology, and cognate subjects compiled by Benjamin Rand (original ed. New York: Macmillan; vols. 1 and 2 reissued by Peter Smith, New York, 1940, vol. 3 1949).

BERKELEY, Bishop George.
   1710.   *A Treatise Concerning the Principles of Human Knowledge*, complete and unabridged text in *The English Philosophers from Bacon to Mill*, ed. E.A. Burtt (New York: The Modern Library, 1939), pp. 509-579.

   1732.   *Alciphron, or The Minute Philosopher*, Volume III of *The Works of George Berkeley, Bishop of Cloyne*, ed. T. E. Jessop (London: Thomas Nelson and Sons, 1950).

BEUCHOT, Mauricio.
   1980.   "La doctrina tomista clásica sobre el signo: Domingo de Soto, Francisco de Araújo y Juan de Santo Tomás", *Critica* XII.36 (México, diciembre), 39–60.

1983. "Lógica y lenguaje en Juan de Sto. Tomás", *Diánoia* 17.

1987. *Metafísica: La Ontología Aristotelico-Tomista de Francesco de Araújo* (México City: Universidad Nacional Autónoma de México).

1987a. *Aspectos históricos de la semiótica y la filosofía del lenguaje* (México City: Universidad Nacional Autónoma de México Press).

1988. *Significado y Discurso. La filosofía del lenguaje en alguno escolásticos españoles post-medievales* (México City: Universidad Nacional Autónoma de México Press).

1991. Introduction and text revision of Ferrer 1991, q.v.

1993. "El Pensiamento y su Relacion con el Signo en Peirce y la Escolastica", *MORPHÉ* (Puebla, México: Universidad Autónoma de Puebla), año 5, no. 8 (enero-junio), 133–142.

1994. "Intentionality in John Poinsot", *ACPQ* Special Issue on Poinsot, Vol. LXVIII, No. 3 (Summer), 293-310.

BEUCHOT, Editor and Translator.
1989. Independent Spanish translation of what in the 1985 Deely edition is Books I-III of Poinsot's *Tractatus de Signis* (= Logica 2. p. qq. 21-23, I 64sa-749b47), but without the First and Second Preambles on Mind-Dependent Being and Relation: Juan de Santo Tomás, *De Los Signos y los Conceptos*, Introducción, traducción y notas de Mauricio Beuchot (México City: Universidad Nacional Autónoma de México, 1989).

BIRD, Otto A.
1987. "John of St. Thomas Redivivus ut John Poinsot", *The New Scholasticism* LXI.1 (Winter), 103–107.

BOSWELL, James.
1793. *The Life of Samuel Johnson, LL.D.* (revised and augmented ed. of 1791 original publication; London: printed by Henry Baldwin for Charles Dilly).

BRÉHIER, Émile.
1938. *Histoire de la philosophie: La Philosophie moderne. I: Le dix-septième siècle* (Presses Universitarie de France), trans. as *The Seventeenth Century* by Wade Baskin (Chicago: University of Chicago Press, 1966).

BURKS, Arthur W.
1958. "Bibliography of the Works of Charles Sanders Peirce", in *The Collected Papers of Charles Sanders Peirce*, Volume VIII ed. Arthur W. Burks (Cambridge, MA: Harvard University Press, 1958), 249-330.

CAHALAN, John C.
>   1985.   *Causal Realism* (= Sources in Semiotics II; Lanham, MD: University Press of America).
>   1994.   "If Wittgenstein Had Read Poinsot: Recasting the Problem of Signs and Mental States", *ACPQ* Special Issue on Poinsot, Vol. LXVIII, No. 3 (Summer), 311-332.

CAJETAN, Thomas de Vio.
>   1506, 1511.   *De Nominum Analogia* (first ed. Venice, March 9; corrected ed. Paris, 1511). Trans. Edward A. Bushinski in collaboration with Henry J. Koren as *The Analogy of Names and the Concept of Being* (Pittsburgh, PA: Duquesne University Press, 1953).
>   1507.   *Commentaria in summam theologicam. Prima pars* (Rome), reprinted in *Sancti Thomae Aquinatis Doctoris Angelici Opera Omnia*, vols. 4 and 5 (Rome: Leonine, 1888-1889).

CIAPALO, Roman, and Joseph PAPPIN III.
>   1995.   *Postmodernism and the Perennial Philosophy* (Notre Dame, IN: Indiana University Press).

COMAS DEL BRUGAR, Miguel ("Michael Comas").
>   1661.   *Quaestiones minoris dialecticae* (Barcelona: Antonius Lacavalleria). Available at the Lilly Library of Indiana University, Bloomington, and on microfilm at the Wahlert Memorial Library of Loras College, Dubuque, IA.

COOMBS, Jeffrey S.
>   1994.   "John Poinsot on How To Be, Know, and Love a Nonexistent Possible", *ACPQ* Special Issue on Poinsot, Vol. LXVIII, No. 3 (Summer), 333-346.

COPENHAVER, Brian P., and Charles B. SCHMITT.
>   1992.   *Renaissance Philosophy* (Oxford University Press).

COTTINGHAM, John, Robert STOOTHOFF, and Dugald MURDOCH, Translators.
>   1985.   *The Philosophical Writings of Descartes* (Cambridge, England: Cambridge University Press), 2 volumes.

CRAIK, K. J. W.
>   1967.   *The Nature of Explanation* (Cambridge: Cambridge University Press).

CUMMINS, Phillip D., and Guenter ZOELLER, Editors.

1992.   *Minds, Ideas, and Objects. Essays on the Theory of Representation in Modern Philosophy* (= North American Kant Society Studies in Philosophy, Vol. 2; Atascadero, CA: Ridgeview Publishing Co.).

DALCOURT, Gerard J.

1994.   "Poinsot and the Mental Imagery Debate", *The Modern Schoolman* LXXII.1 (November).

DEBROCK, Guy.

1989.   "Peirce, Philosopher of the 21st Century", colloquium held 18-19 December 1989 at Catholic University, Nijmegen, The Netherlands, with the papers published in the *Transactions of the Charles S. Peirce Society*, Vol. XXVIII, Nos. 1 and 2. De Brock's own paper introducing the symposium (*loc. cit.* No. 1: 1-18) undertakes the justification of the title without once mentioning the word "semiotic" (or "semeiotic"), even though the ideas and issues he discusses are centrally semiotic ones.

DEELY, John.

1969.   "The Philosophical Dimensions of the Origin of Species," *The Thomist* XXXIII (January and April), Part I, 75-149, Part II, 251-342.

1971.   *The Tradition via Heidegger* (The Hague: Martinus Nijhoff).

1971a.   "Animal Intelligence and Concept-Formation," *The Thomist* XXXV.1 (January), 43-93.

1975.   "Reference to the Non-Existent", *The Thomist* XXXIX.2 (April), 253-308.

1977a.   "Metaphysics, Modern Thought, and 'Thomism'", *Notes et Documents* 8 (juillet-septembre), 12-18.

1977b.   "'Semiotic' as the Doctrine of Signs", *Ars Semeiotica* 1/3, 41-68.

1978.   "What's in a Name?", *Semiotica* 22.1/2, 151-181.

1978a.   "Toward the Origin of Semiotic", in *Sight, Sound, and Sense*, ed. Thomas A. Sebeok (Bloomington, IN: Indiana University Press), 1-30.

1978b.   "Semiotic and the Controversy over Mental Events," *ACPA Proceedings* LII (1978), 16-27.

1982a.   *Introducing Semiotic: Its History and Doctrine* (Bloomington: Indiana University Press).

1982b.   "On the Notion of Phytosemiotics", in *Semiotics* 1982, ed. John Deely and Jonathan Evans (Lanham, MD: University Press of America, 1987), 541-554; reprinted with minor revision in *Fron-*

tiers in Semiotics, ed. John Deely, Brooke Williams, and Felicia Kruse (Bloomington: Indiana University Press, 1986), 96–103.

1985.   "Editorial Afterword" and critical apparatus to *Tractatus de Signis: The Semiotic of John Poinsot* (Berkeley: University of California Press), 391–514; electronic version hypertext-linked (Charlottesville, VA: Intelex Corp.; see entry under Poisnot 1632a below).

1985a. "Semiotic and the Liberal Arts", *The New Scholasticism* LIX.3 (Summer), 296–322.

1986.   "Doctrine", terminological entry for the *Encyclopedic Dictionary of Semiotics*, ed. Thomas A. Sebeok et al. (Berlin: Mouton de Gruyter), Tome I, p. 214.

1986a. "John Locke's Place in the History of Semiotic Inquiry", in *Semiotics 1986*, ed. Jonathan Evans and John Deely (Lanham, MD: University Press of America, 1987), 406–418.

1986c. "Semiotic in the Thought of Jacques Maritain", *Recherche Sémiotique/Semiotic Inquiry* 6.2, 1–30.

1986d. "Idolum. Archeology and Ontology of the Iconic Sign", in *Iconicity: Essays on the Nature of Culture*, Festschrift volume in honor of Thomas A Sebeok, edited by Paul Bouissac, Michael Herzfeld, and Roland Posner (Tübingen: Stauffenburg Verlag), 29–49.

1986e. "A Context for Narrative Universals, or: Semiology as a *Pars Semeiotica*", in *The American Journal of Semiotics* 4.3/4, 53–68.

1987.   "On the Problem of Interpreting the Term 'First' in the Expression 'First Philosophy'", in *Semiotics 1987*, ed. J. Deely (Lanham, MD: University Press of America, 1988), 3–14.

1987b. "A Maxim for Semiotics", Editor's Preface to *Semiotics 1987*, ed. John Deely (Lanham, MD: University Press of America, 1988), pp. iii–v.

1988.   "The Semiotic of John Poinsot: Yesterday and Tomorrow", discussion of reviews of and theoretical issues in Poinsot 1632a, *Semiotica* 69.1/2 (April), 31–127.

1989.   "The Grand Vision", presented in a Friday, September 8 morning session of the September 5–10 Charles Sanders Peirce Sesquicentennial International Congress at Harvard University; published in *Transactions of the Charles S. Peirce Society* XXX.2 (Spring, 1994), pp. 371-400, but with horrible errors introduced after the correction of proofs.

1989a. "A Global Enterprise", Preface to Thomas A. Sebeok, *The Sign & Its Masters* (= Sources in Semiotics VIII; Lanham, MD: University Press of America, 1989), vii–xiv.

1990.   *Basics of Semiotics* (Bloomington, IN: Indiana University Press).

1990a. "Logic within Semiotics", in *"Symbolicity"*, ed. Jeff Bernard, John Deely, Vilmos Voigt, and Gloria Withalm (Lanham, MD: University Press of America, 1993), 77–86.

1991.   "Semiotics and Biosemiotics: Are Sign-Science and Life-Science Coextensive?", in *Biosemiotics. The Semiotic Web 1991*, ed. Thomas A. Sebeok and Jean Umiker-Sebeok (Berlin: Mouton de Gruyter, 1992), 45–75.

1992.   "Philosophy and Experience", *American Catholic Philosophical Quarterly* LXVI.3 (Summer), 299–319.

1992a. "From Glassy Essence to Bottomless Lake", in *Semiotics 1992*, ed. John Deely (Lanham, MD: University Press of America, 1993), 151–158.

1993.   "Locke's Proposal for Semiotics and the Scholastic Doctrine of Species", *The Modern Schoolman* LXX.3 (March) 165–168.

1993a. "Vindicación de la filosofía hispana: la semiótica como restauración de la cultura intelectual ibérica", trans. Benjamin E. Mayer *Revista de Filosofía* (México D.F.: Universidad Iberoamericana), año 27, no. 80 (mayo-agosto, 1994), 310–324.

1993b. "How Does Semiosis Effect Renvoi?", the Thomas A. Sebeok Fellowship Inaugural Lecture, delivered at the 18th Annual Meeting of the Semiotic Society of America in St. Louis on Friday, October 22, and subsequently published in *The American Journal of Semiotics*, Vol. 11, No. 1/2, 3-55.

1994.   *The Human Use of Signs, or Elements of Anthroposemiosis* (Lanham, MD: Rowman & Littlefield).

1994a. "Membra Ficte Disjecta (A Disordered Array of Severed Limbs)", Editorial Introduction to the electronic edition of Peirce i.1866-1913 (see "Note" beginning Peirce entry below).

1995.   "Quid Sit Postmodernismus?", in Ciapalo and Pappin 1995.

1995a? "Locke's Philosophy *versus* Locke's Proposal for Semiotic", *The American Journal of Semiotics* 10.3/4, forthcoming.

DEELY, John, Guest-Editor.
1994.   Special Issue on John Poinsot, *American Catholic Philosophical Quarterly* (ACPQ) LXVIII.3 (Summer).

DEELY, John N., and Raymond J. NOGAR.
1973.   *The Problem of Evolution. A Study of the Philosophical Repercussions of Evolutionary Science* (New York: Appleton-Century-Crofts).

DEELY, John, and Susan PETRILLI, Guest Editors.
  1993.   Urbino Special Issue of *Semiotica* 97.3/4, papers occasioned by the
          seminar held July 6-10, 1992, at the Universitá degli Studi di Ur-
          bino Centro Internazionale di Semiotica e di Linguistica on the
          basis of Sebeok 1991.
DEELY, John, and Terry PREWITT.
  1989.   "A Reference Style for Semiotics: Notes on Historical Layering",
          Semiotic Scene (Summer), n.s. Vol. 1, No. 2, 10.
DEELY, John, Terry PREWITT, and Karen HAWORTH.
  1990.   "On the SSA Style Sheet", *Semiotic Scene*, n.s. Vol. 2, No. 2, 9.
DEELY, John, and Anthony F. RUSSELL.
  1986.   "Francis Bacon", bibliographical entry for the Encyclopedic Dic-
          tionary of Semiotics, Thomas A. Sebeok, General Editor (Berlin:
          Mouton de Gruyter), Tome 1, 68-70.
DEELY, John N., Brooke WILLIAMS, and Felicia E. KRUSE, editors.
  1986.   *Frontiers in Semiotics* (Bloomington: Indiana University Press).
          Preface titled "Pars Pro Toto", pp. viii-xvii; "Description of Con-
          tributions", pp. xviii-xxii.
DESCARTES, René.
  1628.   *Rules for the Direction of the Mind*, trans. Dugald Murdoch in Cot-
          tingham, Stoothoff, and Murdoch 1985: I, 9-78.
  1637.   *Discourse on the Method of rightly conducting one's reason and seeking truth
          in the sciences*, trans. Robert Stoothoff in Cottingham, Stoothoff,
          and Murdoch 1985: I, 111-151.
  1641.   *Meditations on First Philosophy*, trans. by John Cottingham in Cot-
          tingham, Stoothoff, and Murdoch 1985: II, 3-62.
DOYLE, John P.
  1984a. "The Conimbricenses on the Relations Involved in Signs", in
          Semiotics 1984, ed. John Deely (Proceedings of the Ninth Annual
          Meeting of the Semiotic Society of America; Lanham, MD:
          University Press of America, 1985), 567-576.
  1984b. "Prolegomena to a Study of Extrinsic Denomination in the Work
          of Francis Suárez, S.J.", *Vivarium* XXII.2, 121-160.
  1987.   "Suárez on Beings of Reason and Truth (1)", *Vivarium* XXV.1,
          47-76.
  1988.   "Suárez on Beings of Reason and Truth (2)", *Vivarium* XXVI.1,
          51-72.
  1990.   Review of Tachau 1988, q.v., in *The Modern Schoolman* LXVII
          (May 1990), 320-325.

1990.   "'Extrinsic Cognoscibility': A Seventeenth Century Supertran-
scendental Notion'', *The Modern Schoolman* LXVIII (November),
57-80.

1994.   "Poinsot on the Knowability of Beings of Reason", *ACPQ* Special
Issue on John Poinsot, Vol. LXVIII, No. 3 (Summer), 347-373.

ECO, Umberto.

1976.   *A Theory of Semiotics* (Bloomington, IN: Indiana University Press,
1976).

1990.   "Unlimited Semiosis and Drift: Pragmaticism vs. 'Pragmatism'",
in his collection *The Limits of Interpretation* (Bloomington: Indiana
University Press), 23-43.

ECO, Umberto, Roberto LAMBERTINI, Costantino MARMO, and Andrea
TABARRONI.

1986.   "Latratus Canis or: The Dog's Barking", in *Frontiers in Semiotics*,
ed. John Deely, Brooke Williams, and Felicia E. Kruse (Bloomington: Indiana University Press, 1986), 63-73. For background on
this essay, see the editors' note on p. xix.

ÉLIE, Hubert.

1950-1951.   "Quelques maîtres de l'université de Paris vers l'an 1500",
Archives d'histoire doctrinale et littéraire du moyen âge 18, 193-243.

FERRER, Gabriel, Translator.

1991.   *Libro de los Predicables de Juan de Santo Thomas*, selection from Poinsot, Logica 2. p. (1632) "Explicatio Textus Isagogis Porphyrii",
qq. 6-12, Reiser ed. I 376-472b48, with revision of the translation
and introduction by Mauricio Beuchot (México City: Universidad
Nacional Autónoma de México Press).

FISCH, Max H.

1978.   "Peirce's General Theory of Signs", in *Sight, Sound, and Sense*, ed.
T. A. Sebeok (Bloomington: Indiana University Press), 31-70.

1986a.   Review by Max H. Fisch of Poinsot 1632a in *New Vico Studies*, ed.
Giorgio Tagliacozzo and Donald Phillip Verene (New York: Humanities Press for The Institute for Vico Studies), Volume IV, pp.
178-182.

1986b.   "Philodemus and Semeiosis (1879-1883)", section 5 (pp.
329-330) of the essay "Peirce's General Theory of Signs" reprinted in *Peirce, Semeiotic, and Pragmatism. Essays by Max H. Fisch*, ed.
Kenneth Laine Ketner and Christian J. W. Kloesel (Bloomington, IN: Indiana University Press), 321-356.

FISCH, Max H., Kenneth L. KETNER, and Christian J. W. KLOESEL.
  1979.   "The New Tools of Peirce Scholarship, with Particular Reference to Semiotic", in *Peirce Studies* No. 1, ed. K. L. Ketner and Joseph M. Ransdell (Lubbock, TX: Institute for Studies in Pragmaticism), pp. 1–17.

FITZGERALD, Desmond J.
  1986.   "John Poinsot's Tractatus de Signis", *Journal of the History of Philosophy* XXVI.1 (January 1986), 146–149.

FONSECA, Petrus ("Pedro da").
  c.1564.   *Instituições Dialecticas* (*Institutionum dialecticarum libri octo*), ed. Joaquim Ferreira Gomes, 2 vols. (Instituto de Estudos Filosoficos da Universidad de Coimbra, 1964).

FRASER, Alexander Campbell.
  1894.   "Prolegomena", Notes, and Critical Apparatus to edition of *John Locke, An Essay concerning Human Understanding* (Oxford University Press).

FURTON, Edward J.
  1987.   Review of Poinsot 1632a in *The Review of Metaphysics* 40 (June), 766–767.

GANNON, Timothy J.
  1991.   *Shaping Psychology. How We Got Where We're Going* (Lanham, MD: University Press of America).

GAUTHIER, René Antoine.
  1970.   "Introduction" to *L'Ethique a Nicomaque*, traduction et commentaire, R. A. Gauthier et Jean Yves Jolif (12th ed., avec une introduction nouvelle; Paris: Beatrice-Nauwelaerts), Tome I, première partie.

GILSON, Étienne.
  1913.   *Index Scolastico-Cartésien* (thesis at the Université de Paris; Paris: Alcan).
  1937.   *The Unity of Philosophical Experience* (New York: Scribner's).
  1955.   *History of Christian Philosophy in the Middle Ages* (New York: Random House).
  1968.   Personal letter to the author dated 28 August.
  1974.   Personal letter to the author dated 10 July.

GOULD, Stephen J., and Elisabeth S. VRBA.
  1982.   "Exaptation—A Missing Term in the Science of Form", *Paleobiology* 8.1 (Winter), 4–15.

GRACIA, Jorge J. E.
1992.   *Philosophy and Its History. Issues in philosophical historiography* (Albany, NY: State University of New York Press).
1993.   "Hispanic Philosophy: Its Beginning and Golden Age", *The Review of Metaphysics* 46 (March, 1993), 475-502. This paper was originally presented as the opening address at the October 14-17 "Hispanic Philosophy in the Age of Discovery" conference, Catholic University of America, Washington, DC.

GRACIA, Jorge J. E., Guest-Editor.
1991.   Special Issue on Suárez, *ACPQ* LXV.

GREDT, Josephus.
1899.   *Elementa Philosophiae Aristotelico-Thomisticae* (Barcelona: Herder), 2 Vols.
1936.   7th edition, last in author's lifetime.
1961.   13th (5th posthumous) ed. recognita et aucta ab Euchario Zenzen, O.S.B.

GUAGLIARDO, Vincent.
1989.   "Aquinas and Heidegger", *The Thomist* 53.3 (July), 407-442.
1992.   "Hermeneutics: Deconstruction or Semiotics?", in *Symposium on Hermeneutics*, ed. Eugene F. Bales (private circulation; Conception, MO: Conception Seminary College, 1992). An original and valuable investigation, but poorly vetted by those who put it in circulation without first submitting proofs to authors.
1993.   "Being and Anthroposemiotics", in *Semiotics 1993*, ed. Robert Corrington and John Deely (Lanham, MD: University Press of America, 1994).
1994.   "Being-as-First-Known in Poinsot: A-Priori or Aporia?", *The American Catholic Philosophical Quarterly* LXVIII.3, 375-404.

HARDWICK, Charles S.
1977.   *Semiotics and Significs: The Correspondence between Charles Sanders Peirce and Victoria Lady Welby* (Bloomington, IN: Indiana University Press).

HAWKING, Stephen A.
1988.   *A Brief History of Time, from the Big Bang to Black Holes* (New York: Bantam Books).

HEIDEGGER, Martin.
1927.   *Sein und Zeit*, originally published in the *Jahrbuch für Phänomenologie und phänomenologische Forschung*, ed. E. Husserl; trans. John Mac-

quarrie and Edward Robinson as *Being and Time* (New York: Harper & Row, 1962). Page references in the present work are to the 10th German edition (Tübingen: Niemeyer, 1963).

1929.   *Vom Wesen des Grundes* (Frankfurt: Klostermann, 1955).

1943.   *Vom Wesen der Wahrheit* (Frankfurt: Klostermann, 1954; actual composition 1930). The English translation by R. F. C. Hull and Alan Crick, "On the Essence of Truth", in *Existence and Being*, ed. Werner Brock (Chicago: Gateway, 1949), pp. 292–324, was consulted in preparing the present work.

1947.   *Platons Lehre von der Wahrheit mit einem Brief über den Humanismus* (Bern: Francke).

1951.   *Kant und das Problem der Metaphysik* (Frankfurt: Klostermann, 1951), trans. by James S. Churchill as *Kant and the Problem of Metaphysics* (Bloomington, IN: Indiana University Press, 1962).

HENDERSON, Lawrence J.

1913.   *The Fitness of the Environment* (Boston: Beacon Press).

HENRY, Desmond Paul.

1987.   "The Way to Awareness", review of Deely edition of Poinsot's *Tractatus de Signis* in *The Times Literary Supplement* no. 4,413 (October 30–November 5), p. 1201.

HJELMSLEV, Louis.

1961.   *Prolegomena to a Theory of Language*, being the second, revised translation by Francis J. Whitfield of *Omkring sprogteoriens grundlaeggelse* (Copenhagen: Ejnar Munksgaard, 1943), incorporating "several minor corrections and changes that have suggested themselves in the course of discussions between the author and the translator" from the Preface, p. v).

HUME, David.

1739–1740. *A Treatise of Human Nature*, ed. Selby-Bigge (1896), second ed. with text rev. and variant readings by P. H. Nidditch (Oxford: Clarendon, 1978).

1748.   *An Enquiry Concerning Human Understanding* (originally published under the title *Philosophical Essays concerning the Human Understanding*, but retitled as of the 1758 edition), ed. P. H. Nidditch (3rd ed.; Oxford, 1975).

1776 (April 18). "My Own Life", Hume's autobiography, reprinted in *An Enquiry Concerning Human Understanding*, ed. and intro. by Charles W. Hendel (New York: Bobbs-Merrill, 1955), pp. 3–11.

JAKOBSON, Roman.
1974.   "Coup d'oeil sur le devéloppement de la sémiotique", in *Pano-rama sémiotique/A Semiotic Landscape*, Proceedings of the First Con-gress of the International Association for Semiotic Studies, Milan, June 1974, ed. Seymour Chatman, Umberto Eco, and Jean-Marie Klinkenberg (The Hague: Mouton, 1979), 3–18. Published separately under the same title by the Research Center for Lan-guage and Semiotic Studies as a small monograph (= *Studies in Semiotics* 3; Bloomington: Indiana University Publications, 1975).
1980.   "A Glance at the Development of Semiotics", English trans. by Patricia Baudoin of Jakobson 1974 in *The Framework of Language* (Ann Arbor, MI: Michigan Studies in the Humanities, Horace R. Rackham School of Graduate Studies), 1–30.

JOHANSEN, Jørgen Dines.
1993.   "Let Sleeping Signs Lie. On signs, objects, and communication", in Deely and Petrilli Eds. 1993: 271–295.
1993a.   *Dialogic Semiosis* (Bloomington, IN: Indiana University Press).

KANT, Immanuel.
1784, September 30. "Was Ist Aufklarung?", trans. "What Is Enlighten-ment?" by Lewis White Beck in *Foundations of the Metaphysics of Morals* (Indianapolis, IN: Bobbs-Merrill, 1959), pp. 85–92.
1781, 1787. *Kritik der reinen Vernunft* (Riga); trans. Norman Kemp Smith, *Kant's Critique of Pure Reason* (New York: St. Martin's Press, 1963).

KECKERMANN, D. Bartholomew.
1614.   *Scientiae Metaphysicae Brevissima Synopsis et Compendium*, in *Operum Omnium* Tomus Primus. In the matter of a doctrine of signs, Keck-ermann principally looks to Timpler.

KENNY, Anthony, Ed.
1970.   *Descartes. Philosophical Letters*, trans. and ed. by Anthony Kenny (Oxford, England: Clarendon Press).

KETNER, Kenneth Laine.
1993.   "Novel science; or, How contemporary social science is not well and why literature and semeiotic provide a cure", *Semiotica* 93.1/2, 33–59.

KRAMPEN, Martin.
1981.   "Phytosemiotics", *Semiotica* 36.3/4, 187–209; substantially reprinted in Deely, Williams, and Kruse 1986: 83–95.

KREMPEL, A.
1952. *La doctrine de la relation chez saint Thomas. Exposé historique et systéma-tique* (Paris: J. Vrin).

LAVAUD, M.-Benoît.
1928. "Jean de Saint-Thomas, l'homme et l'oeuvre", Appendix II to *Introduction à la théologie de saint Thomas*, being Lavaud's French translation of Poinsot's "Isagoge ad D. Thomae Theologiam" (in the *Tomus Primus Cursus Theologici* [1637], Solesmes ed., 1931: 142-219) (Paris: André Blot), pp. 411-446.

LEIBNIZ, G. W. F.
1704. *Nouveaux Essais sur l'entendement humain* (first published posthumous-ly in Amsterdam, 1765), English trans. and ed. by Peter Remnant and Jonathan Bennett, *New Essays on Human Understanding* (Cam-bridge University Press, 1981).

LOCKE, John.
1690. *An Essay Concerning Humane Understanding* (London: Thomas Bas-sett); the Fraser 1894 and Nidditch 1975 eds. were also consult-ed. Note the "e" at the end of "Human" in Locke's original title. The later modern editions drop it. In Chapter 5, page references are to the Fraser text.

LOVELOCK, J. E.
1972. "Gaia as Seen through the Atmosphere", *Atmosphere and Environ-ment* 6, 579-580.
1979. *Gaia. A New Look at Life on Earth* (Oxford, England: Oxford Univer-sity Press).
1988. *The Ages of Gaia: A Biography of Our Living Earth* (New York: W. W. Norton).

MARITAIN, Jacques.
1922. *Antimoderne* (Paris: Revue des Jeunes).
1953, November 1. "Preface" to Simon et al. 1955: v-viii.
1957. "Language and the Theory of Sign", originally published as Chapter V of the anthology *Language: An Enquiry into Its Meaning and Function*, ed. Ruth Nanda Anshen (New York: Harper & Bros.), 86-101, is reprinted with the addition of a full technical apparatus explicitly connecting the essay to Maritain's work on semiotic begun in 1937 and to the text of Poinsot 1632 on which Maritain centrally drew, in Deely et al. 1986: 51-62, to which reprint page references are keyed.

1959. *Distinguish to Unite, or The Degrees of Knowledge*, trans. from the 4th French ed. of 1932 entry above, q.v., under the supervision of Gerald B. Phelan (New York: Scribner's).

1962, May. Three seminars given in Toulouse and published under the title *Dieu et la Permission du Mal* (Paris: Desclée de Brouwer, 1963), English trans. by Joseph Evans, *God and the Permission of Evil* (Milwaukee: Bruce, 1966). Page references in the present essay are to the Evans trans.

1963. *Distinguer pour Unir: Ou, les Degrés du Savoir* (orig. ed. 1932; Paris: Desclée de Brouwer). Page references are to the French text of the 7th edition as reproduced in the definitive text of *Jacques et Raissa Maritain Oeuvres Completes*, Vol. IV, édition publiée par le Cercle d'Études Jacques et Raïssa Maritain (Éditions Universitaires Fribourg Suisse et Éditions Saint-Paul Paris), 257–1110. See 1959 entry above for available English trans.

MARMO, Costantino.
1987. "The Semiotics of John Poinsot", *Versus* 46 (gennaio-aprile), 109–129.

MAROOSIS, James.
1981. *Further Consequences of Human Embodiment: A Description of Time and Being as Disclosed at the Origin of Peirce's Philosophy of Community* (unpublished doctoral dissertation; University of Toronto, Department of Philosophy).

1993. "Peirce and the Manifestation of Self-Transcendence", in *Semiotics 1993*, ed. Robert Corrington and John Deely (Lanham, MD: University Press of America, 1994).

MATSON, Wallace I.
1987. *A New History of Philosophy* (New York: Harcourt Brace Jovanovich), in two volumes.

MAURER, Armand.
1962. *Medieval Philosophy* (New York: Random House), being Volume II of a projected 4–volume *History of Philosophy* under the general editorship of Etienne Gilson.

MAYR, Ernst.
1974. "Teleological and Teleonomic: A New Analysis", in *Methodological and Historical Essays in the Natural and Social Sciences*, 4, ed. Robert S. Cohen and Marx W. Wartofsky (Dordrecht, Holland: D. Reidel Publishing Co.), 91–117.

1983. Adaptation of 1974 entry with unchanged title as Chapter 25 of *Evolution and the Diversity of Life. Selected Essays* (Cambridge, MA: The Belknap Press of Harvard University Press), 383–404.

McKEON, Richard M., Editor.
1941. *The Basic Works of Aristotle* (New York: Basic Books, 1941).

MERTON, Thomas.
1951. *The Ascent to Truth* (New York: Harcourt, Brace and Company).

MESSENGER, Theodore.
1974. "From Σημειωτική to Semiotic", in *A Semiotic Landscape/Panorama sémiotique* (Proceedings of the First Congress of the International Association for Semiotic Studies, Milan, June 1974; The Hague: Mouton, 1979), 326–328.

MILES, John Russiano ("Jack").
1985. Text of the original announcement by the University of California Press of the publication of *Tractatus de Signis: The Semiotic of John Poinsot*. See Poinsot 1632a.

MILLER, Eugene F.
1979. "Hume's Reduction of Cause to Sign", *The New Scholasticism* LIII.1, 42–75.

MILLER, James.
1993. *The Passion of Michel Foucault* (New York: Simon & Schuster).

MORRIS, Richard J.
1986. Review of Poinsot 1632a in *The Book Review of The Los Angeles Times*, Sunday, 11 May 1986, p. 8.

MUÑOZ DELGADO, Vicente.
1964. *Lógica formal y filosofía en Domingo de Soto* (Madrid).

MURPHY, James Bernard.
1990. "Nature, Custom, and Stipulation in Law and Jurisprudence", *The Review of Metaphysics* XLIII.4 (June), 753–790.
1991. "Nature, Custom, and Stipulation in the Semiotic of John Poinsot", *Semiotica* 83.1/2, 33–68.
1994. "Language, Communication, and Representation in the Semiotic of John Poinsot", *The Thomist* 59.4 (October).

NADLER, Steven.
1992. "Descartes and Occasional Causation", paper presented at a University of Chicago sesson of The Midwest Seminar in the History of Early Modern Philosophy, 5 December.

1992a.   "Intentionality in the Arnauld-Malebranche Debate", in Cummins and Zoeller eds. 1992: 73–84.

NIDDITCH, Peter H.

1975, 1979. Foreword, Notes, and Critical Apparatus to new edition of John Locke, *An Essay concerning Human Understanding* (Oxford).

NUCHELMANS, Gabriel.

1987.   Review of John Poinsot: *Tractatus de Signis: The Semiotic of John Poinsot*, ed. John N. Deely with Ralph A. Powell, in *Renaissance Quarterly* XL.1 (Spring) 146–149.

PAPE, Helmut.

1993.   "Final Causality in Peirce's Semiotics and His Classification of the Sciences", *Transactions of the Charles S. Peirce Society* (Fall), XXIX.4, 581–607.

PARKINSON, G. H. R., Editor.

1993.   *The Renaissance and Seventeenth-century Rationalism*, Volume IV of the *Routledge History of Philosophy* (London: Routledge). The promising title of this volume proves a disappointment in the end, for the construction of the volume breaks no new ground but follows only the received outlines of the period from c.1350 to Descartes, outlines which, it is the argument of the present book to demonstrate, screen out the developments of greatest philosophical interest for the contemporary scene.

PARKINSON, G. H. R.

1993.   "Introduction" to Parkinson Ed. 1993: 1–15, q.v.

PEIRCE, Charles Sanders.

Note: The designation CP abbreviates Peirce i.1866-1913 below. This abbreviation, followed by volume and paragraph numbers with a period between, has become the standard reference form for this work.

The designation NEM abbreviates *The New Elements of Mathematics*, ed. Carolyn Eisele (The Hague: Mouton, 1976), 4 volumes bound as 5.

The designation W followed by volume and page numbers with a period in between abbreviates the ongoing *Writings of Charles S. Peirce: A Chronological Edition*, initiated as the Peirce Edition Project at Indiana University-Purdue University/Indianapolis by Edward C. Moore under the general editorship of Max H. Fisch, now under the direction of Christian Kloesel (Bloomington: Indiana

University Press, 3 vols.—1982, 1984, 1986—published so far of a projected 20).

Unpublished mss. are cited by number, using the pagination made by the Institute for Studies in Pragmaticism at Texas Tech University in Lubbock.

Chronology and identification of the Peirce materials is based on Burks 1958, Fisch et al. 1979, Hardwick 1977, and Robin 1967, 1971, as indicated at specific points.

i. 1866-1913. *The Collected Papers of Charles Sanders Peirce*, Vols. I–VI ed. Charles Hartshorne and Paul Weiss (Cambridge, MA: Harvard University Press, 1931–1935), Vols. VII–VIII ed. Arthur W. Burks (same publisher, 1958). Available in electronic form as a full-text database (both in a stand-alone disk version and on CD-ROM), with hypertext-links based on Burks 1958 and an editorial introduction (Deely 1994a), in the Past Masters series (Charlottesville, VA: Intelex Corporation, P.O. Box 859; FAX 804-979-5804).

1867.   "On a New List of Categories", CP 1.545–567 (Burks p. 261); W 2.49–59.

1868.   "Questions concerning Certain Faculties Claimed for Man", *Journal of Speculative Philosophy* 2, 103–114, reprinted in the *Writings of Charles S. Peirce. A Chronological Edition, Volume 2*, ed. Edward C. Moore, Max H. Fisch, Christian J. W. Kloesel, Don D. Roberts, and Lynn A. Ziegler (Bloomington, IN: Indiana University Press), 193–211. Page reference in this paper is to the *Writings* reprint or CP, as indicated.

1868a. "Some Consequences of Four Incapacities", in CP 5.310–317; W 2.241.

1892.   "The Law of Mind", *The Monist* (2 July), 533–559; reprinted in CP 6.102–163.

1892a. "Man's Glassy Essence", *The Monist* (3 October), 1–22; reprinted in CP 6.238–271.

c.1896. "The Logic of Mathematics; An Attempt To Develop My Categories from Within", CP 1.417–520 (Burks p. 281).

1897.   "The Logic of Relatives", CP 3.456–552 (Burks p. 287).

c.1897. "Ground, Object, and Interpretant", CP 2,227–229 (see Burks p. 287).

1901.   A passage editorially deleted from the "Sign" entry for Baldwin 1901-1902 (q.v.), Vol. 2, pp. 527–528. In CP 2.303–304 (Burks p. 292).

1902. "Sign", entry for Baldwin 1901-1902: II, 527.

1903. "The Ethics of Terminology", from *A Syllabus of Certain Topics of Logic* (Boston: Alfred Mudge & Son), pp. 10-14; reprinted in CP 2.219-2.226 continuing 1.202 (Burks p. 295).

1904. Letter of 12 October from Peirce to Lady Welby, complete in *Semiotics and Significs. The correspondence between Charles S. Peirce and Victoria Lady Welby*, ed. Charles S. Hardwick (Bloomington, IN: Indiana University Press, 1977), 22-36; excerpted in CP 8.327-341 (Burks p. 321).

1904a. Letter to William James dated 7 March, partial in CP 8.258-259.

1905. "Prolegomena to an Apology for Pragmaticism", *The Monist* 16 (October 1906), 492-546; with an "Errata" published in vol. 17 (January 1907), p. 160. Reprinted with the published corrections and additional material in footnotes in CP 4.530-572 (Burks p. 297).

1905a. "What Pragmatism Is", *The Monist* 15 (April), 161-181; reprinted in CP 5.411-437.

1905-1906. Ms. 283, partially published under the title "The Basis of Pragmaticism" in CP 1.573-574 (= ms. pp. 37-45), 5.549-554 (= ms. pp. 45-59), and 5.448n. (= ms. pp. 135-148). (See Robin 1967: 28; Burks 298).

1906, March 9. 52-page draft letter to Lady Welby (under Robin L463, p. 200), ms. pp. 24-30 excerpted in Hardwick 1977: 195-201, to which published excerpt page reference is made in this book.

c.1906. Excerpt from "Pragmatism (Editor [3])", in CP 5.11-13 (except 5.13n1), and 5.464-496, with 5.464 continuing 5.13, both dated c.1906, are from it (Burks 1958: 299).

c.1907. "Pragmatism", MS 318 in the Robin *Annotated Catalogue* (1967). (A small segment of this ms. appears under the title "From Pragmatism" in NEM III.1: 481-494).

c.1907a. Excerpt from "Pragmatism (Editor [3])", published under the title "A Survey of Pragmaticism" in CP 5.464-496 (Burks p. 299).

1908. Letter to Lady Welby begun December 14 (in Hardwick 1977: 63-73) and continued December 23 (ibid.: 73-86); the "sop to Cerberus passage" occurs in the latter part.

1908a. Draft of a letter dated December 24, 25, 28 "On the Classification of Signs", CP 8.342-379 except 368n23 are from it (Burks p. 321 par. 20.b).

1909. From a letter dated March 14, printed under the heading "Signs" in CP 8.314 (Burks p. 320 par. 14.b).

c.1909.   "Some Amazing Mazes, Fourth Curiosity", CP 6.318–348.

PENCAK, William.
   1993.   *History, Signing In. Essays in History and Semiotics* (New York: Peter Lang).

PÉREZ-RAMOS, Antonio.
   1993.   "Francis Bacon and Man's Two-Faced Kingdom", in Parkinson Ed. 1993: 140–166, q.v.

PHILODEMUS.
   a.79AD   *On Methods of Inference*, ed. with trans. and commentary by Phillip Howard De Lacy and Estelle Allen De Lacy (rev. ed. with the collaboration of Marcello Gigante, Francesca Longo Auricchio, and Adele Tepedino Guerra; Naples: Bibliopolis, 1978).

PITTENDRIGH, Colin S.
   1958.   "Adaptation, Natural Selection, and Evolution", Chapter 18 of *Behavior and Evolution*, ed. Anne Roe and George Gaylord Simpson (New Haven: Yale University Press), 390–416.

POINSOT, John.
   Note: A complete table of all the editions, complete and partial, and in whatever language, of Poinsot's systematic works in philosophy and theology is provided in Deely 1985: 396–397. The description of the contents of the individual volumes of the *Cursus Theologicus* provided below is taken from Jacobus Quetif and Jacobus Echard, *Scriptores Ordinis Praedictorum, Tomus Secundus* (Paris, 1721); a narrative review of these contents can be found in Lavaud 1926: 424–435 (see Deely 1985: 398n3). The principal modern editions referred to in this work are abbreviated as follows:
   R followed by a volume number (I, II, or III) and pages, with column (a or b) and line indications as needed = the *Cursus Philosophicus Thomisticus*, ed. by B. Reiser in 3 volumes (Turin: Marietti, 1930, 1933, 1937).
   S followed by a volume number (I–V) and page numbers = the five volumes of the incomplete critical edition of the *Cursus Theologicus* ed. at Solesmes (Paris: Desclée, 1931, 1934, 1937, 1946; Matiscone: Protat Frères, 1953).
   V followed by a volume number (I–IX) = the complete edition of the *Cursus Theologicus* ed. by Ludovicus Vivès published in Paris between 1883 and 1886.

1631.   *Artis Logicae Prima Pars* (Alcalá, Spain). The opening pages 1–11a14 of this work and the "Quaestio Disputanda I. De Termino. Art. 6. Utrum Voces Significant per prius Conceptus an Res" pages 104b31–108a33, relevant to the discussion of signs in the *Secunda Pars* of 1632 (entry following), have been incorporated in the 1632a entry (second entry following, q.v.: pp. 4–30 and 342–351 "Appendix A. On the Signification of Language", respectively), for the independent edition of that discussion. From R I: 1–247.

1632.   *Artis Logicae Secunda Pars* (Alcalá, Spain). From R I: 249–839.

1632a.   *Tractatus de Signis*, subtitled *The Semiotic of John Poinsot*, extracted from the *Artis Logicae Prima et Secunda Pars* of 1631–1632 (above two entries) and arranged in bilingual format by John Deely in consultation with Ralph A. Powell (First Edition; Berkeley: University of California Press, 1985), as explained in Deely 1985: 445ff. Pages in this volume are set up in matching columns of English and Latin, with intercolumnar numbers every fifth line. (Thus, references to the volume are by page number, followed by a slash and the appropriate line number of the specific section of text referred to— e.g., 287/3–26.)

An independent translation of what in the 1985 Deely edition is Books I-III of Poinsot's *Tractatus de Signis* (= Logica 2. p. qq. 21-23, I 646a-749b47), without the First and Second Preambles on Mind-Dependent Being and Relation, is available in Spanish: Juan de Santo Tomás, *De Los Signos y los Conceptos*, Introducción, traducción y notas de Mauricio Beuchot (México City: Universidad Nacional Autónoma de México, 1989).

The Deely edition of Poinsot's *Tractatus de Signis* is also available in electronic form as a full-text database (both in a stand-alone disk version and as part of the Aquinas CD-ROM database), enhanced with new material on relation, and with cross-references and editorial materials fully hypertext-linked, in the Past Masters series (Charlottesville, VA: Intelex Corporation, P.O. Box 859; FAX 804-979-5804).

1633.   *Naturalis Philosophiae Prima Pars: De Ente Mobili in Communi* (Madrid, Spain). In R II: 1–529.

1634.   *Naturalis Philosophiae Tertia Pars: De Ente Mobili Corruptibili* (Alcalá, Spain); in Reiser vol. II: 533–888.

1635.   *Naturalis Philosophiae Quarta Pars: De Ente Mobili Animato* (Alcalá, Spain); in Reiser vol. III: 1–425.

1637.   *Tomus Primus Cursus Theologici* (Alcalá, Spain). V I & II; S I complete & II through p. 529. **Contents of T. I:** *Tres Tractatus ad theologiae tyrones praemissi: Primus* in Universum textum Magistri sententiarum in ordinem redigit; *Secundus,* omnium quaestionum D. Thomae et materiarum in sua summa ordinem explicat; *Tertius,* vindicias D. Thomae pro doctrinae ejus puritate probitate et singulari approbatione offert. *In Iam Partem, de Deo, qq. 1-14,* et *Tractatus de opere sex dierum.*

1640.   "Lectori", Preface added to the 4th edition (Madrid) of the Second Part of the *Ars Logica,* calling attention to the uniqueness, position, and utility of the text of the *Treatise on Signs* within the *Ars Logica* and *Cursus Philosophicus.* Included in the 1930 Reiser ed. p. 249, the 1985 Deely ed. pp. 34–35.

1643a.   *Tomus Secundus Cursus Theologici* (Lyons). The Solesmes edition of this work (Vol. II p. 531–end and Vol. III; Paris: Desclée, 1934 and 1937) is the best modern edition. **Contents of T. II:** *In Iam Partem, de Deo,* qq. 15-26.

1643b.   *Tomus Tertius Cursus Theologici* (Lyons). The Solesmes edition of this work (Vol. IV; Paris: Desclée, 1946) is the best modern edition. **Contents of T. III:** *In Iam Partem, de Trinitate et Angelis.*

1645a.   *Tomus Quartus Cursus Theologici,* ed. Didacus Ramirez (Madrid). The Solesmes edition of this work (Vol. V; Matiscone: Protat Frères, 1946, 1953) is the best modern edition. **Contents of T. IV:** *In Iam IIae, de Ultimo fine et de actibus humanis,* qq. 1-20.

1645b.   *Tomus Quintus Cursus Theologici,* ed. Didacus Ramirez (Madrid). The Vivès edition of this work (Vol. VI; Paris, 1885) is the best modern edition. **Contents of T. V:** *In Iam IIae, qq. 21-70 et 109-114.*

1649.   *Tomus Sextus Cursus Theologici,* ed. Didacus Ramirez (Madrid). The Vivès edition of this work (Vol. VII; Paris, 1885) is the best modern edition. **Contents of T. VI:** *In IIam IIae, qq.. 1-23, 64, 81, 82* [inserting the correction of Simonin, 1930: 147 note 1], *83, 88.—VIII Quaest. Quodlibetales.*

1656.   *Tomus Septimus Cursus Theologici,* ed. Didacus Ramirez (Madrid). The Vivès edition of this work (Vol. VIII; Paris, 1885) is the best modern edition. **Contents of T. VII:** *In IIIam Partem, de Incarnatione, qq. 1-26.*

1667.   *Tomus Octavus Cursus Theologici,* ed. Franciscus Combefis (Paris). The Vivès edition of this work (Vol. IX; Paris, 1885) is the best modern edition. **Contents of T. VIII:** *In IIIam Partem, de Sacramentis in genere, de Eucharistia, de Poenitentia.*

PORPHYRY.
c.271.   *Porphyrii Isagoge et in Aristotelis Categorias Commentarium* (Greek text),
ed. A. Busse (Berlin, 1887). English trans. by Edward W. War-
ren, *Porphyry the Phoenician: Isagoge* (Toronto, Canada: Pontifical
Institute of Mediaeval Studies, 1975).

POWELL, Philip Wayne.
1971.   *Tree of Hate: propaganda and prejudices affecting United States relations
with the Hispanic world* (New York: Basic Books; reprinted, with
a new "Introduction" by the author, Vallecito, CA: Ross House
Books, 1985).

POWELL, Ralph A.
c.1967.   "The Problem of Identifying More or Less Unitary Beings in Our
World" (unpublished and perhaps lost manuscript).
1969.   "The Late Heidegger's Omission of the Ontic-Ontological Structure of Dasein", in *Heidegger and the Path of Thinking*, ed. John Sallis (Pittsburgh, PA: Duquesne University Press, 1970), 116-137
(volume presented on the occasion of Heidegger's 80th birthday,
September 26, 1969).
1983.   "Poinsot as Foil for Doctrinal Considerations on Inexistent Personality in Existent Substance According to C. S. Peirce", in *Semiotics 1983*, ed. Jonathan Evans and John Deely (Lanham, MD:
University Press of America, 1987), 93-104.
1983a.   *Freely Chosen Reality* (Washington, DC: Univ. Press of America).
1984.   "Kant's Thought Interpreted through Peirce's Categories", in
Semiotics 1984, ed. John Deely (Lanham, MD: University Press
of America, 1985), 325-332.
1985.   "The Evidential Priority of Unindividuated Realities: The Philosophy of Science of Willard Van Orman Quine", in *Semiotics 1985*,
ed. J. Deely (Lanham, Md: Univ. Press of America, 1986), 45-55.
1986.   "From Semiotic of Scientific Mechanism to Semiotic of Teleology in Nature", in *Semiotics 1986*, ed. John Deely and Jonathan
Evans (Lanham, MD: University Press of America), 296-305.
1987.   "Democracy's Causal Signs of Primitive Justice", in *Semiotics
1987*, ed. John Deely (Lanham, MD: University Press of America, 1988), 414-422.
1988a.   "Degenerate Secondness in Peirce's Belief in God", in *ACPA
Proceedings* LXII, 116-123.
1988b.   "Epistemology's Minimal Cause as Basis of Science", *Semiotics
1988*, ed. Terry Prewitt, John Deely, and Karen Haworth (13th

Annual Proceedings of the Semiotic Society of America; Lanham, MD: University Press of America), 180–188.

1988c.   Personal correspondence to author dated 16 December.

1989.   "The First Amendment Become Causal Sign of Freely Avoiding Injustice over Abortion", in *Semiotics 1989*, ed. John Deely, Karen Haworth, and Terry Prewitt (Lanham, MD: University Press of America, 1990), 130–137.

1990.   "Dicent Signs as Signs of Mechanist Causality in a Totally Intelligible Universe", in *Semiotics 1990*, ed. Karen Haworth, John Deely, and Terry Prewitt (Lanham, MD: University Press of America, 1993), 354–361.

1991.   "Mechanist Justice Limits U.S. Politics", in *Semiotics 1991*, ed. John Deely and Terry Prewitt (Lanham, MD: University Press of America, 1993), 308–318.

1992.   "Voter's Peircean Free Non-Existence", in *Semiotics 1992*, ed. John Deely and Robert Corrington (Lanham, MD: University Press of America, in press).

RAMIREZ, Didacus.

1645.   "Vita Rmi P. Joannis a Sto Thoma", earliest biography of Poinsot, originally published at the beginning of the first posthumous volume, i.e., *Tomus Quartus*, of the *Cursus Theologicus*; reprinted as Appendix I to Solesmes, 1931: xxv–xliij, to which reprinting page references in this work are made.

RAMIREZ, J.-M.

1924.   "Jean de St. Thomas", *Dictionnaire de théologie catholique* (Paris: Letouzey), Vol. 8, 803–808. (Note: This work is not reliable for chronology. See Reiser, 1930: XV, par c.).

RANDALL, Jr., John Herman.

1962.   *The Career of Philosophy*. Vol. 1: *From the Middle Ages to the Enlightenment* (New York: Columbia University Press).

RANSDELL, Joseph.

1977.   "Some Leading Ideas of Peirce's Semiotic", *Semiotica* 19, 157–178.

RAPOSA, Michael.

1994.   "Poinsot on the Semiotics of Awareness", *ACPQ* Special Issue on John Poinsot, Volume LXVIII, Number 3 (Summer), 405-418.

RASMUSSEN, Douglas.

1994.   "The Significance for Cognitive Realism of the Thought of John Poinsot", *ACPQ* Special Issue on Poinsot, Vol. LXVIII, No. 3 (Summer), 419-433.

REISER, B.
    1930.   "Editoris Praefatio" to Ioannes a Sancto Thoma (Poinsot), *Ars Logica* (1631-1632), nova editio a Reiser (Turin: Marietti), pp. VII-XVIII.
    1933.   "Editoris in Secundum Volumen Praefatio" to Ioannes a Sancto Thoma (Poinsot), *Naturalis Philosophiae I. et III.* Pars (1633-1634), nova editio a Reiser (Turin: Marietti), pp. V-VIII.
    1937.   "Editoris in Tertium et Ultimum Volumen Praefatio" to Ioannes a Sancto Thoma (Poinsot), *Naturalis Philosophiae IV. Pars* (1635), nova editio a Reiser (Turin: Marietti), IX-X.

REY, Alain.
    1984.   "What Does Semiotics Come From?", *Semiotica* 52, 79-93.

ROBIN, Richard S.
    1967.   *Annotated Catalogue of the Papers of Charles S. Peirce* (Worcester, MA: The University of Massachusetts Press).
    1971.   "The Peirce Papers: A Supplementary Catalogue", *Transactions of the Charles S. Peirce Society* VII.1 (Winter), 37-57.

ROMEO, Luigi.
    1977.   "The Derivation of 'Semiotics' through the History of the Discipline", in *Semiosis* 6, Heft 2, 37-49.

ROSS, W. D.
    1928-1952. *The Works of Aristotle Translated into English*, in XII vols. (Oxford: The Clarendon Press).

RUSSELL, L. J.
    1939.   "Note on the Term ΣΗΜΙΩΤΙΚΗ [sic] in Locke", *Mind* 48, 405-406.

SANTAELLA-BRAGA, Lúcia.
    1991.   "John Poinsot's Doctrine of Signs: The Recovery of a Missing Link", *The Journal of Speculative Philosophy*, New Series, 5.2 (1991), 151-159.
    1992.   "Time as the Logical Process of the Sign", *Semiotica* 88.3/4, 309-326.
    1994.   "Peirce's Broad Concept of Mind", *European Journal of Semiotics*, Special Issue on Mentality Guest-Edited by Mariana Neţ (in press).

SCAPULA, Joannes.
    1579-1580. *Lexicon Graeco-Latinum* (Basel: Ex officina Hervagiana). This work went through several editions: *Lexicon Graeco-Latinum novum*

(Basel: Per Sebastianum Henricpetri, 1605); *Lexicon Graecorum novum* (London: Impensis Ioscosae Norton, 1637); *Lexicon Graeco-Latinum* (Lyons: Typis B. & A. Elzeviriorum & F. Hackii, 1652). Romeo (1977: 46 n.5) explains this series of editions as follows: "Henricus Stephanus' *Thesaurus Graecae linguae* was first published in 1572. Joannes Scapula's pirated abridgment of the *Thesaurus* started in 1579 and generated several editions until the nineteenth century". It must be noted that Romeo (1977: 43) mentions a 1663 edition of Scapula as in Locke's possession along with the 1605 edition, but Romeo gives no bibliographical information whatever concerning this 1663 edition.

SCHEIBLER, Christoph.
1617.   *Opus Metaphysicum.* (Giessen).

SCHMITT, Charles B., and Quentin SKINNER, Eds.
1988.   *The Cambridge History of Renaissance Philosophy* (Cambridge, England: Cambridge University Press).

SEBEOK, Thomas A.
1968.   "Is a Comparative Semiotics Possible?", in *Échanges et Communications: Mélanges offerts à Claude Lévi-Strauss à l'occasion de son 60ème anniversaire*, ed. Jean Pouillon and Pierre Maranda (The Hague: Mouton), 614–627; reprinted in Sebeok 1985: 59–69, to which page reference is made.

1971.   "'Semiotic' and Its Congeners", in *Linguistic and Literary Studies in Honor of Archibald Hill, I: General and Theoretical Linguistics*, ed. Mohammed Ali Jazayery, Edgar C. Polomé, and Werner Winter (Lisse, Netherlands: Peter de Ridder Press), 283–295; reprinted in Sebeok 1985: 47–58, and in Deely, Williams and Kruse 1986: 255–263.

1974.   "Semiotics: A Survey of the State of the Art", in *Linguistics and Adjacent Arts and Sciences*, Vol. 12 of the *Current Trends in Linguistics* series, ed. T. A. Sebeok (The Hague: Mouton), 211–264; reprinted in Sebeok 1985: 1–45, to which page reference is made.

1975.   "Zoosemiotics: At the Intersection of Nature and Culture", in *The Tell-Tale Sign* (Lisse, Netherlands: Peter de Ridder Press), 85–95.

1977.   "The Semiotic Self", discussion paper presented at the Werner-Reimers-Stiftung, in Germany, and subsequently included as Appendix I in Sebeok 1989: 263–267.

1977a.   "The French-Swiss Connection", *Semiotic Scene* I, 27–32.

1984.   "Vital Signs", Presidential Address delivered October 12 to the ninth Annual Meeting of the Semiotic Society of America, Bloomington, Indiana, October 11-14; subsequently printed in *The American Journal of Semiotics* 3.3, 1-27, and reprinted in Sebeok 1986a: 59-79, to which last reprint page reference is made here.

1985.   *Contributions to the Doctrine of Signs* (= Sources in Semiotics IV; reprint of 1976 original with an extended Preface by Brooke Williams, "Challenging Signs at the Crossroads" [Williams 1985], evaluating the book in light of major reviews; Lanham, MD: University Press of America).

1986.   "A Signifying Man", feature review of *Tractatus de Signis* in *The New York Times Book Review* for Easter Sunday, 30 March 1986, pp. 14-15; German trans. by Jeff Bernard in *Semiotische Berichte* Jg. 11 2/1987: 234-239, with translator's "Anmerkung" p. 240.

1986a. *I Think I Am a Verb. More Contributions to the Doctrine of Signs* (New York: Plenum Press).

1987.   "Language: How Primary a Modeling System?", in *Semiotics 1987*, ed. John Deely (Lanham, MD: University Press of America, 1988), 15-27.

1988.   "The Notion 'Semiotic Self' Revisited", in *Semiotics 1988*, ed. Terry Prewitt, John Deely, and Karen Haworth (Lanham, MD: University Press of America, 1989), 189-195.

1989.   "The Semiotic Self Revisited", in *Sign, Self, and Society*, ed. Benjamin Lee and Greg Urban (Berlin: Mouton de Gruyter).

1989a. *The Sign & Its Masters* (= Sources in Semiotics VIII; Lanham, MD: University Press of America. Corrected reprint, with a new Author's Preface and an added Editor's Preface [Deely 1989a], of the University of Texas Press 1979 original imprint).

1991.   *Semiotics in the United States* (Bloomington, IN: Indiana University Press).

1993.   "A Origem da Linguagem", trans. by Fernando Clara for *Semiótica e Linguística Portuguesa e Românica. Homenagem a José Gonçalo Herculano de Carvalho*, ed. Jürgen Schmidt-Radefeldt (Tübingen: Gunter Narr Verlag), 3-9.

SEBEOK, Thomas A., General Editor; Paul BOUISSAC, Umberto ECO, Jerzy PELC, Roland POSNER, Alain REY, Ann SHUKMAN, Editorial Board.

1986.   *Encyclopedic Dictionary of Semiotics* (Berlin: Mouton de Gruyter), in 3 Volumes.

SHORT, Thomas L.
>   1983.   "Teleology in Nature", *American Philosophical Quarterly* 20.4, 311-320.

SIMON, Yves R.
>   1955.   "Foreword" and "Notes" to *The Material Logic of John of St. Thomas*, trans. Yves R. Simon, John J. Glanville, and G. Donald Hollenhorst (Chicago: University of Chicago Press), pp. ix–xxiii and 587-625.

SIMON, Yves R., John J. GLANVILLE, and G. Donald HOLLENHORST.
>   1955.   *The Material Logic of John of St. Thomas,* selections trans. from Poinsot's *Artis Logicae Secunda Pars* of 1632 (Reiser ed.; Turin: Marietti, 1930). Detailed discussions of the Simon trans. in the context of Poinsot's doctrine of signs are in Deely 1985: 117 n. 6, 406 n. 15, 459 n. 93.

SIMONIN, H.-D.
>   1930.   "Review" of the 1930 Reiser edition of Poinsot's *Ars Logica* of 1631-1632, in the *Bulletin Thomiste* (septembre), 140-148.

SIMPSON, George Gaylord, Colin S. PITTENDRIGH, and Lewis H. TIFFANY.
>   1957.   *Life. An Introduction to Biology* (New York: Harcourt, Brace and Co.).

SOLESMES.
>   1931.   "Editorum Solesmensium Praefatio" to Joannes a Sancto Thoma (Poinsot, 1637) *Cursus Theologici Tomus Primus* (Paris: Desclée), i–cviij.

SOTO, Dominic.
>   1529, 1554. *Summulae* (1st ed., Burgos; 3rd rev. ed., Salamanca; Facsimile of 3rd ed., Hildesheim, NY: Georg Olms Verlag).

STEPHANUS, Henricus.
>   1572-1573. *Thesaurus Graecae Linguae*, 6 vols. (Geneva: excudebat H. Stephanus). Paris edition of 1831-1865, *Thesaurus Graecae linguae ab Henrico Stephano constructus. Post editionem Anglicam novis additamentis auctum ordineque alphabetico tertio ediderunt*, ed. C. B. Case and others, reprinted in Graz, Austria, by Akademische Druck-u. Verlagsanstalt, 1954-1955.

STOOTHOFF, Robert.
>   1985.   "Translator's Preface" to *Discourse and Essays* in Cottingham, Stoothoff, and Murdoch 1985: I, 109-110.

SUÁREZ, Francis.
  1597.   *Disputationes Metaphysicae* (Salamanca: Renaut Fratres). Vols. 25
          and 26 of the Opera Omnia, editio nova a Carolo Berton (Paris:
          Vivès, 1861), were used in preparing the present work. I am in-
          debted to Professor Jack Doyle for the following note: ''The *Dis-
          putationes Metaphysicae* was first published at Salamanca in 1597 by
          the brothers Juan and Andres Renaut under the title, *Metaphysica-
          rum disputationum, in quibus et universa naturalis theologia ordinate traditur,
          et quaestiones omnes ad duodecim Aristotelis libros pertinentes accurate dis-
          putantur ... Tomus prior — Tomus posterior*. The two volumes were
          published at almost the same time. On the editions of Suárez's *Dis-
          putationes*, see E. M. Riviere, *Suárez et son oeuvre a la occasion du
          troisieme centenaire de sa mort. I: La bibliographie des ouvrages imprimes
          et inedits* (Toulouse and Barcelona, 1917), esp. p. 14.''
  1605.   *De Sacramentis* (Venice: Apud Societatem Minimam). Vol. 20 of
          the Opera Omnia, editio nova a Carolo Berton (Paris: Vivès,
          1860), was used in preparing the present work.

TACHAU, Katherine H.
  1988.   *Vision and Certitude in the Age of Ockham. Optics, Epistemology and the
          Foundation of Semantics 1250–1345* (Leiden, The Netherlands: E.
          J. Brill, 1988).

TIMPLER, Clemens.
  1604.   *Metaphysicae Systema Methodicum* (Steinfurt).
  1612.   *Logica Systema Methodicum* (Hanover).

TIPTON, Ian.
  1992.   '' 'Ideas' and 'Objects': Locke on Perceiving 'Things''', in Cum-
          mins and Zoeller eds. 1992: 97–110.

von UEXKÜLL, Jakob.
  1934.   *Streifzuge durch die Umwelten von Tieren und Menschen* (Berlin), trans.
          by Claire H. Schiller as 'A Stroll through the Worlds of Animals
          and Men' in *Instinctive Behavior: The Development of a Modern Con-
          cept*, ed. by Claire H. Schiller (New York: International Univer-
          sities Press, Inc., 1957), 5–80.

VILLLOSLADA, Garcia.
  1938.   *Universidad de Paris durante los estudios de Francisco de Vitoria, O.P.,
          1507–1522* (= Analecta Gregoriana XIV; Rome: Gregorian
          University Press).

WALLACE, William A.
  1972.   *Causality and Scientific Explanation I. Medieval and Early Classical Science* (Ann Arbor: University of Michigan Press).
  1974.   *Causality and Scientific Explanation II. Classical and Contemporary Science* (Ann Arbor: University of Michigan Press).
  1977.   *Galileo's Early Notebooks: The Physical Questions*, a translation from the Latin with historical and paleographical commentary (Notre Dame, IN: Notre Dame University Press).
  1981.   *Prelude to Galileo*, essays on medieval and sixteenth century sources of Galileo's thought (= Boston Studies in the Philosophy of Science 62; Dordrecht, Holland: D. Reidel Publishing Co.).
  1984.   *Galileo and His Sources*, the heritage of the Collegio Romano in Galileo's science (Princeton, NJ: Princeton University Press).
  1991.   *Galileo, the Jesuits, and the Medieval Aristotle* (= Collected Studies 346; Hampshire, UK: Variorum Publishing).
  1992.   *Galileo's Logic of Discovery and Proof*, the background, content, and use of his appropriated treatises on Aristotle's Posterior Analytics (= Boston Studies in the Philosophy of Science 137; Dordrecht, Holland: Kluwer Academic Publishing).
  1992a. *Galileo's Logical Treatises*, a translation with notes and commentary of his appropriated treatises on Aristotle's *Posterior Analytics* (= Boston Studies in the Philosophy of Science 138; Dordrecht, Holland: Kluwer Academic Publishers).

WALLACE, William A., Editor.
  1986.   *Reinterpreting Galileo* (= Studies in Philosophy and the History of Philosophy 15; Washington, DC: The Catholic University of America Press).

WALLACE, William A., and W. F. EDWARDS, Editors.
  1988.   *Galileo Galilei, "Tractatio de praecognitionibus et praecognitis" and "Tractatio de demonstratione"* (Padua, Italy: Editrice Antenore).

WATT, William C.
  1993.   "Signification and Its Discontents", in Deely and Petrilli Eds. 1993: 427–437.

WELLS, Norman J.
  1993.   "*Esse Cognitum* and Suárez Revisited", ACPQ LXVII.3 (Summer), 339–348.
  1994.   "Poinsot on Created Eternal Truths vs. Vasquez, Suárez and Descartes", *ACPQ* Special Issue on John Poinsot, Vol. LXVIII, No. 3 (Summer), 435-457.

WHITEHEAD, Alfred North.
  1925. *Science and the Modern World* (New York: The Free Press).
  1933. *Adventures of Ideas* (New York: The Free Press).

WILLIAMS, Brooke.
  1982. "The Historian as Observer", in *Semiotics 1982*, ed. John Deely and Jonathan Evans (Lanham, MD: University Press of America, 1987), 13–25.
  1983. "History as A Semiotic Anomaly", in *Semiotics 1983*, ed. Jonathan Evans and John Deely (Lanham, MD: University Press of America, 1987), 409–419.
  1985. "Challenging Signs at the Crossroads", prefatory essay to Sebeok 1985: xv–xlii.
  1985a. "What Has History To Do with Semiotic?", *Semiotica* 54.3/4, 267-333; preprinted in revised monograph form with index and historically layered bibliography under the title *History and Semiotic* (Victoria College of the University of Toronto: Toronto Semiotic Circle Number 4, Summer).
  1986. "History in Relation to Semiotic", reprint with modest revisions of 1983 above in Deely, Williams, and Kruse 1986: 217–223.
  1987. "Introducing Semiotic to Historians", paper presented in the first AHA History and Semiotics session, at the One Hundred Second Annual Meeting of the American Historical Association, Washington, DC, 27–30 December 1987; available on microfilm or in xerographic form as part of the *Proceedings of the American Historical Association, 1987*, reference #10485 (from: Order Fulfillment, University Microfilms International, 300 North Zeeb Road, Ann Arbor, MI 48106).
  1987a. "Historiography as a Current Event", in *Semiotics 1987*, ed. John Deely (Lanham, MD: University Press of America, 1988), 479–486.
  1988. "Opening Dialogue between the Discipline of History and Semiotics", in *The Semiotic Web: 1987*, ed. Thomas A. Sebeok and Donna Jean Umiker-Sebeok (Berlin: Mouton de Gruyter, 1988), 821–834.
  1991. "History and Semiotics in the 1990s", concluding essay to *Semiotica* Special Issue on History, Guest-Edited by Brooke Williams and William Pencak, 83–3/4, 384-420.

WILLIAMS, Brooke, and William PENCAK, Guest Editors.
  1991. *Special Issue: History and Semiotics, Semiotica* 83.3/4.

WILSON, Margaret D.
   1992.   ''History of Philosophy in Philosophy Today; and the Case of the
           Sensible Qualities'', *The Philosophical Review* 101.1 (January),
           191-243.

WINANCE, Eleuthère.
   1983.   Review of *Introducing Semiotic* (Deely 1982), *Revue Thomiste* LXXX
           (juillet-aôut), 514-516.

Index

Rey, Alain 161n6, 287, 289
Riviere, E. M. 291
Roberts, Don 280
Robin, Richard S. 280, 287
Robinson, Edward 274
Rome 24
Romeo, Luigi 109n1, 113, 287
Ross, W. D. 263, 287
Rubio, Antonio 33
Rules for the Direction of the Mind (Descartes) 53-5
Russell, A. F. 40, 270
Russell, L. J. 109n1, 113, 287

Salamanca 23, 33, 58n8
Salazar, Francisco de 33
Sallis, John 284
Santaella-Braga, Lúcia xiii, 9, 14, 30, 145, 191n3, 243, 287
Sarria, Thomas of 24
Saussure, Ferdinand de 189, 202
Scapula 111, 287-8
Scheibler, Christoph 124, 288
Schiller, Claire 291
Schmidt-Radefeldt, Jürgen 289
Schmitt 125n8, 143, 287
Scholastic 57
Science 221-2
- contrasted with philosophy 29-30, 85-6
Scotus, John Duns 32n4, 39, 39n1, 124, 129n11, 130
Sebeok, Thomas A. 9, 80n35, 106, 109n1, 113, 114, 161n6, 168, 178, 183, 192-4, 200, 205, 209, 217, 221, 234n18, 244, 248, 262, 268, 288, 289
Second intentions as logical relations 90n45. *See* Intention
Secondness 204. *See* Brute force
Secundum esse. See Relatio secundum esse; Ontological relation
Segovia 33

Selby-Bigge 274
Sem- (Greek root) 113
Semeion (Greek) 113
Semeiosy (synonym for action of signs or semiosis) 114, 204, 226n11, 236. *See also* Action of signs; Semiosis; Triadic
Semeiotic (variant of semiotic) 113
Semeiotike (Greek) 113, 117n6
Semeiosis (variant spelling of semiosis). *See* Semiosis
Semiosis 10, 15, 114, 121, 141, 157, 166-78, 175n18, 179, 180, 181, 184, 186-8, 193, 200, 209, 225, 227, 234, 239-43, 246-7, 271, 275
- Aristotle's four causes inadequate to 95, 198-9
- common ground of 105
- distinctiveness of 226n11
- Greek term for 114
- role of fundament in 199, 229-31, 231n15
- unlimited 95n54, 166n10, 175, 222-3
- virtual 173-8
- why unlimited 73n27, 93-5, 94n53.
- *See also* Action of signs; Biosemiosis; Physiosemiosis
Semiotic 5, 6, 7, 41, 43n4, 52, 72-3n27, 80n35, 109, 111, 114, 117n6, 136, 143, 185-6, 195, 276
- standpoint proper to 101-2
- unified subject matter for inquiry 69-70, 105
Semiotic consciousness 246
Semiotic Marker, device of explained 74n28
Semiotic Maxim 85n39, 246
Semiotic Scene (bulletin) 261
Semiotic web 169
"Semiotica" as transliteration of Locke 117n6, 118